White Out
THE CONTINUING
SIGNIFICANCE OF RACISM

White Out
The Continuing
Significance of Racism

Edited by
Ashley "Woody" Doane
and Eduardo Bonilla-Silva

ROUTLEDGE
NEW YORK & LONDON

Published in 2003 by
Routledge
29 West 35th Street
New York, NY 10001
www.routledge-ny.com

Published in Great Britain by
Routledge
11 New Fetter Lane
London EC4P 4EE
www.routledge.co.uk

Routledge is an imprint of the Taylor & Francis Group.

Printed in the United States of America on acid-free paper.

10   9   8   7   6   5   4   3   2

Library of Congress Cataloging-in-Publication Data

White out : the continuing significance of racism / edited by Ashley W.
    Doane and Eduardo Bonilla-Silva.
        p.   cm.
    ISBN 0-415-93582-2 (Hardcover : alk. paper)—ISBN 0-415-93583-0
    (Paperback : alk. paper)
    1. United States—Race relations.   2. Whites—Race identity—United States.
    3. Racism—United States.   I. Doane, Ashley W., 1954–   II. Bonilla-Silva,
    Eduardo, 1962–

    E184.A1 W3995
    305.8′00973—dc21   2003005712

CONTENTS

PART V: CONCLUSION

Preface

This book had its genesis in a hallway conversation at the August 2000 Annual Meeting of the American Sociological Association. Both of us (the editors) shared our frustration with what we felt were barriers to publishing critical work on race and whiteness in the mainstream sociological journals. We also felt a sense of dissatisfaction with much of what had been published on whiteness, even though we had both been contributors to the literature. From our perspective, too much of what had been written was in fields such as cultural studies and education and failed to connect whiteness to what Joe Feagin (2000) has called "systemic racism." While other work in fields such as legal studies and history was valuable, we were concerned that there was a clear danger of "whiteness studies" degenerating into a field that reflected the self-absorption of whites and deflected attention from critical and persistent issues of racism in the United States. We believe that there is a place for the study of "whiteness" but that it must be connected to study of the systemic practices that reproduce racial inequality and of the ideology of "color blindness" that provides legitimacy and political cover for the persistence of racism.

In countless telephone conversations and e-mails over the past two years, we continued to develop our vision for this book. We wanted a book that would contain original material from both established scholars and a new generation of scholarly voices. We wanted chapters that would critique existing work on whiteness and contribute to a repositioning of the field. We also wanted empirical work that would provide new insights into the relationship between whiteness, color-blind ideology, and the persistence of racism. With the inspired work of a wonderful array of contributors, this vision has become a reality.

We hope that this book will provoke further debate and research and contribute to a rethinking of the role of whiteness studies. Ultimately, we also hope that it makes some small contribution to the movement for a racially just society.

Acknowledgements

Eduardo Bonilla-Silva

I would like to acknowledge my family: my parents, Jacinto Bonilla and Ruth M. Silva; my sister, Karen Bonilla-Silva; my brother, Pedro Juan Bonilla-Silva, who passed away tragically while we were working on this book; my son, Omar Francisco Bonilla; and my partner in life, the "good Mary," as she is known at Texas A&M. All of them have given me the emotional juice to move on and survive the American sociological jungle.

I would be remiss if I did not acknowledge my three outstanding graduate students at Texas A&M: David G. Embrick, Paul Ketchum, and Karen Glover. They have worked on projects with me, assisted me in research, and given me more support than I have probably given them. Therefore, EBS thanks profusely DE, PK, and KG!

It is during hard times that one realizes who your true friends are. In this regard, my colleague and boss Rogelio Saenz deserves special mention because he gave me the space and support I needed slowly to come back after Pedro's death. Similarly, Tyrone A. Forman, Amanda E. Lewis, and Alford Young went beyond the call of duty and volunteered to come to College Station during the period where my soul and mind were out of whack. For that I will be eternally grateful.

I did some of the final work on this book while on sabbatical at the Research Institute for the Comparative Study of Race and Ethnicity (RICSRE). There I want to thank all the staff (Awino, Leanne, and the genteel Dorothy) as well as the codirectors of RICSRE, Hazel Markus and George Fredrickson. Thanks for giving me the time, space, and support to do my job.

Finally, I would like to acknowledge all my colleagues at Texas A&M for providing me intellectual respect, friendship, and love. I would also like to thank the regular members of the Faculty Development Seminar held on Wednesdays and Fridays at Fitzwilly's in College Station. Life needs balance, and that seminar—and the many pitchers of cheap beer we have consumed there—has become the balance that Mary and I longed for in other places.

Woody Doane

I would like to acknowledge my many intellectual debts: to my parents, Mary Dodge and Ashley Doane, who encouraged me to think critically and instilled a sense of social justice; to my graduate mentor, Bud B. Khleif, who taught me the "craft" of sociology and encouraged me to appreciate the breadth and depth of race and ethnic relations; to the many friends and colleagues with whom I have exchanged ideas of race and ethnic relations, especially Lelia De Andrade, Dan Santoro, Chip Gallagher, and Joyce Hamilton; to all those whose writings on race have inspired me, from W. E. B. Du Bois to Robert Blauner, Stephen Steinberg, Edna Bonacich, Joane Nagel, Joe Feagin, Richard Alba, and Michael Omi and Howard Winant.

A special note of appreciation to Eduardo: transcontinental coediting is a daunting proposition, but we made it work. Amid the countless e-mails and telephone calls, we slipped in tidbits on surviving everything from a move into academic administration to extrahot buffalo wings. It's been fun!

And thank you to family and friends who share so much with me; to Wick Griswold, who always keeps me centered; and to Tam, Justin, and Faith, who make every day meaningful—and who tolerated the many hours this book took away from family time.

BOTH EDITORS

We would like to express our appreciation to our editor, Ilene Kalish, and to all of the production staff at Routledge. And our deepest thanks to all of the contributors: for your creativity and for your patience with our editorial suggestions and oft-frantic e-mails. You made it all worthwhile!

PART I

Rethinking Whiteness Studies

Rethinking Whiteness Studies

WOODY DOANE

One important recent development in the study of race and ethnic relations is the emergence of "whiteness" as an area of investigation. "Whiteness studies" is part of an interdisciplinary project that brings together insights from fields as diverse as legal studies, history, cultural studies, anthropology, education, and sociology.[1]What is new and unique about "whiteness studies" is that it reverses the traditional focus of research on race relations by concentrating attention upon the socially constructed nature of white identity and the impact of whiteness upon intergroup relations. In contrast to the usual practice of studying the "problem" of "minority groups," the "whiteness studies" paradigm makes problematic the identity and practices of the dominant group (Gabriel 1998).

The emergence of "whiteness studies" can be seen as an extension of recent critiques of the sociology of race and ethnic relations. Historically, students of race and ethnic relations focused on subordinate or "minority" groups; that is, those defined as the "other" by the dominant group. This reflected both the social context and relations of power in the larger society. The study of race and ethnic relations—and sociology in general—in the early and mid-twentieth century was shaped by the concerns of the dominant white/Anglo-American group, especially the "social problems" of immigration and urbanization (Coser 1978). Dominant-group social and political interests led to a focus on assimilation, particularly with regard to European immigrants. This was compatible with the more general trend in sociological theory of viewing race and ethnicity as a phenomenon that would wither away in the face of modernization—as a result of either rationalization or the increasing primacy of class conflict. In any event, assimilation theory was as much political prescription as social theory—it was a white, Anglo-American blueprint for what "ought" to happen. Moreover, both perspectives on assimilation, the political and the sociological, envisioned assimilation into "mainstream" American society—a mainstream that was dominated by white, Anglo-American interests.

Well before mid-century, social and sociological attention began to be directed towards the glaring inequality and subordinate status of African-Americans, a situation that was often referred to by the telling label of "the Negro problem" (McKee 1993; Steinberg 1995). Although the racial problems of the United States were certainly viewed as difficult, many theorists (e.g., Robert E. Park, Gunnar Myrdal, Everett Hughes) expected that the assimilation process would eventually expand to include African-Americans. While the focus of research continued to be upon subordinate groups, some observers began to consider the role of whites in the racial problems of the United States. For example, Myrdal (1944:li–lii) spoke of the need to study "what goes on in the minds of white Americans." Unfortunately, this attention was limited to studies of prejudice, with the underlying assumption being that the major obstacle to the integration/assimilation of African-Americans was the prejudicial attitudes of whites. Other dimensions of white domination remained unexamined.

The research program outlined above led to the failure to foresee the Civil Rights and other race-based social movements, the failure to account for the persistence of ethnic assertion, and the failure to explain the continuing significance of race in the United States. Indeed, it has seemingly become a commonplace to describe this as one of the great failures of social science (McKee 1993; Steinberg 1995; Omi and Winant 1986). In response to these changes, post-1960s study of race and ethnic relations has focused upon subordinate groups, with particular emphasis placed upon issues of identity, inequality, change, and resistance. New critical perspectives have examined institutional racism and internal colonialism (e.g., Carmichael and Hamilton 1967; Blauner 1972), explanations for the *persistence* of racial inequality and conflict (e.g., Blumer 1965; Bonacich 1972, 1980), the evolution of racial ideologies (e.g., Omi and Winant 1986), the resurgence of submerged or suppressed identities (Nagel 1996), and the impact of new patterns of immigration (e.g., Portes and Rumbaut, 1996). It is probably safe to say that little of the pre-1960 sociological thinking on race and ethnic relations has gone unchallenged.

Throughout the early stages of this paradigmatic crisis, whiteness—and its role in intergroup relations—remained unexplored territory. For the most part, whiteness was treated as a default category, as textbooks (a major medium through which sociologists present scholarship to the larger society) continued to focus upon subordinate groups—the one exception being studies of "white ethnics," who, it was argued, were still being assimilated into the ("white") mainstream. When explicit attention was directed toward whites, it was to continue the tradition of studying white attitudes (i.e., prejudice) toward subordinate groups. What emerged from this downplaying of "whiteness" was a one-dimensional perspective on race relations, a sociology that by its neglect of the identity of the dominant white group has treated majority-minority relations as if it were necessary to understand only one actor.[2] Thus the more recent emergence of "whiteness studies" is an important component of the rethinking of the study of race and ethnic relations.

One important observation is that "whiteness studies" is not as new as it seems. To some degree, it constitutes the "repackaging" of earlier insights about the nature of whiteness. For example, W. E. B. Du Bois was speaking about "white privilege" when he described the "public and psychological wage" enjoyed by even the poorest whites" (1956 [1935]:700–701). His (Du Bois 1969 [1920]) chapter "The Souls of White Folk" explores whiteness and white supremacy in more detail. Other African-American writers (e.g., Ralph Ellison, Kenneth Clark, James Baldwin) also commented upon the nature of whiteness (cf. Baldwin 1984; Roediger 1998). Tellingly, the primacy of African-American writers in the early investigation of "whiteness" underscores the invisibility of whiteness to white Americans, while the relative lack of recognition received by this work highlights the marginalization of the contributions of African-Americans to the study of race relations.

As I noted earlier, what is new about "whiteness studies" is the *explicit* focus upon whiteness as a subject of study and the deliberate use of labels such as "whiteness studies" to describe the field. This recent emergence of whiteness studies gives rise to several important questions. Why was whiteness essentially ignored in the sociological study of race and ethnic relations? Why did "whiteness studies" emerge when it did in the late 1980s and 1990s? How is its emergence linked to broader trends in society and in the study of race and ethnic relations? A sociology of knowledge perspective can provide some essential insights into the rise of whiteness studies.

As Karl Mannheim (1936) observed, ideas are grounded in changing social and economic circumstances. Following Mannheim, I suggest that the emergence of the idea of "whiteness studies" is the result of the confluence of several social dynamics—new social contexts and new intellectual perspectives. Perhaps the key factor is the "crisis" of whiteness: the continuing challenge to white supremacy and normative whiteness in social institutions and in American culture, and the withering away of white ethnic identities. This occurred in concert with increasing economic change and insecurity and the restructuring of the racial/ethnic demography of the United States as a result of post-1970 immigration. These forces not only changed racial understandings but they also made whiteness more visible. At the same time, sociological perspectives and social thought on race relations were slowly being recast by the new, more critical paradigms described above. These perspectives were more receptive to "seeing" whiteness, particularly to the extent that they focused upon issues of racial stratification and white racism. Interestingly, "whiteness studies" *still* emerged initially outside sociology—in legal studies, history, and cultural studies—a testament to the powerful impact of earlier "minus-one" approaches to race relations that examined all groups *except* the majority (Banton 1983; Doane 1997b).

On the microlevel, trends within the academy may also have played a significant role in the emergence of whiteness studies. To some degree, academic discourses on race (and other social issues) have incorporated a concern with the social location of the researcher, often implying that some voices or perspectives could be more "authentic" than other voices. In this context, whiteness studies offered whites a venue in which they could claim authenticity and expertise and make a contribution to the recasting of the study of race and ethnic relations (Bonnett 1996b). Thus the rapid growth of "whiteness studies" may also reflect the individual and collective self-interest of white researchers—an attempt to retain a grip on the mainstream of the study of race and ethnic relations (see Andersen, Chapter 2 in this volume).[3]

Also significant is the connection between whiteness studies and antiracist politics. As a paradigm, the field of whiteness studies generally claims an avowedly antiracist perspective to the extent that it is as much political project as critical paradigm. By focusing upon the oft-hidden aspects of whiteness and by taking a critical perspective, practitioners of whiteness studies hope to force whites to confront issues of race, to make white dominance problematic, and to work toward—to use the title of David Roediger's 1994 book—"the abolition of whiteness." Beyond the academic realm, confronting "whiteness" has also become a core task for antiracist activists (Bonnett 1996a) to such an extent that there exists a Center for the Study of White American Culture and national conferences of antiracist activists dedicated to challenging white hegemony. The study of "whiteness" seems to offer a vehicle through which progressive whites believe that they can mobilize to challenge white racism.

In sum, I maintain that the emergence of "whiteness studies" is grounded in social change, particularly changes in the social relations reflected in the idea of "race." Social movements challenging white hegemony and social changes in American society created space for the inclusion of "whiteness" as a key concept in our understanding of race and ethnic relations. Also significant is the fact that whiteness studies itself—by its very existence—is (often consciously) contributing to the reshaping of the relationships that it attempts to study.

Given the emergence and explosive growth of "whiteness studies" during the past decade, we have reached the point where it is useful to reflect upon the contributions of this new venture. My objective in this chapter is to present a critical assessment of the implications of "whiteness studies" for the sociology of race and ethnic relations, one in which I consider both the strengths and weaknesses of the paradigm. This will involve several interrelated tasks. First, I examine two of the essential insights of recent scholarship on white racial identity: the invisibility (particularly to whites) and socially constructed nature of "whiteness." Second, I begin to reposition the study of whiteness by emphasizing the *effects* of "whiteness" upon intergroup relations in the United States, particularly its role in the reproduction of white hegemony. Third, I consider the current crisis of "whiteness" and the potential implications of this event for the evolution of white identity. I conclude with an outline for the future development of the sociological study of whiteness and an overview of the remainder of this book.

THE ESSENTIAL INSIGHT: WHITE RACIAL INVISIBILITY

The central component of the sociology of whiteness is the observation that white Americans have a lower degree of self-awareness about race and their own racial identity than members of other racial-ethnic groups. While the nature of white racial identity remains, for the most part, uncharted territory for sociological research, a growing body of research suggests that whiteness is a "hidden identity" (Doane 1997b:378); that is, that it does not generally intrude upon the everyday experiences of most whites. In interviews with white subjects, Robert Terry (1981:119), Joe Feagin and Hernán Vera (1995:139), and Beverly Tatum (1997:93) found that the most common answer to questions concerning the meaning of whiteness was "I never thought of it." Similarly, Judith Martin and colleagues (1996:137) found that college students who adopted the white label were generally unable to provide any meaning for the identity beyond "white means white." To some degree, then, it is possible to speak of whites' unconsciousness or "transparency" (Flagg 1997:629) with regard to their own racial identity. An important aspect of transparency in whiteness studies is the emphasis on "white privilege"—the unearned benefits that flow to whites in the American racial order—as well as the "lack of awareness" of this privilege by whites (McIntosh 1989; Wildman 1996; Rothenberg 2002).

The "hidden" nature of whiteness is grounded in the dynamics of dominant group status. As a sociopolitically and numerically dominant group, whites in the United States have used their political and cultural hegemony to shape the racial order and racial understandings of American society (on the process of "racial formation," see Omi and Winant 1986:57–69). Historically, white-dominated racial understandings have generally focused upon the characteristics (i.e., "differences") of subordinate groups rather than the nature of whiteness. This emphasis by whites upon the racial "other" has gone hand in hand with the politically constructed role of whiteness as the "unexamined center" of American society. Because whites have historically controlled the major institutions of American society, they have been able to appropriate the social and cultural "mainstream" and make white understandings and practices normative (on the "Anglo core culture," see Feagin and Feagin 1996).

The mainstreaming or normalization of whiteness has in turn had important implications for white racial consciousness. Unlike members of subordinate groups, whites are less likely to feel socially and culturally "different" in their everyday experiences and much less likely to have experienced significant prejudice, discrimination, or disadvantage as a result of their race. Given that what passes as the normative center is often unnoticed or taken for granted, whites often feel a sense of culturelessness and racelessness. For most whites, this socially constructed centering is magnified by the decline in ethnic affiliations and ethnic differences among whites, a process that has reduced group identities to "symbolic" individual affiliations or mere "descent categories" (Gans 1979; Alba 1990; Waters 1990; Doane 1997b). The overall effect of these dynamics is to reinforce a lack of self-consciousness among whites, both individually and as a group. Consequently, in a discourse that focuses upon differences and the racialized "other," white becomes a default category—whiteness is defined through boundaries and exclusion, by being "not of color." It is not surprising, then, when whites conclude, as did one of Ruth Frankenberg's (1993:198) respondents, that "they are different, but I'm the same as everybody else."

In essence, the mainstreaming of whiteness and white racial unconsciousness interact in a mutually reinforcing relationship. To the extent that whiteness is the unexamined center of American society, whites are less likely to consider their own white identity. Conversely, to the extent that white racial unconsciousness persists, whites are less likely to perceive the degree to which whiteness permeates cultural understandings and institutional practices—and are thereby more likely to resist attempts to redefine the white "center" of American society. This relationship is at the core of the hidden nature of whiteness at both the individual and societal levels.

While the "hidden" nature and institutional and cultural embeddedness of white racial identity are important insights, it is essential not to overstate the case for white racial unconsciousness. Historically, white racial identity has been asserted and group mobilization has occurred when whites felt threatened by social changes, immigration, and challenges from subordinate groups. This *defensive* assertion (centering on claims of superiority and out-group inferiority) has taken such forms as Anglo-Saxonism, the Ku Klux Klan, immigration restriction movements, the White Citizens' Councils, and the current resurgence of white-supremacist groups (Higham 1988; Horsman 1981; J. Daniels 1997; Dobratz and Shanks-Meile 1997; Ferber 1998a, 1998b). On a microlevel, white racial awareness can increase because of "momentary minority" status (Gallagher 1997:7) or exposure to racialized environments and challenges to white dominance (Gallagher 1995; Saito 1995; Helms 1990; Tatum 1997). As will be discussed below, the dynamics of white racial awareness and group mobilization may become increasingly important in the future.

RETHINKING WHITENESS STUDIES

"WHITENESS": THE PROBLEM OF DEFINITION

One major challenge for those in the field of "whiteness studies" is the need to analyze the core concept. What, sociologically speaking, is "whiteness?" What does it mean to claim a "white" identity? Unfortunately, this issue has for the most part not been addressed. To some degree this reflects the general trend of overlooking whiteness; however, much of the recent literature on "whiteness" also fails to examine this question in any systematic manner. This is dangerous terrain. To focus upon issues of "whiteness" while treating it as conceptually unproblematic is to risk essentializing "whiteness," even if it is generally recognized that "whiteness" is a social construction. More important, to fail to consider the social meaning attached to "whiteness" is to miss a key element of the role of whiteness in race and ethnic relations.

The sociological significance of "whiteness" is closely connected to the meaning of "race." As we conclude the twentieth century, there is a growing consensus among social scientists that "race" has no scientific validity but that it is a *socially constructed* category based upon the arbitrary (and imprecise) evaluation of physical characteristics (Montagu 1974; Gould 1981). Thus "racial groups" are social creations and "racial identities" reflect a process of both affiliation and external ascription. Moreover, as Michael Omi and Howard Winant (1986) remind us, the racial understandings of a society undergo a constant process of re-formation as a result of political struggle and social change. Racial classification schemes in the United States have experienced continual revision, as evidenced by the changing categories employed by the U.S. Census Bureau (Lee 1993). Even the conceptualization of "race" itself has evolved, both among social scientists and in the everyday understandings of social discourse, as the "biological" definitions of the nineteenth and early twentieth centuries have given way to more ambivalent social schema. If "race" can be defined at all today, it is as a contradictory complex of the vestiges of earlier "natural" definitions that are merged uneasily with assumptions of ethniclike traits drawn from the common experiences of groups.

It is not sufficient, however, merely to state that "race" is "socially constructed." The process of racial formation occurs not in a vacuum but under a specific set of social and material circumstances. Race is not a socially created classification scheme that (imperfectly) describes "differences" between groups; it characterizes social relationships between groups having unequal levels of power. As Barbara Fields (1990:101) has observed, race is an "ideology"—a belief system and social discourse that is grounded in and explains social practice. As an ideology, race maintains intergroup boundaries and widens the social distance between groups. More important, it has served to legitimize social inequality by grounding it in pseudoscientific "innate" distinctions. In the United States, the historical role of racial ideologies was to legitimize dispossession, enslavement, and marginalization and to neutralize opposition to elites by creating a basis for forging cross-class alliances within the dominant group. With changing social and economic circumstances, racial ideologies provided the underpinnings for debt peonage and caste, as well as discrimination, superexploitation, and exclusion. Currently, a "color-blind" racial ideology continues to support racial inequality and more subtle forms of exclusion (Carr 1997; Bonilla-Silva 2001), simultaneously denying and reinforcing racial boundaries.

In the context of the ideology of race, "whiteness" must be understood as a position in a specific set of social relationships—a *"racialized social system"* (Bonilla-Silva 1997)—and as a *historically contingent* social identity. While "white" has been used in a descriptive sense in a variety of settings, including China and the Middle East, the hardening of group boundaries and the racialization of whiteness are modern phenomena linked to European conquest and colonialism (Bonnett 1998) and the spread of global capitalism. In the United States, "whiteness" slowly emerged as a socially constructed identity in concert with the racialization of dispossession and enslavement and in response to ruling-class strategies to separate indentured servants and landless free persons on the basis of race (Fields 1990; Takaki 1993; Allen 1994, 1997). "Whiteness," then, was constructed as a claim to superiority and privilege in contradistinction to a racial "other"—groups defined as inferior in an emerging racialized social system and its supporting ideology of "race." As Roediger (1991, 1994) has observed, "white" became discursively linked to such statuses as "free" and "worker"—a definition grounded in negative images of the "other."

The historically contingent nature of "whiteness" is perhaps best reflected in the evolution of group boundaries as socially constructed "racial" categories change in response to changes in racialized social systems (Bonilla-Silva 1997). In its first iterations, "whiteness" was seemingly coterminous with "English," as reflected in Benjamin Franklin's famous quotation regarding the "tawney" complexion of Swedes, Germans, and the French (cited in R. Daniels, 1990:110). With the upsurge in immigration during the nineteenth century, the racial status of various immigrant groups became a matter for social and political debate (Roediger 1991; Allen 1994; Ignatiev 1995). As part of this process, an Anglo-Saxon racial ideology served to facilitate the designation of Southern and Eastern European immigrants as "racially" different—and to legitimate policies of exclusion (Higham 1988; Horsman 1981; Grant 1916). Clearly, the boundaries of "whiteness" were historically problematic.

Historically, "whiteness" has exhibite tremendous flexibility in redefining itself and group boundaries in order to maintain a dominant position (Doane 1997b). To paint with a broad brush, we can conclude that over the past two centuries, there has been a gradual expansion of "white" group boundaries to include all "European" (another socially constructed term) groups. This ongoing redrafting of intergroup boundaries took place in a social environment that was continually evolving as a consequence of such forces as demographic change (particularly changing patterns of immigration) and capitalist development (especially industrialization and the emergence of new forms of labor control). The difficult and contested nature of this process of boundary expansion was captured in the emergence of discourses of ethnicity and assimilation, discourses that reflected the continual re-formation of "whiteness" amidst ongoing political struggle. From the standpoint of the dominant classes and ethnic groups (e.g., Anglo-Americans, white Protestants), the expansion of boundaries was politically advantageous in that it both incorporated social groups (especially the immigrant working class) who potentially could have allied themselves with peoples categorized as "nonwhite" and expanded the numerical hegemony of "white" Americans. For "European" immigrants, incorporation or assimilation as "white" Americans led to enhanced political and economic opportunities— what Roediger (1991) has termed the "wages of whiteness."

In sum, "whiteness," like race, is a socially constructed category that reflects social relationships: *it cannot be understood apart from racialized social systems.* In the context of the U.S. racial system, "whiteness" evolved from a relatively nebulous descriptive term to a basis for the rights and privileges of citizenship and—with the rise of "scientific" racism—a claim to superiority on the basis of "biological" differences. Despite the failure of attempts to define "whiteness" administratively and legally (cf. Lee 1993; Haney López 1996), it remained an important social and political fiction. Following the expansion of the boundaries of the "white" group described above, the emergence of modern industrial/postindustrial economic institutions, attacks on "scientific" racism (Montagu 1974), and the decline of formal racial segregation in the face of pressures from oppressed groups, "whiteness" continued to evolve—and to become increasingly "transparent." In this new social terrain, claims to "biological" superiority were generally discredited. Instead, "whiteness" emerged in late-twentieth-century public discourse as an identity having some vague phenotypical basis (e.g., "skin color") but whose social role was to serve as an oft-hidden claim to the social and cultural "center." As we will see below, this aspect of whiteness has played a key role in maintaining white supremacy.

In considering the evolution of the social forms of "whiteness," it is important to assert that this process is *not* one of simple historical periodicization or a "straight-line" transformation from more overt to relatively hidden displays of identity. As I noted earlier, the expression of "whiteness" was often variable in nature as it fluctuated between periods of assertion and quiescence. Even during the ascendancy of overt racism and white supremacy, "whiteness" exhibited elements of transparency, a reflection of dominant group position. Likewise, as "whiteness" became more hidden, overt white supremacy may have been consigned to the margins but it did not disappear. The essential point is that different—and even contradictory—forms of "whiteness" may coexist.

WHITENESS AND THE REPRODUCTION OF RACIAL HEGEMONY

One focus of "whiteness studies" has been to examine, albeit in an unsystematic way, how transparent forms of "whiteness" reinforce the existing racial understandings and racial order of society. Unfortunately, too much attention has been devoted to cultural images or microlevel discussions of "white privilege" (see the critique by Andersen in Chapter 2). The significance of racial ideologies and categories is not in their content but in how they affect social interaction and social stratification. Ideologies "explain" (i.e., legitimate) social relationships, while categories reflect placement within a set of relationships. They function to justify social arrangements, mobilize in-group members, and marginalize members of dominated groups. During the ascendancy of "biological" or "scientific" racism, the role of racial ideologies and of the notion of "whiteness" was to justify (in an explicit manner) conquest, enslavement, disenfranchisement, exclusion, and unequal treatment. Even seemingly opposing discourses—those advocating the abolition of slavery or fair treatment of Native Americans—served to reinforce rather than challenge the underlying racial understandings by failing to challenge assumptions of racial inferiority.

In contrast, to the extent that "whiteness" is transparent or hidden, its political and social role in reproducing white supremacy is much less visible.

A core element in the relationship between the transparency of "whiteness" and the reproduction of white hegemony is what could be termed the normalization or "universalization" (Gabriel 1998:12) of whiteness. The combination of existing domination with transparency enables "whiteness" to be cast—but not named—as the larger society, the cultural mainstream, and the nation. As Toni Morrison (1992:47) has observed, "deep within the word 'American' is its association with race . . . American means white." Politically, this means that government activities promoting white interests can masquerade as those of American society as a whole. Throughout American history, the U.S. government has acted to protect white power—from immigration restriction to Native American policy to co-opting African-American challenges to the racial order (e.g., Piven and Cloward 1971; Nagel 1996). To the extent that the prevailing political ideology portrays the state as a neutral agent in a pluralistic democracy, such state actions are cast as representing the interests of the "larger society." This *legitimation* of the actions of the "racial state" (Omi and Winant 1986:110–113) eases the tasks of domination and reproduction of the system of racial stratification. In such a context, even legal decisions that maintain racial boundaries or fail to challenge white interests can be presented as the neutral adjudication of "constitutional" issues (cf. C. Harris 1993; Haney López 1996). Given this masking of relatively overt state actions, the racial content of other government activities that exacerbate racial inequality (e.g., federal housing policy, urban policy, social welfare policy—cf. Massey and Denton 1993; Oliver and Shapiro 1995; Lipsitz 1998) is even less likely to be detected.

White transparency also affects white racial discourse—the ways whites construct or frame understandings about race and the ways in which they articulate these understandings in public forums (Doane 1996). The significance of racial discourse is twofold: it reflects existing social relations and cultural understandings, and, more important, it is part of the process through which racial understandings or ideologies are created and redefined. In other words, how whites view themselves and the dominant ways in which they define racial issues and their position in the U.S. racial order will shape intergroup relations, political agendas, and the dynamics of group mobilization. This is not to suggest that whiteness is monolithic and that all whites share the same perspective, but rather to examine significant and recurring themes in white racial discourse.

One central dynamic in white racial discourse is what we might refer to as the "color-blind" package of racial understandings. Summarized in very general terms, this discursive frame emphasizes the role of the Civil Rights movement in eliminating state-supported segregation and blatant forms of discrimination while transforming white racial attitudes. Particularly important are the purported decline in the acceptability of overt expressions of racism and the claimed increase in white acceptance of subordinate-group participation in

American society, a trend that is repeatedly cited in survey data (Schuman et al. 1997; Firebaugh and Davis 1988). What emerges is an image of a "postracial"or "color-blind" society, one in which race is no longer viewed as a significant obstacle to social and economic participation and where racism is no longer a structural phenomenon but is limited to hate crimes or other acts of discrimination committed by a small number of prejudiced *individuals* (who may be of any race).

Color-blind racial ideology has combined with the transparency of white identity and white privilege to create a new set of racial understandings for white Americans. Within this new racial discourse, race no longer "matters"— except perhaps as a private or symbolic identity (cf. Gans 1979) vaguely linked to "culture" in a "color-blind" society. In this "color-blind" society, the prescription for dealing with racial issues is not to "see" race and to claim that "everyone is the same." In other words, race is defined as an illegitimate topic for conversation. This means that those who are conscious of race or who inject racial issues into a debate may be accused of complaining, of seeking special treatment, of "playing the race card," or even of being racist (Blauner 1992:57; Doane 1996:39–40; Hartigan 1997b:496).

I contend that "color-blind" ideology plays an important role in the maintenance of white hegemony. As an organized set of claims about race, "color blindness" rests on the seemingly unassailable moral foundation of "equality," which is the basis for its political strength. What is overlooked—or deliberately masked—is the persistence of racial stratification and the ongoing role of social institutions in reproducing social inequality (on "color-blind racism," see Carr 1997; Bonilla-Silva 2001). In essence, the "color-blind" society is not a utopia where racial inequality has been eliminated; it is simply a discourse in which it is not permissible to raise issues of race—except perhaps to condemn *individual* acts of racism. Within the discourse of "color blindness," inequality is explained away as the result of individual or communal failings, not the persistence of racism, and is therefore not considered a problem requiring structural change. Given the transparency of "whiteness" and of racial inequality, the "denial" or "strategic avoidance of race" is an effective political strategy (Frankenberg 1993; Doane 1996:40) for legitimizing the persistence of white hegemony. It is not necessary that the "color-blind" discourse be universal (to take such a position would be a gross oversimplification) but merely influential enough to neutralize or redirect potential challenges to the existing racial order.

Another political effect of the melding of color blindness and the transparency of "whiteness" is the marginalization of the social and political claims of subordinate groups. If "whiteness" assumes a position as the unexamined center of American society, then the identities and practices of racially oppressed groups become something that must be changed in order to increase participation in a white-dominated society. Similarly, if race no longer "matters," then attempts by subordinate groups to engage in group political mobilization, to make social institutions more responsive, and to include their perspectives in American history and culture are defined as inherently illegitimate and derided as "politically correct." In the absence of a *named* "White History Month," Black History Month is criticized as unnecessary and unequal. Color-blind ideology seemingly adapts well to events. Following the September 11, 2001, attack on the United States, claims that race is irrelevant in a "united America" potentially make it unpatriotic or even subversive to raise questions of racial injustice. This creation of a "one-dimensional" framework of domination that eliminates opposing discourses—and its routinization in the understandings of everyday life (Marcuse 1964)—makes it more difficult to challenge white hegemony.

Perhaps the most significant political effect of the transparency of "whiteness" and color-blind racial ideology is on white explanations for the persistence of racial stratification in the United States. The "hidden" nature of whiteness and white privilege in turn shapes whites' views of inequality (indeed, the core of "white privilege" is the ability to be treated as *individuals* in a white-dominated society, as opposed to being "profiled" by police or viewed as a representative of one's race). Because whites tend not to see themselves in racial terms and not to recognize the existence of the advantages that whites enjoy in American society, this promotes a worldview that emphasizes *individualistic* explanations for social and economic achievement, as if the individualism of white privilege was a universal attribute. Whites also exhibit a general inability to perceive the persistence of discrimination and the effects of more subtle forms of institutional discrimination. In the context of color-blind racial ideology, whites are more likely to see the opportunity structure as open and institutions as impartial or objective in their functioning (Kluegel and Smith 1982; 1986; Kluegel 1990). This combination supports an interpretative framework in which whites' explanations for inequality focus upon the cultural characteristics (e.g., motivation, values) of subordinate groups, a finding that repeatedly surfaces in national surveys (Kluegel 1990; *New York Times* 1991; Schuman and Krysan 1999). Politically, this blaming of subordinate groups for their lower economic position serves to neutralize demands for antidiscrimination initiatives or for a redistribution of resources and to legitimize policies (e.g., the retreat from school desegregation and from affirmative action) that serve to defend white advantages. The effects of color blindness and the invisibility of white privilege are that subordinate group claims for a reallocation of political and economic resources can be cast as invalid, as simply another demand for preferential treatment by "special interests."

CHANGING TERRAIN: THE EVOLUTION AND "RECONSTRUCTION" OF "WHITENESS"

As Michael Omi and Howard Winant (1986:68–69) remind us, race is an "unstable and de-centered complex of social meanings constantly transformed by political struggle." During the past few decades, whiteness in the United States has been undergoing a period of crisis and transition. Beginning in the 1950s, the Civil Rights movement and related social movements succeeded in recasting the politics of race in the United States. Particularly significant in this process were challenges to white domination and exclusion, from demands for increased legal protection for civil rights, to group-based claims for the redress of racial inequality, to challenges to white hegemony over "American" culture and national identity. Implicit in this process was a challenge to the historical foundations of whiteness; that is, an attack on the legitimation of a white identity grounded in claims to white supremacy and the casting of whiteness as a positive and normalized alternative to a negatively defined racial "other." In short, it has become more difficult for whiteness to cast itself as the unexamined center of American society.

The impact of this "identity vacuum" was exacerbated by the concomitant decline of ethnic identities among whites, as the boundaries of the dominant group progressively expanded from an original Anglo-American core to include first white Protestant Americans and, more recently, all European-Americans (Doane 1997b). What has emerged is a more general—and often transparent (dominant ethnic identities are as subject to transparency as dominant racial identities)—European-American panethnic identity (Alba 1990; Doane 1997b) that may include "symbolic" vestiges of previous affiliations (Gans 1979). One outcome of this process is that for many whites, ethnic identities are more a descent category (i.e., where one's ancestors came from) than a meaningful social identity. This has created an increasing sense of "hollowness" of identity among white Americans, especially when contrasted with the assertion of cultural uniqueness by peoples of color. This hollowness is frequently manifest in popular discourse; for example, discussions of "diversity" or "multiculturalism" generally exclude whites. Thus the crisis of whiteness has political, cultural, and sociopsychological dimensions.

One response to this "crisis" of whiteness has been what Omi and Winant (1986:109–135) and Stephen Steinberg (1995) have described as the "racial reaction" of the 1970s and 1980s (and now the 1990s and 2000s). This is the attack by conservative countermovements on multiculturalism, affirmative action, the welfare state, and the role of the state as "protector" of minority rights. This political agenda has resonated among a white population that *perceives* itself as economically insecure, facing increasing political challenge, and soon to become a numerical minority (on whites' misperceptions of racial demographics, see Nadeau et al. 1993). What has emerged is what Winant (1997:42–48) has described as a series of white racial "projects" or political agendas ranging from the far right to the "new abolitionists," each of which is attempting to rearticulate the politics of race in the United States.

In some respects, much of what is happening is not new. The white racial projects of recent decades have strong parallels to what I referred to above as the defensive assertion of whiteness, a practice that has deep historical roots. White defensiveness can take the form of either overt expressions of white supremacy (as has occurred among the far right) or, more frequently, the subtle or even transparent (in terms of lack of awareness) use of whiteness as the "mainstream" or unexamined center. To the extent that any shift in strategy has occurred, it is the degree to which both liberal and conservative strategies have melded white transparency to the ideology of "color blindness" (Winant 1997; Carr 1997). This "stealth" project—inasmuch as its benefits for whites are deliberately masked—plays a major role in the drive to maintain white dominance.

At the same time, the present situation does differ from the past. What is new is the beginning of a changing terrain for the politics of whiteness. The political debates of recent decades have initiated a process of "outing" whiteness, exposing the contradictions in past constructions of whiteness and making it more difficult to sustain "white" as a default identity in contrast to a racial "other" (on "white racial dualism," see Winant 1997:41). It is clearly possible to observe a growing racial self-awareness among whites, as whites respond to the identity vacuum, to increased (and politicized) encounters within institutions, and to general challenges to white domination (Gallagher 1995; Saito 1995).

Perhaps the current formation of "whiteness" can best be described as exhibiting contradictory tendencies. The forces challenging whiteness have rendered it more visible, yet it retains many elements of a hidden identity. We can speak of white racial politics or white racial projects, yet in most cases the "white" component remains relatively invisible. These countervailing dynamics are significant in that the recent power of whiteness (in the "post–scientific racism" era) stems from its position as the hidden or normalized center of American society, as currently manifest in the discourses of "color blindness" and individualism. To the extent that whiteness becomes more visible, whites will either have to acknowledge their position as continuing beneficiaries of white supremacy (and perhaps alter the racial status quo) or devise new strategies for maintaining white hegemony. The evolution of whiteness and the implications of these changes should be an important element of the study of whiteness.

One influential discourse that emerges from the crisis and reconstruction of whiteness is one in which whiteness is redefined as a liability and whites are cast as "victims." If society is cast as "color-blind" and racism is reduced to the actions of prejudiced individuals, then it is possible to claim that "minority racism" exists alongside white racism and that whites are equally or even more likely to be targets. As Charles Gallagher (Chapter 10 in this volume) argues, color-blindness also enables some whites to "play the white ethnic card" and claim that their ancestors also experienced oppression, thereby negating any current advantages. On a broader scale, if white privilege is invisible and racial barriers are claimed to be a relic of the past, then race-based claims or challenges to the existing system of racial stratification (which has now been recast as a meritocracy) can be framed as "reverse discrimination" or racism against whites (Gallagher 1995; Doane 1996; 1997a). As Gallagher (1995) and George Lipsitz

(1998) have noted, if whites feel that the major racial problems existed in the past (i.e., slavery) and not in the present, then when issues of racial inequality are raised, they feel picked on, victimized, and "made to feel guilty." In this socially constructed reality, where whites are "victimized" by affirmative action and false accusations of racism, a new generation of whites can claim—as my students have in essays—that their chances for a successful career are lower because they are white. While this model of white victimization may rest on weak empirical foundations, its political significance should not be underestimated. Casting whites as victims provides a strong base for countermobilization and the defense of white privilege—a social movement that ironically can advance under the banner of color blindness. As Ian Haney López (1996) has observed, this has led to a discourse where race can be discussed only in the context of defending white interests in the face of "reverse discrimination."

WHITENESS AND THE SOCIOLOGY OF RACE AND ETHNIC RELATIONS: AN AGENDA FOR THE FUTURE

The title of this book, *White Out,* was chosen very carefully. A whiteout is a winter condition in which clouds and heavy, wind-driven snow combine to obscure vision, distort the horizon, and make it difficult to see anything except *very dark* objects. I believe that this captures the historical impact that whiteness has had on race relations in the United States. At the same time, our title points to another danger, that of seeing nothing but white. As Margaret Andersen so brilliantly argues in the next chapter, whiteness studies also has the potential danger of deflecting much work on race relations toward a relatively meaningless debate on the construction of white identity. I agree. Whiteness cannot and should not be studied apart from white racism and racialized social systems. This is reflected in the second part of our title, "The Continuing Significance of Racism."

The chapters in this volume are a starting point in the project of redirecting whiteness studies in what we believe is a more meaningful direction. This involves several important tasks. First, we need to rethink whiteness in ways that have greater theoretical and analytical complexity. The chapters in the next section both challenge existing ways of viewing whiteness and attempt to conceptualize it in new ways. We need to understand the multidimensional nature of whiteness, to see that it can, as demonstrated by several authors, take on different forms across class lines, among new immigrants, and in the multiracial political movement. There are many other dimensions to be explored, including understanding the effect of globalization upon whiteness.

A second major task is to undertake empirical studies of the role whiteness and color-blind racism play in the reproduction of white dominance. One major shortcoming of much of the existing literature on whiteness is its lack of empirical grounding. The research-based chapters in the third part of the book explore several ways in which whiteness shapes casual conversation, presentation of self, school behavior, and perceptions of workplace issues, affirmative action, and desirable neighborhoods. In each case the final outcome is to reinforce white supremacy and the dominant color-blind ideology. We hope that these works inspire much more sociological research into the dimensions of whiteness and color-blind racism.

Finally, given that whiteness is a position in a racialized social structure and that these structures are constantly changing, we need to move beyond static conceptualizations of whiteness to incorporate ways in which whiteness is being recast. The two chapters in the fourth section of the book explore dimensions and contradictions in the relationship between whiteness and antiracist challenges to white supremacy. If we are to hope for any meaningful challenge to the dominance of color-blind ideology, then we need to understand the impact of whiteness on antiracist efforts. In the final chapter of the book, coeditor Eduardo Bonilla-Silva presents a provocative discussion of the Latin Americanization of the United States—an outline of ways in which the boundaries of white racial identity may change in the twenty-first century and the implications of these changes for the future of race relations in the United States. If indeed race relations in the United States are at the beginning of a period of rapid change, then it is all the more essential that we develop a new direction for the sociological study of whiteness.

PART II

New Perspectives on Whiteness

2
Whitewashing Race: A Critical Perspective on Whiteness

MARGARET L. ANDERSEN*

What does it mean to be white? This is the question being asked in the emergent field of whiteness studies, where scholars are probing how white racial identity is constructed and how systems of white privilege operate. Several ideas have developed from this new work about the social construction of race and the development of white identity and white privilege. Yet there is something fundamentally disturbing about the growth of whiteness studies. I write this essay with a deep sense of ambivalence. Many, including myself, have long argued that studies of racial, gender, and class stratification are inadequate as long as the focus is solely on people of color as victims. Indeed, progressive scholars have asserted that analyzing structures of white privilege must be part of the analysis of racial stratification (Andersen 1984, 1987, 1999; McIntosh 1988; Rothenberg 2002; Wilson 1973). But in shifting the subject of race from the experience of disadvantaged groups to white people, whiteness studies risks eclipsing the study of racial power, focusing solely on white identity, and analyzing "whiteness" in the absence of the experience of people of color.

Many working in this area have cautioned us about the potential for whiteness studies to divert attention from racism (Fine et al. 1997; Frankenberg 1997; Rothenberg 2002), and all of the writers working in this area identify themselves as working for antiracist, progressive politics. Furthermore, most state that their work is situated in an analysis of white privilege, although, as we will see, this is often more promised than realized. The criticisms raised here are not meant to devalue the contributions made by the people working on this subject. Nonetheless, the proliferation of literature in this area suggests that it is

*This paper has grown from many exciting discussions with scholars thinking about race. I thank the following for sharing their ideas as I developed this project: Maxine Baca Zinn, Joel Best, Edna Bonacich, Eduardo Bonilla-Silva, George Frederickson, Estelle Freidman, Elizabeth Higginbotham, Peter Kolching, Carole Marks, Hazel Markus, Joanne Nigg, Peggy Phelan, Matthew Snipp, Claude Steele, Dorothy Steele, Jory Steele, Ben Steiner, Bob Zajonc, and the Multicultural Discourse Group at the University of Delaware. I also appreciate the support provided by the Center for Comparative Studies of Race and Ethnicity at Stanford University.

time to assess critically the value of whiteness studies both for the study of racial inequality and for its implications for action to promote a more racially just society. Most commonly this literature is being written by those in education, legal studies, history, psychology, and literature and by antiracist activists. There is a noticeable absence of sociological work (with the exception of this volume and a handful of others; see Frankenberg 1993, 1997; Gallagher 1999, 2000; Thompson 1996, 1999; Wellman 1997; Winant 1997). The point here is not to guard disciplinary turf but to show how the absence of a sociological perspective leaves whiteness studies without much grounding in the material reality of racial stratification.

WHY WHITENESS? WHY NOW?

Several questions form the core of whiteness studies, including: What does it mean to be white? How has "whiteness" emerged historically? What is the role of law in defining who is white? How has the emergence of whiteness as a racial identity been linked to the social construction of others (i.e., the process of racialization) and to the formation of class structure? Is confronting whiteness a necessary step in progressive politics for racial change?

Whiteness studies originates in several intellectual movements: feminist scholarship on the intersections of race, class, and gender; critical legal studies; critical race theory; cultural studies; poststructuralist and postcolonial scholarship; multicultural education, and historical studies of the emergence of white racism and white racial identity. Several landmark publications have inspired much of this work, especially Peggy McIntosh's essay, "White Privilege and Male Privilege" (1988), Ruth Frankenberg's book, *White Women, Race Matters* (1993), and David Roediger's book, *The Wages of Whiteness* (1991). Together, these authors have asked how the taken-for-granted and invisible character of whiteness reinforces systems of advantage and disadvantage and how the construction of whiteness supports the hegemony of white power and the class structure. Although there are some significant differences in the orientation of those from different disciplines (worthy of further investigation), the major questions asked have forced us to think about how racial identities are created and how systems of privilege operate.

Why whiteness? Why now? Whiteness studies has been the subject of headline articles in *The Chronicle of Higher Education, Newsweek, Time*, and numerous academic periodicals. Since intellectual movements within the academy usually reflect political and social changes in the society writ large, the growth of this field should be understood in the social and historical moment of which it is a part. This includes the growth of conservatism; the emergence of racial identity politics; the backlash against affirmative action; increased and widely acknowledged population diversity—including news about the decline of whites as a majority population; the growth of academic feminism; and the absence of a nationally visible antiracist movement. In this context, the prevailing discourse about race in the dominant culture has been marked by an ideology of color blindness, which both silences discussion of persistent racial inequality *and* asserts that race no longer matters (Bonilla-Silva 2001, 1997; Bonilla-Silva and Forman 2000). Color-blind ideology assumes that society is organized along race-neutral structures. Whiteness studies is a revolt against conservative, color-blind politics (Nyugen 2000). Hence whiteness studies scholars see their work in contrast to reactionary movements to establish white student centers, to reassert white supremacy, and to restrict the academic canon primarily to works by and about white scholars.

Moreover, the focus on diversity and on racial identity and the changing composition of the population have created a society marked by racial anxiety. Assertions about political correctness, the professed decline of "standards," and the call for traditional values are indications of a profound sense of white racial angst; many now think that being white is a handicap, even though the system of white privilege remains. Indeed, affirmative action politics has generated a sense of perceived threat among many white people. The growth of feminism and the rise of racial identity politics mean that the privileges associated with being white and male have called into question (Wellman 1997); hence, many whites think that they are the new losers (Apple 1998). The prospect that whites will no longer be a clear numerical majority in the population—a fact widely disseminated and known—also raises new racial anxieties for some whites as the population becomes more racially and ethnically diverse. At the same time, as Howard Winant (1997) has argued, the communal basis of white ethnicity has disappeared, even though it is maintained as a "status honor" or "ethnicity without cost" (Gans 1979; Waters 1996).

In this context, there is profound confusion for liberals about how to think about and talk about race, even though most liberals would quickly distance themselves from anti–affirmative action efforts and would want to still be "correct" in their support for racial justice. But since conservatives have appropriated the liberal ideology of color blindness as the cultural ideal, liberals have been left with no way to articulate their antiracist politics. Progressives in this context have then asked: What does my whiteness mean and what is my place in progressive antiracist politics? Progressive white men, especially, are likely to perceive their race/gender identity as a marked category, whereas before it could simply be taken for granted. And as David Wellman argues, in experiencing themselves as a marked and suspect category:

> white men have discovered what nonwhites and women living in a pre-dominantly white male (and heterosexual) world have always known: Life in a racial and gendered category is not always comfortable. Thus, white men are beginning to experience what they previously took for granted: for middle-class men, this is a sense of privilege, for working-class men, it is feeling beleaguered and besieged. (Wellman 1997:321).

It is, then, not surprising that, as far as I can tell, the majority of those writing in "whiteness studies" are white men—more so than is the case in the intellectual movements from which these studies emerge. Conditions of the time pose this dilemma: How can white men (and white people, more generally) align them-selves with progressive racial causes when the progressive discourse around race and gender points to them as the cause of the problem? Especially at a time when the dominant discourse over race comes from those defending the status quo *and* in the absence of a visible, antiracist, multiracial movement, progressive white people may be searching for a sense of political and intellectual place. As a young, white, progressive student said to me, "I am trying to figure out my place in this." Whiteness studies seems to provide a solution to this dilemma.

THEMES IN WHITENESS STUDIES: WHITENESS AS NORM, PRIVILEGE, AND SOCIAL CONSTRUCTION

Three major contributions emerge from the new whiteness literature. First is the recognition that *"white" is ubiquitous*, though typically not acknowledged. Second is that *whiteness is a system of privilege*, mapped on to the domination of "others"—that is, people of color. Third is an emphasis on *race as a socially constructed category*; just as people of color have been "racialized," so have whites, although with radically different consequences.

WHITENESS AS THE INVISIBLE NORM

Toni Morrison (one of the few African-Americans writing about whiteness) writes about "the gaze of whiteness as the unacknowledged norm." She con-tinues: "My project is an effort to avert the critical gaze from the racial object to the racial subject; from the described and imagined to the describers and imaginers; from the serving to the served" (Morrison 1992:90). This captures well the orienting theme of whiteness studies: being white is a particular social position that has been largely unexamined; furthermore, whiteness structures racism and racial inequality. Whiteness scholars argue that without examining whiteness per se, we ignore the construct on which race, racism, and racial in-equality are built. Moreover, just as feminist studies has analyzed the distortions that result from taking men's experience as the unacknowledged norm against which women are judged and seen, whiteness scholars assert that "white" has been the unexamined norm, implicitly standing for all that is presumed to be right and normal. Whiteness is the location from which others are defined and judged, since it is white people who hold the power to do so.

In a related vein, whiteness scholars point out that "race" is present even if there are no people of color in the room (Aanerud 1997). Early in feminist studies, Marcia Millman and Rosabeth Moss Kanter (1975) pointed out that gender was operative even in a group of all men. That is, women do not have to be present for gender to be operating; men are gendered subjects, too. The analogy to race is that race is operative even in a group of all white people. (There are suggestions here for future empirical work, though little such empirical work has been done to date.) Hence whiteness studies conclude that "the 'problem' of race now includes those who are raced white" (Nakayama and Martin 1999:5). In other words, just as people of color are racialized, so are whites, though in different social locations.

This scholarship also argues that whiteness is culturally hegemonic and maintains its hegemony by seeming natural or just not being questioned. Hence "as long as race is something only applied to non-white people, as long as white people are not racially seen and named, they function as a human norm. Other people are raced, we are just people" (R. Dyer 1997:1). Because of this, the argument presumes that disrupting whiteness will shake the foundations of racism. Therefore one of the purposes of whiteness studies is to "destabilize" white identity—to expose, examine, and challenge it. Renunciating whiteness as an assumed and normative identity is required, according to this literature, as a step toward creating racial justice. Whiteness scholars presume that studying whiteness will help us understand how white domination continues. Thomas Nakayama and Robert Krizek write, " 'White' is a relatively uncharted territory that has remained invisible as it continues to influence the identity of those both within and without its domain. It affects the everyday fabric of our lives but resists, sometimes violently, any extensive characterization that would allow for the mapping of its contours. It wields power yet endures as a largely unarticulated position" (1999:88).

Some of the new scholarship on whiteness takes its lesson from postmodernist and poststructuralist concepts of positionality—that is, the idea that social location shapes what you perceive. As a long-standing conclusion of the sociology of knowledge, such an argument acknowledges the significance of social location in shaping the worldview of diverse groups. Whiteness studies adds that the "personal interrogation of position" (Patterson 1998:119) will make whiteness visible and thereby undermine the perpetuation of an unjust racial order. There is an assumption here that if white people would only become conscious of their whiteness, more just behavior would follow. One might ask if becoming conscious of whiteness could not just as easily produce white-supremacist movements or lead white people to feel relieved that they have privilege and others do not (a reaction I have found among white students who have read about white privilege). As Parker Johnson puts it: "I hope that we will not reinscribe white hegemony by merely interrogating its subjectivity and particularism, but that we will create new intellectual space for relational understanding and, more importantly, racial justice. . . . What will whites think, be, and do when they are no longer white?" (1999:5).

WHITENESS AS A SYSTEM OF PRIVILEGE

Not only is whiteness conceptualized in this literature as an unacknowledged norm, it is also defined as a system of racial privilege. This is one of the most important points in the whiteness literature. Whiteness is an "invisible bundle of expectations and courtesies" (Delgado and Stefanic 1997:xvii). "An invisible sack of privilege," Peggy McIntosh (2001[1988]) calls it in her highly influential essay, where she details the myriad of ways that whiteness can be taken for granted in everyday life. White people need not wonder, for example, if their achievements (a job, an award, a scholarship) will be seen as happening *because* of their race; they need not worry that if they fail, their failure will be used to judge their race. Whiteness just is; no white person is seen as representing their race. Indeed, most white people do not even think of themselves as raced subjects.

This argument is particularly powerful as a pedagogical tool in teaching about race and racism. Many, including me, have used McIntosh's list of white privileges to reveal to students the unacknowledged privilege associated with being white and to show how this structures a system of advantage and disadvantage. As many in the whiteness literature have argued, whiteness maintains its invisibility by not being questioned (N. Rodriguez 1998). Thus scholars argue that: " 'Mapping whiteness' has the potential not only to raise consciousness about one's own possible complicity in supporting oppressive regimes . . . it also positions one to encounter a multitude of critical languages that can be used to rethink and live whiteness in progressive ways" (N. Rodriguez 1998:31–32). But understanding white privilege only as a repertoire of taken-for-granted advantages is not enough. Without also understanding racism and racial stratification as the foundation of white privilege which is the very structure of society, acknowledging white privilege will only generate a sense of relief for dominant groups and will not dissect the institutional arrangements through which racism continues.

Yet how do we move beyond recognizing white privilege to actually doing something about it? Richard Dyer states: "White power secures its dominance by seeming not to be anything in particular" (1998:1). But in shifting the focus to whiteness, do we sidestep white racism? Think about this: "The shift from race to whiteness is an important conceptual shift in that it allows us to identify the ways that white privilege functions *without having to name anyone a racist*" (emphasis mine; Wander, Martin, and Nakayama 1999:23). Whiteness scholars do situate "whiteness" in a discussion of privilege, but, as we shall see, other than this, seldom is white privilege or white racism actually examined in depth in much of this writing.

THE SOCIAL CONSTRUCTION OF RACE

A third persistent theme in the whiteness literature is that race is a social construction, news perhaps to some, but a point known by sociologists since the founding of the discipline. The argument is that race is not "real" but stems from social relations; therefore, whiteness has constructed "others" while also constructing itself. Whiteness is an unmarked category against which difference is constructed. Hence to be white is to be not black and blackness is created out of the vantage point of white identity.

This contribution of the whiteness literature is especially strong in the historical literature, where the construction of whiteness is understood in the context of the formation of class, nation, and empire (Frankenberg 1997; Ignatiev 1995). Thus David Roediger (1991) argues that we cannot understand the formation of class and race domination in economic terms alone. He argues that historically white workers defined and accepted their position as wage laborers by seeing themselves as "not slaves." The identity as "white" thus emerges from workers' fear of their dependency as a wage class and thus is part of the process of both class and race formation. This analysis also restores human agency to an otherwise more determinist view of class formation and reflects a theme running throughout this literature: that the construction of white identity develops through the creation of "otherness."

This social-constructionist theme is consistent with the new emphasis on racialization in much contemporary race scholarship. This argument in this literature also reflects the discovery (vis-à-vis postmodernism) by humanists and psychologists of the idea of social construction. Whereas in many disciplines race has typically been treated as an attribute, whiteness studies reestablishes the significance of race as a social construction. As a consequence, the methodology of much of this writing is narrative, autobiographical, and textual. Oddly enough, however, little connection is typically made in this literature to the operation of the state and economy in producing racial categories, since the focus tends to be overwhelmingly personal (although this is not true of all the whiteness literature).

Furthermore, as in gender studies, there is a fascination in this literature with transgression-crossing boundaries as we "do race." Race is conceptualized in much of this writing as performance, and the performance of whiteness is said to be dismantled through "interrogation." Thus Chris Cuomo and Kim Hall write: "Scholars and activists critically interrogating whiteness seek to decenter rather than recenter whiteness by making performances of whiteness visible" (Cuomo and Hall 1999: 3). But whiteness is more than a performance. As we shall see, there is little discussion in this literature of an institutional connection with the performative aspects of racial identity. This is the result of so much of this writing originating in cultural and literary studies. Useful as such studies have been in underscoring the social construction of race, when they fail to connect whiteness to material structures and the operation of power, they provide hollow understandings of the structural foundations of racism.

EVALUATING WHITENESS STUDIES

Having seen the major contributions of whiteness studies, how do we evaluate its value? This can be done on several grounds: 1) conceptual and analytic clarity; 2) empirical verification; 3) pedagogical value; 4) the implications for social policy and social change.

Conceptually, one of the major problems in the whiteness literature is the reification of whiteness as a concept, as an experience, and as an identity. This practice not only leads to conceptual obfuscation but also impedes the possibility for empirical analysis. In this literature, "whiteness" comes to mean just about everything associated with racial domination. As such, whiteness becomes a slippery and elusive concept. Whiteness is presented as any or all of the following: identity, self-understanding, social practices, group beliefs, ideology, and a system of domination. As one critic writes, "If historical actors are said to have behaved the way they did mainly because they were white, then there's little room left for more nuanced analysis of their motives and meanings" (Stowe 1996:77). And Alastair Bonnett points out that whiteness "emerges from this critique as an omnipresent and all-powerful historical force. Whiteness is seen to be responsible for the failure of socialism to develop in America, for racism, for the impoverishment of humanity. With the 'blame' comes a new kind of centering: Whiteness, and White people, are turned into the key agents of historical change, the shapers of contemporary America" (1996b:153).

Despite noting that there is differentiation among whites and warning against using whiteness as a monolithic category, most of the literature still proceeds to do so, revealing a reductionist tendency. Even claiming to show its multiple forms, most writers essentialize and reify whiteness as something that directs most of Western history (Gallagher 2000). Hence while trying to "deconstruct" whiteness and see the ubiquitousness of whiteness, the literature at the same time reasserts and reinstates it (Stowe 1996:77).

For example, Michael Eric Dyson suggests that whiteness is identity, ideology, and institution (Dyson, quoted in Chennault 1998:300). But if it is all these things, it becomes an analytically useless concept. Christine Clark and James O'Donnell write: "to reference it reifies it, to refrain from referencing it obscures the persistent, pervasive, and seemingly permanent reality of racism" (1999:2). Empirical investigation requires being able to identify and measure a concept— or at the very least to have a clear definition—but since whiteness has come to mean just about everything, it ends up meaning hardly anything.

The vagueness of whiteness as an analytical and empirically observable concept is coupled with the virtual absence of material analysis in most of this work. One of the oddest things about the whiteness literature is that most authors state that they situate their work in the analysis of privilege, but in most of this writing, there is hardly any mention of white racism, global capitalism, split labor markets, residential segregation, school tracking, and so forth. All of the mechanisms and sites of racial domination and subordination disappear from view. Instead, the focus is on the "norm" that whiteness creates. And in scholarship that purports to be about white privilege, why do so many authors focus on the white working class if they reference any empirical subjects at all (Newitz and Wray 1997)? Where is the middle class in this literature? Where are white elites? In the end, whiteness studies tells us little about the process of racial subordination, focusing instead primarily on white identity. Like study-ing "diversity without oppression" (Andersen 1999), there is little analysis of power and a strange absence of analyses of white racism—except for personal narratives about learning racism—in much of this literature.

Exceptions to this include the works of Heney Giroux (1997), George Lipsitz (1998), Raka Shome (1999), and Peter McLaren (1997, 1999). Giroux writes: "Central to any pedagogical approach to race and the politics of 'white-ness' is the recognition that race is a set of attitudes, values, lived experiences, and affective identification. However arbitrary, dangerous, and variable, the fact is that racial categories exist and shape the lives of people differently within ex-isting inequalities of power and wealth" (1997:294). Shome writes: "Whiteness is not just about bodies and skin color, but rather more about the *discursive practices* that, because of colonialism and neocolonialism, privilege and sustain the global dominance of white imperial subjects and Eurocentric worldviews" (Shome 1999:108). Shome clearly situates whiteness in the context of global power relations. She writes: "Whiteness needs to be studied through the inter-locking axes of power, spatial location, and history" (1999:109), but nonetheless returns to how whiteness has structured her identity in colonized India and as an Indian woman in the United States. An assumption running throughout the literature is that "removing the mystique of the 'center' disrupts its power" (Trinh 1991). Without a discussion of racial power, this seems rather hollow. Rather, there is a tendency for much of the writing in this area to move to-ward self-reflection. A huge portion of the literature is autobiographical writing on becoming white or on white people's first encounters with racism. As a re-sult, much of this literature quickly devolves into highly individualized identity narratives or provides voyeuristic, ethnographic accounts of various aspects of white working-class life and white popular culture.

In addition, in emphasizing the social construction of race, whiteness scholars emphasize the ideological construction of racial meaning and identities but without connecting racialization to the operation of the state (legal scholars are an exception; see C. Harris 1993; Haney López 1996). Thus whiteness becomes conceptualized largely as individual performance, something that means that if whites were to simply denounce white privilege and white identity—that is, become "race traitors" (Ignatiev and Garvey 1993–1994)— racial stratification would go away. Yet, as Joe Feagin has argued in criticizing the overemphasis on social construction of race: "Systemic racism is not just about the construction of racial images, attitudes, and identities. It is even more centrally about the creation, development, and maintenance of white privilege, economic wealth, and sociopolitical power over nearly four centuries" (Feagin 2000:21). Likewise, Cornel West writes: "Categories are constructed, scars and bruises are felt with human bodies, some of which end up in coffins. Death is not a construct" (Klor de Alva, Shorris, and West 1997:485). The idea that whites just individually give up their whiteness seems ludicrous if one understands that racial identity is not just an individualized process but involves the formation of social groups organized around material interests with their roots in social structure, not just individual consciousness.

Much of the whiteness writing originates in the school of thought stemming from educational studies about "unlearning racism." In this argument, racism and prejudice are seen as being learned early in white experience but as being "unlearned" if one reexamines one's past and denounces earlier learned prejudices. This assumes that the problems of racism can be solved by white people changing their minds. Confronting one's own racial prejudice and race awareness is no doubt a part of challenging the racial order, but, like studying prejudice in the absence of racial stratification, leaving things in the hands of "unlearning racism" is likely to do little to unseat the apparatus of racial power. When this is coupled with the obfuscation of thought that appears in some of these individual narratives, we are often left with rhetorical and garbled thinking, such as: "I was raised to be an antiracist, not an antiracist racist." This author goes on to say: "Antiracists do not own the inevitability of their racism. . . . Antiracist racists know that even in the practice of the confrontation of injustice, they are still racist. . . . It [antiracist racism] embodies an honest experience of the complexities of racism occupying one's psyche mediated with a profound commitment to the lifelong confrontation and attempted eradication of it from one's psyche" (Clark 1999:93).

Prejudice and racism do not develop in the absence of material reality, as sociological work that links prejudice to a sense of group position demonstrates (Blumer 1958; Bobo 1999). But without this material foundation, much of the writing on whiteness comes across merely as white angst. Likewise, focusing on "privilege" without any discussion of discrimination and exclusion makes even the concept of privilege an elusive one (Zack 1999).

Even those who acknowledge the material basis of race and racism (and most do in passing) retreat to essentialized notions of whiteness as the thing that holds everything together—as though if white people were to abandon whiteness and change their minds, it would go away. Thus, for example, Giroux argues that "deconstructing whiteness" is the basis for a new democratic practice. He writes that rather than eradicating the concept of race, we should "renegotiate" whiteness, by which he means considering the differences in whiteness and the political possibilities that can be opened up through a "discourse of whiteness." This will "articulate new forms of identity, new possibilities for democratic practices, and new processes of cultural exchange" (1997:265). Whiteness, according to Giroux, promotes race-based hierarchies, and racial identity structures the struggle over cultural and political resources. He writes: "Whiteness' in this context becomes less a matter of creating a new form of identity politics than an attempt to rearticulate 'whiteness' as part of a broader project of cultural, social, and political citizenship" (1997:295). Giroux explicitly advocates "a pedagogy of whiteness" as going beyond identifying whiteness as an ideology of privilege and domination, which he sees as making "white" monolithic and therefore not generating good antiracist politics. Instead he suggests that whites should "understand and struggle against the legacy of white racism while using the particularities of 'their own culture as a resource for resistance, reflection, and empowerment' " (1997:310)—a quote he borrows from Stuart Hall, who in the original used it to refer to black Americans (Hall 1991). The role of people of color in whiteness studies then becomes not only nonexistent, but appropriated.

What about the implications of whiteness studies for classroom pedagogy? Should teachers use their time to teach about whiteness, or does this supplant other efforts for multicultural/multiracial education? Sheets argues that whiteness studies centers the dialogue on white identity rather than on multicultural/multiracial classroom practices and teacher-student relationships (Sheets 2000). Some even say that whiteness studies appropriates the pain of people of color and changes the goal of multicultural education into the transformation of white people, not the education of students of color or the education of whites about the experience of people of color. Seen in this way, people of color become invisible once again as whites become the center of attention. Such critics ask: Is not the goal of multicultural education learning about the experience of others? For whose purposes and to whose benefit does whiteness studies work?

Finally, what kind of politics and social policies does whiteness studies suggest? The political/pragmatic implications of this literature are that we should create instability in racial categories. Is that enough? Two directions are suggested in the literature: abolishing whiteness and transforming/rearticulating whiteness. Thus, in the journal *Race Traitor*, Noel Ignatiev and John Garvey argue: "The key to solving the social problems of our age is to abolish the white race. Until that task is accomplished, every partial reform will prove elusive, because white influence permeates every issue of U.S. society, whether domestic or foreign" (1993–1994:10). They distinguish this from antiracism, claiming that "antiracism admits the natural existence of 'races' " (1993–1994:10) and saying instead that "the way to abolish the white race is to disrupt that conformity. If enough people who look white violate the rules of whiteness, their existence cannot be ignored. If it becomes impossible for the upholders of white rule to speak in the name of all who look white, the white race will cease to exist" (1993–1994:36). There is debate about this position within the whiteness literature, but one cannot help but wonder: If "whiteness" disappeared, would we not still have racial subordination? Or if white people no longer thought of themselves as white, would not capitalism continue to produce a racially segregated and divided society?

Whiteness scholars see whiteness as subject to redefinition resistance and change. Hence Dyer writes: "A crucial political, cultural, and ultimately educational project is to make whiteness strange" (1997:4). Michael Apple notes that there are dangers, because this can have contradictory effects and can "run the risk of lapsing into progressive individualism" (Apple 1998:xi). He continues:

"We must be on guard to ensure that a focus on whiteness doesn't become one more excuse to recenter dominant voices and to ignore the voices and testimony of those groups of people whose dreams, hopes, lives, and very bodies are shattered by current relations of exploitation and domination" (1998:xi).

Whether whiteness studies can provide the grounds for a racially progressive movement is highly questionable. As David Stowe (1996) asks: How many political movements have succeeded based on a renunciation of privilege? In the end, the whiteness literature seems to give whites a place in antiracist politics but does not well articulate a politics of change. If we disrupt the ideology of race and its effects on our interactions and relationships, do we necessarily destabilize white privilege in the material sense? Particularly since this body of literature seldom deals with the material reality of racial segregation and discrimination, this seems unlikely.

We should also ask whose interests are served by the study of whiteness. Many claim that those writing this literature are people of color, but I found writings by people of color in this literature to be very few. (One exception is Roediger's collection, *Black on White* [1998]). Does whiteness studies then just reinforce the central place of white people in race scholarship (Cuomo and Hall 1999)? Compared to the access to mainstream journals and the academic press that ethnic and black studies had in their beginnings, it is worth noting that whiteness studies have early achieved a place in the academy (Sheets 2000).

For many, participation in whiteness literature is itself a new form of privilege. Joe Kincheloe and Shieley Steinberg state that a key goal of whiteness studies is "creating a positive, proud, attractive, antiracist white identity that is empowered to travel in and out of various racial/ethnic circles with confidence and empathy" (1998:12). Who gets the privilege of such "traveling"—that is, assuming the stance of the outsider with the option of leaving at any time? Who gets to be a "race" without the negative consequences of racial stratification? One scholar puts this question well as she writes: "Is the study of whiteness just another untapped arena of investigation that we can now mine—without recrimination—successfully applying the body of our situated knowledge through a kind of naïve and opportunistic theoretical travel?" (Chabram-Dernersesian 1997:109). Whiteness now gets a "class, race, and gender accent" (Chabram-Dernersesian 1997:110).

As Dyson asserts: "Current whiteness studies will only be strengthened as they refer to those texts and figures in black life, and in other minority communities, who have aided in the demythologization of a homogenous, uniform whiteness" (Dyson, quoted in Chennault 1998:305). Although shifting the subject of race to white people has the potential to analyze the operation of systems of advantage, to date it has largely centered around white people again and can be seen as affirming and reifying whiteness even while linking it to racism and social privilege.

CONCLUSION

Although there is a risk in characterizing this literature as a whole, I am not convinced that whiteness studies will either produce analytically strong arguments about race or lead to a progressive politics for racial change. First, it is troubling that the literature on whiteness remains largely uninformed by a sociological perspective. As Howard Winant (1997) has written, race tends to be depicted in much of this literature as *either* a biological fact *or* an illusion. Indeed, some of the whiteness literature treats race as pure illusion. But recognizing the socially constructed nature of race does not mean it is "not there" or that we can just think it away, such as by renunciating white privilege. Race is a social fact in the sense that Emile Durkheim (1964[1895]:13) meant; race can *both* be constructed *and* be real in its consequences. And, as Rubén Rumbaut has creatively articulated (1996:xvi), race is a "pigment of our imagination"; nonetheless, it is real in that it results in a specific distribution of differential resources. Furthermore, we need not "see" race to have race-specific outcomes. As many have demonstrated, race-blind policies can reproduce racial privilege (Bonilla-Silva 1997, 2001; Bobo 1999).

Although there is debate within this literature on whether we should "abandon whiteness" or become fully cognizant of whiteness, the literature shares a conclusion that only by becoming fully conscious of whiteness can we develop progressive action toward the goal of racial justice. Hence the new whiteness literature appeals to white liberals who want to think race should just go away: we can "all just be people." Although I confess to believing in the appeal of that framework, when I think about the agenda for social science and social policy, whiteness studies seem more of a deflection from scholarship that can produce meaningful social policy. At the same time, whiteness scholarship provides a new academic opportunity for white people, thus, ironically, installing a new form of white privilege.

I have no doubt that self-criticism must accompany white people's antiracist work. Too often white progressives leave their own attitudes and behaviors unexamined while working against racism. But politics does not stop there, as the authors in whiteness studies know. Although I think we must destabilize the hegemony of the "color-blind" framework that now petrifies racial progress, I do not think we can simply deconstruct race and make it go away. This is not to say that it is unimportant to study how race is perceived and constructed but, if we see race as overly constructed, then we engage in intellectual games that are meaningless in the society beyond the academy. It is possible to see race in overly constructivist terms (Feagin 2000).

The literature on whiteness, though situated in recognition of the privileges that "whiteness" supports, has a strong tendency to gloss over the material realities of race, since its primary focus is on white identity and white consciousness. In the absence of a material analysis of race and racialization, much of the whiteness studies scholarship devolves into white identity politics. This is why Howard Winant (1997) concludes that without these studies incorporating the state, politics, and economic structures, whiteness studies become just a search for identity. As he explains, racial identities are constructed in the context of racial rule. To cite one of the sociological founders of this work, Ruth Frankenberg: "If focusing on white identity and culture displaces attention as a site of racialized privilege, its effectiveness as antiracism becomes limited" (Frankenberg 1997:17).

3

White Supremacy as Sociopolitical System: A Philosophical Perspective

CHARLES W. MILLS*

In their introductory pieces surveying, from an interdisciplinary perspective, recent "whiteness" literature, it is noteworthy that neither Margaret Andersen nor Woody Doane cite any philosophy text nor indeed refer to the discipline at all. Philosophy's classic pretensions to be able to illuminate the human condition with the light of reason have, to many critics, collapsed in a retreat to an inbred hermeticism, opaque and irrelevant to the outsider. Particularly in the analytic mainstream of the profession, there is a reluctance to engage with the social and historical. Indeed, in an important recent book, John McCumber goes so far as to anoint analytic philosophy with the dubious honor of being "the most resolutely apolitical paradigm in the humanities today." But McCumber argues that it would be a mistake to attribute this disengagement purely to internal factors. On the contrary, he claims that an examination of the pre- and postwar record shows an externalist account to be far more plausible: the impact of McCarthyism, which differentially targeted philosophers, making philosophy, in fact, "the most heavily attacked of all the academic disciplines" (2001:13, 37). Proportionally more philosophers lost their jobs through political harassment in the 1950s than academics in any other field.

So if academic philosophy today seems to have little to say to the uninitiated, this is by no means a matter of disciplinary necessity, for the fear quite recently was that it would say too much. Philosophy at its best does indeed have the capacity to illuminate, to challenge everyday assumptions of normalcy, undermine the taken-for-granted, upend the conventional wisdom—to be, in short, a highly *subversive* discipline. It needs to be remembered, after all, that Karl Marx's radical revisioning of society was (despite his own disclaimers) ultimately rooted in philosophy.

What I will argue in this chapter is that the best way to approach issues of whiteness is in social-systemic terms and that philosophy can make a

---

*This is a revised and expanded version of a chapter, "White Supremacy," that appeared in *The Companion to African-American Philosophy,* ed. John Pittman and Tommy Lott (London: Blackwell, 2003).

contribution to such an understanding by its historic (if not always current) willingness to transgress subject boundaries and map global pictures. I am in complete agreement with Andersen and Doane that contextualization within a racialized social system of white privilege is the most illuminating way to understand the workings of race. In my own work (Mills 1997, 1998), I have sought to expose the conceptual whiteness of mainstream philosophy and have argued that *white supremacy* needs to be taken as a theoretical object in its own right, a global social system comparable in current significance, though not historical age, to Marx's *class society* and feminist thinkers' *patriarchy*. If philosophy is about understanding the human condition, then it needs to understand the condition of humans shaped and molded by these systems into capitalists and workers, men and women, whites and nonwhites.

CONCEPTUALIZATION AND SCOPE OF WHITE SUPREMACY

Marx had to redefine "class" and "class society" in terms of ownership relationships to the means of production; feminists had to adapt the term "patriarchy" from a usage originally significantly different. By contrast, retrieving "white supremacy" from the historical lexicon has the advantage that it is the term that was already traditionally used to denote the domination of whites over nonwhites. When the phrase is used in mainstream social theory, of course, it is usually restricted to *formal* juridico-political domination, as paradigmatically exemplified by slavery, Jim Crow, and black disenfranchisement in the United States and by apartheid in South Africa (Fredrickson 1981; Cell 1982). Since official segregation and explicit political exclusion of this sort no longer exist in the United States, the term has now disappeared from mainstream white American discourse. If it is employed at all, it is only to refer to the unhappy past or, in the purely ideological and attitudinal sense, to the beliefs of radical white-separatist groups (i.e., as white-supremac*ists*). That in important ways the United States could still be white-supremacist would, of course, be rejected out of hand.

A crucial initial step toward reviving the term, then, would be establishing the simple sociological and political truth—not exactly unknown to the Western sociopolitical tradition—that power relations can survive the formal dismantling of their more overt supports. Even for postapartheid South Africa, where whites are a minority, it should be obvious that their strategic economic and bureaucratic power will continue to give them differential power. For the United States, where racialized and vastly disproportionate concentrations of wealth, cultural hegemony, and bureaucratic control are of course reinforced by white political *majoritarianism,* the case should—were it not for ideological blinders—be much easier to make. So the argument would be that American white supremacy has not vanished but has changed from a *de jure* to *de facto* form. The merely formal rejection of white-supremacist principles will not suffice to transform the United States into a genuinely racially egalitarian society, since the actual social values and enduring politico-economic structures will continue to reflect the history of white domination (Crenshaw 1988:1336). White supremacy thus needs to be conceptualized in terms broader than the narrowly juridical. Frances Lee Ansley suggests the following definition: "a political, economic, and cultural system in which whites overwhelmingly control power and material resources, conscious and unconscious ideas of white superiority and entitlement are widespread, and relations of white dominance and non-white subordination are daily reenacted across a broad array of institutions and social settings" (1989:1024n). Though white-black racial domination has clearly been central to this system, a comprehensive perspective on American white supremacy would really require attention to, and a comparative analysis of, white relations with other peoples of color also: Native Americans, Mexican-Americans, and Asian-Americans (Takaki 1990[1979]; Okihiro 1994; Almaguer 1994; Foley 1997).

In this more latitudinarian suprajuridical sense, white supremacy could be said to characterize not merely the United States but the Americas as a whole. For many decades a sharp contrast was drawn in the sociological literature between Anglo North America, racially exclusionary, and the supposedly more egalitarian Iberian societies of Latin America. But in recent years, an increasing body of work has dismantled the promulgated myths of color-blind racial democracy, pointing out that most Latin-American nations have historically stigmatized and subordinated their Afro-Latin populations (Twine 1998). *Mestizaje* (race mixture) as an ideal has in actuality been predicated on the differential valorization of the European component and the goal of *blanqueamiento*, whitening, and to this socially meliorist end many Latin-American nations have had white immigration policies. A color pyramid with multiple subtle steps and shadings has—when set in contrast to the crudely bipolar and explicitly exclusionary U.S. model—been falsely represented as racially egalitarian rather than hierarchical in a different way (Minority Rights Group 1995).

Finally, insofar as the modern world has been foundationally shaped by European colonialism, there is a sense in which white supremacy could be seen as transnational, global, the historic domination of white Europe over nonwhite non-Europe and of white settlers over nonwhite slaves and indigenous peoples, making Europeans "the lords of human kind" (Kiernan 1981[1969]; Cocker 1998). David Theo Goldberg (2001) argues that the European and Euro-implanted state has been racialized from the modern period onward, and Frank Füredi reminds us that before World War II, most of the planet was in fact formally ruled by white nations who, on colonial questions—whatever their other differences—were united on maintaining the subordination of nonwhites. Indeed, in a (today embarrassing) episode now rarely discussed in the historical literature, a Japanese proposal to include "the equality of races" in the League of Nations' Covenant was formally defeated at the 1919 post–World War I Versailles Conference (Füredi 1998:42–45). To the extent that this European and Euro-American domination persists, albeit through different mechanisms (military, economic, cultural), into the postcolonial period, we could be said to be still living in an age of global white supremacy.

ORIGINS AND EVOLUTION OF WHITE SUPREMACY

The verdict on the origins of racism is still out because, though most scholars locate its genesis in the modern period, some theorists argue for antecedents, or even full-blown versions, in the medieval and ancient worlds (Gossett 1997[1963]). But whatever the ultimate verdict on this question, white supremacy as a *system,* or set of systems, clearly comes into existence through European expansionism and the imposition of European rule through settlement and colonialism on aboriginal and imported slave populations—the original racial "big bang" that is the source of the present racialized world (Winant 1994).

But this domination need not itself have taken a "racial" form. The causes for the emergence of "race" as the salient marker of exclusion and the corresponding growth and centrality in the West of racist ideologies continue to be contested by scholars. What are sometimes called "idealist" accounts would focus on the role of culture, color symbolism, and religious predispositions, for example the self-conceptions of "civilized" Europeans opposed to a savage and "wild" Other, the positive and negative associations of the colors white and black, and the assumption of a Christian prerogative to evangelize the world and stigmatize other religions as the devil worship of heathens (Jordan 1977[1968]; Jennings 1976[1975]). On the other hand, so-called "materialist" accounts, primarily Marxist in inspiration, would see such factors as either irrelevant or subordinate to the causally more important politico-economic projects of obtaining a supply of cheap labor, expropriating land, and imposing particular superexploitative modes of production, for which "race" then becomes the convenient superstructural rationale (Cox 1948; Fields 1990). Marxist accounts have tended to the class-reductionistic (famously, for example, in Cox), but they need not necessarily be so. The trick is to explain the emergence of race in historical-materialist terms, with appropriate reference to the interests, projects, and differential power of the privileged classes, while recognizing that—*once created*—race acquires a power, autonomy, and "materiality" of its own, so that white group interests then become a factor in their own right. Unfortunately, few theorists have been able to achieve this delicate balancing act.

Other explanations not readily fitted into a materialist/idealist taxonomy regard white racism as a systematized and sophisticated extrapolation of the primordial ethnocentrism of all humans or as linked with particular psychosexual projections on to the dark body (Kovel 1984[1970]).

Debates over origins also have implications for the conception of "race" itself and the evolution of white supremacy. Until recently race has paradigmatically been thought of as natural, biological, the carving of humanity at its actual ontological joints. By contrast, contemporary radical thought on race almost universally assumes what has come to be called a "constructionist" theory (Omi and Winant 1986; Haney López 1995). From this perspective, "whites" and "nonwhites" do not preexist white supremacy as natural kinds but are categories and realities themselves brought into existence by the institutionalization of the system. The white race is in fact invented (Allen 1994, 1997), though theorists will differ on the relative significance of the role of the state (from above) in making race and whiteness (Marx 1998) as against the role of the Euro working class (from below) in making themselves white (Roediger 1991). Correspondingly, white supremacy evolves over time not merely in its transition from a *de jure* to a *de facto* form but in the changing rules as to who is counted as white in the first place. Matthew Frye Jacobson, for example, has recently argued that U.S. whiteness is not temporally monolithic but should be periodized into "three great epochs": from the 1790 law limiting naturalization to free white persons to the mass influx of Irish immigrants in the 1840s; from the 1840s to the restrictive immigration legislation of 1924; and from the 1920s to the present. In the process, groups once recognized as distinct races (Mediterraneans, Celts, Slavs, Teutons, Hebrews) have now disappeared into an expanded white race (Jacobson 1998). Similarly, other authors have delineated how over time the Irish and the Jews *became* white in the United States (Ignatiev 1995; Brodkin 1999).

WHITE SUPREMACY AS POLITICAL

In radical oppositional political theory, such as that centered on class or gender, a crucial initial conceptual move is often the redrawing of the boundaries of the political itself. In the Marxist model, capitalism is not seen, as it is in neoclassical economic theory, as a set of market transactions disconnected from societal structure. Rather it is viewed as a system dominated by a bourgeoisie whose differential economic power ramifies throughout society, making them a "ruling class," so that even with universal suffrage the polity is still no more than a "bourgeois democracy." Thus the atomistic social ontology of liberalism, most famously manifested in social contract theory, is asserted to be profoundly misleading. Similarly, the radical feminists of the 1970s, who devised the use of "patriarchy," argued that men as a group dominate women as a group, but that this is mystified by another set of conceptual blinders: the limiting of the boundaries of the political to the so-called public sphere. The ubiquity of patriarchy as a political system is therefore obscured through the seemingly "natural" relegation of women to the apolitical domestic space of child-rearing and care of the household. Male domination becomes conceptually invisible rather than being recognized as itself the oldest form of political rule (Clark and Lange 1979; Jaggar 1983; Pateman and Gross 1987).

In both cases, then, the challenge of class and gender theory to mainstream thought involves a revision of what counts as political in the first place and a focus on power relations and manifestations of domination not recognized and encompassed by the official definition of the political (political parties, formal contests in the electoral arena, the actions of delegated representatives in parliamentary bodies, etc.). The deliberate employment of the term "white supremacy" (in contrast to the orthodox paradigm of "race relations") constitutes a parallel challenge. The idea is that it is politically illuminating to see whites in the United States as ruling as a group, thus constituting the "ruling race" of what was originally—and is in some ways still—a "*Herrenvolk* democracy" (van den Berghe 1978), a "white republic" (Saxton 1990), historically founded on a notion of racial, Anglo-Saxonist "manifest destiny" (Horsman 1981).

It will be obvious that such a conceptualization is radically at variance with a mainstream white American political theory that generally ignores or marginalizes race. The hegemonic "race relations" paradigm largely confines discussions of race to sociology—race is not seen as *political* (in the double sense of being created and shaped on an ongoing basis by political forces and as being itself the vehicle of political power). Moreover, apart from this disciplinary confinement, the paradigm itself is fundamentally misguided insofar as it seeks to conflate the experience of assimilating, ambiguously off-white, European *ethnics* (Irish, Jewish, Mediterranean) with the radically different experience of subordinated, unambiguously nonwhite, non-European *races* (black, red, brown, yellow), the former within, the latter beneath, the melting pot. Where race has been dealt with in mainstream political theory, it has either been at the local level of urban politics or, when tackled as a global reality, been standardly framed as an "anomaly" to supposedly central, inclusive, liberal-democratic, political values and conceived of in ideational, attitudinal, and individualist terms: a tragic "American dilemma" (Myrdal 1944). As such, racism is to be redressed through moral suasion and enlightenment, having no substantive conceptual implications for American political theory, which can take over without modification the (facially) raceless categories of European sociopolitical thought in which the ascriptive hierarchy and traditionalism of the Old World are contrasted with the egalitarian and democratic liberalism of the New (R. Smith 1997).

White supremacy as a concept thus registers a commitment to a radically *different* understanding of the political order, pointing us theoretically toward the centrality of racial domination and subordination. Within the discursive universe of white social theory on race, liberal or radical, it disrupts traditional framings, conceptualizations, and disciplinary divisions, effecting what is no less than a fundamental paradigm shift (Blauner 1972; Steinberg 1995).

To begin with, attention is displaced from the moralized realm of the ideational and attitudinal to the realm of structures and power which has been the traditional concern of political theory. Correspondingly, the facile and illusory symmetry of an individualized "prejudice" equally to be condemned wherever it is encountered, which opens the conceptual door to the later notion of "reverse discrimination" and the Supreme Court's opting for the "colorblind" "perpetrator perspective," is revealed as a mystificatory obfuscation of

the clearly *a*symmetrical and enduring system of white power itself. "The perpetrator perspective presupposes a world composed of atomistic individuals
whose actions are outside of and apart from the social fabric and without historical continuity" (Freeman 1996[1990]:30). Second, this conception blocks
mainstream theory's ghettoizing of work on race through rejecting its conceptual framing of the polity as a raceless liberal democracy. Instead, the polity
is conceptualized as a white-supremacist state, a system as real and important
historically as any of those other systems formally acknowledged in the Western
political canon (aristocracy, absolutism, democracy, fascism, socialism, etc.).
Third, the notion of a global racial system with its own partial autonomy constitutes a repudiation of the too often epiphenomenalist treatment of race in the
most important Western theory of group oppression, Marxism. Instead of treating race and racial dynamics as simply reducible to a class logic, this approach
argues that through constructions of the self, proclaimed ideals of cultural and
civic identity, decisions of the state, crystallizations of juridical standing and
group interests, permitted violence, and the opening and blocking of economic
opportunities, race becomes real and causally effective, institutionalized and
materialized by white supremacy in social practices and felt phenomenologies.
What is created, in the words of Eduardo Bonilla-Silva, is a "racialized social
system" in which "the race placed in the superior position tends to receive
greater economic remuneration and access to better occupations and prospects
in the labor market, occupies a primary position in the political system, [and]
is granted higher social estimation" (2001:37).

Finally, it should be noted that this alternative paradigm—race as central,
political, and primarily a system of oppression—is (at least in broad outline) not
at all new but has in fact always been present in oppositional African-American
thought. Over thirty years ago, for example, Stokely Carmichael and Charles
Hamilton argued in their classic *Black Power* that essentially white Americans
"own the society," that the most important kind of racism is "institutional,"
and that blacks should be seen as an internal colony facing whites who, on issues of race, "react in a united group to protect interests they perceive to be
theirs," dominating blacks politically, economically, and socially (Carmichael
and Hamilton 1967:21–23). From the struggles against slavery to the battles
against Jim Crow, from David Walker's militant 1830 *Appeal* (1993[1830]) to
Malcolm X's matter-of-fact 1963 judgment that "America is a white country
and all of the economy, the politics, the civic life of America is controlled by the
white man" (X 1971:91), blacks have historically had little difficulty in grasping
that the central political reality of the United States is, quite simply, that it is a
"white man's country." But this "naïve" perception has apparently been too sophisticated for mainstream, white, political theory to apprehend. Current work
on white supremacy in critical race theory and critical white studies can thus be
seen as a belated catching-up with the insights of black lay thought, simultaneously disadvantaged and advantaged by lacking the formal training of the white

academy, and proper intellectual credit needs to be given to the black pioneers of this conceptual framework.

DIMENSIONS OF WHITE SUPREMACY

White supremacy should therefore be seen as a multidimensional system of domination not merely encompassing the "formally" political that is limited to the juridico-political realm of official governing bodies and laws but, as argued above, extending to white domination in economic, cultural, cognitive-evaluative, somatic, and in a sense even "metaphysical" spheres. There is a pervasive racialization of the social world that means that one's race, in effect, puts one into a certain relationship with social reality, tendentially determining one's being and consciousness.

A. THE JURIDICO-POLITICAL SPHERE

For the alternative paradigm, the state and the legal system are not neutral entities standing above interracial relations but for the most part themselves agencies of racial oppression (Kairys 1990[1982]). To Native Americans, the white man's law has constituted an essential part of "the discourses of conquest" (R. A. Williams 1990). For blacks, the history has been similar. As the late Judge A. Leon Higginbotham, Jr. documented in detail, blacks have consistently been legally differentiated from and subordinated to the white population, not merely with the obvious case of the enslaved but also in the lesser rights of the free black population (1978, 1996). The Philadelphia Convention notoriously enshrined slavery without mentioning it by name through the three-fifths clause, and in 1790 Congress made whiteness a prerequisite for naturalization. The 1857 *Dred Scott* Supreme Court decision codified black subordination through its judgment that blacks were an inferior race with "no rights which the white man was bound to respect." The promise of Emancipation and Reconstruction was betrayed by the Black Codes, the 1877 Hayes-Tilden Compromise, and the 1896 *Plessy v. Ferguson* decision which formally sanctioned "separate but equal." For the next sixty years, Jim Crow was the law of the land, with widespread black disenfranchisement, exploitation, and inferior treatment in all spheres of life (Litwack 1998). Thus for most of U.S. history, white supremacy has been *de jure,* and blacks have either been non- or second-class citizens unable to appeal to the federal government to provide them equal protection (D. King 1995).

While the victories of the 1950s and 1960s over Jim Crow have led to the repeal of overtly racist legislation and thus to real racial progress, substantive racial equality, as earlier noted, has yet to be achieved. The failure to allocate resources to implement antidiscrimination law vigorously, the placing of the burden of proof on the plaintiff, conservatively narrow interpretations of civil rights statutes, the backlash against affirmative action and desegregation, and the general shift since the 1960s from the "victim" to the "perpetrator" perspective (Freeman 1996[1990]) in effect mean that further erosion of white domination is increasingly being resisted. Moreover, since the United States, unlike apartheid South Africa, has a white majority, a democratic vote guided by white group interests will itself continue to reproduce white domination in the absence of opposition from the Supreme Court, which is committed to "veiled majoritarianism" (Spann 1995). Donald Kinder's and Lynn Sanders's research shows that, in contradiction to the expectations of classic postwar pluralist theory, racial-group interests are nationally the most important ones, cutting across and overriding all other identities, and that whites see black interests as antagonistic to their own (Kinder and Sanders 1996). Whether through legalized inferiority, electoral disenfranchisement, or majoritarian group-interest-based domination, then, blacks have been systematically subjugated for nearly four hundred years in the white American polity.

Finally, in mapping the juridico-political, the role of official and unofficial white violence in perpetuating white rule also needs to be taken into account: the sanctioned tortures and informally connived-at killings of slave penal codes; the "demonstration effects" of lynchings in terrorizing the local black population; the freedom to operate given the Klan; the differential application of the death penalty; the race riots which, until well into the twentieth century, were basically white riots; and the part played by the repressive apparatus of the state (slave patrollers, federal militia, police, military, the prison system) in first suppressing slave uprisings and then later targeting legitimate black protest and activism to gain the rights enjoyed by white Americans (Berry 1994[1971]; Garrow 1981; H. Shapiro 1988; O'Reilly 1991[1989]; Dray 2002). In effect, for most of U.S. history the state has functioned as a racial state protecting white supremacy.

B. THE ECONOMIC SPHERE

Marx's theorization of the dynamics of capitalism famously rests on the claim that it is intrinsically an exploitative system, since even when the working classes are being paid a "fair" wage, surplus value is being extracted from them. But with the discrediting of the labor theory of value, this claim is no longer taken seriously in mainstream neoclassical economics. In the case of white supremacy as a system, however, there is a pervasive "exploitation" ongoing throughout society that is, or should be, quite obvious and that is wrong by completely respectable, *non*-Marxist, liberal bourgeois standards (if applied nonracially). As one classic line puts it, white American wealth historically rests on red land and black labor. What could be termed "racial exploitation" covers an extensive historical variety of institutionalized and informal practices operating much more broadly than on the backs of proletarian wage-labor: the expropriation of Native Americans; African slavery; the refusal to blacks of equal opportunity to homestead the West; the debt servitude of sharecropping; the turn-of-the-century exploitation of Asian "coolie" labor; the exclusion of blacks and other nonwhites from certain jobs and trades and the lower wages and diminished promotion chances within those employments that were permitted; the blocking of black entrepreneurs from access to white markets; the denial of start-up capital by white banks; the higher prices and rents for inferior merchandise and housing in the ghettoes; the restricted access of blacks to state and federal services that whites enjoyed; the federally backed segregation and restrictive covenants that diminished the opportunities for most blacks to accumulate wealth through home ownership; the unfair business contracts that took advantage of nonwhite ignorance or that, when recognized as unfair, had to be signed because of lack of an alternative to white monopoly control; and many others (Massey and Denton 1993; Oliver and Shapiro 1995; Lipsitz 1998; Brown 1999).

An adequate theorization of white supremacy would require a detailed taxonomy of these different varieties of racial exploitation that have jointly historically deprived people of color as a group of billions or even (globally) trillions of dollars of wealth and have correspondingly benefited whites, thus in effect constituting the "material base" of white supremacy. (The wealth of the median black American household is less than one eighth the wealth of the median white household.) And globally there is a long-standing black and Third World argument that slavery, colonialism, and the exploitation of the New World were crucial in enabling European development and producing African underdevelopment, so that racial exploitation really has to be seen as planetary in scope (E. Williams 1966[1944]; Rodney 1974[1972]; Blaut 1993). The recently revived struggle for black reparations in the United States and the indictment of the legacy of colonialism at the August 2001 UN Conference in Durban, South Africa, are manifestations of a global movement for compensation for historically unpaid-for land and labor that one hopes will force an official acknowledgment and (partial) reckoning of the terrible human costs of the past few hundred years of white domination.

C. THE CULTURAL SPHERE

Given recent debates about "multiculturalism," the cultural dimension of white supremacy at least is familiar: a Eurocentrism that denigrates non-European cultures as inferior or even nonexistent and places Europe at the center of global history (Amin 1988). What is not usually articulated is the role such denigration played in teleological theories of history that made Europeans the (divinely and biologically) favored race, destined either to annihilate or to lead to civilization all others, generating a discourse that could be regarded as "fantasies of the master race" (Churchill 1992; Said 1993). Colonial peoples in general, of course, have suffered this denial of the worth of their cultures, but the centrality of African slavery to the project of the West required the most extreme stigmatization of blacks in particular. Thus sub-Saharan Africa was portrayed as the "Dark Continent," a vast jungle inhabited by savage "tribes" lost in a historyless and cultureless vacuum, to be redeemed only by a European presence (Mudimbe 1988, 1994). The Tarzan novels and movies and the thousands of African "adventure" stories of pulp and ostensibly highbrow fiction of the last hundred years are all part of this master-narrative of white cultural superiority (Pieterse 1992[1990]). From north to south, from Ancient Egypt to Zimbabwe, the achievements of the continent have generally been attributed to anybody other than the black population themselves. Blacks in the United States and the Americas generally were, of course, tainted by their association with such a barbarous origin (Fredrickson, 1987[1971]). Similarly, after the defeat of Native American resistance, a policy of cultural assimilation to "Kill the Indian but save the man" was implemented.

But apart from this well-known pattern of white cultural hegemony, there is also a phenomenon that deserves more theoretical attention: cultural *appropriation* without acknowledgment, so that civilization in general seems to have an exclusively white genealogy—a form of exploitation that, again, is uneasily fitted within the categories of the best-known mainstream theory of exploitation, Marxism. Cultural white supremacy manifests itself not merely in the differential valorization of Europe and European-derived culture but in the denial of the extent to which this culture—"incontestably mulatto" in the famous phrase of Albert Murray (1970)—has itself been dependent on the contributions of others, hence a "bleaching" of the multicolored roots of human civilization. Ancient Egyptian influences on Ancient Greece, Chinese scientific achievements, Native American mathematics, agriculture, and forms of government, are all denied or minimized, so that Europeans seem to be the only people with the capacity for culture (Bernal 1987; Harding 1993).

D. THE COGNITIVE-EVALUATIVE SPHERE

Systems of domination affect not merely the persons within them but their theorizing about these systems. Integral to both Marxist and feminist thought has been an auxiliary *meta*theoretical aspect, the theorizing about hegemonic theories. In Marx's analysis of fetishism and naturalization, in feminists' exposure of overt and hidden androcentrism, oppositional thinkers have mapped the various ways in which ideas, values, concepts, assumptions, and overall cognitive patterns contribute to the reproduction of group privilege and rule. White supremacy likewise will have associated with it distinctive epistemologies, factual claims, and normative outlooks which need to be exposed and demystified.

The clearest manifestation will be the development of racist ideology itself in its numerous and polymorphic historical variants, theological and "scientific": from the Ham myth through polygenesis, Social Darwinism, and craniometry, to IQ theory and the Bell Curve (S. J. Gould 1981; Hannaford 1996; Gossett 1997[1963]; Jacoby and Glauberman 1995; Herrnstein and Murray 1994). But there will be many other kinds of examples also, sometimes not claims of knowledge so much as claims of ignorance—a nonknowing which is not the innocent unawareness of truths to which there is no access but a self- and social shielding from racial realities that is underwritten by the official social epistemology. Being constructed as white means, *inter alia,* learning to see and understand the world in a certain way. In Ralph Ellison's classic novel *Invisible Man,* the eponymous narrator describes the "peculiar disposition" of white eyes, a blindness arising not out of physiology but socialized cognitive psychology, "the construction of their *inner* eyes," and in *Black Like Me,* white-turned-black John Howard Griffin looks back from the perspective of his newfound consciousness at the "area of unknowing" of Whitetown (Ellison 1972[1952]; Griffin 1996[1961]). Thus there will be characteristic and pervasive patterns of not-seeing and not-knowing—structured white ignorance, motivated inattention, self-deception, and moral rationalization—that people of color, for their own survival, have to learn to become familiar with.

More generally, white normativity in the factual and moral realms will involve taking whites as the normative reference point and illicitly generalizing from their experience, from Eurocentrism in models of history to current "color-blind" denials of the reality of white American racial privilege. The original fusion of personhood—what it is to be human—with membership of a particular race will continue to shape white perception, conceptualization, and affect in unconscious and subtle ways even in apparently nonracist contexts (Lawrence 1995). Since this system will inevitably influence nonwhite cognition also, the racially subordinated will have to learn to challenge white epistemic authority, to think themselves out of conceptual frameworks and value systems that justify or obfuscate their subordination.

E. THE SOMATIC SPHERE

White supremacy also has a central somatic dimension, especially where the black population is concerned. Since this is a political system predicated on racial superiority and inferiority, on the demarcation and differential evaluation of different races, the "body" in the body-politic naturally becomes crucial—and *non*metaphoric—in a way it does not in the abstract polity of (official) Western theory. A white "somatic norm" assumes hegemonic standing, serving as an important contributory measure of individual worth, and the literal lack of incorporation of people of color into the extended white macrobody of the *polis* is written directly on their flesh (Hoetink 1962). In his book simply titled *White,* Richard Dyer (1997) documents the pervasive iconography of the white bodily ideal and shows how over decades it has come to be constructed in movies through special photography and lighting techniques. Not merely in the United States but in its broader external cultural sphere, these images influence both how people see others and how they see themselves. The nonwhite body—red, yellow, brown, black—has been clearly demarcated as alien, flesh *not* of our flesh. The black body in particular, being both the sign of slave status and the body physically most divergent from the white one, has historically been derogated and stigmatized as grotesque, ugly, simian: mocked in blackface minstrelsy, newspaper cartoons, advertising, animated films, memorabilia (Turner 1994; Pieterse 1992[1990]).

The young Marx made alienation from one's labor a central concept in his indictment of class society. Here under white supremacy, it could be argued, one has an alienation far more fundamental, since while one can always come home from work, one cannot get out of one's skin. Nonwhites socialized into the acceptance of this somatic norm will then be alienated from their own bodies, in a sense estranged from their own physical being and being-in-the-world (Russell et al. 1992). Recent philosophical work on the body has generally focused on gender rather than race (Welton 1998), but some philosophers of color, for example Lewis Gordon and Linda Martín Alcoff, are beginning to explore racial embodiment and alienation from a phenomenological point of view (Gordon 1994; Alcoff 1999). Particularly for women, for whom the (patriarchically driven) imperative to be beautiful is most important, this alienation will manifest itself in attempts to transform the body to more closely approximate the white somatic ideal, whether through makeup and cosmetic aids or, in the extreme case, plastic surgery: eye jobs, nose jobs, dermabrasion (Gilman 1998). Moreover, there will be an inevitable racialization of sexual relations in terms of the differential social attractiveness of certain bodies (Fanon 1967[1952]). Toni Morrison's powerful and moving first novel, *The Bluest Eye*, depicts the tragic fate of a young black girl whose dearest wish is to get the blue eyes whose lack, she concludes, is what makes her unloved (2000[1970]). Necessarily, then, the resistance to oppressive corporeal whiteness has taken the form of a guerrilla insurgency on the terrain of the flesh itself (White and White 1998).

F. THE METAPHYSICAL SPHERE

Finally, in a bow to the distinctive insights of my own profession, let me conclude by saying something about what could be termed the "metaphysics" of white supremacy. Whereas mainstream Anglo-American analytic philosophy tends to separate metaphysical issues of being and consciousness, identity and the self, from the social (one thinks of the classic images of the isolated, solipsistic, Cartesian ego, of the atomic and presocial individuals of contract theory), there is far greater appreciation in the Continental tradition in its numerous variants (Hegelian, Marxist, poststructuralist) of the notion of the socially constituted, or at least socially shaped, self. Hence the idea of a *social ontology*.

Now, the mainstream narrative of modernity is nominally egalitarian, in that normative human equality is taken to have been achieved by the Enlightenment. So the metaphysic implicit in the description of the "free and equal" individuals of social contract theory is classically that of an undifferentiated equality. But a case can obviously be made that whiteness was a prerequisite for full personhood—normative, sociopolitical, and "metaphysical" equality. An ontology of society and the self that accurately maps rather than obfuscating these realities thus needs to recognize the centrality of racial *in*egalitarianism. From this "metaphysical" perspective, white supremacy could be seen as a bipolar system whose ontological underpinnings lift a white *Herrenvolk* above nonwhite, particularly black, *Untermenschen*. People of color have always recognized that racial subordination is predicated on regarding them as less than fully human, as subpersons rather than persons. A social theory whose implicit ontology fails to register this reality is getting things wrong at the foundational level, since the nonwhite struggle for equal, socially recognized personhood has in fact been one of the central battles of the past few hundred years.

CONCLUSION

The virtue of using white supremacy as an overarching theoretical concept is that it enables us to pull together different phenomena and integrate these different levels: sociopolitical, economic, cultural, epistemological, somatic, metaphysical. For the elements I have separated analytically are of course interacting with one another in reality, jointly contributing to the reproductive dynamic that helps to perpetuate the system. If race was previously thought of as in the body, it is now too often thought of as merely in the head: claims of nonreality have replaced claims of physical reality. But race is best conceived of not primarily as ideational but as embedded in material structures, sociopolitical institutions, and everyday social practices that so shape the world with which we interact as to constitute an "objective" (deriving from intersubjectivity) though socially constructed "reality." Philosophy's promise to illuminate the world can be realized only by recognizing the whiteness of that world and how it affects its residents. Theorizing white supremacy as objective, systemic, multidimensional, constitutive of a certain reality that evolves over time can contribute both to understanding the world and, ultimately, to changing it.

4

Rethinking Whiteness Historiography: The Case of Italians in Chicago, 1890–1945*

THOMAS A. GUGLIELMO

Over the last decade, historians of the United States such as David Roediger (1991, 1994, 2002), Noel Ignatiev (1995), Matthew Jacobson (1998), and many others have played a crucial role in the growth and popularity of whiteness studies—and with numerous positive results. If much of whiteness studies, as Margaret Andersen convincingly demonstrates in Chapter 2 in this volume, has shifted the focus away from people of color and from issues of power and privilege, whiteness historiography may be an exception. Indeed, scholars such as Roediger have stressed the centrality of people of color in histories and theories of whiteness; and he along with numerous other historians has focused squarely on issues of power and resources, inequality and racism.

Still, this close connection between U.S. historians and whiteness studies has not been an unmitigated blessing. Most important, a faulty assumption—that European immigrants arrived in the United States as "in-between peoples" and became fully white only over time and after a great deal of struggle—stands at the heart of a great deal of U.S. whiteness historiography (Barrett and Roediger 1997; Brodkin 1999; Gerstle 1997; Nelson 2001; Peck 2000; Roediger 1991, 1994; Sugrue 1996) and has been accepted uncritically by scholars in various disciplines (Bonnett 1998; Feagin 2000; Prashad 2000; Warren and Twine 1997; Waters 1999). Focusing on a case study of Italians in Chicago from the turn of the century through World War II, I dispute this core assumption. I argue that many Italians faced extensive *racial* prejudice and discrimination in the United States as Italians, South Italians, Latins, and so forth, but were still largely accepted as white by the widest variety of people and institutions—naturalization laws and courts, the U.S. census, race science, newspapers, unions, employers, neighbors, politicians, and realtors. This widespread acceptance was reflected most

---

*Much of this chapter comes from my book, *White on Arrival: Italians, Race, Color, and Power in Chicago, 1890–1945* (New York: Oxford University Press, 2003a). For those readers who wish to see a more extensive treatment (and documentation) of most of the subjects in this chapter, please consult the book.

concretely in Italians' ability to naturalize as U.S. citizens, work at certain jobs, live in certain neighborhoods, marry certain partners, and patronize certain movie theaters, restaurants, saloons, hospitals, parks, and settlement houses. In so many of these situations, one color line existed separating whites from non-whites; and from the moment they arrived in the United States, Italians were consistently placed on the side of the former. If Italians were racially undesirable in the eyes of many Americans, they were white just the same.

To make better sense of this argument and my critique of whiteness historiography, two conceptual tools should be explained briefly at the outset. First is the simple point made by many of the contributors to this volume that we take the structure of race seriously. Race is still too often talked about as simply an idea, an attitude, a consciousness, an identity, or an ideology. It is, to be sure, all of these things—but also much more. It is also rooted in various political, economic, social, and cultural institutions and thus is very much about power and resources (or lack thereof). Particularly helpful on this point is sociologist Eduardo Bonilla-Silva (1997:469–470), who suggests we use "racialized social system" as an analytical tool. He argues that:

> In all [such] systems the placement of people in racial categories involves some form of hierarchy that produces definite social relations between the races. The race placed in the superior position tends to receive greater economic remuneration and access to better occupations and/or prospects in the labor market, occupies a primary position in the political system, is granted higher social estimation . . . and receives a "psychological wage." The totality of these racialized social relations and practices constitutes [a racialized social system].

Such a social system existed throughout the late nineteenth and early twentieth centuries in Chicago (and, of course, in the United States as a whole). Whether one was white, black, red, yellow, or brown—and to some extent Anglo-Saxon, South Italian, North Italian, or Alpine—powerfully influenced (along with other systems of difference like class and gender) where one lived and worked, the kinds of people one married, and the kinds of life chances one had. Thus race was not (and is not) completely about ideas, ideologies, and identity. It is also about location in a social system and its consequences.

To understand fully these consequences, one more conceptual tool is critical: the distinction between race and color. Several years back, when I began research on Italians and race, I envisioned a "wop to white" story, an Italian version of Noel Ignatiev's *How the Irish Became White* (1995). I quickly realized, however, that this approach had serious shortcomings. For one, Italians did not need to become white; they always were, in numerous critical ways. For another, race was more than black and white. If Italians' status as whites was relatively secure, they still suffered, as noted above, from extensive *racial* discrimination and prejudice as Italians, South Italians, Latins, and so on.

Nor was this simply "ethnic" discrimination. To be sure, few scholars agree on how best to differentiate conceptually between "race" and "ethnicity." Some have argued that whereas race is based primarily on physical characteristics subjectively chosen, ethnicity is based on cultural ones (e.g., language, religion, etc.). Others have maintained that "membership in an ethnic group is usually voluntary; membership in a racial group is not." Still others have argued that "while 'ethnic' social relations are not *necessarily* hierarchical, exploitative and conflictual, 'race relations'" almost always are (Jenkins 1997:81, 74–75). None of these distinctions, while all valid in certain ways, is very helpful for our purposes. None of them, that is, helps us to better understand Italians' social experiences and their particular social location in the United States. After all, a group such as the "South Italian race" was purported to have particular "cultural" *and* "physical" characteristics; included both voluntary *and* involuntary members; and was created in Italy and used extensively in the United States to explicitly rank and exploit certain human beings.

How, then, to navigate between Italians' relatively secure whiteness *and* their highly problematical racial status, without resorting to unhelpful conceptual distinctions between race and ethnicity? The answer, I contend, is race and color. I argue that between the mid-nineteenth and mid-twentieth centuries there were primarily two ways of categorizing human beings based on a range of supposedly inborn traits. The first is color (or what might be called "color race" since this is what many Americans think of as race today): the black race, brown race, red race, white race, and yellow race. Color, as I use it, is a social category and not a physical description. "White" Italians, for instance, could be darker than "black" Americans. Second is race, which could mean many things: large groups like Nordics and Mediterraneans; medium-sized ones like Celts and Jews; or smaller ones like North or South Italians.

This race/color distinction was, of course, never absolute during this time period and it certainly changed over time. But some people and institutions were very clear on the distinction. The federal government's naturalization applications throughout this time period, for instance, asked applicants to provide their race and color. For Italians, the only acceptable answers were North or South Italians for the former and white for the latter. Most important, for all of its discursive messiness, the race/color distinction was crystal clear on the ground in Chicago when it came to resources and rewards. In other words, while Italians suffered for their supposed *racial* undesirability as Italians, South Italians, and so forth, they still benefited in countless ways from their privileged *color* status as whites.

This argument, as noted, squarely challenges a core assumption among whiteness historians about the "in-betweenness" of European immigrants. I want to argue further that this interpretive problem in whiteness historiography stems in part from two larger conceptual problems: first, many whiteness scholars, by failing to understand the distinctions between race and color, have assumed that challenges to a group's racial desirability as, say, Latins or South Italians necessarily called into question their color status as whites. This was not the case; Italians could be both racially inferior "dagoes" and privileged whites simultaneously. This point is vividly apparent when one compares the experiences of Italians with those of groups whose whiteness was either really in question (e.g., Mexican-Americans) or entirely out of the question (e.g., African-Americans and Asian-Americans).

Second, many whiteness historians have not appreciated the structural nature of race and have therefore made arguments about the nonwhiteness of European immigrants based on limited evidence at best. To see race as structural, however, means that to be white or nonwhite involved (and involves) occupying a particular structural location. And to determine this location one must examine a broad range of institutions over time. No whiteness historians that I have read have done this—at least with regard to "in-betweenness" arguments. This essay attempts to address this lack. Drawing on research from a larger project of mine, it examines Italians' race/color location vis-à-vis a broad range of international, national, and local institutions—the Bureau of Immigration, the United States census, the Federal Housing Administration, race science in Italy and the United States, courts, laws, newspapers, neighborhood improvement associations, restrictive covenants, riots, settlement houses, political parties, and so forth—over several decades of time. Only through this sort of analysis, I contend, can scholars determine the whiteness or nonwhiteness of European immigrants in the United States.

Italians are a particularly good group on which to test my "white on arrival" argument, because they faced such severe racial discrimination and prejudice in the United States, which all started prior to migration in Italy. In the late nineteenth century, an influential group of positivist anthropologists such as Cesare Lombroso, Giuseppe Sergi, and Alfredo Niceforo emerged on the scene with scientific "proof" that southern Italians were racially distinct from and hopelessly inferior to their northern compatriots. Sergi, for instance, using skull measurements to trace the various origins and desirability of the Italian people, argued that while northern Italians descended from superior Aryan stock, southerners were primarily of inferior African blood. Similarly, Niceforo argued in his widely read study, *L'Italia Barbara Contemporanea*, that two Italies existed, whose fundamental racial differences made unification impossible. After all, "one of the two Italies, the northern one, shows a civilization greatly diffused, more fresh, and more modern. The Italy of the South [however] shows a moral and social structure reminiscent of primitive and even quasibarbarian times, a civilization quite inferior" (Covello 1967:25).

Such ideas were by no means restricted to the academy; a great deal of Italian mass culture and many public officials absorbed and disseminated them as well. For instance, Italy's leading illustrated magazine of the time, *Illustrazione*

Italiana, repeatedly and "patronizingly celebrate[d] the South's anomalous position between Italy and the Orient, between the world of civilized progress and the spheres of either rusticity or barbarism" (Dickie 1997:135). As one of the magazine's reporters noted after a trip through Sicily in 1893, "in the fields where I interviewed many peasants I found only types with the most unmistakable African origin. My, how much strange intelligence is in those muddled brains." Similarly, Filippo Turati, a Socialist Party leader at the turn of the century, no doubt spoke for many of his compatriots when he referred to the "Southern Question" as a battle between "an incipient civilization and that putrid barbarity" (Gribaudi 1997:96).

Just at this moment—at the height of the scientific and popular racialist assault on the *Mezzogiorno* (South Italy) and its people—the origins of Italian immigration to the United States shifted dramatically from the North to the South. As hundreds of thousands of these much-maligned *meridionali* (southern Italians) arrived in America each year, a wide variety of American institutions and individuals, alarmed by this massive influx, made great use of Italian positivist race arguments. The U.S. Bureau of Immigration, for instance, in 1899 began recording the racial backgrounds of immigrants and distinguishing between "Keltic" northern Italians and "Iberic" southern Italians (McSweeney et al. 1898). In 1911, the U.S. Immigration Commission, throughout its highly influential forty-two-volume report, made a similar distinction. Citing the works of Niceforo and Sergi, it argued that northern and southern Italians "differ from each other materially in language, physique, and character, as well as in geographical distribution" (U.S. Immigration Commission 1911:81). While the former are "cool, deliberate, patient, practical, as well as capable of great progress in the political and social organization of modern civilization," the latter are "excitable, impulsive, highly imaginative, impracticable" and have "little adaptability to highly organized society" (U.S. Immigration Commission 1911:82).

A wide range of Chicago's citizens and institutions shared these views. In 1910, for instance, the *Chicago Tribune* sent anthropologist George A. Dorsey to the *Mezzogiorno* to study immigrants in their homelands. Traveling from one small hill town to the next and writing daily columns for months on his impressions, Dorsey offered the most damning view of southern Italians. These people, he claimed, were unmanly and primitive barbarians who had clear "Negroid" ancestry, who shared much more in common with the East than the West, and who were "poor in health, stature, strength, initiative, education, and money." "They are," concluded Dorsey after five months of daily investigations, "of questionable value from a mental, moral, or physical standpoint" (*Chicago Tribune* 1910b:9).

Dorsey and the *Tribune* had their many allies on these points. The University of Chicago's widely renowned sociology department, for example, conducted many studies of local Italian communities, and their findings, like those of Dorsey, were rarely flattering. One graduate student, for example, declared in her master's thesis that Chicago's southern Italians "are very impractical, they let their imagination run away with them. They are impulsive and excitable. They would rather sit and sing all day than do any work and improve their surroundings" (Sager 1914:16). At times, even social settlement workers—often immigrants' loyal defenders—revealed contempt for southern Italians. Marie Leavitt, for example, the head resident at the Eli Bates House on the Near North Side of Chicago, portrayed local Sicilians as the perfect picture of pathology: "We have about us many hopelessly dependent families, either broken down by disease, or of so low a grade mentally that they cannot compete with normal persons. [They] huddle together in the cheapest tenements, sinking in the social scale, but bearing children whom we must hope to inspire with a desire for better things" (Local Community Research Committee n.d.:9–10).

Meanwhile, everyday Chicagoans had their own ways of expressing their distaste for Italians. As one old-time resident of South Chicago remarked in the 1920s: "The Italians have been coming in here for twenty years but most of them live north of the tracks. There weren't many down in our section. We wouldn't let 'em come south of the tracks. They were afraid of getting pelted with stones and we would have done it too. . . . It is bad enough to work with 'Dagoes.' I wouldn't think of living next to one" (Cressey 1930:256). On the Near North Side, meanwhile, bloody battles involving sticks, guns, knives, and blackjacks occurred regularly between Swedes and Sicilians. The former also held homeowner meetings to devise more genteel ways of ridding the neighborhood of the dreaded "dark people." The problem, in the words of one local Swedish pastor, was that Sicilians "do not keep their places clean; they tear up the cedar blocks of the sidewalk; and they also bring the district into disrepute in many other ways" (*Skandinaven* 1900). Children engaged in similar battles on the playgrounds and streets of the neighborhood, as Swedish girls kept their Sicilian counterparts off the swings and sandboxes at Seward Park by exclaiming: "Get out! Dagoes! Dagoes! You can't play here!" Boys battled too; on one occasion an Italian youngster led a charge of his compatriots against Swedish and Irish boys on horseback (Zorbaugh 1929:160).

Taken together, many southern Italians encountered powerful and pervasive racial discrimination and prejudice during their early years in the United States and in Chicago more particularly. Thus, if *meridionali* emigrated from Italy in part to escape a racialized social system that relegated them to the bottom tier, they entered another social system in the United States fairly close to the bottom again. But the social systems of turn-of-the-century Italy and the United States were very different. Most important, unlike in the Old World, southern Italians never occupied the lowest of social positions in the United States. This was because the United States had both racial *and* color hierarchies, and if Italians were denigrated and exploited in the former, they were greatly privileged in the latter. That is, for all of the racial prejudice and discrimination that Italians faced in these early years, they were still generally accepted as white and reaped the many rewards that came with this status.

To be sure, this statement needs serious qualification, for certainly at no other time in Italian-American history was the color status of *meridionali* more hotly contested. In 1911, for instance, the U.S. House Committee on Immigration openly debated and seriously questioned whether one should regard "the south Italian as a full-blooded Caucasian" (U.S. Congress 1912:77–78). And a range of Americans shared these ideas. From the docks of New York to railroads out West, some American workers carefully drew distinctions between themselves— "white men"—and immigrant foreigners such as Italians (Leiserson 1924:71–72; Barnes 1915:8; Higham 1988:66). In the South, one town attempted to bar Italians from white schools, while Louisiana state legislators in 1898 fought to disenfranchise Italians along with African-Americans at the state constitutional convention (Cunningham 1965:34; Campisi 1942:83). And, of course, lynchings—a punishment often reserved for African-Americans—were none-too-rare an occurrence for Italians throughout the South, West, and Midwest at this time. As late as 1915, an armed posse in Johnston City, Illinois, a mining town only three hundred miles from Chicago, lynched Sicilian Joseph Strando for his alleged murder of a prominent town resident (*L'Italia* 1904:1; *Chicago Tribune* 1915a:13; Brundage 1997:2).

Various Chicago institutions and individuals also had their questions about Italians' proper color status. The city's newspapers, for instance, sometimes drew connections between southern Italians and the "colored races": The former, it was thought, were at least partly the descendants of "Negroid" people; were as frugal, exploitable, and undesirable as the Chinese; hailed from a part of the globe thought to be far more "Oriental" in ways of thinking and living than European; and had swarthy enough features to warrant frequent remark. In one typical front-page story about an Italian murder on the Near North Side, the *Tribune* described the neighborhood of the crime scene: "Squat two-story buildings apparently crammed to bursting with dark skinned men and women and overflowing with dark skinned children, were giving off odors of garlic from midday meals" (*Chicago Tribune*, 1915b:1). At other times, newspapers could be more direct. *Tribune* guest columnist, George Dorsey, in an essay entitled "Ideas of East and West Rub Elbows in Naples," stated openly: "A brunette from the south of Italy looks like a white man in the heart of Africa. [But] the same man in Chicago might be taken for mulatto" (*Chicago Tribune* 1910a:8). In Chicago, as in other parts of the United States, then, Italians' whiteness was the subject of some debate in the early years of migration and settlement.

In the end, however, this debate never led to any sustained or systematic positioning of Italians as nonwhite. That is, if U.S. congressmen openly debated whether southern Italians were full-blooded Caucasians, they never went so far as to deny *meridionali* naturalization rights based on their doubts; and if some Louisianans tried to disenfranchise Italians, their efforts, in direct contrast to those regarding African-Americans, failed miserably.

But it was really at the local level in Chicago where Italians' whiteness was most visible. When famous African-American boxing champion Jack Johnson attempted to marry a "white" woman in 1912, a rowdy and menacing crowd of a thousand "whites" protested on the Near North Side by hanging Johnson in effigy. Meanwhile a nationwide legal and popular campaign was launched to prevent the "interracial" union from occurring. Italians, by contrast, could marry members of any group without anywhere near this level of resistance (*L'Italia* 1912:3; Mumford 1997:3–18; Bederman 1995:3–5).

Regarding housing, battles took place to prevent Italian infiltration in places such as the Near North Side and the Grand Avenue area. These efforts, however, were never as violent as those in areas just west of the Black Belt, where bombings, rioting, and gang attacks against African-Americans occurred regularly as the Great Migration got under way during World War I. As a result, while the few wealthy Italians could move to virtually any Chicago neighborhood that they could afford, African-Americans were forced to live in the most blighted of Chicago's neighborhoods, regardless of their wealth or education. Hence African-American residential segregation was extraordinarily high even as early as 1900 and always much higher than that of any European immigrant group (Philpott 1991:116–182; Spear 1967:21–33; Grossman 1989; Hoyt 1933:315–319; Tuttle 1970:159–176; Abbott 1936:117–126; *L'Italia* 1910a:2).

In the workplace, Italians faced a good deal of discrimination from both unions and employers in these early years. However, they always enjoyed far more employment options and opportunities than did African-Americans and Asians, both of whom worked almost exclusively in either "ethnic enclaves" or the domestic and personal service trades; better-paying jobs in commerce and industry were effectively closed to them (Vecoli 1963:342–345, 350, 360, 419–424; *La Parola dei Socialisti* 1913; Philpott 1991:119; Spear 1967:30–41; Grossman 1989; Tuttle 1970: 108–130).

Finally, as with public accommodations and private agencies, Italians were refused admission to movie theaters and restaurants on occasion (*L'Italia* 1909). But such instances were rare indeed and certainly paled in comparison to what many African-Americans and some Asians had to endure: systematic exclusion from or segregation in countless Chicago restaurants, theaters, hotels, bars, prisons, hospitals, settlement houses, orphanages, schools, cemeteries, and the like (Spear 1967:42–49; Grossman 1989:127–128; *L'Italia* 1910b:2). Taken together, even in this early period when the "colored races" remained a small fraction of the city's population, a distinct and pervasive color line existed separating whites from nonwhites. And for all their alleged racial inadequacies, Italians were placed firmly on the white side.

And this fact, despite some difficult times in the interwar years, never changed for Italians in Chicago. In 1919 when a massive "color" riot engulfed Chicago and divided it unmistakably into two camps—"whites" and "Negroes"—Italians largely abstained from the violence. Those few Italians who did get involved, however, clearly did so on the side of the "whites." Indeed, no one seemed to question Harold Brignardello's rightful membership in the "white" mob that stoned an African-American's home (Chicago Commission on Race Relations 1922:27–28), or that the murder of African-American Joseph Lovings at the hands of Italians on the Near West Side was just another example of "white" rage against "Negroes" (*Il Progresso Italo-Americano* 1919:3; *Chicago Tribune* 1919:2; Chicago Commission on Race Relations 1922:7, 585, 597, 659; U.S. Congress 1919:3392–3393). In all accounts of the riot in newspapers, books, and so on, Italians were (and are) always categorized as "white."

Several years later Italians were involved in another sort of race war—this time, however, on the defensive end. In the early 1920s, anti-immigrant racialists from Madison Grant to the *Chicago Tribune* roundly condemned Italians (particularly those from the South) as an inferior, mongrel race, whose immigration was destroying the United States. Interestingly, however, this racialist assault stopped well short of questioning Italians' whiteness. If all racialists agreed that "new" immigrants were a hopelessly inferior lot, they also agreed that these newcomers were "white" or "Caucasian" just the same. Lothrop Stoddard's popular book, *The Rising Tide of Color* (1920:267), was typical on this point. In this, Stoddard, an ardent Nordic-supremacist, sounded the alarm against the unrestricted immigration of the Alpine and Mediterranean races, who, as "lower human types," "upset standards, sterilize better stocks, increase low types, and compromise national futures more than war, revolutions, or native deterioration." And yet, for all this doom and gloom, Stoddard was far more concerned about "colored" immigrants from Asia, Africa, and Central/South America. "If the white immigrants can gravely disorder the national life," declared Stoddard passionately, "it is not too much to say that the colored immigrant would doom it to certain death." The Immigration Act of 1924 made eminently clear the practical implications of this distinction between "whites" and "coloreds": while "new" European immigrants, branded as racial inferiors, were severely reduced in numbers, the Japanese, branded as racial *and* color inferiors, were excluded altogether.

Mayoral politics in these years offers another picture of Chicago Italians' anomalous social position as racial outsiders and color insiders. That is, in certain campaigns, certain candidates and political parties used crime-wave anxieties to mobilize voters; Italians—often implicitly, but sometimes explicitly too—were the racialized embodiment of these anxieties (as I will discuss below). Hence campaigns that focused on crime must have contributed to the racialization/criminalization of Chicago's Italians. In one blatant case, for example, a Republican mayoral candidate made the following campaign promise in a 1931 stump speech on the South Side: "If I get elected mayor . . . we will start in the first ward and run the Dagoes out of the south end of it. You don't like that word? . . . There is one race that has more killers in it than any other . . . I will say it again. We will run the Dagoes out of the south end of that ward" (Merriam n.d.:6).

At the same time, these projects hardly disqualified Italians from claiming the wages of whiteness in the political arena. Indeed, when in 1927 the Democratic Party attempted to mobilize whites as whites against Republican mayoral candidate "Big Bill" Thompson "and his negroes" (*Chicago Herald Examiner* 1927:9), Italians were certainly among those voters targeted by this most color-conscious of campaigns. Through their Italian Committee for Mayor Dever, they printed pamphlets (reprinted in Italians' foreign-language newspapers), which featured a long list of reasons why Italians should support Dever. The list concluded on this point: "If you do not want your compatriots to lose their position and be replaced by blacks, vote for the faithful and loyal friend of the Italians, WILLIAM E. DEVER" (*L'Italia* 1927:3). Furthermore, during the campaign, some Italians worked for local Democratic politicians to spread the word about Thompson and the so-called African-American menace. On March 26, Joseph Bazzario and Charles Labato, who both lived and worked in Lincoln Park and owed their jobs to local Democrats, crisscrossed their neighborhood "with paste brushes, pails, and posters." According to the county commissioner who spotted them, "one man would daub a telephone post with paste and the other would slap on a poster reading: 'Negroes First—William Hale Thompson for Mayor' " (*Chicago Tribune* 1927:5).

Meanwhile, the rise of Italian organized crime further convinced many Chicagoans of Italians' "natural inclination toward criminality." Indeed it was in the Prohibition years of Al Capone, Johnny Torrio, and others that, in the words of Horace Cayton and St. Clair Drake, "gangsters replaced Negroes in the civic consciousness as Social Problem No. 1" (Drake and Cayton 1993:77[1945]); that the vice president of the United States, Charles Dawes, pleaded with the Senate to "rescue Chicago from a reign of [Italian] lawlessness" (U.S. Congress: 1924:5456); and that the *Chicago Tribune*, in one bold, sensationalistic headline after another, condemned "alien murderers" from Sicily as *the* scourge of the city (see, for example, the following *Chicago Tribune* articles: 1926a:4; 1926b:1; 1926c:1; 1926e:3; 1926d:1).

Still, as was the case with rising anti-immigrant racialism and mayoral politics, criminalizing campaigns had little effect on Italians' whiteness. As the *Chicago Defender* bitterly pointed out in 1928, even the most notorious Italian gangsters were, unlike law-abiding African-Americans, "privileged to live wherever they choose to purchase homes . . . and every community is open to them" (*Chicago Defender*, 1928: pt. 2:2). In the late 1920s, when the Park Manor Improvement Association organized against "undesirables," no neighbors gave the

Capones any trouble; indeed, Al's mom, Theresa, signed the restrictive covenant for her son (Philpott 1991:211).

And of course these residential options were open to all Italians, not just the gangsters among them. To be sure, certain people still resisted having Italians as neighbors throughout the interwar years. In the Calumet Park district on Chicago's Far South Side, for example, one observer noted: "the Slavs are the only ones who fraternize with the Italians. The Swedes regard the 'Wops' as they call them, as sneaky and vicious, and they are continually fighting with one another" (Dempsey n.d.:8). As in the past, however, these forms of resistance to Italian infiltration were never nearly as violent, organized, or relentless as those facing the "colored races," particularly African-Americans. For instance, no all-"white" restrictive covenants or "white" property-owners associations (and there were hundreds of each in Chicago in these years) ever targeted Italians. And the waves of anti-African-American house bombings and violence that swept across the city during World War II and beyond made anti-Italian neighborhood resistance seem like welcoming parties in comparison (Guglielmo 2003a:chap. 8).

Most important, as the federal government in the 1930s and 1940s became increasingly active in private and public housing, it unambiguously classified Italians as "white" and lavished aid upon them because of it. Take Federal Housing Administration (FHA) loans for example. While all-"white" outlying areas and suburbs received thousands of these loans, starting in the 1930s, neighborhoods with any "colored" population, or threat of it, received almost no support. As Kenneth Jackson (1985:215) has shown, "the main beneficiary of the $119 billion in FHA mortgage insurance issued in the first four decades of FHA operation was suburbia." These color inequalities extended to pubic housing as well. On the Near West Side in the late 1930s and 1940s, when quality housing in poorer neighborhoods was exceedingly scarce, the Chicago Housing Authority openly and severely limited African-Americans' numbers at the Jane Addams Houses (one of the city's first three public housing projects and the only one to admit African-Americans) and in turn increased the number of apartments available to "white" tenants. And with over 40 percent of these apartments going to Italians, it was they who benefited most from these discriminatory policies (Guglielmo 2003a:chap. 8).

The story I tell here, as noted, challenges a core tenet in recent whiteness historiography. While some historians have written about "in-between" immigrants eventually becoming white over time, I talk instead of "racially undesirable" Italians, who were still white on arrival in Chicago and who benefited immensely from the arrangement. And it seems to me wholly plausible that this story applies to Italians beyond Chicago and to other European immigrant groups across the United States. I have argued elsewhere that whether Italians happened to settle in San Francisco or San Antonio, New York or the New South, they faced differing degrees of racial discrimination and prejudice. But they were always accepted as white by the widest variety of individuals and institutions. In the South, for instance, where Italian immigrants faced perhaps the most intense racialized/colorized hostility, Italian whiteness was well established and visible on a daily basis. Indeed, I have seen no evidence that Italians were ever disfranchised in any state on account of their color, subjected in any systematic way to Jim Crow segregation, or legally barred from marrying "white" women (Guglielmo 2003b). Similarly, in the West of "white man's towns," where pervasive color lines prevented many "nonwhites" from owning land, marrying freely, serving on juries, joining particular unions, and claiming land to mine, Italians were again unambiguously white. Race and color, to be sure, are geographically contingent and their meaning and power may vary greatly over space. In the case of Italian immigrants to the United States, however, they were white on arrival—regardless of where they happened to arrive (Guglielmo 2003b).

This Italian story may also be more similar to than different from that of other European immigrant groups. It seems wholly plausible, as well, that all other southern and eastern Europeans, such as Jews, Poles, Slavs, Hungarians, and Greeks were white on arrival themselves. Like Italians, these groups may have suffered from their share of racial discrimination as Hunkies and Hebrews, Alpines and Latins; and on occasion a foreman here and a neighbor there might have questioned the whiteness of these "peculiar" and "problematic" newcomers. Still, I have seen precious little evidence to suggest that these groups were ever positioned as nonwhite in any sustained or systematic way.

Of course, far more work needs to be done on these questions. Historians are only just beginning thoroughly to examine European immigrants' precise race/color location in the late nineteenth- and early twentieth-century United States. My white-on-arrival story, then, particularly as it relates to non-Italians, is less definitive and more suggestive—to both historians and nonhistorians alike. Historians, in my view, need to take the structure of race seriously if they wish to have any success determining the whiteness or nonwhiteness of European immigrants. Scholars in other disciplines, to state the obvious, should be careful about accepting historians' arguments at face value. Indeed, as in the case of "new" European immigrants' race/color status in the United States, these arguments could be, at best, poorly substantiated, at worst, dead wrong.

Meanwhile, it is well to note that these arguments are not merely academic ones. First, stories about European immigrants "becoming white" tend to exaggerate the malleability of America's racial categories and structure. In the process, they encourage more sanguine views of the nation's racial future than history teaches and a more timid racial politics than the present demands. Second, appreciating European immigrants' whiteness on arrival is a crucial antidote to many European ethnics' deeply distorted sense of their history in the United States. Working on Chicago Italians, for instance, I discovered in oral histories that numerous interviewees contrasted themselves explicitly with African-Americans and spoke proudly of the ways in which they pulled themselves up by their bootstraps by working hard and shunning government assistance. And, of course, these narratives have some truth to them. Many Italians did work hard, and their success in America is, in part, a testament to this fact. However, the idea that they, unlike African-Americans, did it all by themselves without government assistance could not be more inaccurate. Indeed, the opposite was often the case, as I hope this essay has shown. Italians' whiteness—conferred more powerfully by the state than any other institution—was their single most powerful asset in the New World; it gave them countless advantages over nonwhites in housing, jobs, schools, politics, and virtually every other meaningful area of life. Without appreciating this fact, we have no hope of fully understanding European immigration yesterday or the persistence of racial inequality today.

5

Shades of Whiteness: The Mexican American Experience in Relation to Anglos and Blacks

EDWARD MURGUIA
TYRONE FORMAN

In 1965, the Congress of the United States passed an amendment (the Hart-Cellar Act) to the Immigration and Nationality Act that abolished discrimination based on national origin and enabled, for the first time, large-scale immigration from all countries. Prior to 1965, the majority of immigrants to the United States originated from Europe; however, since passage of the amendment, increasing numbers of immigrants have come from Asia and Latin America. In fact, post-1965 immigration, which Pedraza (1996) labeled the "Fourth Wave of Immigration," has led to a large increase in the Asian and Latino populations in the United States.

The influx of immigrants from Latin America and Asia has altered the racial landscape of the United States. Specifically, the new immigration has led to an increasingly multiethnic and multiracial United States (Farley 1996; McDaniel 1995). As a result of this increasing diversity, the social dynamics of everyday living in U.S. neighborhoods, schools, and workplaces are rapidly changing as well. This shift has not gone unnoticed by students of race and ethnic relations. In fact, at least two basic perspectives regarding the implications of these demographic shifts have emerged. In one account, largely espoused by conservative scholars and political pundits, demographic shifts portend the impending doom of white American culture and identity (Buchanan 2001; Brimelow 1995; Thernstrom and Thernstrom 1997). The driving force behind their concern is demographic projections that by 2050, whites will be a statistical minority in the United States. These analysts have framed these demographic changes as "a problem" of too many of the "wrong kind" of people (e.g., Proposition 187 in California).

The opposing account highlights growing racial and ethnic diversity as initiating new possibilities for coalitions among people of color (Jackson, Gerber, and Cain 1994; Lott 1994; Okazawa-Rey and Wong 1997). These commentators frame the demographic changes as a potential "antidote" to decades of racial exploitation of various racial and ethnic groups, as experienced by Asians (Almaguer 1994; Takaki 1989; Chan 1991), blacks (Franklin and Moss 1994;

Rawick 1972; Takaki 1993), Latinos (Almaguer 1994; Barrera 1979; Montejano 1987), and Native Americans (Cornell 1988; Takaki 1993; Thornton 1987) through conquest, colonization, and enslavement.

Both perspectives, ironically, have paid little attention to the complexities of race and ethnicity in contemporary society. In fact, each has treated race and ethnic categories as if they were fixed and stable. For instance, on the one hand the conservative point of view situates the large numbers of Asians and Latinos as a "problem" likely to dilute the power of whites. On the other hand, the progressive viewpoint sees the large numbers of Asians and Latinos as an "opportunity," as people likely to dilute the power of whites. Both views become problematic if we view race through the lens of social construction. Indeed, some authors, in response to conservative analysts' doomsday outlook, have argued that the social category of "white" is not likely to diminish as a result of increasing numbers of Asians and Latinos. Highlighting the way the category "white" expanded at the beginning of the twentieth century to incorporate new groups (e.g., Italians, Irish, Polish), they argue that "white" may well expand again, sustaining itself by incorporating many of these post-1965 immigrants into the "white" category (Warren and Twine 1997).

Making this picture even more complicated, new immigrants who arrive from Latin America in particular are already a diverse group in terms of racial categorization (C. Rodriguez 2000). For instance, immigrants from Latin America run the gamut in terms of racial identification from "black" to "white" to somewhere "in between" these two racial polarities. Hence it is very likely that some Latinos will become white over time while others will either be folded into existing racial categories such as the black category or will create new categories (see Flores-Gonzalez 1999). These realities call into question the conservative as well as the progressive perspective. The conservative perspective assumes that the white majority will not accept some Latinos as essentially white, and the progressive perspective assumes that Latinos will consider themselves as non-white. In short, to assume that the influx of these new immigrants will lead to outcomes as predicted by either the conservative or the progressive perspective is to obscure the real complexity that is likely to result from these groups' arrival and incorporation into the United States's racial schema.

In this chapter we seek to highlight the problems with these two views by exploring in depth the issue of whiteness with regard to one major group—the Mexican origin population. Although here discussed in the context of new immigration, those of Spanish heritage have been in what is now the United States since the 1500s. Before the Mexican War of 1846 to 1848, what is now the southwestern part of the United States was northern Mexico. Nevertheless, large-scale immigration from Mexico to the United States has been continuous in recent times, and this, in addition to natural increase, has led to the 20,640,000 people of Mexican origin counted by Census 2000.

ADVANTAGES OF WHITENESS

MacIntosh (cited in Mahoney, 1997:331) provides a useful metaphor of what it means to be white in American society. She indicates that it is like having "'an invisible weightless knapsack' of provisions, maps, guides, codebooks, passports, visas, compasses, and blank checks." Her analogy is similar to Bourdieu's ([1973] 1977) concept of "cultural capital" that explains the advantages of elite children in school. According to Bourdieu, children of the well-off have both a general background of knowledge as well as specific information taught to them by their parents which makes understandable what teachers present to them in school. Children without the right kinds of cultural capital valued by the middle and upper classes have a difficult time understanding what is going on in their classes, do not do well in school, and consequently drop out of school (more accurately, are pushed out). In contrast, the advantages of elite children enable them to succeed in school, and they come to believe that they do well in school "naturally."

There is a class- and culture-based self-assuredness possessed by people of middle- or upper-class stature and who are white. For nonwhite nonelites, such an assuredness is either precarious or nonexistent. More generally, being poor and of color in the United States can best be described as a struggle. Externally, it is a struggle for place; internally, it is a struggle to validate the color of one's skin and one's culture. The result of differences between the ways in which lower- and working-class youth and middle-class youth grow up has been called "the hidden injuries of class" (Sennett and Cobb 1973), and these injuries are ex-acerbated if, in addition to social class, race is involved. Needing a term that designates a combination of race and class, we introduce the term, "raceclass," paralleling Milton Gordon's (1964) "ethclass" term. The concept of "whiteness" implies both European ancestry and a middle- or upper-class status, and with terms of color such as "Mexican American" or "black," not only is (a largely) non-European ancestry implied but also a lower- or working-class status is in-dicated. Mexican Americans and blacks are objectionable to majority whites because of "raceclass," the combination of lower-class status and color that the terms for the minority groups imply to the majority. To the extent that mi-nority individuals reach middle-class status, they become less objectionable, al-though not completely, because race remains as a social barrier (Feagin and Sikes 1994).

SHADES OF WHITENESS

There are many forms of whiteness. As one author points out "whiteness may well work in distinct ways for homeless white men, golf club membership own-ing executives, suburban soccer moms, antiracist skinheads, and/or union-card carrying factory workers" (Lewis 2003b). Hence we can talk about the "shades of whiteness." Despite this diversity, however, in the pathways through which whiteness gets enacted daily, there remains what Lewis has labeled "hegemonic whiteness." Hegemonic whiteness captures the simple fact that in any given epoch certain forms of whiteness become dominant. It is the elite that provides the most coherent display of whiteness and it is their embodiment of whiteness that is the hegemonic form. This form of whiteness does the work of securing "the dominant position of Whites" (Lewis 2003b). Before discussing what we call "shades of whiteness" and the possible "whiteness" of members of the Mexican origin population, it is useful to describe in more detail hegemonic forms of whiteness in the United States today.

Worldwide, but from the perspective of the United States, the whitest collection of people is the English aristocracy of the United Kingdom, with the Royal Family at its head (Kelley 1997). In the United States, the most white are members of "old money" families (Aldrich 1989) in the Northeast with inherited wealth, children who go to schools such as the "St. Grottlesex" New England Episcopalian preparatory schools (Andover, Exeter, Choate, St. Paul, Groton, and Middlesex) (Amory 1947:299) and then to Ivy League colleges such as Harvard, Princeton, and Yale. As the children come of age, they inherit money through trust funds, move into family businesses, and become members of interlocking corporate directorships. The members of this class tend to be of English heritage and Protestant, and they would consider no group their superior except for the English aristocracy of the United Kingdom. For numerous reasons (geography, religion, race, culture, social class), the Mexican origin people in the United States have had and for the most part will have little or no contact with this American Northeastern old-money group.

A second elite group in the United States possesses large amounts of money, but rather than being old and inherited, their money is new and earned. Aldrich (1989) calls an individual in this social class "Market Man." While these entrepreneurs may have more money than many members of the old-money elite, they do not have the prestige of members of old-money families. Some, but relatively few, of Mexican origin have made it into this group. A combination of light skin color and large amounts of money are necessary to be included in this group if one is of Mexican origin.

A third level of "whiteness" in the United States includes those of European ancestry in the middle and upper middle class. A considerable number, more than at the second level, of the Mexican origin group can become "white" at this level—for several reasons. First, some people of Mexican origin have a significant amount of European ancestry, which makes them light-skinned and therefore indistinguishable from the majority society. Second, there is upward mobility among the Mexican Americans. As they move into middle-class and upper-middle-class status, they, on at least the most light-skinned of them, will face some but not a great amount of prejudice and discrimination. In any case, they are not likely to receive much more prejudice than white ethnics (such as the Irish, Italians, and Poles) currently receive.

Table 1 Key Variables that Influence Mexican Origin Identification.

VARIABLE	MEXICAN (MEXICAN INDIAN)	NOT MEXICAN (AMERICAN WHITE)
Name	Spanish	English
Command of English	Nonproficient	Proficient
Skin Color/Facial Features	Dark/Indian	Light/European
Height	Short	Tall
Religion	Catholic	Protestant
Social-Class Standing	Lower Class	Middle Class
Ethnic Self-Identity	Mexican	American
Racial Self-Identity	Nonwhite	White

WHITES' EVALUATION OF MEXICAN AMERICANS IN TERMS OF SOCIAL DISTANCE FROM THEMSELVES

Whites do not place Mexican Americans in the same location as blacks in terms of social distance from themselves. For instance, Warren and Twine (1997:212) cite a young white woman's response to their question concerning who was "allowed" to move into her community, "Blacks are not allowed to move into this area, but Mexicans and Asians are different—they can blend."

Generally speaking, having Mexican Indian characteristics as well as having lower-class characteristics places individuals at greater social distance from the U.S. majority society than having characteristics associated with European ancestry and characteristics associated with being in the middle or upper social classes. More specifically, eight factors seem to influence whites' evaluation of Mexican Americans. Two of the eight factors relate to language and are, first, the name of the individual, including given name(s) and surname, and second, the Mexican origin person's command of English. The remaining six variables are phenotype, height, religion, social-class standing, and ethnic and racial self-identity. Given that Anglo-conformity assimilation (Gordon 1964) has been the reality in the United States, to the extent that Mexican origin individuals desire upward social mobility, they may try to minimize social distance between themselves and majority whites by changing their characteristics relative to the above variables, at least the variables over which they have some control. Each variable is considered below in some detail.

Concerning given names, most ethnic would be a first name that is not English and that does not have an English referent, a name such as "Guadalupe" (Guadalupe is a name that can be given to either a male or a female in Mexico). More acceptable to the majority society would be a Spanish name that has an English referent, such as Jose, which is Joseph in English. Still more acceptable would be a Spanish name with an English referent that is spelled the same (or very similarly) in English and Spanish, such as David (In Spanish, there is an accent mark on the "i" in David). An even more "white" first name would be an English name such as "Henry," where the name exists in English but not in Spanish. The Spanish equivalent of Henry is "Enrique" a different word from "Henry." Finally, the most English given name would be a name that has no Spanish equivalent, such as "Geoffrey."

Name changing of first names can be generational, that is, parents who have Spanish given names give English first and second names to their children. It can also be that individuals themselves change their own names, most often through nicknames (Roberto becomes Bob or Bobby, for example), or by giving themselves, in their speech and correspondence, the English equivalent to their Spanish first and second names or, if there is no English equivalent, the closest English equivalent to their Spanish first and second names.

The second variable refers to the last names (surnames) of Mexican Americans. Compared to given names, there is greater reticence in changing a last name from Spanish to English, from Martinez to Spencer, for example, because this places social distance between individuals and their own family members with the same last name as themselves. Some last names are common in Spanish, such as Gonzalez or Martinez, and will be recognized as such, placing social distance between individuals with such names and the majority. Some less common Spanish surnames may not be recognized as such, and individuals with such names may not experience a great amount of social distance between themselves and the majority. Some Mexican origin individuals have non-Spanish surnames either because of a previous intermarriage with an Anglo male or because someone decided to give himself/herself an English last name (despite creating social distance between himself/herself and his/her family), and this is the situation in which the least amount of social distance is placed between persons with such last names and majority whites.

In terms of accent, most prestigious is the ability to speak English fluently and without an accent. Second is the ability to speak English, but with a Spanish accent. Third would be Spanish-only speaking. To the extent that an individual is unable to speak English or speaks only heavily accented English, social distance is placed between the individual and majority whites.

Phenotype is defined as the external physical appearance of a person. While some researchers have argued the social construction of race almost to the exclusion of any consideration of actual difference in phenotype, we would argue that there is an element of measurable difference in phenotype that contributes to social distance from the majority society. In other words, majority whites react to visible differences in phenotype and treat others accordingly. Of course, the meaning given to phenotype itself is socially constructed. The external physical appearance most European is light skin color and facial features similar to people in Northern and Western Europe, that is, a narrow nose, round eyes, thin lips, and so on.

The next variable we consider is height. A major element determining the height of Mexican origin individuals has to do with nutrition. With improved nutrition in the United States has come increased height by generation of those of Mexican origin in the United States (Of course, improved nutrition is also occurring in Mexico as well as in the United States at this time). To the extent that individuals are very short or short, they are seen as less "white," in large part because shortness has been associated with being from an underdeveloped country. Note that this is one of the differences between the Mexican origin group and the African origin group. Among those from Africa, height varies greatly, and a substantial number of both Africans and African Americans are taller than majority whites.

Relative to religion, the most ethnic situation for those of Mexican origin would be being Catholic and belonging to a Mexican Catholic church in a *barrio* (a working-class Mexican origin neighborhood). The circumstance with the least social distance from majority-white society would be belonging to an established upper-middle-class or upper-class Protestant church. Established and prestigious Protestant denominations include, for example, the Episcopalians, Presbyterians, and Congregationalists. Belonging to an affluent Episcopalian church in an elite white neighborhood would be the situation with the least social distance from majority whites.

It should be noted that there is a difference in religious status and upward mobility between Catholics and Protestants. Catholics, when they rise socioeconomically, tend to stay within Catholicism. The change when Mexican American Catholics become upwardly mobile is that of moving from an ethnic lower- or working-class-neighborhood Catholic church to a Catholic church that is nonethnic and is in a nonethnic neighborhood. In contrast, individuals who are Protestant tend to change denominations as they move upward in social class. Denominations with less social prestige tend to be the "storefront" Protestant churches, churches of relatively recent origin. Protestant churches with a greater amount of prestige are those that have been in what is now the United States since colonial times.

We next consider the variable of social class. When we think of majority whites, we think of individuals in the middle or upper classes. In contrast, when we think of Mexicans in the United States, we think of individuals in the lower or working classes. To the extent, then, that a person of Mexican origin moves into the middle class, he or she becomes more "white."

Concerning ethnic self-identity, those who identify exclusively with being "American" would place no social distance between themselves and the majority society. By identifying as "Mexicano" or as "Mexican American," individuals place greater social distance between themselves and the majority. With reference to race, individuals can see themselves as "white" or "nonwhite." In the U.S. Census, respondents have the choice of declaring themselves racially white or of other races.

In sum, we can see how different two individuals would be if they were at opposite ends of continuums on all eight variables. In the case where the individual was at the most "white" end of the continuum along each of the eight variables, the individual would be named, for example, Geoffrey Spencer, would speak perfect English, would be light-skinned, tall, at least in the upper middle class if not in a higher social class, would belong to an affluent Protestant church, and would think of himself as American and as white. Non-Hispanic whites would place little or no social distance between themselves and such an individual.

On the other hand, if an individual were at the other end of each of the eight variable continuums, the individual would be named Guadalupe Martinez, would speak only Spanish, would be short, dark, lower-class, would attend the Mexican Catholic church in the *barrio* and would consider himself a Mexican and a nonwhite. The social distance that non-Hispanic whites would place between themselves and this individual would be very great. Notice that six of the eight variables are changeable—the individual's name, command of English (but not totally, because if a language is learned after a certain age, there is the likelihood of always speaking the language with an accent), religion, social-class standing, ethnic self-identity, and racial self-identity. Only one's height and skin color are relatively immutable. Hence, as part of a process of upward mobility in the United States, some people of Mexican origin engage in a process of changing their location on the continuum of the above variables, minimizing social distance between themselves and majority whites. Others, though, regardless of upward mobility, arrive at a political consciousness where, although participating in the larger American society, they maintain a cultural pluralistic point of view and choose bilingualism and biculturalism rather than assimilation.

MEXICAN ORIGIN TERMS OF SELF-REFERENCE AND SOCIAL DISTANCE FROM MAJORITY WHITES

We have discussed individual characteristics of Mexican origin and the meaning whites give to varying characteristics of members of the group, resulting in social distance imposed on Mexican origin individuals by majority whites. We now look at six terms of Mexican origin self-reference to determine the amount of social distance which people of Mexican origin place between themselves and majority whites through their use of these terms. Four of the terms refer to ancestry from a single country of national origin, Mexico itself. The two remaining terms are "pannational" in that they can refer to individuals from numerous countries where Spanish is spoken as well as to people from Mexico. The national-origin terms are "Mexicano," "Mexican," "Chicano," and "Mexican American," and the panethnic terms are "Latino" and "Hispanic." The four national-origin terms are in order of social distance from whites, with "Mexicano" exhibiting the greatest social distance from Whites and "Mexican American" designating the least amount of distance. The two panethnic terms are also in order of social distance, with "Latino" indicating greater social distance from whites than "Hispanic."

The first term, "Mexicano," exhibits a considerable amount of social distance between individuals who use this term as their preferred term of self-designation and the majority, in part because this term is in Spanish. Unlike the term "Mexican American," there is no reference to the United States in the term "Mexicano." The second term, "Mexican," has less social distance from majority whites than "Mexicano" because the term "Mexican" is in English. Again, "Mexican" implies a considerable amount of social distance from majority whites. As with the term, "Mexicano," if one says, "I am Mexican," there is no mention of the word "American" in it and this makes it a term more distant from the majority society than the term "Mexican American."

The third term, "Chicano," which is probably derived from a diminution of the word "Mexicano," came into popular usage during the late 1960s and early 1970s to designate people who trace their ancestry to Mexico. This word connotes more than ancestry in Mexico, however; it also connotes militance and dissatisfaction with conditions of Mexican origin people in the United States. It has a connotation of pride in one's Mexican heritage and culture. Associated with the word "Chicano" are the civil unrest and the social movements that were occurring when the term came into prominence, including Cesar Chavez's United Farmworkers Union struggle, Reies Lopez Tijerina's Alianza movement in New Mexico, and the creation of La Raza Unida Party, a political party that gained considerable support for a time in Texas. The fourth term, "Mexican American" refers both to possessing a Mexican heritage and to being American, and so it has both ancestry in Mexico and a current nationality and residence in the United States associated with it. Since the noun in the term is the word "American" and the adjective is "Mexican," it more strongly associates one with the United States than with Mexico.

The two panethnic terms, "Latino" and "Hispanic," refer to people of more than one national origin but are being used by those of Mexican origin to refer to themselves. "Latino" technically refers to people from those numerous countries whose language is derived from Latin, although its usage in the context of the United States is limited to those from countries where Spanish or Portuguese is spoken. "Latino" is parallel to the term "Hispanic," in that it is panethnic, encompassing numerous nationalities (Also, unlike "Hispanic," it seems to include those from Portugal and Brazil). However, "Latino" implies a greater social distance between the people to whom it refers and majority whites than does "Hispanic." A group using the term "Latino" in self-reference cannot and does not want to become white. Use of "Hispanic," on the other hand, expresses a desire to achieve white status. The term "Latino" has within it a critical awareness that things are not all well with the minority group. It includes a sense of historical oppression and a struggle for equality among members of the group. In this way, the term "Latino" parallels the term "Chicano," except that "Latino" is a panethnic term, whereas "Chicano" refers to ancestry in the country of Mexico alone. These two terms, "Chicano" and "Latino," one a national term and the second a pannational term, are in opposition to the more conservative terms, "Mexican American" and "Hispanic," "Mexican American" being the national term and "Hispanic" being pannational. With the term "Hispanic," the connotation is not one of questioning the system but rather of obtaining a larger piece of the pie within the system as it is. The term "Latino," on the other hand, connotes a questioning of the system and a sense that the political, economic, and social systems of the United States are unfair and should be changed.

Use of the term "Hispanic" raises additional issues. A large number of those of Mexican origin, particularly in Texas and Arizona, are calling themselves "Hispanic." "Hispanic" refers to all people in the United States who trace their origin back to Spain. Therefore the term "Hispanic" includes not only those of Mexican origin but also those in the United States from Cuba, Puerto Rico, from Central and South America, and from Spain itself (whether or not "Hispanic" includes those from Portugal or Brazil is a major problematic—according to the U.S. Census, it does not). The advantage of this term as a panethnic term is that it significantly increases the number of people being designated, and numbers are, of course, important from a political point of view. Currently, the number of Hispanics is slightly larger the number of African Americans in the United States. Census 2000 counted 35,306,000 Hispanics and 34,658,000 blacks.

Also, while those of Mexican origin have been thought of in the past as a regional group concentrated in the American Southwest (the states of California, Arizona, New Mexico, Colorado, and Texas), Hispanics are to be found throughout the United States. Because "Hispanic" emphasizes the European origin of the group, it minimizes the social distance between the group and majority whites. To the extent that those of Mexican origin want to "become white," this is the term that moves them in this direction. The fact that it is the term used by the U.S. Census is critically important because this legitimizes the term, and census counts and analyses are made based on this term. Its use by the U.S. Census makes it the term of choice for many. It remains to be seen to what extent the fact that it downplays origin from Mexico and non-European ancestry will keep it from being totally accepted by those of Mexican origin, or, on the other hand, to what extent the advantages of larger size and a national rather than a regional presence override the importance of emphasizing Mexican heritage.

INTERGROUP RELATIONS BETWEEN THOSE OF MEXICAN ORIGIN AND BLACKS

Based strictly on social class, it might be assumed that the possibility of a political and social coalition for the improvement of social conditions would be relatively straightforward between Mexican Americans and blacks. Such an assumption, however, ignores important aspects of social reality. The reality is that because European whites conquered the indigenous people of Mexico and have remained the elite in that country ever since, because blacks occupy a low status in the United States and people in the United States tend to want to place social distance between themselves and those lower than themselves in the racial hierarchy, and because a significant percentage of the Mexican origin population in the United States is an immigrant population, the social distance between Mexican Americans and African Americans remains very large. For example, a study conducted in the state of Texas found that Mexican Americans preferred greater social distance from blacks than from whites (Dyer, Vedlitz, and Worchel 1989). Similar results were found in a study of Mexican Americans in Pontiac, Michigan (Lambert and Taylor 1990), where Mexican Americans reported preferring intermarriage with whites and Puerto Ricans to blacks. This pattern held for their preferences of close friends, neighbors, and coworkers (for similar findings, see Grebler, Moore, and Guzman 1970; Robin Williams 1964). In addition, significant numbers of Mexican Americans report viewing blacks as violent, aggressive, lazy, untrustworthy, and unlawful. In fact, a recent study of Mexican American college students showed that they held several negative stereotypes of blacks (Niemann 1994). These results are consistent with previous work that suggests that "Mexican Americans have historically viewed Blacks as 'black Anglo-Saxons' in the negative sense of their being an inferior imitation" (Henry 1980:224). These patterns of intergroup attitudes are also consistent with other research showing that the majority of Mexican Americans do not favor coalitions with blacks (Grebler, Moore, and Guzman 1970; Henry 1980; Henry and Munoz 1991; Jennings and Lusane 1994).

An Empirical Analysis of Mexican Origin Views of Blacks and Whites

In the 1990 Latino Political Survey (de la Garza, et al. 1998), Mexican American racial affect toward blacks and whites was measured using a feeling thermometer scale. Specifically, each Mexican American respondent was asked to indicate on a feeling thermometer scale ranging from 0 to 100 how "warm" or "cold" they felt toward blacks and whites. A score of 0 reflects a very cold feeling, a score of 50 degrees reflects a neutral feeling, and a score of 100 reflects a very warm feeling. The following analysis draws upon data from this survey.

Table 2 reports the distributions of Mexican American racial affect toward blacks and whites. Generally, Mexican Americans felt most warm toward whites and least warm toward blacks. For instance, 60 percent felt very warmly (i.e., 75 degrees or higher on the thermometer scale) toward whites while only 36 percent felt very warmly toward blacks. This pattern is not surprising in light of previous work that has documented strained relations between Mexican Americans and blacks (see Dyer, Vedlitz, and Worchel 1989; Grebler, Moore, and Guzman 1970; Lambert and Taylor 1990; Robin Williams 1964). Others have argued that Mexican American antiblack prejudice is related to the fact that "Spanish culture has traditionally denigrated 'dark skin' and 'inferiorized'

Table 2 Mexican Americans' Warmth toward Blacks and Whites.

| | RACE | |
DEGREES ON FEELING THERMOMETER	BLACKS	WHITES
Mexicans		
0°–24°	7.2%	2.7%
25°–49°	10.5	4.7
50°	33.7	24.0
51°–74°	12.5	8.4
75°–100°	36.1	60.2
(N)	(1544)	
Mean	3.61	4.18
Black-White Difference	−0.57*	

* $p \leq .001$(two-tailed paired sample t-tests)

its possessors." As a result, a key "legacy of that culture persists and translates into . . . negative attitudes toward contact with Blacks" (Oliver and Johnson 1984:66).

Rodriguez and colleagues (1991:47) point out that "a Latino's racial identity is not (just) genetically determined but . . . depends on many variables, including phenotype." Given the above results as well as Oliver's and Johnson's observation, it is necessary to consider other factors such as phenotype in large part because there is considerable heterogeneity in the Mexican American population in terms of skin color (Allen, Telles, and Hunter 2000; Arce, Murguia, and Frisbie 1987; Murguia and Telles 1996; Telles and Murguia 1990). For example,

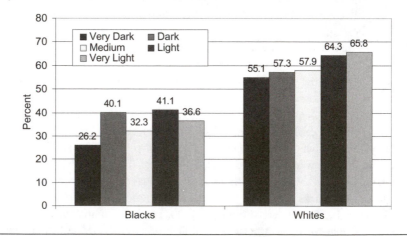

Figure 1 Mexican Americans' warmth toward blacks and whites by skin color.

according to the 1990 National Latino Political Survey (de la Garza et al. 1998), 20 percent of Mexican Americans were considered to have a "dark" skin color, another 44 percent had "medium" skin color, and 36 percent were considered to have "light" skin color. This item was based on the interviewers' assessment of the respondents' skin color.

Figure 1 reveals two important facts. The first is that, on average, Mexican Americans of all colors feel warmer toward whites as compared to blacks. Second, although there does not seem to be a significant pattern relating skin color and Mexican American affect toward blacks, light-skinned Mexican Americans seem to have a significantly warmer affect toward Anglo-Americans than do Mexican Americans of darker skin colors.

THE IMMIGRANT HYPOTHESIS

Part of the social distance found between those of Mexican origin and blacks may be due to the immigrant status of a substantial part of the Mexican origin population in the United States. In one of the few studies of minorities' intergroup attitudes, Lucie Cheng and Yen Le Espiritu (1989) developed what they call the "immigrant hypothesis" to help explain the differing patterns of intergroup attitudes and relations of Asians with Latinos and blacks. As they outline it, the immigrant hypothesis suggests that because of the large proportion of foreign-born people among both the Asian and Latino populations, these two groups share a "frame of reference different from that held by native born Americans" (Cheng and Espiritu 1989:531), in the case of our discussion, blacks. Because, as Cheng and Espiritu (1989:528) note, "immigrants often leave their home countries as a result of economic or political turmoil," they share a belief in an immigrant ideology in which the United States is understood to be a land of opportunity. These shared beliefs result in better intergroup attitudes and relations between Latinos and Asians. As Uhlaner (1991:341) notes, "learning a new language, dealing with new customs, and negotiating the intricacies of the immigration and naturalization process itself present a set of experiences that may generate common interests that bring immigrants together." Although Cheng and Espiritu's immigrant hypothesis was developed to explain the differing intergroup attitudes and relations between Asians and Latinos as compared to Asians and blacks, it also has relevance for understanding Mexican Americans' attitudes toward blacks and whites.

Although Cheng and Espiritu highlight the importance of nativity in distinguishing Asians and Latinos from blacks, we argue that it is more than just the sense of "sameness" derived from being foreign-born that may orient Latinos and Asians to have more positive views toward one another than toward blacks. We argue that the shared immigrant ideology of Latinos and Asians may also translate into distaste for blacks, whom they perceive as not embracing the achievement ideology. Okazawa-Rey and Wong (1997:33) make a similar point, noting that "immigrants judge the lack of success of U.S.-born peoples

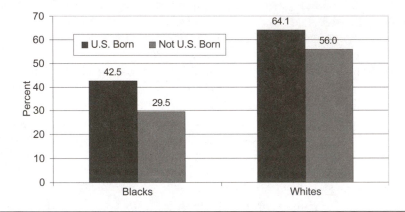

Figure 2   Mexican Americans' warmth toward blacks and whites by nativity.

of color to be the result of intellectual, character, and moral deficiencies rather than the effect of institutionalized discrimination and other real barriers to opportunities for success." A recent study of Latinos (most of Mexican origin) in Houston, Texas, that compared native-born Latinos to foreign-born Latinos found that approximately six in ten foreign-born Latinos believed there was a great deal of conflict between blacks and Latinos, in contrast to the results for native-born Latinos, in which four in ten reported a great deal of tension between blacks and Latinos (Mindiola, Rodriguez, and Niemann 1996). Jones-Correa (1998:120) notes that: "it makes just as much sense to act instrumentally and distance [oneself] from 'being Black' in their home countries as it does in the United States . . . [immigrants] are predisposed, then, even before coming to the United States, to see race as a scale on which one shifts 'upward' to become whiter, if one can." Moreover, Warren and Twine (1997:208) describe this process as "a tactical matter for nonblacks of conforming to white standards, of distancing themselves from Blackness, and of reproducing anti-Black ideas and sentiments." As a result, rather than having empathy with similarly situated minority groups that some might expect, Asian and Latino immigrants may instead express racial antipathy toward African Americans, whom they see as encompassing all that they hope not to become.

Empirically, using data from the 1990 National Latino Political Survey, we demonstrate in Figure 2 that nativity plays a role in Mexican Americans' feelings toward whites and blacks. Mexican origin individuals born in the United States feel significantly more warmth toward blacks and whites as compared to those born outside it. These results are consistent with the immigrant hypothesis. We want to emphasize, though, that concerning Mexican origin black relations, the immigrant hypothesis, while important, provides only part of the answer.

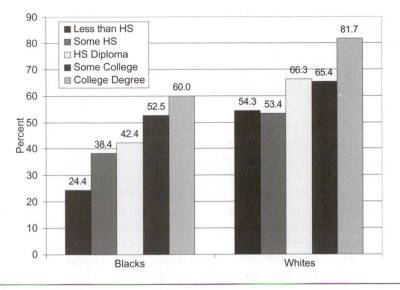

Figure 3   Mexican Americans' warmth toward blacks and whites by educational attainment.

According to the 1990 Census, only 33 percent of the Mexican origin population, admittedly a large proportion of the group but certainly not the majority, are foreign-born. (This differs considerably from other Latino populations; for instance, 72 percent of Cubans, 71 percent of Dominicans, and 81 percent of Salvadorans are foreign-born.) One possible source of Mexican origin-Black social distance is Mexicans' high value for white skin—a holdover from the colonial experience. Another possible source is Mexicans' devaluing of blackness resulting either from current anti-black images and stereotypes that cross over from the U.S. to Mexico in media and popular culture or related to the fact that "Spanish culture has traditionally denigrated 'dark skin' and 'inferiorized' its possessors (Oliver and Johnson 1984: 66)."

Based on data from the 1990 National Latino Political Survey (see Figure 3), the impact of education on Mexican American attitudes toward blacks is striking. There is a linear increase by level of educational attainment in warmth toward blacks, from a score of 24.4 for Mexican Americans with less than high school to 60.0 for those with a college degree. There is a similar, although not perfectly linear, increase in warmth toward whites from a score of 54.3 for Mexican Americans with less than high school to a score of 81.7 for Mexican American college graduates.

This may indicate that with an increase in education, Mexican Americans may have greater social contact with Anglos and blacks, which may lead to a decreased amount of stereotyping of both of them.

Conclusion

At the beginning of this chapter, we noted that demographic projections forecast that by 2050 whites will be a statistical minority in the United States (Farley 1996; McDaniel 1995). A major reason for this demographic shift is the rather large number of immigrants arriving in the United States from Asia and Latin America. In response to these demographic patterns, writers on race and ethnic relations have developed two distinct perspectives on their likely significance. One view suggests that it is doomsday in "America" and that the white values and culture that it largely represents will soon cease to exist. The other view indicates that the numerical shrinkage in the white population virtually assures the possibility for a more just and equitable U.S. society as it pertains to the opportunity structure facing racial and ethnic minorities. In contrast to these perspectives, we have argued instead that the changes in the racial/ethnic composition of our nation over the next five decades are not likely to lead to either of these portraits, in part because both views mistakenly treat racial and ethnic categories as if they are fixed and stable.

According to the 1990 Census, approximately 51 percent of the Mexican-origin population self-identified as "white" and 47 percent identified as "Other." Consequently a third alternative for the future racial schema—that we believe reflects the complexity and fluidity of racial and ethnic categories—is the emergence of a three-way split of whites/browns/blacks, with some Mexican origin peoples, along with other groups from Latin America, seeing themselves in the middle of the United States racial hierarchy as "brown" and others strongly identifying with the white majority (see Bonilla-Silva et al. 2003). One possible indicator for how the Mexican origin population and others from Latin America will identify is their chosen panethnic label as either "Hispanic" or "Latino." For instance, claiming the panethnic label "Hispanic" can be seen as an attempt to become another European-origin white group much like the Italians and Irish. In this scenario, there is a real danger that a significant part of the Mexican origin population will identify with and support policies advantageous to the largely white middle and upper classes but disadvantageous to the lower and working classes of people of color. In contrast, the claiming of the panethnic identity "Latino" can be seen as an attempt to identify as nonwhite. In this scenario, there is the possibility of coalescing with other people of color and supporting public policies that would address common struggles that each group faces, such as the need for better public school funding and inner-city job creation.

In this chapter, we have examined the Mexican origin population in the United States and the issue of whiteness as our lens onto what is likely to occur over the next five decades. Specifically, we have shown that discussing the Mexican origin population as a monolithic entity, especially as it pertains to their relation to blacks and whites, is problematic. For instance, how Mexican origin individuals see themselves (and are viewed) in relation to each of these groups depends on an array of factors such as their name, English-language proficiency, skin color, height, religious orientation, social class, ethnic identity, and racial identity. In short, to speculate that all Mexican origin individuals will align themselves with people of color is no more accurate than to suggest that all will embrace whiteness as a strategy of upward mobility in the United States. It appears that there are a number of possible alternatives for the future of relations among whites, those of Mexican origin, and blacks. Unfortunately, only time will tell which is the most viable.

6

Rejecting Blackness and Claiming Whiteness: Antiblack Whiteness in the Biracial Project

MINKAH MAKALANI

Over the past fifteen years in the United States, there has emerged a concerted push to reclassify people with one Black and one white parent as biracial.[1] Advocates of this biracial project seek to have people of mixed parentage (PMP) recognized as a distinct, biracial race.[2] They maintain that a biracial identity is more mentally healthy than a Black one and challenges popular notions of race in the United States, therefore making it the basis for "ultimately disabus[ing] Americans of their false beliefs in the biological reality of race" (Zack 2001:34). This will lead society away from racial classifications, hasten racism's demise, and bring about a color-blind society (Gilanshah 1993; Spickard 2001; Zack 2001). Still, the progressive qualities of a biracial identity are more apparent than real.

The presence of a biracial race would certainly disrupt popular ideas about race, but to suggest it would precipitate the end of racial classifications is speculation (Parker and Song 2001). Changing popular ideas about race can occur without addressing racial oppression (Mosley 1997), and abolishing racial classifications to create a color-blind society is more likely to contribute to the persistence of racism than to its demise (Carr 1997; Neville et al. 2000; Bonilla-Silva 2001). Additionally, most arguments for a biracial race ignore the sociohistorical character of race and roots biracialty in biological notions of race "mixture" (powell 1997). This raises serious doubts about the biracial project's claim to be a progressive social movement. Rather than seeking to overthrow the racialized social system, it is a reactionary political response to the racialization of people of African descent in the United States as Black. Specifically, it uses whiteness to distinguish PMP from African Americans as a new race that would be positioned between Blacks and whites in a reordered, racialized social system.

Several historians have addressed the historical role of whiteness in ordering racial oppression, giving special attention to how white racial identity develops in different racial formations (Roediger 1991; Allen 1994; on racial formations, see Baron 1985; Cha-Jua 2001). Putting these together with other works on race (C. Harris 1993; Malik 1997; Mills 1997), we can see whiteness as primarily a component part of racism. Cheryl Harris (1993:1735) alludes to this when she argues that whiteness is used by whites to maintain a superordinate position in the racial hierarchy: "the state's official recognition of a racial identity that subordinated Blacks and of privileged rights in property based on race elevated whiteness from a passive attribute to an object of law and a resource deployable at the social, political, and institutional level to maintain control." This identifies a link between white racial identity and Black subordination and more importantly conceptualizes whiteness as a material object used to maintain white supremacy rather than as merely an aspect of white identity.

This chapter analyzes the biracial project's *deployment* of whiteness to argue that PMP constitute a new race. With the role whiteness plays in racism in mind, this accomplishes two things. First, it builds on Cheryl Harris (1993) to argue that whiteness is a dynamic social property that people of color might use to negotiate the racial hierarchy and it cautions against the tendency to essentialize whiteness as something only whites have. Second, it examines the biracial project as a particular instance of people of color using whiteness, by looking at the assertion that PMP are racially distinct from African Americans because whiteness is an immutable biosocial attribute. Using a materialist theory of race and racism, I argue that a biracial race has no social, historical, or cultural basis and that claims for its existence ignore the sociohistorical character of race and conflate racial identity with racial identification. Focusing in part on congressional testimonies on the census, but primarily on biracial-identity Internet Web sites, I examine the arguments of biracial-identity advocates to show how whiteness is deployed as a tool to distance PMP from African Americans politically, socially, and culturally.

RACE, RACISM, AND EMBRACING WHITENESS

There are three arguments for PMP constituting a distinct race: 1) their "racial reality" (i.e., possessing whiteness) sets them apart from African Americans; 2) they have white political interests which can only be expressed by embracing whiteness and rejecting blackness; and 3) PMP can escape the social stigma of "black blood" by asserting their whiteness and institutionalizing their distinction from Blacks. These arguments reflect two distinct perspectives on race and racial identity: *ideological individualism* and *biological determinism* (powell 1997).

Ideological individualism conceives of race as an ideological belief in biologically pure races that, in turn, produces racism. Building on the current racial formations' color-blind racial ideology, it argues that individuals have a right to choose their racial identity, irrespective of their racial classification. In this way, a biracial identity is seen as challenging the basis of racism by highlighting that races are not mutually exclusive, pure biological groupings.

Biological determinism maintains that there are biologically distinct races, and the progeny of interracial unions possess characteristics of both races, making them racially distinct from their parents. Hence a biracial identification recognizes their "racial reality."

While these are two different perspectives on race, their articulation in the biracial project conjoins them in subtle yet important ways. Logically, the ideological-individualist perspective depends on biological determinism in order to substantiate the claim that one can be biracial. To assert that there are no races negates the possibility of a biracial race, since any argument for hybridity depends on two nonhybrid (pure) parts (Dirlik 2000). Similarly, the biological-determinist perspective is undergirded by a liberal emphasis on the individual. Arguing that a person is biracial simply because they have one Black and one white parent is fundamentally identical to arguing they are Black because any African ancestry makes one racially black. The biracial project opposes the sociohistorical definition of who is Black, however, by emphasizing that individuals are forced to negate their racial reality. Hence the biracial project is premised on arguments grounded in long-disproven scientific notions of race and a liberal emphasis on the individual (powell 1997). Ultimately, this veils the major political implication of asserting a racial reality based solely on being part white—granting a biracial race the privileges of whiteness (Baker 2001; Makalani 2001).

The argument for a distinct biracial race also, on a basic level, entails a rejection of blackness. The first argument subtly rejects blackness and apparently has little concern for whiteness, while the other two articulate an explicitly antiblack whiteness. Nonetheless, the practical effects of both are identical. They each result in a new racial group defined primarily (if not solely) by being part white. Though seeming to attack the fallacy of biologically pure races, they nonetheless emphasize white racial parentage and presume the existence of pure racial groups. Finally, they ignore racial oppression. For example, G. Reginald Daniel (1992:340) argues that being biracial "in a hierarchical system simply means being just a little less Black and thus a little less subordinate." Naomi Zack (1993:9, 165) even suggests that defining some people as Black "unjustly excludes [them] from [a] white designation," and since people classified as Black are not treated equally with whites, "perhaps the time has come to reject the concept of a black American race." To paraphrase Christine Hickman (1997), these positions respond to antiblack racism by making PMP nonblack rather than attacking racism itself, which contributes to Black people's continued oppression.

The creation of a new race that possesses whiteness would require a restructuring of the system of racial oppression but not its abolition. Races are historically developed political groupings that always exist in a racial hierarchy (Bonilla-Silva 1997; Makalani 2001). As such, a new race *must* be situated within the racial hierarchy; any discussion of race has therefore to take racism as the principle category of analysis. Racism is the organization of a society's institutional infrastructure so that racial groups are placed in a hierarchical relationship to one another, and the society's laws, policies, and social relationships give preference to a superordinate race and discriminate against subordinate races. It is, however, a dynamic structure that can adjust to new historical circumstances to ensure the dominant racial class's continued economic exploitation and social control of subordinate racial groups. As stated earlier, whiteness functions as a component of this structure, determining which racial group(s) receive advantages and privileges and which receive none. Heretofore, whiteness has largely been at the disposal of whites, but new historical circumstances demand that it become available to nonwhites for white supremacy to survive.

The biracial project actively seeks to redefine the boundaries of whiteness. Whether argued from an ideological-individualist or biological-determinist perspective, it roots whiteness squarely in biology. PMP possess whiteness as a biological fact, and a biracial identity merely acknowledges their racial reality. A major problem has been the conflation of racial identity with racial identification. For Janet Helms (1994:3), racial identity "refers to a sense of group or collective identity based on one's perception that he or she shares a common racial heritage with a particular racial group." This does not mean a person can have a racial identity different from their racial group. Rather, it is how he or she comes to understand his or her racial classification, the positioning of his or her racial group in the racial hierarchy, and its political and economic interests in that hierarchy (Bonilla-Silva 2001). A racial identity, then, develops in a racially oppressive society "in response to or in synchrony with either benefiting from or suffering under [racial] oppression" (Helms 1996:147).

In contrast, biracial identity advocates are actually referring to racial identification. Racial identification is the assertion that a person is a particular race (i.e., I am Black, or I am biracial), which need not coincide with their racial classification. As John powell (1997:799) notes, while it is true that everyone is an individual, "it is a false claim and a flawed hope that we can define who we are in isolation." In conflating racial categorization with identification, the biracial project confuses self-perception with social classification. This disregards racialization as a historically determined phenomenon and conceives race as a basic human attribute rather than a social relationship (Malik 1997) while simultaneously recognizing the economic value in racial identity.

Articulating a racial identification at odds with PMP's racial categorization, the biracial project seeks to gain from claiming whiteness. People with one Black and one white parent have historically been Black and their racial interests have been identical to those of their Black parent. This does not mean an individual *will* invest in a Black racial identity. Claiming whiteness for PMP is therefore more than the assertion of a biological attribute; it is a claim on political and economic privileges. As Cheryl Harris (1993:1735) argues, "a white person 'used and enjoyed' whiteness whenever she took advantage of the privileges accorded white people simply by virtue of their whiteness—when she exercised any number of rights reserved for the holders of whiteness." It imparts certain political, economic, and social privileges that are denied to and premised on the oppression of African Americans. Similar to white racial identity, the claim to whiteness is the basis for a biracial race that would enjoy privileges and advantages denied to Blacks. As such, the creation of a biracial race is premised on the continued subordination of Blacks.

WHITENESS IN THE BIRACIAL PROJECT

The biracial project's use of whiteness is evident most clearly on biracial-identity Web sites, which emerged around the same time the Internet became a popular form of mass communication (the early 1990s). These Web sites have been instrumental in propagating the arguments of lobbyists and lay advocates of biracial identity; the sites maintained by organizations such as Project RACE (Reclassify All Children Equally) and the Association of MultiEthnic Americans (AMEA) and e-zines such as *Interracial Voice* (*IV*), *The Mulatto People* (*TMP*), and *The Multiracial Activists* (*TMA*) have helped forge a popular conception of biraciality. The main Web site in this regard is the electronic magazine *Interracial Voice*. Dedicated to "the universal recognition of mixed-race individuals as constituting a separate 'racial' entity—" (*Interracial Voice* a), *IV* runs bimonthly editorials on a range of issues. Through its "Letters to the Editor" section and "Point 2 Point" discussion board (both with archives dating back to 1995), readers are able to engage editorial writers and one another on the question of a biracial race/identity. Moreover, because both advocates and critics contribute to these discussions, we can outline some of the more pervasive arguments that maintain whiteness is central to the creation of a biracial race. Though the focus is largely on *IV*, critical attention is also given to the articulation of the biracial project on other Web sites.

WHITENESS AND DEFINING "BIRACIAL"

Most of the discussions on *IV* focus on defining who is biracial. The central concern is avoiding a definition that includes the bulk of African Americans. Since an estimated 75 percent to 95 percent of African Americans have white and/or American Indian ancestry, being biracial is valuable only if it excludes the majority of Black people, being biracial looses its value. Such a definition, however, has proven elusive. For example, in 1993 Susan Graham of Project RACE argued that only those people with parents from two of the established racial groups should be classified as biracial (J. M. Spencer 1997). Graham sought to avoid biological determinism, but her definition presents problems of its own. Specifically, how would a person with one biracial and one Black parent be classified? To define them as biracial would, to borrow the reasoning of some advocates, to deny an aspect of their heritage. It also hints at biological determinism, since there is no reason why such a person should be biracial instead of Black, especially considering the social, historical, and cultural basis for that person being Black. Partly in response to this problem, Graham modified her argument to include as biracial anyone with "origins in two or more of the listed [racial] groups" (U.S. Congress 1998:554–555). The main problem here, though, is that it defines who is biracial in such a way as to include nearly all African Americans (Powell 1997). Graham's categorization problems are not replicated on bira- cial identity Web sites, where being biracial is tied to "white blood," looking white, and having few (if any) stereotypic Black features (e.g., dark complexion, kinky hair, full lips, etc.). This is especially so when discussing light-skinned blacks.

A reader on *IV* questioned why light-skinned Black people are identified as "multiracial" on that Web site, particularly when those people clearly identify as Black. In raising this question, Tiffani Whittaker, who identifies as Black, wrote:

> I am black. I have a very mixed ancestry. . . . People ask me if I'm "mixed" and all kinds of other things all the time. . . . Some people in my family look white, but they are not. . . . [T]hat is what black America looks like. (*Interracial Voice* d, September 26, 2000)

Implicitly, Whittaker's point about phenotypic differences among African Americans eschews a biological view of race. Yet most participants in this discus- sion disagreed. Becky, a supporter of biraciality, emphasized how "white blood" distinguishes "mulattos" from Blacks:

> You are not the definition of "Black." You have enough White Blood to only be Mulatto. Do you know what looking White comes from, having lots of White Blood. . . . Do you think you resemble the Black slaves that wa[l]ked off those ships 400 yrs ago, some Blacks do, but people ask you what you are? I don't think so. I don't want to hear that nonsense [that] all Blacks are mixed. (*Interracial Voice* d, September 27, 2000)

Becky links blood and phenotype to suggest that only people who look African (presumably a singular phenotype) are Black, seemingly because they are racially pure. This conceives of race in strict biological terms and moves beyond a question of parentage to include light-skinned Blacks as biracial. A. D. Powell, who identifies as white-biracial, was emphatic on this point:

> Sorry, kid. You're not the child of "two black parents" if you don't LOOK "black." If people are constantly asking you what you are or taking you for something other than "black," it's because you AREN'T Black. (*Interracial Voice* d, September 27, 2000)

Candance Miller, who identifies as black but supports biraciality, echoed this sentiment by declaring to Whittaker: "the fact that you have a very mixed an- cestry means that you're multiracial" (*Interracial Voice* d, September 28, 2000). This betrays a biological-determinist understanding of race, as mixed ancestry or parentage makes a person biracial. Still, not looking black is important.

Whittaker sought to clarify her position by highlighting the social aspects of black racial identity. She wrote, "I think 'Black' can and does include all of those [non-African ancestries] so in no way do I think calling yourself Black denies or ignores mixed ancestry" (*Interracial Voice* d, September 29, 2000). Here, Whittaker's conception of black racial identity acknowledges the history of miscegenation in African-American racialization. Rather than take her seriously, though, participants in this discussion betrayed their antiblack feelings. Becky again responded to Whittaker:

> Yeah, now I get it. You want Black to include all kinds of things because you don't like what Black really stands for. Black isn't White, Latino, European, Indian, Black is Black. Stop taking away from the essence of Black and trying to pretty up the word "Black" with (Black is European, Indian) and all other kinds of no sense nonsense. . . . Black ain't good enough anymore, but you will be quick to pigeon hole a Mulatto as Black. (*Interracial Voice* d, October 2, 2000)

Becky's suggestion that Whittaker perceives "Black" as limited, ugly, and not "good enough," actually exposes her own negative conception of blackness. She restricts who is Black to a stereotypical image of Africans while arguing that those defined as biracial have a non-African phenotype. Interestingly, this denies light-skinned Blacks the very individual right to self-definition that the biracial project claims to champion for all people. Physical appearance becomes the main (if not sole) criteria for defining who is biracial, and it is imposed on anyone deemed to have "enough white blood."

The centrality of "white blood" to a biracial race is underscored on the Web site *The Mulatto People* (*TMP*). Richard Miller, *TMP*'s editor and a regular participant in *IV* discussions, identifies the defining characteristic of "mulattos" as having "too much white ancestry to be the same as Black" (*Mulatto People* a). For Miller this negates the claim that most Black people have white and/or American Indian ancestry, since biologically "mulattos" are not Black. More important, he views this claim as "nothing more than a malicious attempt to defeat the multi-racial movement [to] distinguish ourselves from monoracial groups" (*Mulatto People* b; *Interracial Voice* e, Miller, June 17, 2000). He even proposes replicating the complexional elitism of the nineteenth- and early-twentieth-century Black middle class to solidify this distinction and ensure a biracial race's social position "above blacks":

> [Mulattos] segregated themselves and formed their own communities, clubs, societies, etc.—and they used certain tests, such as the paper bag test, the comb test, and the vein test to keep blacks out, so that mulattos would stay distinguished from blacks. . . . The literature regarding these events will tend to make the mulattos at this time seem evil. If these events are true, then I am very proud of these mulattos who have gone before us. . . . [They] were doing what they had to do—maintain their status as an autonomous people. (Miller, n.d.)

Obscuring more than it reveals about color conflict in African-American history, this clearly demonstrates the social role of whiteness in the biracial project. Lewis Gordon (1995:386) reminds us that such an argument exists within "the matrices of value in a world that is conditioned by two fundamental convictions, (1) it is best to be white, and (2) it is worse to be black." Historically this value system has produced a correlation between skin color and social stratification in the Black community, where social and economic privileges have been extended to light-skinned Blacks (Keith and Herring 1991; Seltzer and Smith 1991). The biracial project would transform this stratification into a racial distinction by deploying one of the central principles of whiteness: excluding blacks. As conceptualized in the biracial project, this would entail "the right to own or hold whiteness to the exclusion and subordination of Blacks" (C. Harris 1993:1736).

Whiteness also imparts white political interests to a biracial race. In discussing Black-mulatto conflicts in the West Indies, Liam Martin declared, "mulattos have claims on whiteness and so can have white interests themselves" (*Interracial Voice* e, September 8, 1999). Though focused on the West Indies, his comments were directed at the United States. Martin even suggests that a Black identity is oppressive and maintains a biracial identity requires "rejecting blackness and claiming whiteness" (*Interracial Voice* b, February 3, 1999). Similarly, A. D. Powell calls "'black' ancestry . . . a stigma which no sane person would want" (*Interracial Voice* f, August 6, 2000), and advises "Mulattos OFFICIALLY [to] separate from Blacks" (*Interracial Voice* c, December 7, 1999).

In this sense, a biracial identification is more than an individual choice. African ancestry is seen as socially undesirable, and embracing whiteness is the only to negate it. Furthermore, a biracial race having political interests identical to whites means this project's racial-political interests are in direct opposition to those of Blacks. Hence claiming whiteness and rejecting blackness to establish a biracial race involves opposing the political interests of African Americans, manifested primarily by attacking the Black community. Charles Byrd, editor of *Interracial Voice*, consistently calls the Black community a false idea that "only exists in the minds of government demographers and certain 'civil rights' leaders" (*Interracial Voice* b, February 21, 1999). In addition, he has opened *IV* for whites to articulate explicitly racist proposals for destroying the Black community. For example, white guest editorialist George Winkel, who regularly participates in *IV* discussions, once argued that since "'white' acceptance & full integration" were the main goals of the Civil Rights movement, "Black ghetto families [should be relocated] into white foster neighborhoods for absorption" (*Interracial Voice* b, July 2, 1999). This letter was published without editorial comment, and Winkel subsequently published editorials on *IV*, despite his gross misunderstanding of the Civil Rights movement and a malevolent relocation scheme. Furthermore, these statements are undergirded by a conception of whiteness as *the* social norm—the Black community is a demographic and political fiction that should be destroyed by forcibly assimilating Black people, since they have failed to replicate the American (white) standard of community (Harris 1993; Hickman 1997; Mills 1997).

This antiblack bias has understandably troubled many who visit these Web sites. One *IV* reader attempted to address this by posing as a discussion topic: "Can multiracial people be racist or embrace ideas of racial superiority?" While the topic "Who is Black?" elicited two hundred responses in forty-five months, and "Passing for Black? " received 219 posts in sixty-eight months, this topic garnered only thirty-one responses in thirty-four months. Additionally, only seven responses actually addressed the question, five of these dismissing the suggestion that biracial people could be racist. When one reader questioned why others failed to address this topic seriously, Byrd called it "the height of arrogance for someone to come into a forum such as this and suggest . . . that people should somehow feel ashamed because they haven't publicly acknowledged their 'racist attitudes' towards Blacks'" (*Interracial Voice* e, November 30, 2000). Still, some on *IV,* like Terry,[3] feel that the majority of people on *IV* "seem to be obsessed with plain old, unmixed black people. As if black people are really making their lives that much of a living hell. . . . I too am multicultural and I identify strongly with both parts of myself," Terry explains, "[b]ut unlike the people at Interracial Voice, I have no problem with being african american" (May 31, 2001). When another person questioned why *IV* readers "harbor[ed] rather hostile attitudes toward black people[,] especially blacks who have a darker complexion?" (*Interracial Voice* b, Simmons, March 24, 1999), Byrd responded:

> Regarding harboring hostile attitudes to self-identified "blacks," I find that most of this stems from some "black" people refusing to believe or accept that there is another identity that a *mixed-race* individual can adopt other than "black" or "white.". . . This is evidence of a simple mind at play, and after you've been in the presence of such ignorance myriad times, you no longer feel the need to bite your tongue. (*Interracial Voice* b, March 24, 1999)

This highlights a fundamental problem in the biracial project. First, Project RACE and *IV* exhibited antiblack hostility well before the validity of a bira-cial identity was challenged, and Web sites such as *The Mulatto People* and *The Multiracial Activist* were founded with an explicitly antiblack orientation. It is also untrue that all African Americans oppose or are even aware of the bira-cial project. In making this charge, advocates represent the opposition of the National Association for the Advancement of Colored People (NAACP) to a multiracial census category as the entire Black community's opposition, which reveals a tendency to view African Americans as a monolith. It is telling, though, that despite the widespread opposition to such a category from various commu-nities of color, African Americans are the primary targets of the biracial project's hostility.

In 1997, during the congressional hearings to determine whether to add a "multiracial" category to the census, several organizations and community groups expressed their opposition to such a category. The National Asian Pacific American Legal Consortium (NAPALC), the National Council of American Indians (NCAI), and the National Council of La Raza (NCLR) all testified that they opposed such a category. These organizations, along with the Chinese for Affirmative Action (CAA) and the Asian Americans for an Accurate Count (AAAC), questioned the appropriateness of using the census to validate personal identity. Census figures are used to monitor and enforce civil rights compliance (R. Spencer 1999), and as Rebecca King (2000:195) notes, using the census to "satisfy individual multiracial goals... may leave many monoracial groups unable to gain the reparations they need." Still, these nonblack communities and organizations rarely receive the level of criticism directed at African Americans and the NAACP.

At this writing, a significantly large segment of *IV*'s editorials criticized African Americans. *The Multiracial Activist* has announced its official opposition to the NAACP, characterizing the organization and its president Kweisi Mfume as racists (Landrith, n.d.). Susan Graham (1997), as executive director of Project RACE, labeled the NAACP as racist for attempting to "define our children" as Black, while making only passing reference to the numerous other organizations who were ostensibly doing the same thing. Ultimately, the contention that this hostility is directed at those who oppose such an identity is disingenuous.

Equally problematic is the contention that a biracial community exists and therefore should be recognized. Every advocacy group and Web site contends they represent a distinct racial community, something with which scholars advocating a biracial identity disagree with. For example, Naomi Zack (1993) states that such an identity lacks a historical basis. Deborah Johnson (1992:44) argues that "the biracial group is most often not available, [and] there are no cultural rituals, values, or artifacts with which to identify." Hence the census has become the focal point of the biracial project. Many view race as an idea created by government agencies and identify the census as the primary medium of racialization (Lee 1993; Nobles 2000). While it is undeniable that the census contributes to racialization, it is a mistake to contend that it is central to that social process. Sociologist Mary Waters testified to Congress that placing a biracial category on the census could exacerbate existing racial tensions. "The fact that this group does not exist now," she maintained, "does not mean that the group cannot come into existence and begin to have social meaning for people" (U.S. Congress 1998:452). This is precisely what many advocates are hoping. For example, Graham (2000) argued that PMP should "have the respect of an appropriate racial label" on the census. Such a category gives them an "accurate" racial label like other racial groups. In his written testimony, sociologist

G. Reginald Daniel carried this point further to argue that a biracial heading is necessary to distinguish between people who identify as biracial and "individuals who have multiple ancestries, but . . . a single-racial identity" (U.S. Congress 1998:575). None of this, however, supports the view that there *is* a "biracial community."

The most recent support of this view is the 784,764 people who checked "Black" *and* "White" on the 2000 Census. These respondents are seen as a rapidly growing, racially distinct group. Charles Byrd even suggests that this community is much larger than the census indicates. "[L]ight-skinned individuals . . . have been told for years that mixed race people are black," which he believes prompted many of them to check "Black" alone on the census (Hubbard 2001). However, a critical analysis of the returns reveals a very different picture. An underlying assumption is that the people who marked "Black" *and* "White" on the 2000 Census in fact identify as biracial, and that those who do identify as biracial have a singular understanding of their identity. Some people were merely noting their mixed parentage or ancestry, but nonetheless identify as Black. Kerry Ann Rockquemore (1998) argues that there are multiple meanings to a biracial identity and it does not necessarily entail rejecting a Black identity or asserting a racial distinction.

Using the census returns as an indicator of the "biracial community's" size also overlooks the age of these respondents. The population cohort marking "Black" *and* "White" on the 2000 census is significantly younger than other single or multiple race response cohorts. While minors constitute only 25.3 percent of all single-race responses, they are 42 percent of all multiple-race responses (Meyers 2001) and 33.4 percent of all responses marking two races (U.S. Census Bureau 2000).[4] By contrast, minors make up nearly 72 percent of all responses marking "Black" *and* "White" (U.S. Census Bureau 2000). This is considerably higher than any other segment of the population that marked "Black" along with one or more other races. Some scholars contend that this reflects the appeal of a biracial identification to younger people (Korgen 1998), but such a conclusion is misleading precisely because of the age of this cohort.

People typically alter their identities (in the psychological sense) as they mature. With a biracial identity being socially unstable, the number of people who used the census as a way to identify as biracial will likely change on the next census. Some will cease identifying as biracial and assume either a Black or white identification, while others may assume a biracial identity latter in life. They may continue to mark "Black" *and* "White" on future schedules, but this does not mean they will mark "biracial" or "multiracial" if such an option becomes available. More important, a majority of the 2000 Census responses with "Black" and "White' marked came from minors, which means that the responses were made by parents or were selected by the minors while under their parents' influence. This is significant because, as several scholars (D. Harris

2002; Morning 2000) suggest, a young child or adolescent with a racial identity different from what their parents desire is likely to express their chosen identity only outside the home. Additionally, if the parent is identifying their child in a way that is uncomfortable for that child, it may be abandoned latter in life. As the child becomes an adult and begins to understand and experience the social, political, and economic consequences of race and racism, how they understand their racial classification will likely change. For many, having no identifiable racial group, being categorized as Black and the sociopolitical reality of racism may lead them to view a Black racial identity as more socially meaningful and mentally healthy than a raceless or biracial identity (Morning 2000; Twine 1996). This is particularly important when we consider the demographics of the parents of this population.

David Harris's (2002) analysis of the National Longitudinal Study of Adolescent Health (Add Health) data set suggests that many, if not most, of the children who identify as biracial are being raised by single white mothers.[5] This does not mean that having a white mother means a person will identify as biracial. Rather, it highlights that race and gender conjoin in curious ways around this issue. France Winddance Twine (1998), in examining white mothers of Black children in Britain, found that politically progressive white mothers tended to encourage a Black identity for their children and to teach them proactive methods for dealing with racism. Twine (1996) also found that when white suburban mothers in the United States did not discuss race with their children, these children held race-neutral identities that were eventually disrupted upon entering puberty. The difference lies in the former group's willingness to involve their children in the cultural practices, social institutions, and political functions of blacks in Britain and the latter group's failure to even discuss race in the home.

Unlike in previous generations, white women are currently more likely to parent a mixed-parented Black child than are Black women. Natality records from five years in the 1990s show that white women 77 percent of all birth mothers of mixed-parented Black children in that decade (U.S. Department of Health and Human Services 1994, 1995, 1996, 1999, 2000). Given the persistence of social prohibitions against Black/white interracial relationships, it is not at all surprising that many of these children are raised in single-parent households. Given the reality of racial segregation (Massey and Denton 1993) and the patriarchal practices of mothers being primary caregivers, a significant number of mixed-parented children are being raised in predominantly white neighborhoods. Many of these children never have significant involvement in the institutional, political, cultural, and intellectual life of the Black community. Consequently, they grow up with few, if any, meaningful interpersonal relationships with African Americans outside their family, are socially illiterate in Black social settings, and may interpret communal cultural practices as rejection or marginalization, which contributes to feelings of alienation from other Blacks. This does not constitute a biracial community but rather a growing number of Black people who are removed socially and geographically from the Black community.

CONCLUSION

Heretofore, studies of whiteness have quite logically focused on its use by groups now categorized as white. Nevertheless, in looking at only how the Irish, Southeast Europeans, Jews, and others used *their* whiteness to become white, we run the risk of essentializing whiteness as something available *only* to whites. The present study builds on Cheryl Harris (1993) to demonstrate that people of color can also use whiteness to negotiate the racial hierarchy. Specifically, I have focused on the claim that people of mixed parentage possess whiteness as an immutable biosocial attribute. The main concern is how they seek to use that property to distinguish themselves from African Americans, position themselves above Blacks in the racial hierarchy, and receive some of the privileges of whiteness. Having no historical basis for asserting such a "racial reality," as well as lacking an identifiable community, a culture, and the social institutions necessary to socialize a person as biracial, advocates are mistaken in assuming an inherent value or necessity in such an identity.

This is not to say that every person with a biracial identity is a racist or that every biracial-identity advocacy group is invested in whiteness (e.g., see *Hapa Issues Forum* <http://www.hapaissuesforum.org>), but that antiblack whiteness dominates this racial project. Moreover, while the examples provided in this paper reveal an overt antiblack whiteness, the available evidence suggests that many who identify as biracial have internalized latent antiblack sentiments (Rockquemore 2002). The absence of an internal challenge to the antiblack whiteness of this racial project suggests it will contribute to the persistence of racial oppression and that a politically progressive alternative is unlikely.

Black studies scholars must give this racial project more attention. At present, it is little more than a lobbying effort to establish a census category, but this is tied directly to an attempt to create a new race. As such, it would contribute to the growing attacks on the Black community characteristic of the current racial formation (Cha-Jua and Lang 1999). We must give more attention to how race, class, gender, and geopolitical location have come together in this initiative, as well as address the continued privileging of light skin over dark skin both among African Americans and in the larger society. Additionally, we need to approach this issue with a greater sense of history. The predominance of social science scholarship on this issue has led to a discourse of biraciality that acts as if Blacks have only recently began to have children with whites and places too great an emphasis on the census.

Nor has there been a good analysis that explains why this issue has arisen at this particular historical moment (J. M. Spencer 1997; R. Spencer 1999). This is particularly important when we note that the biracial project has emerged and made its greatest strides amid predictions that by the year 2050 whites will be a numerical minority. While it may seem coincidental, history demonstrates that when whites are a numerical minority, they maintain social control of the racial order by positioning the progeny of Black-white unions as an intermediary race between themselves and blacks (Horowitz 1973). Given this racial project's concern for expanding the boundaries of whiteness so that having "white blood" makes one nonblack and socially positions a biracial race above Blacks, we cannot ignore its potential to further whites' social control over people of color. Indeed, the attempt to restructure the racialized social system so that whiteness becomes available to more nonwhites could frustrate social movements intent on destroying whiteness and racial oppression.

7

Who Are These White People?: "Rednecks," "Hillbillies," And "White Trash" As Marked Racial Subjects

JOHN HARTIGAN, JR.

There are few better critical openings onto the operations of whiteness than through its meaty, soft underbelly, as represented by "rednecks," "hillbillies," and "white trash." These terms are applied to vast numbers of white people, in each instance emphatically inscribing a charged form of difference marked off from the privileges and powers of whiteness; each term demarcates an inside and an outside to mainstream white society. Though it is easy to assume these racial epithets are synonymous, the differences from which they are historically derived and that they continue to inscribe depict fundamental social dimensions of whites' lives and interests that are both obscured by the concept of whiteness and critical to the task of rendering this racial identity in specific terms rather than abstractions or generalizations. The manifold uses of these derogatory labels in U.S. popular culture offer an excellent means to grasp both the enduring intraracial dynamics that have long maintained the unmarked status of whiteness and the intriguing, complex current forms of name-calling that whites engage in as they attempt to navigate increasingly fraught social terrains in the United States from economically tenuous subject positions.

The active uses of these terms in popular cultural discourses today are one aspect of the current "crisis of white identity," a concept that references the drastic changes in the political and social landscapes of the United States (Winant 1994). Whites' majority status in this country is crumbling, beginning first with the nation's largest cities during the 1970s and 1980s and continuing now with its largest states (California and Texas), and is forecasted to be a *fait accompli* for the United States as a whole by 2050. However, "whiteness" as it is frequently deployed in various antiracist or academic accounts reduces the multilayered spatial and temporal dynamics of this process by deploying a uniform, essentialized, analytic construct to explain how white racial privilege and power are maintained (Bonnett 1997). This construct is poorly suited to the task of analyzing the distinct processes, first, by which whites are racialized and, second, how the unmarked character of that racial identity is undermined for certain class-based or regional groupings of whites.

Part of the challenge facing whiteness studies is to treat whites as full racial subjects—that is, as subjects whose identity is nested within a variety of overlapping, often conflated discourses on belonging and difference generated in particular social relations and indexing a host of cultural positions or statuses—and not simply as bearers of latent or blatant forms of racism. Just as the broad cultural and political dimensions of "blackness" cannot be reduced to a response to racism, the significance of white racial identity—developed through class- and gender-based intraracial contests over belonging and difference—cannot be wholly equated with racist perceptions, beliefs, or actions. This essay offers a view of how to begin this work by sketching some of the contours of popular culture in the United States today where the racialness of whites is close to the surface—moments where, quite in contrast to the social circumstances of most middle-class whites, their racial and class markings are the object contests over belonging and difference.

In the following survey of current uses of "white trash," "redneck," and "hillbilly" in a variety of popular cultural mediums, my objectives are threefold, each opening distinct venues for the goal of deconstructing whiteness. First, in contrast to the view that whiteness generically constitutes a position of power and authority, I depict the social contours and discrepant circumstances that comprise the lives of lower-class whites. These labels are each applied to whites with tenuous economic and social circumstances, teetering on the edge of society and hardly privileged or powerful in any conventional sense. Second, these racial epithets are a means to objectify specific forms of cultural content or at least distinct social positions (regional and class identity, in particular) that are located disruptively within the homogenizing discourses and practices of whiteness. The stratification of power and privilege within whiteness hinges upon rural versus urban identity and the relative degrees of education versus "backwardness"; these labels all work to animate these key contours of difference within whiteness. Finally, these instances of name-calling demonstrate the charged intraracial dynamics that both support and reproduce whiteness—dynamics that are perhaps as critical to the maintenance of whiteness as are interracial inscriptions of otherness and difference. What counts as white in many social situations depends on class identity, and the terms of racial belonging and difference are importantly inflected by the markings of class.

Hence the following, by way of deconstructing whiteness, surveys simultaneously the stratified social terrain of white social identity and the rhetorical means of boundary maintenance work that whites pursue in stabilizing and reproducing the homogenizing practices that both occult these differences and project an ostensibly nonracialized (i.e., unmarked) social position of authority and dominance. These instances of name-calling evidence the forms of decorum or etiquette that whiteness depends upon for its hegemonic position and which is consistently threatened by the words, actions, bodies, and lifestyles of various strata of whites who reveal the tenuous and artificial nature of these social conventions by their inability to conform to the decorums of whiteness. Tracking these terms in popular culture is a means to view gaps within the body of whiteness in order to understand how they may be further exploited.

Perhaps the best place to start is with one of the more sensational racial episodes on a national stage from the past few years. John Rocker, a pitcher initially with the Atlanta Braves, incited a flurry of antiracist protest and commentary across the nation when he voiced his dislike for New York City in an interview in *Sports Illustrated* magazine (Pearlman 1999). Rocker explained that his loathing for the city derived from: "taking the 7 train, looking like you're going through Beirut with some kid with purple hair and some queer with AIDS right next to you." He also complained about all the foreigners: "You can walk an entire block in Times Square without hearing a word of English." These comments, along with with others reported from the interview, instigated a wave of public protests against Rocker and led the commissioner of baseball to levy a stiff twenty-eight-game suspension and $20,000 fine on Rocker. The beleaguered Rocker tried an interesting tack to counter his depiction as a clear public example of the enduring operation of white racism. In a subsequent ESPN interview (Rocker 2000), he insisted that he was not a "racist," just a "redneck." Rocker was soon traded to Cleveland, where he once again struggled to fit in with teammates and to get along with fans—in part because of his public notoriety. One source of conflict in the clubhouse came to light when Rocker derisively labeled one of his former Atlanta teammates as "white trash" (Rogers and Rogers 2001). However, this epithet received scant media attention and provoked no public outcry at all.

The example of Rocker lays out two of these three terms and makes clear some distinctions in their usage. Quite simply, "redneck" is something Rocker doesn't mind being; it is an identity that can be invested with valor, in contrast to the loathsome image of the white racist (though, for some, "redneck" and "racist" are synonymous). In contrast, "white trash" is something even John Rocker holds in low esteem. It operates here intraracially, inscribing a sense of contempt and distinction that even a self-identified "redneck" and publicly pilloried "racist" feels is critical to maintain. The lack of public outrage over his use of "white trash" evidences a key component of this term's operation. It is often noted how white, middle-class liberals learn very young not to use epithets with racial connotation, while they receive different messages from their parents concerning labels for poor whites, the most naturalized of which is "white trash." The dynamics of this marking are explored in detail below, but first to the matter of current uses of "redneck."

Rocker's is only one of many instances of "redneck" in popular culture, but this form, when the term is used as a means of self-identification, is the most common. There are certainly instances where "redneck" is applied in public contexts in a disparaging and dismissive manner, but most usage involves individuals claiming a certain social identity. These forms of self-identification are distinctive in that they continually allude to charged terms of difference within whiteness; they underscore rather than efface the distinctions that inform the severely sloped terrain of power and privilege of whiteness by animating and inhabiting the most extreme caricatures of white rural poverty and ignorance. Within this position of marked whiteness, two distinct strategies employed by those who self-identify as "redneck": one approach seeks actively to counter the stereotyped features of this label, while an opposite tack asserts a stance squarely within these disparaged features.

Two great examples of these different strategies of self-identification are the Redneck Games, held annually in Dublin, Georgia, and the American Redneck Society. Membership in the latter comes with a year's subscription to the society's newsletter, the *Mullet Wrapper,* along with a certificate of membership, an inscription of the redneck creed—"just because we talk slow doesn't mean we think slow"—and two bumper stickers. The American Redneck Society uses the *Mullet Wrapper,* with a subscription base of some ten thousand people, to counter stereotypes of poor whites such as those voiced by one reporter covering the society, who noted: "Apparently, not all rednecks look like extras from *The Dukes of Hazard* and decorate their lawns with old appliances. In fact, they come from all walks of life and from every corner of America" (Marchand 1997). This observation indicates both the assertion and the acknowledgment that "redneck" is not bound to its region of origin—a point best evidenced by the enormous popularity of Jeff Foxworthy's comic routine, "You might be a redneck if . . ."—and is taken up as a means of self-identification in locations far and wide. But a very loud contrary claim, underscoring the enduring centrality of the South to the term's usage, is made by the Redneck Games.

This annual event, which has drawn a combined crowed of fifty thousand people over the past six years, puts on display a range of buffoonish activities that purport to represent this distinctive white tribe. Contests feature bobbing for pigs feet, hubcap hurls, seed spitting, the "armpit serenade" and "dumpster diving"; festivities commence with a ceremony displaying a propane torch. As the torch suggests, the games spoof respectable and established athletic venues such as the Olympics. Confederate flags are displayed enthusiastically, worn emblazoned on shirts, hats, bikinis, or pants, hung on boats and campers, or carried about on poles. The mud pit produces a bit of "color" to whiteness, literalizing the "red" imagery as one after another pale white body plunges into a red dirt pool and emerges dripping in red.

The games seem to teeter on the fault line between "respectable" and "transgressive" responses to the label "redneck." Such public performances attempt to critique the stereotypes but end up actively reproducing them, perhaps because, in the end, participants tangibly feel the weight of the social distinctions that animate the stereotype and recognize that these cannot be easily dispelled. In that regard, why not at least retain an identity, one that does provide performative room for maneuver. As one of the Redneck Games organizers put it, observers "seem to think we are portraying Southern people as unintelligent, beer-swilling hicks." Rather, "we just like to have fun" (Pappas 1999).

Such public displays by "rednecks" are not merely reflexive responses to widely circulated, disparaging depictions of lower-class whites. Each element of these performances bears some link to actual social practices and a certain cultural condition. The most systematic attempt to survey the cultural content of "redneck" is quite likely Bethany Bultman's *Redneck Heaven: Portrait of a Vanishing Culture* (1996). Bultman compiles beliefs and practices, stories and traditions, even recipes and advice that define and inform "redneck culture"— one that she repeatedly suggests is derived in part from the heritage of the Celts. Bultman travels the nation interviewing people who both claim this charged label and follow a set of "codes" or "values" that she discerns as central to "redneck ideology." These largely hinge on "Attitude": "a genetic inability to kiss butt," derived from both the necessity and the willingness to flaunt social conventions.

Jim Goad's *Redneck Manifesto* asserts a similar definition: "A redneck, as I define it, is someone both conscious of and comfortable with his designated role of cultural jerk. While hillbillies and white trash may act like idiots because they can't help it, a redneck does it to spite you. A redneck is someone who knows you hate him and rubs that in your face" (Goad 1997). This antagonistic, disparaged stance can be seen as informing all manner of cultural practices, from music to athletics to work. Bultman's compilation of aphorisms, culinary practices, forms of ingenuity, sexual habits, styles of labor and recreation, and devotional dispositions all turns on this amplification of social rejection; though, as Goad notes with the contrast to "white trash" and "hillbillies," the question of economic and social necessity is somewhat less emphatic than for other labels for poor whites.

Invocations of a distinctive "Attitude" are the baseline by which positive cultural contents of "redneck" are proffered, but this is a meager basis for asserting a collective identity in the face of social contempt. Hence the transgressive and self-debasing dimensions of "redneck" countervail against efforts at asserting a "respectable" identity in the stratified terrains of whiteness. No better examples of this are two Web sites that, at first impression, seem to have a good deal in common. Dixienet.org and RedNeck.org each assert a form of separate Southern white identity, but each do so in radically different manners that reflect class divisions marked by "respectable" and "disreputable." Dixie-Net features petitions for "Southern Reparations" as well as various "states rights" efforts and in opposition to "Southern ethnic cleansing." The site also features the League of the South's Declaration of Southern Cultural Independence, which opens: "We, as citizens of the sovereign States of the South, proclaim before Almighty God and before all nations of the earth, that we are a separate and distinct people, with an honourable heritage and culture worthy of protection and preservation. Standing in the very place where our President Jefferson Davis stood in 1861, we declare that Southerners are entitled, like all peoples, to self-determination." The site is packed with notices of conferences and associations, links to journals and to newsletters, and copious events that promote white Southern distinctiveness. Interestingly, my keyword search of the site for "redneck" revealed "no matches on this site."

RedNeck.org, on the other hand, wallows in many debasing images of poor, rural whites. The page opens with a warning that immediately asserts a sense of difference from the mainstream of white society: "Caution. You are entering RedNeck.org. Sissy Yankee Boys and eny uh y'all born north of the Red River, may need to git a note from yore mamma's or flash a lil red skin round tha neck ta git in. Don't step in anything, stomping around in here." This warning features the self-deprecating use of vernacular English and misspellings that reflect the transgressive emphasis of the site, a point that is further underscored by the site's claim to be "more fun than stomping on baby chickens in yore barefeet." Links, images, and text on the site conform to an aesthetic of the grotesque, featuring deranged deer hunters, sex with farm animals, public urination, and a slew of redneck jokes. Each caricatured depiction asserts a stance that, quite in contrast to the efforts of a site like Dixie-Net, inhabits, ratifies, and indulges stereotypes of poor rural whites, finding them enjoyable rather than abhorrent.

Tara McPherson, in "I'll Take My Stand in Dixie-Net: White Guys, the South, and Cyberspace," assesses how such sites operate in the post-civil rights public discourse of the United States. McPherson deftly uses Dixie-Net as an example of how "cyberwhitening" occurs in online discussions or virtual communities. She finds that "the default setting is all too white" at this site, because discussions of racism are directly squelched and the invocations of the South as an imagined community consistently promote an implicitly white racial subject. But McPherson suggests that it takes more than an attention to racism to analyze these sites because participants "do not believe themselves to be racist," and "labeling them and their cyberspaces as 'racist' does little to help us understand how they understand either whiteness or blackness" (McPherson 2000). After detailing how the play of images and texts interpolates the viewer into a white subject position, she then demonstrates how, by coining new languages and investing old signs with new meanings, these sites surprisingly fashion a "subaltern counterpublic." This leads McPherson to a challenging question: "What does it mean that white, mostly middle-class men—the group that we usually see as important players in the public sphere—feel the need for alternative publics?" (McPherson, 2000:126). McPherson adds, "these men clearly see themselves as marginalized because of their southernness, and they actively construct spaces in which this origin can be discussed, celebrated, and protected from attacks, real or imagined."

Whiteness, as McPherson observes, is reproduced through these sites, particularly as discussions of white Southernness couched in terms of ethnicity deflect attention away from "the privileges whiteness confers and often functions as yet another form of covert racism." Yet McPherson also regards this experience of perceived marginality—exaggerated or not, and certainly varied in its intensity along a continuum of class positions—as a means "to make whiteness strange" by amplifying the forms of differences its homogenizing practices obscure. Furthermore, in terms of the experience of social marginalization, we can discern in these sites two general strategies, one striving for the "respectability" of social practices such as conferences, petitions, and redemptive, scholarly research to valorize this condition, the other, conversely, flaunting social conventions and underscoring the debasing differences. This latter approach perhaps acknowledges the indelibleness of class markings and the interminable importance of class in determining matters of belonging and difference.

Hence the work of "redneck" in popular culture in the United States opens up a space within whiteness, one that clearly features the diacriticals of class and regional difference that importantly score the social landscape of white identity. "Redneck" demarcates a sharp division among whites, distinguishing those who are indelibly marked or unmarked in terms of class or region in relation to whiteness. Caricatured behaviors and beliefs may be claimed as forms of self-identification under the label "redneck," but the obverse situation also pertains—"redneck" still does a great deal of work of representing a debased other. Here the example of the computer game "Redneck Rampage" stands out. Its designers claim that it is "far and away the most profane computer game in the history of mankind," which, along with the excessive amounts of blood and gore, is clearly a strong selling point of the game.

The distinguishing feature of this game is the way "Redneck Rampage" systematically mobilizes and animates the most debasing tropes from the poor rural white stereotype. The othering dynamic is clear: "rednecks" are the ones being slaughtered in the game. The storyline features "Leonard and Bubba's" efforts to "get back their prize-winning pig who's abducted by aliens . . . in the fictional town of Hickston, Arkansas." Players blast their way through country bars and trailer parks, slaughtering rednecks left and right. As the game's promo reads: "If you thought navigating a melted-down Los Angeles or sneaking around ogres' castles was tough, then just try your hand a-whoppin and a-stompin the good ole boys at Stanky's Bar & Grill." Clearly, part of the allure here is bloodletting in a scene of socially marked others.

"Hillbilly" applies to a social landscape reminiscent of the terrain covered by "redneck," but with greater regional specificity and perhaps more historical depth and coherence. As well, the critical reaction to "hillbilly" is more developed than with "redneck." "Hillbilly" burns sharply and poignantly in the memory of those so labeled, and the textures of its current usage reflects the strong antipathy some whites have to this rhetorical identity. "Hillbilly" also has a longer record of usage in the public domain; it entered the popular lexicon quite early and served active duty as an acceptable derisive term. Hence current usage reflects a more polarized set of relations and a good deal more ambivalence than does "redneck." But its usage also depicts a social collective, in a manner contrary to "white trash," a term that inscribes severe social isolation. As evidenced in the long-running popularity of the television show *The Beverly Hillbillies*—which is currently being redeveloped by CBS as part of their "reality" programming, featuring a new family of "real" hillbillies cast in today's Beverly Hills—the connotations of "hillbilly" are more comic than threatening.

The most common current usage of "hillbilly" is in relation to music, reflecting the term's historical status in popular culture. In the 1920s, "hillbilly" was used by record companies to characterize and market the music being produced by whites in both rural and urban areas throughout the South. This marketing practice paralleled the "race records" approach of the major labels, segregating early jazz and blues recordings. In this regard, "hillbilly" was racialized as white but also clearly marked as distinct from the mainstream audiences and musical practices of white society broadly. The name said it all, as Tony Scherman suggests. "The new genre still lacked a name. Record companies restlessly tried out 'Old Time Songs,' 'Old Familiar Tunes,' 'Mountain Ballads.' Gradually a single name emerged; mingling amusement and derision, it neatly encapsulated America's feeling about the new genre: hillbilly" (Scherman 1994). Through fits of fashion and in conjunction with the dramatic mid-century demographic shifts in the United States as rural peoples migrated to industrialized urban areas, the popularity of "hillbilly" rose and fell through the next eight decades. Rural whites, derided as "hillbillies" in the North, at first took solace in the image and the music; then, as they assimilated to middle-class urban lifestyles, they gradually rejected the genre and the label. Beginning in the 1980s, "hillbilly" commenced one of several "returns" to modest popularity, reflecting discontent with suburbia or the disillusionment of downward mobility and deindustrialization.

Currently, "hillbilly" is enjoying a resurgence, as noted by *Billboard* magazine. "Now, a crop of current entertainers, including Toby Keith and Montgomery Gentry, are bursting out of the proverbial closet and proudly waving the hillbilly banner" (Jessen 2000). These performers appeal to whites who find themselves distanced from white middle-class society or on the fringe of economic survival. Montgomery Gentry's hit, "Hillbilly Shoes," earned an early release from Columbia "because radio jumped on it early." Audiences were enthused over the song's depiction of righteous rejections of condescending social judgments. "You want to judge me by the whiskey on my breath/You think you know me but you ain't seen nothing yet/Till you walk a while, a country mile/In my hillbilly shoes." Studio executives characterize the group as "raw" and "gritty," claiming "there's nothing slicked up here." While music industry representatives in Nashville continually try to distance themselves from the "hillbilly stereotype," they are consistently drawn back into reproducing and marketing just this imagery largely because it is lucrative, with a strong appeal to those who feel distanced from white social forms of respectability and belonging (Appel 2000).

While "hillbilly" may command a significant market share in current popular culture, it is not hard to find many accounts of those who are perhaps closest to the stereotype, those most easily marked by its charged characterization, who abhor and resent the term, refusing its relevance and rejecting it as a form of self-identification (Goster and Richard 1997). Nationally, attention to the disparaging features of this stereotype was strongest during the period when Bill Clinton campaigned for and won the presidency. "Hillbilly" was a label applied alternately to Clinton, his running mate, Al Gore, and a key portion of his constituency—mostly rural Southern whites. Particularly affected were white residents of Arkansas. As recently noted in the *Los Angeles Times*, "Eight years after Bill Clinton first ran for president, reporters there still seethe at the hillbilly image produced by outside reporters" (Kolker 2000). One sustained response to this image is the documentary *The Ozarks* (1999) which (according to a promotional flyer) "attempts to counter the stereotype of the lazy, moonshining 'hillbilly' image of Ozarkers with a view of a strong, proud, hardworking and independent people."

But more typical are the kinds of first-person accounts featured in an essay in *Newsweek* titled "Who's a Hillbilly?, relating stories of rural whites who are unable to escape from the "hillbilly stigma." Author Rebecca Kirkendall, drawing on her personal experiences of being derided and disparaged through jokes, comments, and looks about her rural upbringing, reflects both on the reproduction of "hillbilly" stereotypes in popular culture and the curious way some whites participate in these forms of commercialization. "Despite their disdain for farm life—with its manure-caked boots, long hours and inherent financial difficulties—urbanites rush to imitate a sanitized version of this lifestyle. And the individuals who sell this rendition understand that the customer wants to experience hillbillyness without the embarrassment of being mistaken for one" (Kirkendall 1995).

Social commentators, political observers, editorialists, and comedians throughout the 1990s dealt in "hillbilly" stereotypes without much restraint, reflecting little of the self-consciousness that is increasingly afforded to depictions of ethnic and racial groups. Most notoriously, perhaps, the *Wall Street Journal* did not hesitate to ask in a headline, referring to Bill Clinton, "Who is this sex-crazed hillbilly?" (Ferguson, 1996). But the most intriguing dimension of uses of "hillbilly" in the last three presidential campaigns is the way it materialized across party lines. The same imagery that was invoked to characterize Bill Clinton's supporters was also mobilized in relation to George W. Bush's 2000 campaign. In both cases, what mattered most was the sense of difference posed by lower-class, rural, Southern whites.

One story in *Time* featured a first-person account of a campaign reporter, Steve Lopez, who leaves Bush's bus to head out on his own through the rural areas of South Carolina in order to understand Bush's popularity. Along Highway 178 Lopez stumbles into the Roadkill Grill and meets the people of the "hillbilly nation." "The hillbillies, it turns out, liked Bush, as did plenty of God-fearing family folk, party loyalists and the professionals who fit more comfortably into the new South Carolina." But in pursuing reasons for this support, Lopez found only confirmations of the most stereotyped features of "hillbillies." "More often than not, when I asked people, 'Why Bush?' it was as if they had a zinc deficiency. The smile would freeze, the eyes would cloud and all signs of intelligence would fade" (Lopez 2000). This image is the most enduring representation of rural poor whites: faded or absent intelligence. Obviously, despite challenges to such stereotypes in the popular media, this image is sufficiently entertaining and gives voice to anxieties sufficiently deep to warrant its continued circulation.

Though "hillbilly" imagery is caustically active from California to Washington, D.C., it has burrowed mostly deeply into Appalachia, where concentrations of poverty and illiteracy have long nourished its most disparaging connotations. Residents feel the impact of stereotypes that construe them as "backward," lazy, and dangerous. This region has been exploited for over a hundred years by various corporate interests and government agencies, producing a degrading dynamic of dependence that continues to this day, highlighted by rampant environmental destruction caused by ongoing mining operations. The majority of whites in this region are far from powerful or privileged. School programs in Kentucky work to counter "hillbilly" stereotypes by imbibing a sense of positive cultural content in children through exposure to bluegrass music and other aspects of "mountain culture." Dan Hays, executive director of the International Bluegrass Music Association, relates "many kids who live in these mountain areas still suffer under the hillbilly stereotypes. If you can take something that's an important part of their culture and history and turn it into something they can be proud of, then they don't have to be ashamed of where they came from" (Simon 2001). But what is tricky about such a strategy is that it does nothing to drain the reservoirs of contempt that feed such stereotypes in the first place; hence these efforts risk reanimating the cultural differences that are the bases for "hillbilly."

Countering poverty-related shame is certainly a challenge in Appalachia, but more difficult problems arise for the poor whites with Appalachian roots scattered in pockets of inner-city neighborhoods in the Midwest. The prejudice and discrimination confronting urban Appalachians is well documented (Mead 1995, Obermiller and Philiber 1987, Pasternak 1994). Their rates of unemployment and dropping out of high school are double that of African-Americans in some neighborhoods of Cincinnati, the city with probably the largest concentration of urban Appalachians. As has been the case since these people first migrated to Midwestern cities, urban Appalachians face discrimination in hiring and housing because their accents, lifestyles, and relations are indelibly marked as "hillbilly." Their situation underscores a basic point in relation to each of these forms of name-calling: these rhetorical identities make it clear that whites are not uniformly privileged or powerful because of their skin color. But the more fundamental point to be drawn from "hillbilly," as well as "redneck" and "white trash," is that these stereotypes derive their enduring currency from the way they ratify a host of anxieties that white, urban Americans hold concerning the white underclass.

This nexus of anxiety and contempt is clearest in uses and depictions of "white trash." If "hillbilly" burns, "white trash" brands. What distinguishes this term from the others is not the cultural content that it grounds but rather the highly emotional response of loathing and disgust the image generates among the white middle class. Even among the white lower classes, "white trash" is primarily a distancing technique before it is an identity. As with John Rocker's quote, claims to a "redneck" identity are frequently accompanied by disavowal of and distancing from "white trash." A central dictum of the "redneck value system," according to Bultman, is "never accept a handout, 'cause if you do you're white trash"; Goad favorably contrasts "rednecks" to "white trash," and as the RedNeck.org site emphatically asserts, the first in the list of "What a Redneck Ain't" is "white trash." Thus we see in "white trash" the dynamics of distancing and boundary maintenance that inform "redneck" and "hillbilly" distilled into a most concentrated and virulent form.

Further evidence of this distillation is the effect on social perception of this rhetorical identity. "Hillbilly" and "redneck" each easily conjure collective images of poor whites as a social order, but "white trash," perhaps because it so keenly draws attention to breeches of racial decorum, singularly renders poor whites in isolation, as evictees from the social compact. "Redneck" anxiety over being perceived as "white trash" highlights a crucial aspect of this rhetorical identity. The ease of this "misperception" reflects the fact that, in terms of cultural content (the bodily type, lifestyle, and beliefs), these two terms can be regarded as synonymous. Thus it is not the "content" to which "white trash" refers that distinguishes this terms' usage. Rather, its rhetorical uses distinguish an order of whites definable strictly by transgressions of the social expectations that maintain the unmarked status of whiteness and facilitate its claims to power and privilege.

There are many complex dynamics to the rhetorical identity "white trash" that exceed the scope of this essay. I have written extensively on the history of "white trash" and its uses in films, music and novels elsewhere (Hartigan 1992, 1996, 1997b), so here I will offer a more cursory account of current uses that relate to the task of deconstructing whiteness. Notably, of the three prevailing terms for poor whites, only "white trash" makes the racial stakes explicit by specifying "white." There are two critical dimensions to this specificity. The first is that whiteness is at stake in inscription of this label, for it marks white people who are rupturing decorums associated with whiteness. The second dimension closely follows: "white trash" is consistently applied to whites who live closest to blacks, either in a literal proximity or in a more symbolic social sense, in terms of lifestyle or (limited) economic circumstances (Hartigan 1999). That is, these are the whites who make the arbitrariness of the "color line" apparent by the way their predicaments undermine racial conventions. Hence it is with "white trash" that the opportunities for deconstructing whiteness become most tangible.

"White trash" also demarcates the end of the class spectrum, where extremes are heightened, allowing for bizarre transpositions to occur. "White trash" becomes chic in a way neither "redneck" nor "hillbilly" could ever attain. "White trash charms" is a line of jewelry from a designer in Los Angeles who bedecks Hollywood stars with bracelets, earrings, and necklaces festooned with diamonds, rubies, and sapphires bearing "trashy" logos, like "Lady Luck" or "Punk Rock." Across the country, in Manhattan, the East Village store, "White Trash," sells "kitschy items" that cost hundred of dollars. Another dimension of the way "white trash chic" operates is its invocation as an aesthetic, a representational approach that purports to merge "high" and "low" culture. The most recent example is the movie *Scotland, PA*, an adaptation of Macbeth set amidst the fast-food pits of rural Pennsylvania. Billy Morrissette, the film's director and writer asserted, "I tried to keep it just pure white trash, with a touch of Shakespeare." Similarly, Peter Steinfield, the screenwriter for *Drowning Mona*, characterized that movie's motif as "the white-trash *Murder on the Orient Express*." In addition to these, films such as *Poor White Trash* and *Joe Dirt* claim free license to use poor whites as a stage for fashionably depicting themes that breech an array of social decorums.

The forms of defensiveness that accompany "redneck" and "hillbilly," discussed above, are not similarly generated by such appropriations or deployments of "white trash," perhaps because the term's boundary maintenance work allows little room for valorized self-identification. As well, maybe with "white trash" we reach a terrain where the depravities facing poor whites are so stark or severe that representational struggles are simply not a priority. Among the various strata of poor whites, "white trash" most readily applies to those who cannot afford membership in the American Redneck Society or who have neither the time nor social capital required to write angry letters to the editor over depictions of "hillbillies" in the *Wall Street Journal* or the *New York Times*. These extreme social conditions have long animated "white trash," yet there are interesting developments in the fast-changing realm of popular culture whereby some poor whites have fashioned for themselves a charged speaking position out of the degraded status of "white trash." But grasping the cultural significance of the rise of rap star Eminem or the popularity of comedian Roseanne first requires an attention to the way the label has long policed the spheres of public discourse in the United States.

The rise of these and other self-professed "white trash" performers flies in the face of the traditional usage of this term to restrict a segment of whites, their interests and concerns, from being regarded seriously in public forums. Social critics have used the term not just to specify a particular group, but to degrade a certain condition. This is evident from Charles Murray (1993) berating "white trash culture" in the *Wall Street Journal* and Oklahoma governor Frank Keating (Dallas Morning News 1999) characterizing methamphetamines as "a white trash drug." Governor Keating made the purpose of his use of this label explicit, explaining that such drug use is practiced "by the lower socioeconomic element of white people, and I just think we need to shame it." The distinctive characteristic of this very public form of debasement or name-calling is to depict certain behaviors or thoughts, words or actions, as outside the realm of social acceptance. And it applies wherever the traces of poor white social conditioning can be detected, as is evident in the surge of "white trash" references to Bill Clinton following his departure from office. As Howie Carr (2001:14A) proudly declared the day following George W. Bush's inaguration, "The white trash is out of the White House. Our long national nightmare is over."

But as Clinton's resilience in the face of social contempt perhaps indicates, a notable transformation may well be underway in U.S. public discourse, a possibility best glimpsed in the rise of Eminem. Here is a public performer whom critics were initially ready to dismiss. In so doing, and as with Kid Rock before him, critics mobilized "white trash." For example, P. J. O'Rourke characterized Eminem as "a beyond-Faulknerean specimen of double-Y chromosome white trash who mimics all that's loathsome and stupid in ghetto thug culture—resulting in a toilet mouth recording" (O'Rourke 2001). This characterization reproduces a hackneyed image of "bad breeding" in the extreme, but one that has yet to loose its social luster for "respectable" whites staring out at the likes of "white trash."

But Eminem, as with Roseanne before him, beats critics to the punch by making their condescension explicit and claiming the degrading epithet first, as a form of self-identification. In a variety of interviews, Eminem described his impoverished childhood in Detroit as a "white trash" existence. He (Eminem 1999) makes the claim lyrically as well, when he describes his Detroit upbringing in "If I Had": "Tired of being white trash, broke and always poor/Tired of taking bottles back to the party store/ Tired of not having a phone, tired of not having a home to have one in if I did have it on." Certainly, a significant portion of his marketing success is the fact that many poor white kids identify with this gesture. As Eminem notes: "what people don't realize is that there are so many poor white kids in America. They just go unnoticed, know what I'm sayin', just because of like, statistics. There's white trash in America, and as soon as they see a white-trash kid like me that lived a [expletive] life that they can relate to, then they go buy it because they understand it" (Wartofsky 1999).

While these are certainly telling instances of "white trash" being deployed in public discourse, the greatest power of the term derives from its operation away from the glare, where it works its effects sharply and insidiously without besmirching the person who hurls the epithet. After all, the negative charges associated with "white trash" can reflect badly on the user, especially since the term is often used to respond to breaches of decorum. The work this label does usually goes unnoticed and draws little comment, except for those rare occasions where the boundary maintenance work of the term is dragged into the open, as it was when Lizzie Grubman, a New York publicist, rammed her wealthy father's Mercedes-Benz SUV into a crowd of people outside a Hamptons nightclub, injuring sixteen people before fleeing the scene. This appalling scene was instigated when a bouncer asked her to move the vehicle from a fire lane. She spat the epithet, "white trash," at him, then turned the SUV into a weapon, injuring the bouncer and others in the crowd in the process. This incident is instructive not simply because Grubman used the term; rather, this was one of those rare instances when usage of "white trash" was publicly critiqued and evaluated for its implications and assumptions. A host of social critics commented on her usage of "white trash," and their reflections offer an excellent synopsis of the boundary work accomplished via this label.

For upper-class whites who noticed, Grubman's usage was primarily a mortifying breech of etiquette, in that it led to a public spectacle. An essayist for the *Washington Post* used this incident as an opportunity to opine on how "it has not been a well-mannered summer" and to relate her investigation of whether the "social graces have disappeared"—an endeavor that involved keeping close "track of every service interaction I've had" over the summer and assessing the distinction between informality, indifference, and plain rudeness and disrespect (Janis 2001). Another essayist, in the *Hartford Courant,* also used this incident to nominate Grubman as "the poster girl for bad behavior" for her indiscretions. However, she was listed as just one among a host of "famous faces [who] seem to be working overtime these days at cursing, bending the truth, evading responsibility and airing their dirty laundry" (Morago 2001).

Keen social insights into the relational dynamics of class identity were also generated in relation to this incident. Roberto Santiago, in an editorial in the New York *Daily News,* pointed out that in her use of "white trash" Grubman "made a social statement: 'white trash' remains the only slur that is not labeled as hate speech—and the only slur used unabashedly by all races." Santiago insightfully remarked, too, on the uneven rhetorical ground mobilized by "white trash": there is no reciprocal, equally visceral, debasing, or morally charged name for upper-class whites. "In a fair world, 'white trash' would refer to those who sneer at maids, doormen, messengers and minorities. But because the slur is all about white class distinctions, the worst one can call Lizzie Grubman is a pampered, spoiled brat." Perhaps reflecting on the rise in "white trash chic," Santiago commented further: "Sad to say, the final arbiters of what is 'white trash' and what is 'cool' are the world's Grubmans. Body piercings, tattoos and Harleys used to be 'white trash' but now are embraced by the socially hip" (Santiago 2001).

A view from England, the land where class culture has always been a central obsession, was conveyed in the *Daily Telegraph* by Zoe Heller, who observed:

> For the most part, the media have pitched the Grubman story as class war—a story about rich, "arrogant" blonde girls using enormous cars given to them by their daddies to mow down the little people. This doesn't preclude a certain kid of aspirational voyeurism of Miss Grubman's "lifestyle"—gleeful accounts of where Lizzie gets her hair blown out, articles of advice from fashion experts on how she should "tone down her pampered look" for her court appearances, and so on. (Heller 2001)

Heller's attention to the upper-class fascination with this spectacle extended further as she commented on the multivalent nature of this epithet and the way its derisive social charge can cut in many directions at once: "For all their private outrage on behalf of the humble working stiff, the reporters covering this debacle have betrayed a distinct snobbery of their own—a disdain for uppity Jewish princesses with too much privilege and no real 'class.' As far as the hacks are concerned, it's Miss Grubman who's white trash and this, no doubt, is why they have felt so free to stick the boot in." Quite in excess of whatever cultural content or social position may be considered proper as this term's range of reference, Heller identified the premier purpose of "white trash" as a form of social distancing, inscribing an inaccessible "upper" sphere as well as a debased "lower" realm.

Finally, an editorial in the *Washington Post* (Kelly 2001:A21) suggested, in what I assume to be a sarcastic vein, that we "pity Miss Grubman. She is a victim of our culture if ever there was one. How was she to know that it was impermissible to run over white trash? Miss Grubman knows what we all know. There is us—us in the VIP rooms, us in the VIP schools, us in the VIP jobs. And there is not-us, the white trash, and there are very different rules for what each can do to each other." Uses of "white trash" inscribe and make emphatic a realm of "us" and "not-us" for whites. On one side are all the social practices, conventions, and resources, access to which assures whites a privileged and powerful status in this society. On the other side are all those reminders of both the artificial nature of these conventions and the tenuousness of claims to these resources. Antiracist critiques have long targeted "naturalizing" discourse in relation to assertions of social superiority, but the manifold ways these discourses operate in relation to class identities is largely unacknowledged in the public sphere. "White trash" insists on the naturalness of class identities, but in every instance of its usage one can detect as well the anxious uncertainty as to how long or how well those identities will be maintained in the face of changing economic or social circumstances.

The distinctions between these key terms are tangible and active, reflecting historical developments and varied current circumstances for lower-class whites. But these distinctions do not countervail against the fundamental similarity that links each term. "Redneck," "hillbilly," and "white trash" each share a common property: they are deployed and projected in order to maintain the unmarked status of whiteness. In each instance of these labeling practices, a normative status of whiteness is affirmed, one that is free of the blemish of poverty and protected from the ruptures of decorum that might undermine its hegemonic status. These disparate uses are also all linked in that they reference a condition of relative disadvantage within the privilege of whiteness, one that is tangible but multivalent, shifting in intensity of its effects—at times no more "real" for whites, in social terms, than any other "symbolic" ethnicity, while for some whites it is a daily inscription of social contempt and distance.

Each of these epithets hence assembles a host of stigmatized "traits" that can be mobilized either to assert distance from this disparaged social condition or to affirm one's position squarely within this space of difference. Each of these terms is useful to the project of deconstructing whiteness because they make race tangible in relation to class distinctions in a manner that is often forestalled by assertions of white normativity. These terms, used to police the unmarked status of whiteness, are also useful in undermining the same in that they all introduce specificity to the blank slate of whiteness. By specifying class and regional distinctions, the notion of whiteness as an unmarked normative identity is usefully assailed. If we are to do more than reproduce the logic of racial thinking by generalizing about "whiteness" and "blackness," it is exactly this kind of attention to the specifics of social positioning and predicaments that needs to be the basis for analysis.

The uses of these white epithets sketched here suggest several critical considerations in the interests of deconstructing whiteness. First, it is important to be clear what the target of deconstruction is. "Whiteness," broadly applied, fixates on homogenizing practices and assumes a generic position of racial dominance; but this mode of attention will not bring into view the charged intraracial contests that whites engage in as they strive to maintain an unmarked social status. In projecting a uniform condition of privilege and power onto whites, the many fault lines where these assumptions break down will be obscured, thus undercutting a potent means to consider how whites might "disinvest" from whiteness. As well, each of these terms sounds off or amplifies a range of cultural practices or situations with substantial historical depth. It is this cultural content, via considerations of how it is distinctly inflected or signified in terms of class distinctions, that must be drawn into view in analyzing white racial identity, rather than abstract assertions that whiteness represents the absence of culture (Roediger 1994). The general point here is that attention to these terms provides the means by which the density of these racial subjects can be fully considered, and it is this perspective, rather than an attention to whiteness generally, that offers the greatest critical purchase on the ways in which white racial identity is experienced, reproduced, and undermined. These contests over belonging and difference, in all their intricacies, surely inform the interracial contests over whiteness in the public sphere as well.

One final point regarding these stereotyped, rhetorical identities. This imagery and the epithets associated with it perform an additional critical function in the maintenance of whiteness, for these are the figures whites use to delimit an attention to the subject of racism. Consistently, these are the images and people that whites turn to when they need to think about or are confronted with the reality of racism in this country. News features, movies, novels, and editorials rely upon images of poor, often rural whites to address the subject of racism. This economy of examples works to delimit a broader attention to both the "possessive investment in whiteness" (Lipsitz 1998) and the racist dynamics of white society. After all, poor whites are not the bank officers who deny mortgages and other loans to African-Americans of all classes at rates two to three times that of their white counterparts; poor whites are not among the landlords who refuse housing to African-Americans, nor are they the human resources managers who are racially influenced in their hiring and firing decisions. Yet representations of racism in popular culture continue to rely disproportionately upon images of "rednecks," "hillbillies," and "white trash." Hence one critical tack to deconstruct whiteness involves recognizing the complex and emotionally charged contests over belonging and difference that engage whites intraracially. Then recognize the important work these stereotypes perform in maintaining a prevailing image of whiteness as racially unmarked and removed from the blot of racism.

8

The Beautiful American: Sincere Fictions of the White Messiah in Hollywood Movies

HERNÁN VERA
ANDREW M. GORDON

> A good deal of time and intelligence has been invested in the
> exposure of racism and the horrific results on its objects.
> But that well-established study should be joined with an-
> other, equally important one: the impact of racism on those
> who perpetuate it . . . to see what racial ideology does to the
> mind, imagination, and behavior of masters.
> —Toni Morrison, *Playing in the Dark,* pp.11–12

The movies we analyze in this chapter are produced by white Americans. These are fictional creations that are made believable by portraying things and persons we recognize because of their likeness to elements in our social environment. These "social representations" make sense to us because of the ideas and experiences we share with the moviemakers. But movies do not merely mimic reality; they also invent new ways of acting, feeling, and thinking.

The concept of social representations allows us to pay particular attention to the "version" of events, things, and persons proposed by the movies. The fact that most people consider movies as "just entertainment" makes films very effective means of disseminating images and ideas we would reject if they were proposed in other ways. This is particularly the case with our study of the white self, the concept of white Americans proposed by white American moviemakers. Since we live in a cinematic society, one that "knows itself in part through the reflections that flow from the camera's eyes" (Denzin 1995:1), what the movies present is a crucial part of what passes for real in society.

Since Gordon Allport's groundbreaking work (1954), the study of race relations has been dominated by the concept of prejudice. The word denotes judgments and sentiments toward others; prejudices are representations *of others.* But the term makes no reference to the representations *of self* that the encounter with the "other" evokes in the racist person. The self-concept of the perpetrator, as much as his or her prejudice about the other, explains racist oppression. For example, by seeing the other as lazy and dirty, we see ourselves as industrious and clean. The extermination of the natives in the Americas helped to confirm the European self-identity as the master race (Churchill 1992).

Our use of the term "sincere fiction" (Bourdieu 1977b:112) assumes that we make sense of the world through stories we tell each other. It also implies that people act according to what they learn from these stories. The fictions are sincere because most people are unaware of alternative ways in which they could portray themselves and others in these stories and unaware that what they believe about themselves as whites is a myth, a social invention (Feagin and Vera 1995:13).

According to Pierre Bourdieu, culture is not constructed rationally but derives from power. "Symbolic violence" refers to the imposition of systems of meaning upon people so that the symbols are recognized as legitimate. Culture is accepted as simply "the way things are," which obscures power relations and contributes to their reproduction. Specifically, we assert that the white American self-concept is a sincere fiction that is maintained with intense symbolic labor (such as movies) so that people fail to recognize the brutal reality of American race relations (Feagin and Vera 1995:136). White hegemony is a violent, irrational, unstable system that needs to make itself appear natural and benign in order to perpetuate itself.

The power to redefine or to force misrecognition of social reality is a significant power. Divisions of race are arbitrary constructions, fictions. For example, for centuries, the Irish were not recognized as "white" and the Jews were seen as a separate race. In the United States, whites have seen themselves as the norm while seeing racial others as all alike. Whites have seen and portrayed people of color in distorted ways that spread negative images throughout our culture and, via our media, throughout the world. Films must appeal to mass audiences to be profitable. Audiences must be able to identify the things, persons, and social relations on the screen. This is why films are an ideal way in which to observe representations of the dominant group in a culture.

Other visual representations, such as comic books and television, are also worth studying for the sincere fictions they contain. We choose film because it has existed for the entire twentieth century, allowing us to witness the development (or lack of development) of the white American self across the century. Hollywood movies could be considered sincere fictions of American culture, made by a major American industry, and for American (and ultimately worldwide) consumption. To cite Toni Morrison once again: "the subject of the dream is the dreamer" (1992:17).

WHITES IN HOLLYWOOD MOVIES

The epic *Birth of a Nation* (1915), the propaganda film for the Ku Klux Klan, the notorious American terrorist organization, inaugurated what we call the "Hollywood movie." *Birth* "represents two historical landmarks: an incomparable racial assault and a major breakthrough for subsequent filmmaking technique" (Taylor 1996:15). The blatant racism in this movie rewrites history. Its vicious portrayal of blacks and mulattoes provoked an outcry that made this film "the first media event of a type that complements the definition of mass culture" (Taylor 1996:15).

In addition to its aesthetic components—on which so much has been written—*Birth* inaugurates a representation of the white self in movies that survives to this day and that has been neglected by scholars. The central character in *Birth*, Ben Cameron, founds the Ku Klux Klan to save white women from the lust of blacks and to restore the order of white supremacy in the nation. The Camerons are introduced in the antebellum South as living in a familial paradise of kindly masters with puppies that frolic at their feet. When the family visits the plantation, blacks pick cotton in the background, and happy blacks dance for the white masters.

Ben Cameron, affectionately called the "Little Colonel," is part of this idyllic white family and later serves as a brave officer of the Confederacy. He is presented as a noble hero: at the battle of Petersburg, as the title card reads: "The Little Colonel pauses before the last charge to succor a fallen foe" as he gives water to a wounded Union soldier. His courtship of a Northern woman presents him as a sensitive, entirely proper suitor, in contrast with the coarse rape attempts made by a black soldier and by a mulatto politician. Ben Cameron is among the Southern whites oppressed by Northern carpetbaggers, excluded from political participation by venal black election officers, and victimized by all-black juries. He is presented as the messiah who conceives of an army of horseback riders dressed in white sheets that becomes the Ku Klux Klan and protects the South and white Southern womanhood. His intentions are presented in the movie as entirely altruistic.

WHITE MESSIAHS

Hollywood films are replete with the self-serving fantasy of entirely altruistic white men, alienated heroes who are often misfits within their own society and are even mocked and rejected until they become leaders of a rejected group. Like Ben Cameron in *Birth of a Nation*, they find themselves by sacrificing themselves to liberate the oppressed. White messiahs are overwhelmingly male; women seldom qualify for this exalted status. Often the natives treat the white outsider like visiting royalty or a god, instantly worshipped. This is presented as to be expected, no less than he deserves. The messiah is marked by what Max Weber (1958 [1922]: 245) called "charisma," an extraordinary quality that legitimizes his role as leader and savior of darker-skinned followers.

The image of the white messiah is ubiquitous in recent American action-adventure movies, especially hit series such as *Die Hard, Superman, Batman, Indiana Jones, Rocky, Rambo, Terminator, Alien,* and *Men in Black.* Such films typically concern a white hero or superhero (only in *Alien* or *Terminator* is it a heroine) who triumphs despite impossible odds against arch villains and saves the city, the nation, or the world. Often he defeats evil megalomaniac "others": foreigners, Nazis, or extraterrestrials who want to rule the whole world. This is a reflection of American civic religion, which transforms collective endeavors into the battle of a lone individual against the forces of organized evil. Hollywood favors stories about strong individuals. The white action messiah reaffirms the fantasy of an autonomous individual. The action hero is typically a loner, although in more recent films such as *Indiana Jones and the Temple of Doom* (1984) and *Three Kings* (1999), the white messiah brings with him a multicultural team of helpers.

LEADERS OF PEOPLE OF ANOTHER COLOR

In this chapter, we focus on white messiahs who lead people of another color. This is a powerful cultural myth because it presents whites with pleasing images of themselves as saviors rather than oppressors of those of other races. The adventure of a white messiah is an ideal vehicle for propaganda movies. The messiah fantasies are essentially grandiose, exhibitionistic, and self-serving. In the white mind, the racial other does not exist on its own terms but only as what the psychiatrist Heinz Kohut (1971) calls "a selfobject," bound up with the white self.

From among the plethora of such films, for the purposes of this argument we have chosen a sample from the 1960s through the 1990s of stories about Americans encountering the exotic East or a facsimile of Asia: *Stargate* (1994), *Indiana Jones and the Temple of Doom* (1984), *The Man Who Would Be King* (1975), *City of Joy* (1992), *The Green Berets* (1968), and *Three Kings* (1999).

To summarize our argument: first, the ideal white self is constructed as powerful, handsome, brave, cordial, kind, firm, and generous: a natural-born leader. Other races exist as dependent, faithful followers to bolster the grandiose white self-image. And second, in many of these movies, there is a split in the white self that can be resolved only through violence. The sincere fictions encoded in these movies enable the white self to live with itself and to absolve the guilt of racism by portraying the white as noble and self-sacrificing on behalf of other races.

The makers of myths such as *Stargate* and *Indiana Jones and the Temple of Doom* justify imperialism in the name of higher goals: religious, democratic, or humanitarian. White Americans are there not to get wealthy from the natural resources or to exploit the population but to liberate them from slavery. The oppressors are an extraterrestrial tyrant in *Stargate* and Indian aristocrats in *Temple of Doom*. Two critics write: "*Indiana Jones* is a cinematic variant on the theme of the 'white man's burden.' It seeks to represent imperialism as a civilizing, socially progressive force and so to legitimize Western domination of others. It does so by identifying oppression with the indigenous system of rule" (Postone and Traube 1985:12).

STARGATE

Stargate, one of the most popular films of 1994 and the basis for a subsequent television series, is a good starting point since it presents an almost pure mythic paradigm. Its hero possesses all the typical messianic traits. The film borrows from a wealth of myths, including the legends of Moses and of Christ, and from previous science-fiction films using the myth of the birth of the hero, such as *Star Wars* (1977) and *Dune* (1984). But its more directly relevant myth pertains to American foreign policy in the 1990s, particularly to the relationship of white Americans to Middle Eastern peoples.

Stargate begins with the discovery of an ancient, giant, metal ring during an archaeological excavation in Egypt. Decades later, an American government project activates the ring, aided by Dr. Daniel Jackson, an Egyptologist and linguist, who decodes the hieroglyphic inscriptions on its face. Apparently, the ring serves as a gateway to distant stars. The government sends a military team, led by Colonel Jack O'Neill, to investigate the planet on the other side of the portal, at the other end of the universe. Jackson accompanies them. The men discover a desert planet with a population of dark-skinned slaves dressed in Arab garb who labor in the mines. An alien being who calls himself Ra, the Egyptian sun god, keeps the slaves in ignorance and ruled by terror. Ra created the ancient Egyptian civilization and built the pyramids on Earth as landing sites for his spaceship. Jackson, able to read the hieroglyphs, reveals the truth to the people and persuades them to revolt, and Colonel O'Neill and his men aid them. Through the creative use of an atomic bomb, they finally defeat Ra in a climax similar to that of the first *Star Wars* (1977) movie.

The mythic elements in *Stargate* are obvious. Jackson is an orphan and an outcast, scorned by the scientific community, which refuses to believe his theories. The only one who has faith in him is a wise old woman, a mother figure who recognizes his talent. He shows his extraordinary ability by decoding the symbols, which no one else could do. Next, the soldiers resent Jackson as an outsider and mock him as a hopeless "dweeb." In contrast, the natives immediately bow down before him, believing him to be the chosen one because he wears an amulet with the sign of Ra, given him as a good luck charm by the old woman. Jackson is tested by various ordeals: he maintains his chastity in the face of sexual temptation; he descends into the underworld (the pyramid); he dies and is resurrected (in one of Ra's machines); he refuses to kill his comrades when ordered to by Ra; he resurrects his slain lover; he is almost killed again by Ra, but he escapes; and he successfully leads the people in their fight for freedom.

A split in the white self occurs between the two heroes of the film, who are foils. Jackson represents knowledge, but O'Neill represents military might. Jackson has faith, while O'Neill is embittered (suicidally depressed over the death of his son). Jackson is a man of an extraordinary destiny, a mythic hero; O'Neill is a conventional military leader. At first, the two have nothing in common, and they clash, but later they unite to liberate the natives and both are redeemed by the experience. At the end, Jackson stays behind on Ra's planet, having found a wife and a place as leader of the tribe. O'Neill returns home, but he has found a substitute son in one of the native boys and has overcome his suicidal grief. The explicit message is that white men can overcome their differences and find themselves by fighting together to liberate natives from slavery in an alien land. The natives exist for the white men to realize their potential, and immersion in the exotic other will heal the split in the white self.

Nevertheless, the implicit message of *Stargate* is quite different. The natives are portrayed as credulous, ignorant, and superstitious. If you wear the right amulet, they will bow down and treat you like a god. Like the natives in Hollywood jungle movies of the 1930s and 1940s, they are amazed by a pocket lighter and can be won over with a candy bar. The people on Ra's planet, who are descendants of the Egyptians, have been slaves for thousands of years, and without the coming of the white men, they would have remained slaves for thousands more. All it takes is two smart, white Americans to lead them to freedom. According to the logic of *Stargate*, if Columbus had been an American, he would have come to the New World not to exploit, enslave, convert, or exterminate but as a humanitarian to liberate the enslaved masses from tyranny. These white Americans are good guys, even though they carry an atomic bomb.

Stargate uses a mythic plot to convey its ideological message. The film, which appeared in 1994, contains a thinly disguised allegory about the Gulf War of 1991. The American government, solely out of kindness of heart and love of freedom everywhere, sends its armed forces to liberate desert people from a tyrant who has invaded their country. The evil Ra, who is a monstrous, androgynous alien (played by Jaye Davidson, who portrayed a transvestite in *The Crying Game* [1992]), is a version of Saddam Hussein.

INDY SAVES!

Indiana Jones and the Temple of Doom is similar to *Stargate:* another myth about the white messiah who liberates the slaves in an Eastern land. *Temple of Doom* indulges in even more blatant stereotyping and caricaturing, justifying this by setting the action in the 1930s, using 1930s movie conventions from the action-adventure and cliff-hanger genres and playing the clichés larger than life and close to preposterous. The tongue-in-cheek retro mode is established in the opening sequence, an elaborate, Busby Berkeley—style song- and -dance sequence supposedly set in a Shanghai nightclub in 1936. A blonde American woman sings "Anything Goes" in Chinese. We are signaled that "anything goes" in this movie, including old movie clichés and outdated racist and sexist stereotypes. On his adventures, "Indy drags with him an oriental orphan (the only male his equal) and a screeching, hysterical woman" (White 1984:413).

In *Temple of Doom,* we are in *Gunga Din* (1939) territory, in which the natives are either loyal subjects of the British Crown or rebellious, blood-crazed Thuggee cultists. The division of racial others into the good—faithful helpers of the white man—and the bad—murderous thugs—is introduced in the opening sequence, in which Indy's life is threatened by Chinese gangsters, who try to poison and shoot him. He is aided by a loyal Chinese partner who dies saving him and by a Chinese street kid whom he has adopted.

In the next sequence, Indy shows up in an impoverished Indian village. As in *Stargate,* the natives treat him as their savior and put on a feast in his honor. In both movies, the hero shows his respect by eating the native cuisine, even though his companions find the food repulsive.

There are in fact many similarities between Daniel Jackson in *Stargate* and Indiana Jones, who both represent the mythic white hero, the best of the American self. Both are learned men with doctorates in archaeology and respect for other cultures. Both know languages, so they can communicate with the natives, and both put their learning to use to free the slaves (the whites are not the oppressors—extraterrestrials or other natives are the villains). Even though they are scientists, both are also men of action willing to use violence to defend themselves and the innocent. Both are tested by the same series of ordeals: they maintain their chastity in the face of temptation, descend into the underworld, die and are resurrected (Indy becomes a zombie slave of the Thuggee cult until he returns to normal), refuse to execute their comrades when ordered to by the villain, rescue a lover, escape and lead the people to freedom. Most important, both these fictional characters are kind and fearless, mythic heroes who risk their lives for people of an oppressed race, the polar opposite of real-life colonial masters.

Jackson, however, is selflessly pure, whereas Indy is an ambivalent character who seems to include both sides of the split white self. *Temple of Doom* seems to be trying to have it both ways about the character. Indy is both a scientist and a soldier of fortune, an archaeologist who respects other cultures and a grave-robber and thief of valuable antiquities. In the opening sequence, he attempts to sell for profit an urn containing the remains of a Chinese emperor. When the Indian villagers ask him to return a sacred stone to their village, one is never quite sure whether he wants the stone for their sake or for the "fortune and glory" to which he often refers. The greedy, self-serving side of Indy is caricatured in Willie Scott, the gold-digging American woman who accompanies him.

The white American self who is torn between serving himself and serving others embodies the contradictions of capitalism. He is the classic American hero seen in such characters as Rick in *Casablanca* and Han Solo in *Star Wars.* And in movies such as *Stargate* and *Temple of Doom,* although white Americans may initially have a profit motive in going to foreign lands, they soon abandon it to free the oppressed masses.

As in *Stargate,* the natives in *Temple of Doom* are helpless to liberate themselves. There seem to be no strong men in the Indian village, only women and old men. All it takes is one enterprising American, the great white God sent by destiny, to free the people. Near the end of the movie, when Indy confronts the villainous Mola Ram, high priest of the Thuggees, Indy accuses him: "You betrayed Shiva!" The white American has now appropriated the Indian identity and speaks with the voice of Hindu orthodoxy to denounce the heretic.

In elevating the white American self to the stature of a mythic superhero, both *Stargate* and *Temple of Doom* distort history. While seeming to respect other cultures, they actually insult them, implying, for example, that the ancient Egyptians were incapable of building the pyramids or that twentieth-century Indians eat monkey brains, indulge in devil worship, unspeakable rituals, and human sacrifice, and exploit children as slave labor.

In the Remote Land of Kaffiristan

The Man Who Would Be King is a similar story of a mythic superhero, a great white god come to enlighten the poor, ignorant heathen. However, director John Huston's version of Rudyard Kipling's story presents the myth ironically, as a cautionary tale about the disaster that can ensue when a white imperialist starts believing that he is a god. Among the movies we consider about the white messiah, *The Man Who Would Be King* seems at first to demonstrate the delusive nature of the sincere fictions of the white self. Unfortunately, it ends up reaffirming them by glorifying its roguish heroes and stereotyping the natives.

Huston's movie is framed as a tale told to Kipling by his acquaintance, Peachy Carnahan. Carnahan and his best friend Daniel Dravitt (another Biblical Daniel, like Jackson in *Stargate*) are former British soldiers who stayed on in late-nineteenth-century India to exploit the opportunities there rather than return to dull, working-class lives in England. Carnahan and Dravitt are soldiers of fortune, not ambivalent ones like Indiana Jones, but rogues out to steal whatever they can. They retain audience sympathy because they are loveable scoundrels, loyal to each other, fun-loving playactors and bold adventurers. After trying various swindles, they decide to pull their boldest con job yet: they undertake an expedition to the remote land of Kaffiristan, a country no white man has seen since Alexander the Great. They intend to awe the natives with firepower, set themselves up as kings, and return rich with loot. No one in the movie ever questions the morality of such exploitation and theft.

Kipling first meets them when Carnahan steals his watch and returns it because the watch bears a Masonic emblem. Their membership in this secret society forms a bond between these two white men, even though they are of different classes. Later, the Masonic emblem serves Dravitt well when the natives take it as the sign of his godhood, just as the natives in *Stargate* bow down because Jackson wears the emblem of Ra. According to the movie, the conqueror

Alexander the Great was the founder of the Freemasons, forming a secret fraternity of white men that has lasted throughout most of the history of Western civilization. Huston says, "I used a Masonic emblem to symbolize a universal connection between men..." (Kaminsky 1978:199). Nevertheless, in the plot the native recognition of a supposedly universal symbol serves the purposes only of Western male imperialists.

At first, all goes according to plan. Dravitt is set up as king and god, and even serves the people well, dispensing justice and improving conditions. However, things go awry when Dravitt suffers delusions of grandeur. He thinks he is a god and the reincarnation of Alexander and that events have been determined by destiny. When his terrified bride bites him during a ceremony, he bleeds, revealing he is not a god. The angry natives turn against the Englishmen. Dravitt falls to his death when they cut a rope bridge over a chasm. (There is a similar scene in *Temple of Doom*, except that Indy survives the cutting of the bridge.) Carnahan is crucified but lives to tell the tale, although he is crippled and half-crazy.

Unfortunately, despite its ironic point of view about the white savior, *The Man Who Would Be King* is as condescending in its view of the natives as are *Stargate* and *Temple of Doom*. Indians and other Asians are seen in clichés: as exotic others, comic buffoons, or ignorant primitives. The main Indian character is a Gurkha soldier nicknamed Billy Fish, as if his real name were unimportant. Although he knows the two Englishmen are con artists, he serves them loyally, finally dying on their behalf like Gunga Din. Because of the childlike portrayal of the natives, Afghanistan (where the action is supposedly set) refused to allow the movie to be shown in its theaters.

One critic claims the racism in the film is due to Huston's attempt to be faithful to Kipling and not to impose contemporary attitudes on the film (Hammen 1985:130). But according to another critic: "Huston has traditionally viewed... natives as amoral, entertaining creatures who need to be taken care of, admired, amused, and used but never trusted or treated as equals" (Kaminsky 1978:202). If Huston is faithful to Kipling, it is probably because he shares Kipling's racism.

The Man Who Would Be King resembles Huston's earlier film, *The Treasure of the Sierra Madre* (1948), in which white American men dig for gold in Mexico. Both films are cautionary tales about the corruption caused by excessive greed or power, but they both see racial others as childlike primitives and never question the logic of white supremacy or of imperialism. For all its irony, *The Man Who Would Be King* is a narcissistic fantasy, like *Stargate* and *Temple of Doom*, in which the natives have been waiting for a white savior. The difference is that Huston portrays ironically what happens when narcissism goes to the extreme of megalomania.

The plot of *Man Who Would Be King* was borrowed for the recent, sentimentalized, animated feature *The Road to El Dorado* (2000). The retelling of these myths in Hollywood fictions over the decades suggest the persistence of the sincere fictions of the white self.

SERVING THE POOR

City of Joy is a more realistic portrait of Indian culture than *Temple of Doom* or *The Man Who Would Be King,* showing a wide variety of Indian characters of more than one dimension. Unlike the previous three movies, it is not about a mythic superhero. The protagonist, Max, is a disillusioned white American doctor who comes to India to find enlightenment. But an ashram cannot help him. Instead, he realizes himself by serving the poor and the lepers in a free clinic in "the City of Joy," a ghetto in Calcutta. Max begins as a reluctant messiah, but by the end he has become committed to the people and decides to stay with them.

The story of Max is paralleled by the story of Hasari, a poor farmer driven off the land who comes to Calcutta with his family to start a new life. At first, the family is swindled and forced to sleep in the streets. But eventually Hasari gets work as a rickshaw driver and the family finds a home in the City of Joy. The lives of these two displaced people, the American physician and the Indian farmer, become intertwined, and each helps the other. Max gives Hasari courage to stand up to the gangsters who control the rickshaw business and terrorize the community. And Hasari gives Max a family to which he can belong. At the end, Max sits in a place of honor at the wedding of Hasari's daughter. Like Hasari, he has found a home in the City of Joy. Both become leaders of the community.

Unlike the two male protagonists, women are consigned to conventional, secondary roles in *City of Joy,* except for the Irish nurse, a tough, dedicated, truly admirable woman who runs the clinic alone until she recruits Max. But her function is really a maternal one: to prop up the hero. Like the wise old woman in *Stargate,* she recognizes and nurtures the messiah's potential.

City of Joy is, however, exceptional for a Hollywood film in giving equal time to an American and an Indian and respecting a foreign culture. Nevertheless, it shares the same arrogant assumption as the other movies discussed: the notion that all it takes is one white man to rescue or transform a foreign community. Max will save the City of Joy by helping the Indians to overcome their cultural passivity and to stand up for their rights.

Despite their colonialist assumptions and cultural arrogance, there is an opposite notion often implied in the white messiah movies: that white American culture is incomplete, and exotic foreigners have more soul, so that one can realize oneself in another country in a way one never could in the United States. Hence, what happens in the white messiah movies is usually a two-way process: not only does the messiah influence the community, but he himself is also changed by contact with the people. Jackson in *Stargate* and Max in *City of Joy* are American outcasts who decide to stay in a foreign culture because they have become identified with it. Jackson is an orphan who never really had a father, and Max always resented his; in fleeing America, he is trying to escape his father. What happens to both Jackson and Max is a kind of rebirth or re-oedipalization through entry into a substitute family of another race.

THE INVINCIBLE JOHN WAYNE

In contrast, *The Green Berets,* the weakest movie of the lot, presents us with a cardboard white messiah who never changes. It is prowar propaganda, released in 1968 during the height of the Vietnam War. The movie failed, perhaps because it was a vanity production of John Wayne, by John Wayne, and for John Wayne, who codirected and starred, or because the American public was divided at the time about the war. Wayne plays Colonel Kirby, the usual invincible John Wayne military commander, a Green Beret who leads all the operations and never suffers a scratch. Unlike the other white messiahs in the movies, Kirby is never tempted, never doubts, and never develops. *The Green Berets* is static, with many battle scenes but no dramatic tension.

The movie opens with a press conference in which the army explains that the United States is fighting for the South Vietnamese, who need and want Americans to protect them from brutal Communists. The sole black character in the film is a spokesman for the U.S. government position. A cynical antiwar reporter accompanies Colonel Kirby to Vietnam, where of course he undergoes a change of heart when he sees how the Green Berets offer free medical assistance to poor villagers, adopt a cute little war orphan (a stock character, like Short Round, the Chinese orphan in *Temple of Doom*), and fight valiantly against the evil Viet Cong, who slaughter civilians. The Vietnamese are either loyal allies or treacherous enemies who must be killed. Like Kirby, everyone in this movie is constructed of cardboard.

In the final scene, Kirby comforts the cute little Vietnamese war orphan, giving him his Green Beret and saying, "you're what this war is all about." And they walk off hand in hand to the tune of "The Green Berets," a song in which this elite force of Cold Warriors is called "America's best." The sincere fiction of the white messiah has rarely been presented so crudely: the Vietnamese population is reduced to a grateful little boy who must be protected by John Wayne. How can Americans be wrong or racist when "the best" of the white American self is fighting to protect innocent foreign children of color against aggression? (Indiana Jones is also a kind American warrior, the liberator of children, although *Temple of Doom* is not such naked propaganda.)

Green Berets uses sentimentality to disguise the fact that the Vietnam War was a narcissistic conflict for America. As the recent memoir of Robert S. McNamara reaffirms, U.S. involvement had little to do with the welfare of the Vietnamese but a lot to do with the ideological struggles of the Cold War and with American self-esteem. American intervention in fact produced millions of war orphans, both North and South Vietnamese and American as well. But to recognize this fact would cause intense discomfort to the white self-image as the savior of people of color.

IN THE GULF

The plot of the more recent *Three Kings* (1999) rests upon an updated white messiah aided by a racially mixed team. Although the film is harshly critical of the confused messianism of American foreign policy in the Gulf War, it nevertheless creates another American hero who risks his life to rescue people of color.

The question the film raises is: What was the purpose of the Gulf War? This same question is voiced by two characters: the television journalist Adriana Cruz and the hero, Special Forces Major Archie Gates. Did the United States fight the war to liberate the people of Kuwait, to teach a lesson to Saddam Hussein, or simply to protect the oil reserves? The war liberated Kuwait but stopped short of liberating Iraq, leaving the anti-Saddam rebels twisting in the wind at Saddam's mercy without American military assistance.

Movies often rewrite history, expressing ideological wish fulfillment. *Stargate* and *Three Kings* both rewrite the Gulf War: in *Stargate* the U.S. Army uses an atomic bomb to blow up an evil dictator who oppresses Arabs (a stand-in for Saddam Hussein), and in *Three Kings* the U.S. Army aids the Iraqi rebels after the war ends.

Unlike *Stargate, Temple of Doom,* or *Green Berets,* however, *Three Kings* is thoughtful, distinguished by its pointed political contradictions and deliberate moral ironies. For example, an Iraqi officer who was trained in interrogation by the American military when Iraq was at war with Iran tortures a captured American soldier.

The film also criticizes the racism of the American troops, who show ignorance about and contempt for Arabs. Although a black American sergeant objects to the terms "dune coon" and "sand nigger," he has no objection when a white comrade suggests they use instead the more acceptable alternatives of "towelhead" and "camel jockey." The movie opens with the shooting of an Iraqi soldier. We see the man get hit and die in painful close-up, which induces sympathy for him, yet the American troops call him a "raghead" and snap photos of the corpse as victory trophies.

But the film also shows the conversion of a group of American soldiers, who come to sympathize with the plight of a group of Iraqi refugees and decide to rescue them. The white messiah here is Major Archie Gates, who begins as a cynical opportunist who, to cushion his imminent retirement from the U.S. Army, sets out to steal for himself and his men the Kuwaiti gold held by Saddam's troops (a plot device borrowed from *Kelly's Heroes* [1970]). Nevertheless, when the major witnesses the killing of an unarmed Iraqi woman in front of her husband and little daughter, he suddenly changes his mission to rescuing these Iraqi rebels from Saddam's Republican Guards. It is as if the soldiers of fortune in *The Man Who Would be King* were suddenly transformed from self-serving thieves into champions of oppressed peoples. Hence despite its acid critique of

American foreign policy in the Gulf War and its persistent black humor, the film is at heart a sentimental story about an American good guy standing up to absolute evil (in contemporary American popular mythology, Saddam Hussein is linked with Satan—see for example the satiric *South Park* movie [2000]), giving up the gold and risking his life to save Iraqi refugees.

As a nod to diversity, the film includes a range of white, black, and Latino characters. The two television journalists are a Latina and a blonde woman. Major Gates's team consists of three young, working-class men: one uneducated white Southerner, one naïve white store clerk from California, and one black baggage handler. There is also a black colonel in command. Nevertheless, the leader of the mission and the hero of the film is Major Gates, the white messiah who commands the loyalty and respect of his team and of the Iraqi rebels.

The same pattern, in which the goal of the white protagonist changes from greed to rescuing oppressed ethnic or racial others, is seen as well in *Stargate* and *Temple of Doom* and in the recent animated features *Pocahontas* (1995), *The Road to El Dorado* (2000), and *Atlantis* (2001).

PROJECTIONS OF THE OTHER

In the movies about the white messiah we have discussed, with the possible exception of *City of Joy*, we do not see real Indians, Arabs, or Vietnamese. Instead, we see projections, fantasies created by the white filmmakers. The foreigners and minority characters are usually docile and grateful. If they are active figures, they are either loyal disciples of the white messiah or evil heathens. The white messiah movies tell us little about those of other races but much about the desire of the white self to avoid guilt and to see itself as charismatic and minorities as needing white leadership and rescue.

In the language of object relations, "the central meaning of narcissistic libido is an erotic or libidinal attachment with oneself, even if an object is the vehicle for such involvement" (Eagle 1984:59). As Erich Fromm puts it: "for the narcissistically involved person, there is only one reality, that of his own thought processes, feelings and needs. The world outside is not experienced or perceived *objectively*, i.e., as existing in its own terms, conditions and needs" (Fromm 1955:35–36). Since European culture is hegemonic in the United States, this white narcissism—which we call "sincere fictions of the white self"—is presented and represented in the moving pictures of film and television.

The representations in Hollywood movies are carefully crafted, deliberate attempts to communicate, educate, move and inspire. Movies want, in addition to profits, to bring into being new—or to reinforce old—ways of seeing, feeling, and thinking. The stories told by films in the darkened spaces of the movie theater and now on television, in Denzin's (1995:14) words: "effectively erased the corrosive consequences and features of an oppressive racial and gender stratification system in the United States." In the twentieth century, Hollywood fictions of the white self did much to legitimize white privilege.

PART III

Whiteness and Color-Blind Racism: Empirical Studies

9

White Fright: Reproducing White Supremacy through Casual Discourse

KRISTEN MYERS

Recently, a colleague stopped by my office after her class. She was laughing because her students had just asserted that 65 percent of the population of nearby Chicago was African-American. They based their estimate on the anecdotal evidence gained through everyday observations of those whom they see waiting for trains, taking their money in checkout lines, and shopping in stores. When she corrected them, the students were stunned. In fact, according to the 2000 U.S. Census, the percentage of blacks in Chicago is only 37 percent.

How do people acquire such misinformation? Jonathan Warren and France Twine (1997) argue that there is a perception, especially among whites, that racial and ethnic minorities are exponentially growing. Analysts predict that soon whites will become the "new minority." Indeed, the percentage of whites (both Spanish- and English-speaking) in Chicago is only 42 percent. Whites see their own numbers decreasing and they are on the defensive.

I call this defensive perception "white fright." As a result of white fright, politicians have launched official attacks on immigration, affirmative action, welfare, and a "lenient" justice system. Programs designed in the 1960s to protect civil rights are being abandoned under the rubric of color-blind fairness (Feagin 2000). Thus whites' everyday perceptions may heavily impact social and political policy for generations to come.

As Margaret Andersen states in this volume (Chapter 2), a goal of whiteness studies is "to 'destabilize' white identity—to expose, examine, and challenge it." She asserts that most literature on whiteness ignores the "mechanisms" and "sites" of racial domination and subordination. This study aims to fill the gaps in the literature by examining the ways that a sample of whites subscribe to and help perpetuate white fright through casual, private conversations among themselves—or through "racetalk."

According to Morrison (1993:57), racetalk is "the explicit insertion into everyday life of racial signs and symbols that have no meaning other than pressing African Americans to the lowest level of the racial hierarchy." Racetalk is symptomatic of a racial structure in which some racial/ethnic groups enjoy more privileges than others. Because our society has built race-based assumptions into every level of our social lives and organizations (schools, media, criminal justice system, politics, housing, etc.), racism is always present in social interactions (Bonilla-Silva 1997, Bonilla-Silva and Lewis 1999; Feagin 2000). As Paul Kivel (1996:9; emphasis in original) says, "racism affects each and every aspect of our lives, *all the time,* whether people of color are present or not."

Measuring whites' racism is tricky (see Bonilla-Silva and Forman 2000). The post–civil rights climate makes the public expression of racist ideas unacceptable, so its articulation becomes more subtle (see Gibson 1998). New forms of racism maintain privileged status for the dominants without being openly antagonistic (Bobo et al. 1997). Bonilla-Silva and Lewis (1999) argue that there is a "new racism" in the United States which destroys the fruits of civil rights while claiming color blindness. New racism is increasingly covert, unlike racism of the past. The extant research on racist discourse uses primarily survey and interview data as well as texts and speeches (see Bonilla-Silva and Forman 2000; Doane 1996; Steeh and Schuman 1992). All of these forms of data are public talk—ideas knowingly shared with outsiders. Bonilla-Silva and Forman (2000) show that when speaking publicly, whites use semantic maneuvers to "white-wash" or sugarcoat their arguments so as to avoid being labeled racist.

My research looks behind closed doors to investigate the ways in which whites use racetalk to bolster white privilege and generate white fright. Examining private discourse among whites helps to understand the paradox of continued white supremacy in a context of color blindness. Analyses of racist discourse provide a link between people's discriminatory actions and the structure of racial inequality. Van Dijk (1993) argues that discourse itself is a "surface structure"—words, gestures, and expressions—that has no meaning without the "underlying structure." In racetalk, the surface structure is viable only because of the larger racist context. The meanings of racetalk are continually contested (Omi 1999; Winant 1999; Doane 1996). Winant (1999:15) argues that "to represent, interpret or signify race, then, to assign meaning to it, is at least implicitly and often explicitly to locate it in social structural terms." By engaging in everyday racetalk, whites help to legitimate and reproduce the existing racist structure (van Dijk 1993; Bonilla-Silva and Lewis 1999; Bonilla-Silva and Forman 2000; Doane 1996). My research underscores this point. Using participant observation, my informants (N = 22) recorded 282 incidents of casual racetalk by whites. I find that whites' racetalk serves to contain ideologically and demean people of color while simultaneously insulating and celebrating white privilege. Racetalk, then, is a mundane yet pernicious enactment of white supremacy.

METHODS

Because most people avoid using racetalk publicly except by accident (van Dijk 1993), racetalk has a covert quality that makes it difficult to capture. I therefore used informants who acted as "participants as observers," secretly recording racetalk used in their daily encounters.[1] They logged data through field notes, recording any racetalk they overheard as well as that in which they participated. There were two layers of confidentiality: informants created aliases for their subjects as well as for themselves. This paper uses data from two collection periods. The first set of data came from a collaborative research project between myself and an undergraduate student (Myers and Williamson 2001).[2] Additional data were collected through a project in two sections of a qualitative research methods course.[3] All data were collected within a year.

SAMPLING

The selection of informants posed interesting methodological questions. On the one hand, I wanted a broad, random representation of informants to represent best the character and level of racetalk in our community. On the other hand, I wanted informants who knew how to recognize and record racetalk in a qualified manner (see Lofland and Lofland 1995:61). As a compromise, I used various techniques to solicit informants in the first phase of data collection: 1) I posted fliers around campus, targeting black, Southeast Asian, and Latino studies, as well as dorms and classrooms; 2) I published advertisements in the campus newspaper; 3) I contacted "qualified" informants who had previously taken qualitative methods and/or race and ethnicity classes; 4) I made announcements in classes dealing with issues of race/ethnicity. The second phase of data collection was more opportunistic in that I required my students to collect racetalk data as part of a course project. If students consented to donate their data, I included them in this analysis.

Although I recruited a diverse group of informants, in this paper I use primarily data from the white informants. People of color are included only when they report racetalk by whites. Most of the informants were undergraduate sociology majors or minors. Most could be characterized as what Eduardo Bonilla-Silva and Tyrone Forman (2000) call "racial progressives" who recognized and problematized relations of ruling even though they tended to benefit from the power structure. Although students collected this data, the data are not restricted to students.

OPERATIONALIZATION AND DATA-COLLECTION TECHNIQUES

In preparing the informants to collect data, I operationalized racetalk broadly so as to encompass various forms. I explained that racetalk can be used to denigrate any person due to their race/ethnicity. It may be used to celebrate the racial/ethnic pride of any group. Racetalk can be coded language concealing a racialized subtext (e.g., "welfare mother," "urban," and "ghetto"). People may use racetalk in sociopolitical commentaries about racial inequality, such as "Mexicans always get pulled over!" Racetalk includes the denial of the importance of race, such as "I'm not a racist, but. . ." or "I am color-blind."

Informants adhered to several data-collection guidelines. They participated in social interactions as naturally as possible, making and responding to racial/ethnic comments as they normally would. They compiled field notes for fifteen to twenty minutes a day, keeping their notes unobtrusive and secret. They described incidents fully so that an outsider could glean context (Dennis 1993), but they disguised their subjects for confidentiality reasons. They did not incite any racetalk (unless they normally would have), and they avoided judging themselves and their intimates. I assured them that everyone engages in some form of racetalk and that "the emphasis is not racist individuals per se but rather on racist practices and their implications" (Tamale 1996:472).

FINDINGS

Informants' field notes documented casual racetalk by and among college students, family members, employers and coworkers, parishioners, professors, as well as strangers. I find that the whites in this study actively interrogated and resented the presence of people of color. Consistent with Morrison's (1993) original definition of racetalk, whites in this study primarily used it to degrade "others." According to Michelle Fine and Lois Weis (1998), whites create an "other" with "unpleasant personal characteristics," upon whom they project the causes of—and deny personal responsibility for—their problems. The construction of an "other" demarcates whiteness as the standard by which everyone else must be measured (Fine and Weis 1998; Frankenburg 1993). Consistent with this perspective, the racetalk recorded in this study constructed whites as a unified, superior group whose interests were threatened by the very presence of people of color. A grounded coding process (Glaser and Strauss 1967) revealed two strategies used for elevating and protecting white status: categorization and surveillance (see Table 3).[4]

CATEGORIZATION: PUTTING PEOPLE INTO BOXES

In a racist society, difference is not just observed, it is quantified and condemned (see Feagin 2000). When confronted with racial/ethnic difference, whites in this study constructed mythic categories that allowed them ideologically to contain the "other" in boxes. They did this in three ways. 1) Whites created demeaning caricatures and slurs. This language clearly demarcated an "us" from a "them." 2) Once categorized, people were easily dehumanized. White subjects likened people of color to objects and animals. 3) The twin practices of caricaturing and dehumanizing tainted the "others," turning them into contaminants to be avoided or eliminated.

Slurs and Caricatures   Whites used an expanding vocabulary to refer to the "other." Old slurs were used, including brother/sister, nigger/nigga, spic, colored, Chink, Gook, dog eater, cracker, honkey, raghead, towelhead (both of which enjoyed a post-9/11 renaissance), dothead/dot, dago, sand nigger, and "those people." Other terms have morphed and been updated. "Niglet" referred to anyone/anything black, although it was usually used to talk about children. Ranchero, beaner, and brazer suggested Latinos, especially Mexicans. Hispanic

Table 3 Types of Observed Racetalk Incidents by Informant.

INFORMANT'S RACE/ ETHNICITY	INFORMANT'S ALIAS	CATEGORIZATION	SURVEILLANCE	TOTALS
	Barbara[b]	2	0	2
	Carmen[ab]	23	13	36
	Cher[a]	25	22	47
	Cheyenne[b]	4	4	8
	Flora[b]	4	2	6
	Gail[b]	1	3	4
	Harley[a]	6	5	11
	Jessica[b]	4	4	8
White	Joan[b]	1	2	3
	Jonathan[a]	9	10	19
	Kenny[b]	8	5	13
	Lars[b]	2	2	4
	Lavinia[a]	6	14	20
	Rocker[b]	8	5	13
	Rodger[b]	19	19	38
	Sigmund[b]	1	2	3
	Sophia[a]	18	4	22
African-American*	Amber[a]	2	0	2
	Elizabeth[a]	0	2	2
	Coco[a]	5	5	10
Latino/a*	Guido[b]	10	2	12
	Sena[b]	7	2	9
Totals		160 (57%)	122 (43%)	282 (100%)

[a] Data collected in period 1
[b] Data collected in period 2
* Data from informants of color is included in this analysis only if the observed incident involved a white speaker.

children were called "spiclets." "Chiefing" was slang for smoking marijuana. East Indians were referred to as "Gandhis." Colombians were associated with drug dealers. "Panface" referenced Asians.

To mask racial coding, people have innovated. The term "Canadians" was used by whites to refer secretly to African-Americans. An inner-city teacher explained that she and her peers used it to refer to their black students; a police officer reported that he and his colleagues used it when talking about blacks over the radio. Several restaurant workers reported using "Canadians" to refer to black customers—one server went to the kitchen as soon as black customers entered the restaurant (before they were even seated) and announced: "We're going to need some lemonade and chicken wings for the Canadians." "Bubblins" (shortened from "Bubblin' Brown Sugar") referred to African-Americans, and Baby Bubblins referred to black children.

Whites caricatured various cultures. For example, Carmen's white friend planned to go camping. Carmen reported: "Jenn had to go to get her gear from the recreation center. When she came back, she said she felt like a Vietnamese refugee with all the stuff on her bike." Jonathan and his friends made a game out of stereotyping:

> All of us skipped our classes today. We were sitting around watching TV. There was the typical conversation while watching; all niggers are criminals, funny little gooks. This all has become commonplace in our conversations. It goes back and forth until all of the stereotypes are out. Then it stops until something else happens. If this is considered racist, I guess we all are.

Racial caricatures defined behavior that only "those people" do. For example, Sophia entered her dorm room to find her white roommate watching *Ricki Lake*. Typical of sensationalized talk shows, the audience was "going crazy." Sophia reported:

> I asked what the heck was going on. My roommate said, "Someone must have dropped some chicken on the floor." She said it because most of the people on the screen were black.

Programs like *Ricki Lake* and *Jerry Springer* intentionally caricature people of color, perpetuating destructive stereotypes for profit. However, subjects in this study caricatured them as well. Sophia wrote about her brother:

> He does these "impressions" of what he calls "brothers." He was telling about one of his friends and he mentioned something about a black guy. He started moving his hands around, flashing what he thinks to be gang signals, and talking crap. Then he went on to tell his story. I asked him why he felt the need to do that. He replied, "That was how the guy was."

Accents were commonly mimicked. For example, Lavinia and her white roommate wondered who had changed their burned-out lightbulb. The roommate speculated: "One of the [Latina] housekeepers probably said, 'Lightbulb is no working.'" This same woman called her professor Obi Wan Kenobe; the alliteration of her name rhymed and she spoke with a Jamaican accent. A white English major argued that British and Jamaican accents have definite linguistic structure, but "the American Southern accent and Ebonics both destroy grammar patterns written in English." Jonathan's friend criticized his Asian professor: "Goddamn gooks. Can't speak our language, I can't understand what the hell they're saying." Taken together, slurs and caricatures reified damning stereotypes and helped define us/them boundaries.

Dehumanization   Once people were defined as "other," negating their humanity was simpler. Whites in this study attached racial caricatures to myriad objects including clothes, animals, movies, music, and jewelry. For example, a white male pointed at Cher's black cat and remarked, "Look at the little niglet." In the same vein, Rodger reported this incident:

> We were watching a chimpanzee on T.V., and Sam said, "Shit! Look at that monkey!" So we all did and the chimp was running around and did a back flip and climbed a tree. Sam said, "How'd they get that Black guy to do that?" We all laughed.

If whites found an object remarkable, they derisively associated it with people of color. For example, Carmen's white roommate informed her that her headphones made her look "like a nigger." Later, the same woman proclaimed that her new shoes made her look like she had "nigger feet." Harley reported: "We saw an SUV with low rider type tires. I giggled because it looked funny, and my dad said, 'Mexicans,' in a tsk-tsk manner." Carmen and her friend called a slow-moving car driven by Latinos a "Mexi-mobile," concluding, "the reason it was going so slow is because they are so poor and they cannot get insurance." Driving "Mexican style" meant packing a car full of people—even if all of the passengers were white.

Body parts were racialized as well. For instance, Carmen's white friends bantered: "Audrey began to rip on her roommate about how big her butt was. She called her butt a ghetto butt; her butt might rip through her pants." Flora required knee surgery, and she had two options: surgically stretch her own ligament to fit the kneecap, or receive a donated ligament. She asked her friend Tony for advice. When Tony had knee surgery, he chose the donated ligament. The ligament failed, as he explained: "The first donor's ligament came from a lazy Black man. Blacks are so lazy, even their body parts are lazy. Their parts don't want to work either."

Even smells were racially coded. When Sophia's family's van was stolen, a white police officer found it abandoned and returned it to them, saying: "'You could tell it was one of them. You could because of the way it smelled.' Then he gestured to his hair on his head. He mumbled something under his breath about Afro-Sheen." By racially coding objects and animals, whites articulated the message that people of color are less than human.

Contamination   A dehumanized group or object became contaminated. For instance, Flora reported an incident where she and some white friends carpooled their kids to Hooters for a birthday party. Flora's husband put on a rap CD. One friend said, "Shut off the fucking nigger music!" Flora asked him if he disliked Black people. The friend replied, "Yes, they are a bunch of niggers!" He asked his son to pass him the CD case. He looked at it and said, "Yep, he looks like a nigger to me." Anything associated with people of color became defined by those people of color and subsequently devalued.

In this study, whites characterized people of color as contaminated and then invoked this pejorative image to underscore contempt in any situation. Although this tactic involved a logical fallacy—the glittering association (Browne and Keeley 1998)—the rhetorical strategy was effective and pervasive. For example, Jessica quarreled with her white friend, Adam: "I made a suggestion to him. He didn't agree with me, and after hearing my suggestion, he said, 'That is black.' I asked him what he meant by that and he said, 'It's not important. Don't worry about it.' "

Although Jessica was unsure of what Adam meant, Rocker more clearly reported a use of glittering association:

> We sat around on Saturday night, and sometimes we called each other niggers because something stupid would happen. I guess we sometimes refer stupidity to black people. For example, we were playing a card game called circle of death. I did something wrong, and my friend asked me, "Why are you such a black person?"

Guido's white roommate acted similarly: "Throughout the day, he used the word 'nigger' to refer to anything that was negatively happening to him, even if it was something humorous."

The ideological origins of this association are clear. "White" and "black" have long correlated with good and evil (Kivel 1996). Informants provided concrete evidence of the continued salience of this white-supremacist association. For example, Carmen observed a white teacher interacting with white preschoolers in a Sunday school class.

One of the group's activities was to discuss what sin means. The teacher used two sheets of paper: one was black and the other was white. She held up the black piece of paper and said this was sin. Then she held up the white sheet and said something to the effect that this was goodness.

Barbara's white friend "was describing her work and said, 'I am working like a white woman,' describing how hard she was working." Similarly, when Rodger almost rear-ended a car, his girlfriend said, "Jesus! Drive like you're white!" Rodger responded: "Bitch! I ain't white. Now shut yo' damn mouth!"

Some whites constructed gradients of evil regarding blacks. At Barbara's church potluck, a white woman stated. "Jesse Jackson is an example of a black nigger," supposedly distinguishing him from typical, benign blacks. Similarly, Guido's white friend asserted to their black friend that "niggers are lower class Blacks that commit crimes."

Whites sorted people into tidy, toxic boxes that dehumanized people, reinforced damaging stereotypes, and helped reproduce racial/ethnic inequality on a larger level. This conversation recorded by Jessica helps to illustrate the negative consequences of racialized characterizations:

> After visiting my grandma in the hospital, I was telling my friends a story about two men who came into the hospital after being shot. Adam asked, "What were they?" I asked what he meant. He said, "They were niggers, right? Figures, that is just population control."

As Doane says in this volume (Chapter 1), "whiteness is defined through boundaries and exclusion, by being 'not of color.'" Taken together, categorization is the process by which whites construct boundaries through stereotypes, generalizations, and typifications of people of color. By converting real people into harmless categories, whites alleviate white fright. This ideological filing system disarms the threat of difference by dehumanizing and degrading the "other." Intrinsic to this process is the fortification of white privilege.

SURVEILLANCE

The second strategy for insulating white privilege was surveillance. Once they had neatly packaged people of color into boxes, whites interrogated every move that they made. They interpreted the actions of people of color through a racist lens. Patricia Hill Collins (1998) asserts that people of color are under surveillance when they are in the white-controlled public sphere. Seen as uninvited intruders, people of color are interrogated officially by the police and store security guards. They are unofficially interrogated as well, through casual racetalk. To explain the roots of surveillance, Fine and Weis (1998) argue that whites—especially poor and working-class white men—feel an increasing sense of loss due to recent structural changes. Such whites have experienced shrinking wages, the demise of all-white neighborhoods, and the decline of the male role as head of the household. Fine's and Weis's white respondents explain their "package of loss" by blaming minority insurgence rather than critiquing the changing social structures. They argue that whites police their borders—literally though neighborhood clubs, and figuratively through racetalk—in order to "reclaim their waning dominance."

In my study, white subjects' surveillance of people of color was multifaceted, consistent with Fine's and Weis's analysis. White racetalk critiqued people of color according to their presentation of self as well as their use of space and resources. Whites expressed concern that their power and resources were being usurped by people of color. Last, whites perceived that people of color succeeded only due to special treatment.

Presentation of Self: White Like Me   Much of whites' racetalk critiqued and generalized the ways that people of color presented themselves publicly. In addition to mimicking dialects (discussed above), whites privately attacked people of color when they heard them speak at all. Jessica's white friend, Sarah, condemned the African-Americans standing in front of a classroom building: "You know how they stand in one group and they don't move. The only words you hear in each of the circles of conversation is mother fucker—it's like those are the only words they know."

Sigmund and his white coworker had this conversation:

Sigmund: Have you ever noticed with Spanish-speaking customers that they always come in groups of three?

Ned: Three or four.

Sigmund: ...and only one of them knows English? All speak Spanish but only one can translate the English?

Ned: Nothing against their people, but that's just how they are.

Sigmund: I don't have anything against them.

Ned: Well, me either, but if you're going to come to this country you should learn how to speak the language.

Rodger's friends talked about the bad service at McDonald's, saying that if you want to get what you order, "you have to speak Ebonics." Whites criticized whoever did not blend in according to white standards of speech.

Whites also judged people of color by their physical comportment in public spaces. For example, Sena's white roommate noticed that "all Black people congregate all over the buildings [on campus]. She said they stand in front of all the doors: 'They are so ghetto.'" Jessica's friend also attacked African-Americans: "I hate how they cross the street with their nose in the air like they own everything. They don't even say thank you when you stop. Do they think we won't hit them?" Similarly, Rocker's friend said, "Blacks don't look anywhere when they cross the street." White subjects tensed when people of color refused to defer to them in public spaces. Such whites interpreted differences as racial inferiority.

At the same time, whites resented any success on the part of people of color. For instance, whites showed turned a critical eye to the ways that people of color spent money. Kenny's friends wondered how black people can afford "such nice cars." Rocker recorded the following rant in his field notes:

Dude, I hate all these fucking niggers. They drive these nice cars, wear nice clothes. They have their fucking bass on so loud you can't even hear anything else. How do they afford it? Well, they don't pay for school, because they're poor. So they get free tuition, and when they sell their drugs, they buy this shit.

Similarly, Gail reported this:

I overheard two white guys talking about how much they had to work to get what they have. One guy said to the other: "These black people don't even work and they have cell phones and designer clothes." The other guy said, "Yeah man, I work so much just to pay my bills and these people just go and spend money like it's water." I had to agree that I had seen more black people with cell phones than white, but I don't think that we should be so judgmental about it just because they are black.

Carmen's field notes captured financial surveillance:

My [white] roommate was telling us about when she used to work at the grocery store, and behind the store were what she described to be housing projects. She said that all of the black people spent money on useless items like Nike shoes for very young children, instead of spending it on reasonable things like food and shelter.

White subjects spoke as fiscal experts, openly evaluating African-Americans' material consumption. In the racetalk, people of color were damned for being different from whites, and damned if they tried to approximate or surpass whites.

THAT'S MINE: USE OF SPACE AND RESOURCES

Surveillance occurred because of white fright. That is, whites perceived a threat—to their possessions, neighborhoods, safety, jobs, and their overall way of life (Warren and Twine 1997). Whites in this study were hyperaware of the boundaries of their own spaces. They remarked upon attempts by people of color to infiltrate the "white space." Kenny's friend feared an "Asian invasion," saying that too many Asians is as bad as too many blacks. Sigmund's girlfriend said: "Nothing against Black people, but it's like they have to have something of everything, you know." Sigmund replied: "Like BET: [they say,] 'we have to have our own TV station.'" Whites in this study perceived that people of color were "gaining on" them, ignoring the vast white privileges structured into American institutions.

When whites had to share "their space"—broadly construed to include universities, neighborhoods, workplaces, even sidewalks and parking lots—with people of color, racial surveillance ensued. Here, Jonathan's friends compared their majors: "Brad said there were many 'Indians' in his major, while Chris commented that his major had a lot of 'Blacks.' Brad then commented that 'They're trying to take back the night.'" Cher's friend said: "I hate fuckin' niggers. They're always in my club. No one dances better than me. Why do they try to disrespect me and my club? Why can't they just stay in their projects and not bother me?"

The perception that whites were being overrun and possibly surpassed stemmed in part from the sense that whites were losing their jobs to "them." Cher reported a comment by her friend's father: "I used to work for minimum wage in a grain plant. All these Black people started taking the jobs. Since then, the plant has gone to shit." Flora's sister-in-law voiced a similar concern:

She said that when she worked with [Mexicans] in a factory, she found it unfair that they did not have to pay taxes because they were not residents of the U.S. She said all they did was receive wages and save it so they could go back to Mexico. She didn't care about the Mexicans who live here permanently and pay their taxes. She felt it was unfair that Mexicans took jobs away from other people who needed employment to pay their mortgage and chase the American dream.

Cher's friends discussed a solution:

Friend 1: I have a plan.
Friend 2: Huh?
Friend 1: My dad was bitchin' about this dumb ass spic at his work. So I have a plan. We [whites] should move to Mexico because all the Mexicans moved here.
Friend 2: I want to go to Cancun.
Friend 1: I thought we already took that from Mexico.
Friend 2: No, it's still Mexican.

Living in integrated neighborhoods elicited hostility. Carmen's father observed a new family that moved into their neighborhood:

First my dad said something about the African-American man and how he looked like a big hairy gorilla. The he made a comment about the family of "dot heads" that were walking up the driveway to their house. Then a car came with two men in it and he said, "First we have niggers, then dots, and now gay men—what else?"

Carmen's roommate voiced similar concerns about people of color in the dorm: "My roommate and I frequently have our door open. One time when an Indian passed by she said, 'Why does he always look in here?' She doesn't have a problem normally when other people pass by."

Cher's friend reported, "the Mexicans in my town are like flies on horse shit. There are 70 to one house. That's the only way they can live." Harley wrote: "My dad and I were driving around, looking for dinner, when he asked, 'Are there more blacks than whites?' He then told me that when I travel, that's how I can tell if it's a bad neighborhood."

Observing the number of Indians living in their apartment complex, Kenny's friend remarked that "they must ship them in." Carmen and Rocker both observed that one of the dorms on campus housed a disproportionate number of African-American students. Consequently, white students referred to this dorm as a "project" or a "ghetto."

Whites expressed resentment and anger at having to share with the "other." For example, Rocker relayed an incident incited by the need to share a scarce resource: parking spaces.

Me and Cat were waiting for a parking spot and this black guy with ski glasses walked out [to the parking lot]. He walked to a car, then across the parking lot. I said, "You fucking crack head—go rob a store." I was pissed because I was going to be late for class and he made it look like he was going to a car but he didn't. I hate these fucks. They make it look like they're the best when they're not.

Similarly, Sophia's white friend balked at the inconvenience of slowing down his car:

There was this black guy walking by the sidewalk, crossing the street. The guy I was with yelled, "Come on you fucking nigger!" I was all, "Hey watch it!" to my friend. The guy crossing the street couldn't hear because the windows were rolled up (thank God!). But I was really pissed. I asked him why he would say that. He came back with "They have been pissing me off lately."

Most disturbing in the data were the violent overtones in much of the whites' surveillance. As Cher's friend said, "My dad wants to take a gun to all the Mexicans around here." Jonathan's field notes were laced with images of lynching. He reported this conversation between coworkers:

Dave: I have a new enemy here.
Chris: Who's that?
Dave: That nigger from down the hall.
Chris: Why?
Dave: He acts like he runs the place. Tells me what I should be doing.
Chris: I don't like him either.
Dave: I'm going to get a rope. (He said this sarcastically).

Here is another conversation among the same group:

Chris: Why is that black guy standing by that tree?
Dave: He's waiting to be hung in it.
Chris: (laughs) Oh man . . . we can get some rope.
Dave: (laughs) string him up!

Whites' concerns about "impending invasions" underscored their sense of absolute racial entitlement. Indignant, angry, and violent, whites actively resisted sharing "white space," that is, any space, with people of color.

Special Treatment   As a result of their surveillance, whites in this study concluded that advancement by people of color could not be meritocratic, since they were not worthy (not white). According to this logic, progress resulted only from special treatment or "reverse discrimination." Harley reported this about her coworker on the student police patrol:

Jerry told me at work that he is sick of "them," save a few exceptions, saying that we owe them. He said he doesn't like that he can get hurt and it's okay, but he can't hurt one of them without all hell breaking loose. He is upset with people who expect overcompensation for something that is done and over with. His last statement was, "Let it go!"

Harley herself echoed these ideas in her field notes:

> I find a lot of black people I've met overcompensate in areas, and often put their suffering above others. I feel my anger rise when they say things like my ancestors oppressed theirs when it is completely untrue simply because I am white. Many times I have felt discriminated against because I am white, like I owe them for the stupidity of whites in the past.

Whites ironically expressed concern that they were being excluded from "special" black activities. Sophia reported a couple of incidents like this:

> I was standing in line today to get some cash from the bank. I was in line with my friend and there were several other people around us. There was a girl passing out little fliers. She was black. The five people in front of me happened to be black. The girl handed the fliers to each other people in front of me. She was making small talk with them and everything. She came up to us and was about to turn away. I made eye contact with her. Then, reluctantly, she handed me one of the fliers and then just walked away. The flier was for a deejay party that was going on that weekend. It was weird.

Weeks later, Sophia had a similar encounter: two "Black guys" were handing out fliers to other black students. This time, making eye contact did not work. Sophia was befuddled about being "left out" just because of her whiteness. Harley's friends debated why there was a black choir and not a white choir on campus. Cher's friends fought about why there was a black caucus. Most of their analyses portrayed blacks as insurgents attempting to amass special privileges that might unjustly usurp white resources.

Taken together, white surveillance was not harmless curiosity about "the other." At its heart, it concerned territorial rights and white supremacy. These data indicate that the presence of people of color in public arenas elicited angry racetalk focused on putting "them" back in their place—out of the public eye and away from "white" (any) resources. Through surveillance, whites amassed anecdotal data to support their hypotheses that "those people are taking over" (Fine and Weis 1998; Warren and Twine 1997). White fright may aid what Patricia Hill Collins (1998:17) calls a "politics of containment" geared toward limiting if not reversing the expanding rights of subordinates.

DISCUSSION

As other authors in this volume assert (see Andersen, Chapter 2, and Doane, Chapter 1, for examples), race is a social construct. These data provide insight into the ways that whites construct racial meanings and conceptualize and people of color—particularly African-Americans. Whites are disturbed when blacks congregate together in public, when they display self-confidence or pride, when they seem to usurp resources. These data allow us to see the ways in which whites construct blacks as threatening and undeserving of resources and self-confidence, because they conceptualize blacks in a very narrow way. In their talk, whites paint a picture of blacks that resembles Elijah Anderson's (1999) description of the "hyperghetto." In this rendering, African-Americans are drug dealers who spend their ill-gotten money on nice clothes and cars. They walk about with hostile attitudes designed to keep potential attackers at bay. They are uncivil and dangerous. Although few whites in this study have likely spent any time in a hyperghetto, their perception of blacks as "ghetto" has been successfully fabricated by media generalizations. Individuals' talk helps reify this distorted image. Hence whites get worried or angry when they see black people in white spaces, taking this as evidence that the ghetto is seeping into their own communities. Other ethnic groups are suspect as well, but few elicit the same level of hostility as African-Americans. These findings are consistent with Warren's and Twine's (1997) argument that whiteness has meaning only in opposition to blackness.

Based on the white talk in this study, it seems that whites are wistful for the days of Jim Crow. Gone are the glory days when blacks in public spaces kept their eyes down and tried to pass unnoticed. In the olden days, blacks knew their place as inferiors and deferred to superior whites, as dictated by an extensive racial etiquette.[5] As Charles Johnson (1943:123) wrote in the Jim Crow era: "Generally speaking, there is no problem in casual public contacts if the Negroes do not make themselves conspicuous by their aggressive behavior." Modern white talk tries to make sense of unapologetic, "aggressive" African-Americans by implicitly juxtaposing the (bad) present with the (good) past. Other ethnic groups are seen as out of line as well, exacerbating the threat to white supremacy.

CONCLUSION

Survey and interview methodologies miss a great deal of white fright. Although people publicly claim to be color-blind and antiracist, examining their private talk reveals a different reality. Indeed, this research indicates that "old" racism has not died out—it has simply gone underground and become more nuanced. Whites now keep such talk private. Although cautious about saying racist things in "mixed company," whites talked freely among themselves. Talkers assumed that the content was acceptable to the participants in conversations. Indeed, having white skin itself served as a "ticket" to racetalk. Covert participant observation provided access to this talk that until now has not been captured.

Whites fear an impending takeover and they strive to contain people of color safely by categorizing/dehumanizing them and keeping them under surveillance. Whites' overall approach to people of color seems bifurcated: on the one hand, whites disdain them for failing to meet the white standard. On the other hand, whites resent and fear any advancements made by people of color. In either case, people of color bear the brunt of the attacks. As Warren and Twine (1997) argue, there's a racial polemic in the United States that consistently values and protects whites over "others." My data underscore their conclusion.

The casual talk captured in this study was everyday banter among friends, family, lovers, students, and teachers. This talk was Americana. It is precisely the mundane nature of this talk that makes it so compelling. One need not wear a white sheet and whistle "Dixie" to celebrate the structure of racism. Everyday people help to reproduce white supremacy through their casual talk. That is, racetalk is not simply the individual expression of prejudice. It is political in that it expresses an agreed-upon racist ideology among whites. This ideology embodies a folk knowledge that makes sense of the world and it is used to assess right and wrong on a larger scale (Bonilla-Silva 2001).

Bonilla-Silva (2001:63) argues that ideologies are meanings that express "relations of domination." Dominant ideologies become "master frameworks" used to measure all other races/ethnicities. Bonilla-Silva asserts that white ideology reproduces white supremacy in that it accounts for (justifies) racial inequality; it normalizes whiteness; and it provides the basic scripts and rules of engagement for all actors. Dominant ideologies help whites to maintain power by manufacturing consent—both among whites and among people of color, who internalize white supremacy as well. As Teun van Dijk (1993) asserts, the white dominant group is able to reproduce its abuse of power only through an integrated system of discriminatory practices and sustaining ideologies. Everyday conversation helps these ideologies take root, and these in turn justify discrimination. Structure and action are dialectically interconnected, and racetalk helps link white-supremacist ideology with practice. Therefore white fright is a tool for continued oppression of people of color.

10
Playing the White Ethnic Card: Using Ethnic Identity to Deny Contemporary Racism

CHARLES A. GALLAGHER

The ethnic revival among many whites in the 1960s and 1970s has been de-scribed as a "'dying gasp' on the part of ethnic groups descended from the great waves of immigration of the nineteenth and early twentieth centuries" (Steinberg 1989:51) to reassert or return to a real or imagined ethnic heritage. If this period was a "dying gasp" at attempting to revive a moribund sense of ethnic identity for whites, then the end of the twentieth century could be viewed as its funeral. A majority of white respondents I interviewed came from families so ethnically mixed, so far removed from the immigrant experience, and so thoroughly reconstituted through assimilation, divorce, remarriage, and relo-cation that the traits that once distinguished ethnic groups from various parts of Europe have become incidental background information. The overwhelming majority of whites in this study did not live in ethnic neighborhoods, did not feel compelled to date within their own ethnic group, did not have the ethnic traditions of their older kin, and did not obtain employment through ethnic networks. Most have undergone such extensive generational, spatial, and cul-tural assimilation that the "option" to engage in the activities or traditions that forge and give shape to an ethnic identity no longer exists (Waters 1990).

Even in its most diluted, tenuous, or symbolic forms, knowledge of one's ethnic ancestry did, however, perform important psychological, ideological and political functions for some whites. Many respondents selectively resurrected and appropriated ethnic family history to compare and equate the immigration experiences of older, typically deceased kin to Asian migration and the African-American experience of the Middle Passage, slavery, and institutional racism. In this way the "immigrant tales" or even a general knowledge of how white ethnic immigrants were treated by the dominant group upon arrival to the United States provided later-generation whites with the idioms and narratives to create a history of past white-group victimization and hardship.

Playing the "white ethnic card" was the means by which whites could con-struct a story of how ethnocentrism towards whites and racism against blacks and Asians were an equally shared part of white, black, and Asian history.

Historian Matthew Jacobson argues that by fashioning their distant ethnic ancestors as a racialized ethnic "other," whites can now "disavow any participation in the twentieth-century white privilege on the spurious basis of their parents' and grandparents' racial oppression" (Jacobson 1998:8). Selectively recalling ethnic family history provided whites in this study with the language, experiences, and metaphors to discuss past and present white ethnic victimization. Most importantly, the off-the-boat and up-to-the-suburbs success story provided some whites with a safe rhetorical space to champion a philosophy of color-blind universalism rather than the racial particularism many whites associate with identity politics. Ethnic identity was "used" by later-generation whites to evoke stories of immigrant relatives who overcame adversity by thrift, self-improvement, and hard work that made upward mobility and achieving the American Dream possible. These accounts validated many whites' beliefs that if past generations could climb the social and occupational ladder in an environment brutally hostile to white ethnic newcomers without government help, nonwhites, particularly blacks, should have been able to mirror their grandparents' mobility path.

Many whites who were still able to draw on these immigrant tales played the "ethnic card" to maintain, ignore, or discount white racial privilege by using ethnic narratives as a medium through which they could list a host of race-based grievances without appearing racist. With this ahistorical sleight of hand, the real discrimination white ethnics were temporarily subjected to upon arrival to the United States becomes analogous to and indistinguishable from three centuries of slavery, Jim Crow, legal segregation, and state-sanctioned "benign neglect." Within this perspective, where white ethnicity is reconstructed as the social equivalent of being black or Asian, whites are able to maintain the fiction that every group, regardless of color, has been equally victimized by racial and ethnic prejudice. Robert Blauner suggests that the immigrant analogy in which "the historical experience of European ethnic groups and the contemporary situation of racial minorities" (Blauner 1972:10) are equated allows whites to discount white privilege while ignoring the extent to which race and racism continue to shape the life chances of racial minorities.

Based on my interviews, it appears little has changed since Blauner first made his observations thirty years ago: the immigrant analogy remains part of many whites' "commonsense" understanding of race and ethnic relations and is used to dismiss charges of white privilege while negating claims of contemporary racism. Along with being able to deny that whiteness carries with it any unearned privileges, this everyone-was-a-victim mentality serves another important function for whites: framing discussions of contemporary race relations within the lens of ethnicity allows whites simultaneously to be victims and not to be held accountable for the past and present social arrangements that maintain white racial privilege (Gallagher 1997).

Not only does a color-blind perspective negate white privilege but it also allows blame to be placed on racial minorities for lagging economically behind whites. In his research of whites in the Detroit area, Eduardo Bonilla-Silva (2001:161–162) found that his respondents routinely used a mix of political and economic liberalism in order to assert that since "discrimination is no longer a salient factor in the United States, [whites can] believe that blacks' plight is the result of blacks' cultural deficiencies (e.g., laziness, lack the proper values, and disorganized family life)." The color-blind perspective does an enormous amount of ideological work, as the structural advantages that flow to whites because of their skin color is assumed to flow to other racial groups as well.

The Declining Significance of White Ethnicity

Among the eighty-nine white respondents[1] who were asked about their ethnic background in this study, only twelve respondents (13 percent) indicated that their ethnicity was a salient and important part of their identity. Individuals in this "ethnicity matters" category included respondents who had a parent born in Europe or lived in neighborhoods they defined as being ethnic. Respondents in this category typically celebrated some ethnic traditions or had a family member who spoke the mother language.

Fourteen respondents (16 percent) were "symbolically ethnic." Their ethnic identity was completely situational, typically gaining salience during the holidays or at family functions. Their ethnicity was, as Herbert Gans put it, "more a leisure time activity" (Gans 1999a [1979]). Respondents in this category quickly identified a European ancestry then proceeded to explain that their ethnicity was important to them only in very specific circumstances, such as holidays, eating ethnic foods, interacting with grandparents, or discussing family history. For many in this group, symbolic ethnicity came to mean Polish cookies at Christmas, grandmom's spaghetti dinners, or drinking beer on St. Paddy's Day.

The single largest category (thirty-five respondents or 39 percent) was what I term "name-only ethnics." These respondents explained that the only thing about them that was ethnic was their last name. The idea of being ethnic or having an ethnic identity did not resonate with them on any level. Most respondents knew that their ancestors came from various European countries, but outside of a vague geographic link to the continent, they lacked an ethnic identity as it is commonly understood. No cultural traits, shared heritage, or attachments to ethnic communities shaped their identity. One respondent summed up the feelings of persons in this category by explaining that while his name may sound Polish, he was Polish "just by name." Another response typical of those in this category was given by a young white woman from a large Northeastern city who identified her ethnic background as "Irish, Scotch (sic) and German." When asked, however, if these ancestries held any meaning for her she responded,

"No, just when someone says what's your ethnic background." The majority of my respondents reduced their ethnic identity to a list of nations in Europe without the cultural connections. For many whites, citing an ethnic ancestry was culturally analogous to stating that one had been born in California or New Jersey or preferred football over baseball, that is, ethnic ancestry carried little or no cultural weight.

The final category was those respondents who defined themselves as not having a European-based ethnic identity. The twenty-eight respondents (32 percent) who fell into this category eschewed reference to lineage from Europe and instead defined themselves in what they defined as nonethnic terms, labeling themselves as "Heinz 57," "American," "white," or "Caucasian." The responses in this category mirror those given in the U.S. decennial census. Over 13 million Americans in the 1990 census either identified themselves as American or simply did not answer the question. Stanley Lieberson describes this group's identity as having a "recognition of being white, but lack of any clear-cut identification with, and/or knowledge of, a specific European origin" (Lieberson 1991). Subsequent investigation of this nonresponding group suggested that its members did not "feel" ethnic enough to warrant a response. This lack of ethnic affiliation may also explain the almost 1.8 million individuals who defined their ancestry as "white" in the 1990 U.S. census.

A rather surprising finding was that 68 percent of my sample fell into categories where ethnic identity no longer had any bearing on how respondents defined themselves or their day-to-day activities. Respondents in the "ethnicity matters" and "symbolically ethnic" categories were able to draw on ethnic histories in ways that respondents from "name-only ethnicity" and "not ethnic" categories were not. Unlike those who can still draw on real and symbolic forms of ethnicity, the respondents who were ethnic "in name only" or did not define themselves as ethnic at all did not have a repertoire of ethnic experiences to tap. One cannot be nostalgic for a usable ethnic past if the traditions, superstitions, folk wisdom, and stories of family life in the "ethnic neighborhood" have not been passed down from parent to child.

Marcus Hansen's famous aphorism of third-generation return—"What the son wishes to forget, the grandson wishes to remember" (Hansen 1952:492–500)—requires that subsequent generations are told the immigrant tales of migration to the United States: What was everyday life like in ethnic communities? Who discriminated against "our" group and why? What hardship and struggles did "our" ancestors face? What did our ancestors eat? How was home life organized? How was entry into the dominant group and upward mobility achieved? The story telling required to answer these questions have not been told to those now four, five and six generations removed from the immigrant experience. Hansen's adage for the twenty-first century should read: "What the grandson wished to remember, the great-great-granddaughter has never been told." With some noticeable exceptions, the white Americans of European ancestry in this study are exemplars of "straight-line" intergenerational assimilation. The children and grandchildren of Michael Novak's "unmeltable ethnics" have melted rather rapidly into a cultural group that is rather homogenous, discarding almost all of their ethnic background (Novak 1971). For the majority of my respondents, ethnicity was not a salient part of their social identity. However, individuals from each of these four categories of ethnic salience did draw on immigrant tales either explicitly or indirectly through critiques of racial but not ethnic identity politics.

EVERYBODY GOES THROUGH IT: IRISH = ITALIAN = WHITE = BLACK = ASIAN

Tom, a twenty-two-year-old from New Jersey, defined himself as being Italian-Irish-American but does not "have a preference for Italians or Irish or Germans; it doesn't really matter to me." Like Tom, Shannon puts little emphasis on her ethnic background, describing herself as "American but my background is Irish." Both Tom and Shannon do however draw on the white ethnic experience of immigration and their observations that Asians possess a strong work ethic to refute blacks' claims that past and present racism explains contemporary racial inequality. Tom explains that:

> I wouldn't be surprised if people just said [about blacks], "get off your butt, get an education, go to work." These people [Asians] came into this country not having anything. They worked hard, that's how they got here. *There's no difference between what they did now and what my grandparents did eighty, ninety, hundred years ago when they came to this country.* They didn't know anything. They worked hard and survived. They didn't even think of looking at the government or turning to the government and saying this isn't fair because I'm Italian that you are not giving me a job. You know, Koreans work very hard. I've met a lot of Korean people and they are very, very hardworking people.

Like Tom, Shannon also suggests that blacks lack the strong work ethic that made upward mobility possible for white ethnics and Asian-Americans. Tom's response is a example of how the color-blind immigrant analogy is still used by whites first to equate the historical experiences of white immigrants to the experiences of blacks and then to blame blacks for not climbing the socioeconomic ladder as quickly as the whites' ancestors.

When pressed about why she believed blacks see racial inequality where she does not, Shannon said:

> I think that the black people have a very hard time accepting that they are not succeeding because they don't want to work, when they could work and they could succeed just like—I mean look at all the black people who have succeeded in this world—even in this county how can we say

that we're like, suppressing them in any way. I mean look at all the ways you can succeed. I think that they are blaming the wrong people, and I think that the Korean and the Chinese, I don't think they do that.

When asked to clarify how assigning "blame" shapes white attitudes towards blacks, Shannon offers the explanation that whites think:

That they're [blacks] the losers. That they're putting the blame on somebody who's not—it's an excuse for them—it's your fault; it's the white society's fault. I think it just makes them [whites] think less of them. It makes them think that they don't have a work ethic. *I mean when we came to this country no one had anything—I mean they [Asians] had less than the blacks when they came over to this country, way less.* And look at where this country has come. They [blacks] can work just as hard and succeed way above their expectations if they just stopped and looked at themselves.

In these accounts, white immigrants of the past and newly arrived Asians are "model minorities" who succeeded without the help of government intervention. As a discursive strategy this narrative equates the historical experiences of Asians, whites, and blacks and then assigns blame to blacks (or any nonwhites) for not following the same mobility path or achieving economic parity with whites. Talk of institutional racism and discrimination were dismissed as excuses by blacks for not engaging in the type of work and thrift needed to achieve the American Dream. Both these responses are illustrative of what Lawrence Bobo and James Kluegel have termed laissez-faire racism: whites blame blacks for high rates of black poverty by using stereotypes to justify their beliefs ("they don't want to work" and "blacks need to get off their butts") while ignoring the structural conditions that perpetuate such inequality (Bobo and Kluegel 1997). By ignoring how racism is structured into everyday life, many whites are able to view hate crimes or other racially motivated acts as anomalies perpetrated by "a small number of prejudiced individuals (who may be of any race)" (Doane, Chapter 1 in this volume).

Tom's and Shannon's belief about blacks lacking a work ethic or relying on government assistance rather than gainful employment is consistent with national surveys of whites' attitudes towards blacks. A National Opinion Research Center study found that 78 percent of whites believed that blacks were more likely to prefer to live off welfare, 62 percent believed that blacks were less hardworking, 56 percent responded that blacks were violent, and 53 percent believed blacks were less intelligent (*New York Times* 1991).

In an insightful account of how white immigrant ethnic communities were constructed in the early 1970s as the cultural antithesis of nonwhite communities, Micaela di Leonardo outlines the importance of the "model minority" in creating dichotomy between white ethnics deserving of our respect and admiration and the demonization of blacks:

> Model minorities—constructed as various Asian groups and, more re-
> cently, some Latins—are those who "work hard," have "traditional fam-
> ily values," "respect their elders," and thus succeed in the United States
> without any help . . . it is simply an extension into the present, and onto
> different populations, of the ahistorical and antiempirical ethnic report
> card model" (di Leonardo 1999:61).

Several respondents described backgrounds rooted in ethnic traditions with
close ties to immigrant parents or grandparents or living in communities that
were ethnically homogeneous. Mary, a thirty-year-old who grew up in a Polish
and Ukranian neighborhood in Philadelphia, links the "race as ethnicity" perspective to a belief that we have moved to a color-blind society. Asked why she
sensed black-white tensions, she explained:

> I think if the world thought of people as people and if people left the
> past in the past, I think a lot more things could be accomplished. I think
> everyone thinks they have to pay for the sins of their fathers or whatever,
> because every time somebody does want to complain about racial or
> minorities they always go back to when there were slaves in the United
> States. Well you can't blame me. None of my relatives owned slaves,
> so why should I be, like, singled out for that. *My relatives were people
> who came over from Poland who didn't have two nickels to rub together,*
> you know, so I just think it's the past and some people don't want to
> let that go and want to keep saying, well because of this that happened
> a hundred years ago it's everyone's fault. Well it's not. Everyone has a
> chance nowadays to go for an education and everyone has a chance to
> learn.

Mary draws on and equates the hardships her relatives endured as white
ethnic newcomers to the historical experiences of nonwhites. She also believes
that the "chance to learn" is equally available to all and presumably, if taken
advantage of, would provide upward socioeconomic mobility. Joey, a fifty-one-
year-old butcher who grew up in a predominately Italian neighborhood of
Philadelphia, defines himself as Sicilian, although he is half Italian and half
Irish. Joey, like Mary, discerns little difference between the experiences of white
ethnics and those of nonwhites. Joey voices his outrage that blacks are all too
willing to rely on the government for assistance rather than engage in the type
of "honest" work he and his janitor father embraced.

> Like, as far as I'm concerned, this affirmative action to me didn't make
> no sense, cause *nobody gave my grandfather a break* because he couldn't
> speak English . . . he had to learn and he had to—and then my view-
> point again on the influx of immigrants in America today is this . . . my

grandfather came here to put something in America. Today you're taught that the government gives you this, the government gives you that, and they come here and take out.

Joey distinguishes between the hardworking, independent immigrants of yesterday and those immigrants (and blacks) who are viewed as being socially and economically parasitic. Like Joey, Carmelo was also raised in a "traditional" ethnic environment. His parents are Italian, he was raised in an Italian neighborhood, acquired his first jobs through ethnic networks, has some command of the Italian language, and married his Italian high school sweetheart. Although he has since moved to what he calls a "white-bread" upper-middle-class suburb, he owns and operates a very successful and upscale Italian cheese shop in the "Italian" part of the city. Like Mary and Joey, Carmelo embraces an understanding of social mobility that levels racial and ethnic differences:

> You realize that Italians, when they first came over, were treated like blacks think they are being treated. And they think they are the only ones being treated like this. . . . *Everybody goes through it.* Every ethnic group, every race is going through this persecution for being different in the beginning.

Carmelo's historical revisionism allows a story to be told that equates the experiences of blacks and immigrant Italians. Rewriting the past as a place that was equally hostile to all newcomers regardless of race allows some whites to argue that, since everyone started at the socioeconomic bottom, everyone has the same opportunity to achieve the American Dream (Steinberg 1995). Viewing ethnic and racial history as being similar for all groups is, as sociologist Charles Jaret puts it, a "self-serving ideology" because it justifies the structural advantages whites have received because of their skin color (Jaret 1995).

SLAVERY IS OVER: "JUST GET ON WITH IT"

Other young whites did not want to be held accountable for slavery, its legacy, or the ways whites benefit by racial oppression. Slavery was viewed as tragic and regrettable, but it happened "a long time ago." These respondents were oblivious to how the racial caste system, which structured and touched almost every aspect of society, privileged and continues to privilege whites in innumerable ways. References to slavery also provided a comparative historical reference point for some whites to demonstrate how enlightened were their views on race relative to those of their parents and grandparents. James, who "thought" his parents "might" be German or Irish but viewed himself as "just plain old American" was adamant that neither he nor his ancestors were complicit in the slave trade and as such should not be held accountable for society's past sins. When asked why he thought blacks were quick to point out racial discrimination when discussing occupational mobility, James gave this account:

> They want more. They have some crazy grudge about what went on
> with slavery and all that stuff, and they want to get us back for it . . . they
> [blacks today] weren't slaves and they have no right to say that I was a slave
> owner because I wasn't a slave owner. My parents weren't slave owners.
> Your parents weren't slave owners. If you want to make a controversy
> about it and stuff like that, fine, there was a time for it. A hundred years
> ago. It's over. Let it go . . . they say they don't get treated equally because
> they had to go through a long struggle to get from where they were,
> slaves, to get up equal with everybody. But I think the struggle is over.

Unsure of her ancestors' role in slavery, Lori explains she gets "angry when I
hear black people say your people enslaved us—my people, I don't even know
if we were in the country back then. I have no clue." Lucia grew up in a middle-
class suburb outside Philadelphia. Her parents were both born in Italy. She, too,
was angered that slavery continues to be raised by blacks as an explanation for
contemporary racial inequality. Blacks, she laments, should "like, stop living in
the past, with what your ancestors went through and live for yourself. If you
want to make it a better world, then stop fighting a fight that ended a long time
ago. Just get on with it."

If, as some white respondents see it, blacks cannot claim victim status because
slavery, Jim Crow, and institutional racism have been dismantled, then whites
can maintain that white privilege is also a thing of the past. This point was
raised several times when respondents pointed to how much race relations have
changed over the last few decades. Respondents generally believed that inequality
and the lack of access to opportunity were fully addressed in the 1960s. As Jason
put it, "why it is still such a problem when everything is, like, over and done
with since like the sixties." Joe criticized blacks who use the past to complain
about their lack of mobility today. As he sees it:

> they don't know what in the world happened back in the fifties and
> the forties with slavery. They're just going on what they read in books,
> you know, what their great-great-great-grandparents have been passing
> down. They have nothing to do with what happened back then. I don't
> know why they have to keep bringing it up, you know, keep causing
> stuff—well, we were slaves. You weren't a slave. Your great-great-great-
> great-great-great-grandparents were slaves. There is no reason to cause a
> fight now. You know, like Michael Jordan is, like, one of the highest paid
> athletes in the sports business. . . . He gets paid more than the president.
> Michael Jackson. Look at his house. You know. You're black, you're white,
> you're Hispanic, you're Asian. You can do it, too.

For my white respondents, Michael Jackson and Michael Jordan are larger-
than-life examples that race has declined in significance. Joe's equating being

black, Asian, or Hispanic with being white suggests there is no social cost to being a racial minority, nor is there any social benefit to being white. Reflecting on race and opportunity, James explains that "the struggle is over. I think there was a long, hard climb that they took and I think they made it. So let it go, don't keep carrying it on." As Joe reminds us, anyone "can do" the American Dream. Joe sees an America where skin color no longer matters. The irony is the way white respondents explain that race no longer matters for blacks but in real and direct ways matters immensely for them.

Writer Ellis Cose asks this question, which is central to understanding the ideological nuance of Joe's comment: "Life is rough for a lot of people, not all of whom are black, so why, given the advantages at least some African-Americans so conspicuously enjoy, should whites feel any guilt whatsoever" (Cose 1995[1993]:190)?

To feel or express guilt would suggest that whites may have certain advantages in a social system based on the principles of equal opportunity, meritocracy, and color blindness. Ignoring the role of race in American history erases any sense that whites should feel any guilt for the privileges that have provided them with greater economic mobility relative to blacks. As Stephen Steinberg wryly puts it: "No guilt, no obligation to redress wrongs" (Steinberg 1995:59).

Like Joe, Jeff also believes that dwelling on past wrongs is both counterproductive and ultimately unfair to whites. He explains:

> I don't personally feel responsible for my father's sins. Uh, I also don't believe in reparations for something that cannot ever be erased or changed. The past has happened. We can try to make the future better. I don't think that by making me personally pay or by making anybody of my race pay because at one time my race was the perpetrators of sins is going to do anything for the future except keep it going in a vicious cycle.

There is an inherent racial logic in discounting the role slavery has played in shaping contemporary race relations. In order to make the assertion that we now live in a color-blind America where equal opportunity is normative, the social and economic consequences of slavery and the impact of past discrimination on racial minorities today must be negated. Looking back and reconstructing a white ethnic experience that varies little from the experiences of nonwhites creates a happy and guilt-free revisionism where whites did not benefit from the social, economic, and political arrangements of slavery and Jim Crow. The ethnicity-is-race perspective also allows ethnic identity to operate as a carrier of racial group interest. Refuting or denying any historical connection to slavery serves to erase or minimize past and present white privilege. Once this erasure is complete, it is possible to talk of white ethnics and racial minorities as having similar life chances. The ethnic reductionism so central to the "ethnic paradigm," writes David Theo Goldberg:

> reduces racial formations to ethnicity and analogizes the future trajectory of the racial condition to the melting pot experience of immigrant assimilation . . . it takes the formative experience of ethnic groups as generally similar, it overlooks the particular experience in a groups' social constitution of oppressive conditions such as colonialism, slavery, exclusion and in some cases virtual extirpation . . . this paradigmatic disposition to blame the victim implicitly reifies as given the very racial definition of otherness it is claiming to erode. (Goldberg 1993:78)

Goldberg's treatment of the future of race relations is explicitly connected to the past. The color-blind narrative which now dominates political discourse engages in historic revisionism in order to present a story of contemporary race relations where being white is not synonymous with being privileged. It is this denial of privilege and reworking of the past that allows Leslie Carr to argue that "color blindness is not the opposite of racism, it is another form of racism" (Carr 1997).

"BE PROUD OF WHAT YOU ARE . . . NOT OVERLY PROUD"

Suggesting that ethnic identity is an option that whites can ignore or attend to when the situation, mood, or season arises, Mary Waters observes that whites "do not understand why blacks make so much of their ethnicity. They see an equivalence between the African-American and say, Polish American heritages" (Waters 1990:167). Like those whites in Waters's study, many of my respondents felt their ethnicity was primarily ornamental or a way to accessorize culturally. As Waters insightfully points out, the flexibility and play whites have in "choosing" an ethnic identity when the mood or social circumstances warrants do not exist for blacks and Latinos.

Viewing racial identity as a minor variation of ethnic identity, many whites were bothered that racial minorities, particularly blacks, focused on the extent to which they felt race shaped their daily experiences. When asked about her ethnic background, Theresa explains that she is: "Irish and German and English. But I'm not really into it. . . . I just, kind of, I mean, I'm aware of it and around the holidays I kind of get proud of it, but that's it. It's not like really overexcessive or anything."

Not having an "overexcessive" ethnic identity means that Theresa can engage in the kind of ethnic grazing that does not constrain, dictate, or circumscribe individual behavior. She is not linked and obligated to communities that are organized around ethnicity. Expressing an ethnic identity is a private affair. Later in the interview the discussion turned to racial identity politics. In angry tones

Theresa made this point:

> I mean you should be proud of who you are, be proud of what you are, and not overly proud, accept who you are and don't make a big deal about it. I mean, I think they tend to make a big deal out of it. It's like well, I can see that you're black. You don't have to wear the shirt telling me that you are, you know.

Theresa is not part of any ethnic community. The social and political functions ethnicity may have served at one time have in large part been lost or are instrumentally obsolete. She has no ethnic group identity that she can use as a "carrier of group interests." She is unable or unwilling to use her racial identity as a way to discuss racial politics because she might appear racist. She is unable to rely on an immigrant analogy because she lacks the knowledge about the experiences of her immigrant ancestors. The ethnic symbols that Theresa sees African-Americans use to evoke a sense of group solidarity, in this case a black pride T-shirt, do not exist for this admittedly nonethnic white.

Jill, a young white female, defines herself as being a German-American who takes pride in her German ancestry and finds comfort in the German community of the small town in which she was raised outside Pittsburgh. Jill makes the point that expressing an ethnic identity is a valid, legitimate expression for white ethnics, but focusing on one's whiteness is not:

> It's like those black T-shirts they wear, "It's a black thing, you wouldn't understand." I think that's exactly how I think their attitude is toward white people...I mean you could wear something that said "It's a German thing" or "It's a Polish thing," but you couldn't say "it's white thing." Because I guess they view themselves like a huge ethnic culture, and white people aren't really an ethnic culture because their ethnicity comes from Europe or Canada or something.

There is the sense among some whites that there is a double standard that violates two strongly held cultural beliefs. The first is that we are a society based on individual, not group, rights. They feel that race-based organizations or petitioning for civil rights based on group membership is inherently unfair because it subverts deeply help beliefs concerning individual agency, equal opportunity, and the meritocractic ideals. The second point of anger and contention is that blacks could organize around their race, but if whites used their whiteness to discuss race relations they would be viewed as racists. Jen, a middle-class women from a suburb of a large city, was enraged by the way blacks could use their blackness to promote various agendas but whites could not. In an attack on racial identity politics and her perception of a racial double standard, she complains that:

> [the street vendors] had a picture of Jesus, but he was black, OK, now what about if I took Malcolm X and made him white? They'd like, they'd kill me. But that just bothers me. That they can do whatever they want but as soon as we retaliate and say something against them, then they make a big uproar. I mean, I don't really care about the clothes. If they want to say that they're black and proud of it, then be proud of it. But if you want to turn around and say that I'm white or Italian or whatever, that they shouldn't put me down for that, either.

Jill points to what she perceives is a racist double standard. Blacks are able to organize around race, but whites cannot because it would be labeled racist and most whites are too far removed from their ethnic ancestry to draw upon it as a meaningful social identity.

CONCLUSION

Herbert Gans observes that symbolic ethnicity is "characterized by a nostalgic allegiance to the culture of the immigrant generation, or that of the old country; a love for and a pride in a tradition that can be felt without having to be incorporated in everyday behavior" (Gans 1999[1979]:422). Richard Alba notes that "symbolic ethnicity makes few and intermittent demands on everyday life and tends to be expressed in the private domain of leisure-time activities" (Alba 1990:306). In both its symbolic and "name-only" forms, ethnic identity is understood as a personal, private orientation that, like a hobby, makes those who express it feel good. However, ethnic identity, even in its most diluted form is not, as much of the ethnic identity literature implies, benign. Many of the respondents who had little in the way of an ethnic identity or consciousness selectively resurrected ethnic family history to create a rather ahistorical record that equated the experiences of their ancestors with the experiences of blacks. For many of my respondents, ethnic identity was "hidden" and emerged only when, as Ashley Doane notes, the "dominant group interests are threatened by challenges from subordinate groups" (Doane 1997b:378).

Ethnic identity was asserted when white privilege was implied, perceived, or alleged, and that identity was used to reassert, defend, or rationalize those privileges. In this way, ethnic identity performed an important function. Whites could argue that all racial and ethnic groups had a difficult time adjusting to a new nation and had their own set of obstacles and prejudices to overcome. A recent Kaiser/Harvard Survey confirms these beliefs. Almost two-thirds (64 percent) of whites in a national survey believed that whites have not benefited from past or present discrimination and that whites should not be obliged to right any wrongs. The survey also found that 69 percent of whites agreed with the statement: "The Italians, Irish, and many other groups overcame prejudice and worked their way up, African-Americans should do the same thing without any special help from the government" (Kaiser Family Foundation 1997). A recent Gallup poll found that almost 70 percent of whites felt that whites were treated no differently from blacks in their neighborhood (Gallup Organization 1997). Those obstacles specific to the black population, such as institutional racism, voting rights, job discrimination and civil rights were, as many whites see it, addressed and rectified during the Civil Rights movement (Gallagher 1995).

Playing the white ethnic card was the foundation by which some whites could negate contemporary racism and defend white privilege while espousing the American creed of equal opportunity for all. The immigrant analogy rewrites white and black history as being the same, while an all-things-are-now-equal view of race relations promotes the view that we now live in a color-blind society. Once the color-blind narrative is established, internalized, and made hegemonic, it is possible to interpret Martin Luther King's plea that "individuals should not be judged by the color of their skin but by the content of their character" to mean that blacks are racist because they continue to argue that skin color remains an important component of allocating resources and upward social mobility. Not only does laissez-faire, color-blind racism preserve and rationalize white privilege, it ignores the institutional arrangements that maintain white supremacy while framing black grievances as being illegitimate. Ruth Frankenberg suggests "whiteness is often renamed or displaced within ethnic and class namings" (Frankenberg 2000). Playing the "white ethnic card" allows whites with little ethnic identity to rename their whiteness as an expression of ethnic ancestry while displacing the ways in which whites are privileged by their skin color.

11

Some Are More Equal than Others: Lessons on Whiteness from School

AMANDA E. LEWIS

In this chapter I build on Woody Doane's critical appraisal of the whiteness literature (Chapter 1 in this volume) to argue for the necessity of further research and to contribute several theoretical concepts that I think will enrich sociological research on whiteness. As Margaret Andersen (Chapter 2 in this volume) argues, the lack of a sociological perspective within the whiteness literature has too often meant a lack of focus on the "material reality of racial stratification." However, despite agreeing with many of the very real concerns she raises about the field of whiteness studies, I think that there are good reasons (many of those laid out by Doane) to continue to place whiteness under sociological scrutiny. Such research does face some quite real challenges.

CHALLENGES TO STUDYING WHITENESS

In the years that I have taught race relations courses—courses designed at least in part to fulfill university race and ethnic relations or diversity requirements—there is always a moment in the course where I have the following kind of exchange with a student. Near the end of the semester, a white student in the class will express (in some variation) that he/she was "glad to have had the chance to learn about minority groups." When I ask in reply, "What did you learn about your own group?" the response is invariably, "What group?" No matter what we are studying about the history of race relations—about genocide, slave trade, segregation, and so on, these are often read by white students as subjects about others—other people's history, not their own. It was not until I put whites on the syllabus as a specific and explicit topic that this became clearer. This more explicit discussion of the whiteness of whites generated immediate resistance. This resistance on the part of whites to recognizing their own racialness is not unique to college undergraduates.

In the early 1990s, after I had delivered a talk about current patterns of white racial identification, a faculty member in the audience began his comment/question by saying: "You sound like Pat Buchanan." Fundamentally he was asserting that while I might have thought I was studying white racism, it was, he believed, racist of me to talk about whites as a group. He suggested that

I was essentializing race in discussing "white" as if it were a coherent category. He might have had a particularly creative or provocative way to make his point, but he is by no means the only person around making the argument that talking about race is racist. While I vehemently disagree with this last point, his question did raise the importance of theorizing ways of thinking about whites as a social collective that do not imply that all whites are the same, sharing some natural essence.

A third story raises more concretely what the stakes are in doing research on whiteness and racism at the present moment. Essentially, it highlights what it means to try to talk to white folks about race in the current context. In recent interviews with white suburban parents in California, they generally expressed the belief that we should all be color-blind, that they taught their children to be color-blind, and that they for the most part did not care about the color of someone's skin. However, this explicit color-blind discourse was expressed at the same time as other quite contradictory ideas (Lewis 2001). For example, when I asked Mrs. Karpinsky what lessons she tried to impart to her children with regard to race, she explained that she regularly told them that everyone was equal. Later in the interview, however, she provided a more nuanced sense of exactly how equal.

I: Um hm. Do you think it would be a problem for you or your husband, if your daughter marries or you son married someone from a different race.

R: It depends what race . . . I do, to me, Asians aren't—to me it is, I hate to say this, it sounds so prejudiced, but to me it's more like blacks are, African-Americans would be the only . . . to me Asians are just like—white. And I guess I just am realizing I am saying that (laughs). . . . But I wouldn't feel um, uncomfortable at all if my daughter, you know, married a, an Asian person or I wouldn't have felt strange dating an Asian person in college, but I would have felt a little bit—I would have felt uncomfortable dating a black man.

She was not the only parent who expressed rather contradictory ideas in the same breath—everyone is the same, I'm color-blind, but I'd rather be around those with whom I feel comfortable. In fact, her contradictory assertions are emblematic of a particular kind of moment in U.S. racial history in which it is generally not acceptable to express explicit racism but in which people still believe groups are different.[1] Mrs. Karpinsky was similar to the faculty member quoted above and many others today who claim that race is no longer important, that we should all be color-blind, that even talking about race or racial groups is racist in that it perpetuates racial classification. Described variously as the new racism, color-blind racism, or laissez-faire racism (Bobo, Kluegel, and Smith 1997; Bonilla-Silva 2001; Carr 1997; M. Gould 1999), these new racial logics assert a race-neutral social context but do so within a context of persisting racial inequalities across a range of social institutions and daily experiences (Feagin 2000; Oliver & Shapiro 1995).

These color-blind racial discourses have gained prominence at the very moment that many institutional efforts to ameliorate racial inequality are being challenged or abandoned. They are the ideological weaponry of post–civil rights racial projects (Bonilla-Silva 2001; Omi & Winant 1994), what Gramsci has called "wars of position" (Gramsci 1971)—struggles with important implications for the life chances of those still confronting the historical legacy and current manifestations of white supremacy in the United States. Michael Omi and Howard Winant (1994: 56) define a racial project as "simultaneously an interpretation, representation, or explanation of racial dynamics, and an effort to reorganize and redistribute resources along particular racial lines."

As a kind of a racial project, color blindness, then, is not merely about ideas or ways of thinking about race but about defense of a currently unequal status quo. It tells a particular kind of story about the social world ("a representation or explanation of racial dynamics") that necessitates particular kinds of framings of social problems and thus very particular solutions to those problems. In this case, color-blind narratives assert that race is no longer relevant and suggest that any lingering racial inequality is a result of individual or group-level deficiencies (or old problems that will fade with time) rather than a result of current and past racial discrimination. They serve as protection for the existing unequal distribution of resources and as a justification for ending what few programs still exist to try and address racial inequality.

Are we in fact color-blind? Is it becoming less necessary to study race in the United States today? As the stories above demonstrate, many whites do not necessarily recognize their own status as racial actors or consciously identify as belonging to a racial group. This does not mean we should not study race in general or whiteness in particular. In fact, as Doane argues in Chapter 1, the rise of color-blind ideology and the general invisibility of race for whites is indicative of precisely why this work is especially important. In the current moment, where many declare race is not longer relevant and some even argue that it is racist to say whites are members of a racial group, it is particularly important to understand the parameters and functions of whiteness, of what it means to say someone is white.

In this chapter I argue that whites are in fact a "group" of sorts—that not only can we think about whites as a social collective, but we really must. Despite Andersen's very correct caution about the field of whiteness studies, I argue that critical studies of whiteness are essential for struggles for racial equity. However, concurrent with her, I argue that the work we need is work of a particular kind—studies that recognize that studies about race are always studies of power and struggles for material resources. Moreover, given the fact that in many cases whites do not feel they belong to a group, I also argue that it makes sense to talk about whites as a collective only under certain parameters. That is, any attempt to discuss whites as a social collective should do so in ways that do not essentialize—suggest that all "whites" share some unique natural essence or even necessarily a racial identity. In order to demonstrate both the variable meanings and experiences of whiteness and its persistent connection to issues of power and resources, I will draw on some ethnographic data from schools.

Description of Schools and Settings

The data I draw on were collected in three public elementary schools (two urban and one suburban) in California. All three schools were drawn from Hillside, a large metropolitan area in the California.[2] Each was selected with several criteria in mind. I sought to find three different kinds of schools: 1) a fairly typical and diverse urban school (West City); 2) a fairly typical and homogenous suburban school (Foresthills); and 3) a school that was structurally and culturally a bicultural or nonwhite space (Metro 2).[3] By the terms *bicultural* or *nonwhite*, I am signaling more than the racial composition of the students and include also the racial composition of staff, the explicit and implicit focus of the curriculum, and the school's culture and expressed values and goals. In this way, for setting 3 (the biracial or nonwhite space) I looked for a place where, unlike in settings 1 and 2, whiteness was less likely to be hegemonic and where the current racial formation and racial schemas might get challenged. All three were small-to-mid-sized elementary schools and were neither the best nor the worst schools in their respective districts.

Drawn from a larger project (Lewis 2003a), the examples I discuss are meant to be illustrative of the kinds of processes involved in how whiteness works in the everyday rather than to be representative of how this works for all people in all places. Moreover, one of my key arguments is that context will change what is relevant and how racialization works. What does not vary is that race is a part of what is going on in every context within a racialized social system (Bonilla-Silva 1997) and that it is always being made and remade rather than existing forever in some fixed and permanent way. Hence I have drawn on examples that exemplify a particular kind of process or are representative of the kinds of things people talked about.

Who Are We Talking About Anyway: Are Whites a Group?

In many ways current denials of the "groupness" of whites are a variant on a tradition of liberal individualism that denies the reality of groups. In this denial, however, such formulations ignore or obscure the fact of group-based oppression. Importantly, as Iris Young (1994:718) has argued, it becomes impossible "to conceptualize oppression as a systematic, structured, institutional process" if we cannot conceptualize both dominant and subordinate groups as collectivities in some sense. Aside from just my students and Mrs. Karpinsky, some academics have scoffed at the idea that whites are a group, arguing that whites generally do not share a common self-conscious identity. The stakes here, however, are not in claiming that racial groups all have coherent and consistent self-conscious group identities—*none do*—but that they have similar locations within the racial structure—locations that have material implications. Here I am arguing that whiteness is a social location, as opposed to any shared, collective identity.

Following Iris Young's specification with regard to the category "woman," I argue that we are able to talk about whites as a social collective if we draw upon Sartre's notion of seriality (Young 1994; Lewis 2003b). Young and Sartre provide a useful distinction between *groups* identified as self-conscious and mutually acknowledging collectivities and *series* that are passive collectivities. The key distinction here is between the social reality of the material conditions of one's life and a felt internalized identity. For example someone's statement that he or she is "a worker" may not designate an identity so much as a social fact. In her article Young provides a useful example of this distinction. A collectivity of people standing at a corner waiting for a bus stop is a series. They are unified by their shared relationship to a set of objects (the bus or bus schedule) but not in a way that they must recognize or necessarily consider. Their lives and actions are similarly constrained by these objects (e.g., if the bus is late or crowded), but they do not necessarily think of themselves as a "group." If this same collection of people were to come together and to self-consciously organize themselves into a collective to lobby the bus company for better schedules or cheaper fares, then they would become a "group" of bus riders, an active and self-conscious collective, rather than just a "series" or passive collective.

With regard to whites, it is useful to distinguish between various kinds of white collectives, some of which we would define as "white groups" because they come together with explicitly racial purposes (e.g., neo-Nazi, white-supremacist, or even antiracist groups) and others that have nonracial goals and purposes but are still all-white (e.g., many neighborhood watch collectives, community organizations, and children's groups are all-white even though they may not have a self-conscious racial identity or purpose). Although, as in the latter examples, numerous all-white groups do not have explicitly racial goals, their racial composition is not an accident but a result of whites' status as members of a passive social collectivity whose lives are at least in part shaped by the racialized social system in which they live and operate.

The racial composition of all-white settings can result from self-consciously exclusive racial polices (e.g., country clubs that do not allow blacks to join), can just be one of many outcomes from exclusive policies at a different level (e.g., housing segregation shapes who belongs to neighborhood organizations, shops at local grocery stores, attends local schools, and plays at local parks), or can be an outcome of long histories of racial exclusion, even if those discriminatory policies are not actively or aggressively pursued today (e.g., past racial discrimination in the labor market influences what kinds of "work experience" people can draw on today in applying for promotions and better jobs and thus who utilizes executive dining rooms, serves on the board of directors, or attends partners' meetings). Though white collectives may not be self-consciously organized around group racial interests or identities (in fact most are not), their member-ships are not entirely random or accidental. Those who participate are unified at least in part through their similar relation to historic and present-day racial structures.

One of the powerful things about color-blind ideology is the way it naturalizes the outcomes of such racial structures, particularly the whiteness of many social collectives (Bonilla-Silva, Chapter 18 in this volume). Thus, for instance, while organizations or settings that are predominantly black are thought of as "black colleges, black fraternities, black companies," predominantly white equivalents are seen as generic and nonracial.[4] Racialized realities and outcomes are under-stood as natural or merely a result of chance. Whereas in the past many white organizations or collectivities actively policed their boundaries, today many op-erate under a system of *de facto* segregation in which the explicit articulation of exclusive racial policies is not necessary. For example, the fact that many institu-tions and establishments (e.g., schools, restaurants, social clubs, law firms) even within multiracial urban areas are all-white or have all-white clientele is thought to be the result of chance rather than racial practices at any level. Were these in-stitutions to be all-black, all-Latino or all-Asian, understandings of their demo-graphics might well be different. For example, in another interview, Mrs. Grant offered an interesting response to the question of how she would define racism for her children.

I: If, if um, one of the kids asked what racism was, how would you define it for them?

R: Um . . . I guess I would define it that, there's different cultures, and, with different races—um, like Chinese—they have their own culture and their own churches that they go to, and their own food that they eat, and the same way with black people. I mean they . . . like certain things, and when they go to their place of God or whatever, um, it seems to be more . . . when I drive around or whatever, you know you see all these blacks coming out of a church, well that's where they go—I don't know what goes on in there and stuff, but it seems that certain—people seem to gravitate, and, and live in certain areas. I don't know why, but that's the way it, it seems. I mean personally, I don't think that we'd go looking in a neighborhood that was black.

Here Mrs. Grant claims that segregation is the result of happenstance. She doesn't express explicit distaste for others—just a sense that they are a different breed and that it is quite "natural" for people to want to be around people who are like them. This argument that racial inequality is either accidental or a result of preferences which are imagined to be almost natural or innate ("people tend to gravitate") is a central aspect of color blindness and its defense of the status quo—acknowledging our role in creating racism would necessitate having to do something about it.

Moreover, though clearly identifying other racial groups as different, this mother did not have a coherent or self-conscious identity as a white person. When I asked her whether she ever thought of her own racial identity, she explained that she just had not been around it much in her life. The "it" here is a reference to racial others. As far as she was concerned, race was about others. Hence saying that a person is white does not necessarily predict anything specifically about how *or even whether* they take up their social positioning. It does, however, predict something about the relative constraints and expectations they must deal with. In this way, no person or institution within a racialized society escapes the markings of race, but how it marks their life varies considerably. Both individually and in more general ways, what whiteness means varies from one context to the next. For example, not only does whiteness undoubtedly work in distinct ways for homeless white men, golf-club-membership-owning executives, suburban soccer moms, antiracist skinheads, and/or union-card-carrying factory workers, but it also works differently in all-white suburban communities, nonwhite urban spaces, and multiracial progressive political spaces. To illustrate both the variability of the meanings of whiteness in different settings and its consistent role as a signifier of both meaning and social location, I will draw on data from three school communities.

LESSONS ON WHITENESS FROM SCHOOL

FORESTHILLS

In recent ethnographic research in this white, suburban, West Coast community, I found the simultaneous existence of color-blind discourse as the explicit racial logic/talk side by side with quite pervasive color-consciousness in both talk and action. People verbally expressed the idea that "everybody is human" just as they expressed, in various forms, beliefs in group-level racial differences. For better or worse, these were differences that mattered to them—that shaped where they chose to live, whom they wanted their children to marry, whom they chose to play with in the schoolyard, what television shows they liked to watch, and how they understood gaps in achievement. These were not part of contrived arguments to defend privilege but just what they believed "to be true," a result of "natural" instincts to be around people who are "like themselves" or of "cultural differences" in values. In fact, almost all the white people I spoke to rarely, if ever, thought about their own "racialness." In response to questions about what impact they thought race had had on their lives, they said things like Mrs. Grant: "I haven't been around it very much." These patterns illustrate the unique ability of whites today to live their lives in multiple, racialized ways and simultaneously to deny the salience of race generally and not to think about their own whiteness—not to see themselves as racial actors.

That those living in this white suburb situated within a multiracial metropolis fail to understand even their social space as racially coded belies not only the wider reality of the racialized history of suburbanization (Lipsitz 1998;

Massey and Denton 1993; Oliver and Shapiro 1995) but also their own (racially coded) explanations for choosing not to live in the nearby city where many of them work. For example, while none articulated race as the primary factor in deciding where to buy a house, many offered only mildly racially veiled explanations for why they had chosen not to live elsewhere.[5] Existing with the contradictions of living in racialized ways while ignoring or refuting whiteness is in this way made possible by color-blind racial narratives. These narratives resolve such conflicts by providing a seemingly progressive discourse for avoiding race generally ("we are all color-blind; race doesn't matter") and by providing apparently nonracial language (racial code words) for discussing such things as racial preferences when it is necessary to express such desires or to explain one's behavior.

WEST CITY

Unlike Foresthills, the next two school communities are situated within a very diverse city. Both are multiracial spaces; however, while one, West City, is a fairly traditional urban school with 90 percent students of color and a mostly white teacher staff, the other, Metro 2, is a progressive, dual-language, alternative school with over 30 percent white, middle-class students and a predominately Latino staff.

At West City, whiteness had multiple meanings. Bob's son Alex was one of the few white students in the school. Like most of them, he was attending the school temporarily as they made efforts to get him into an alternative school nearby. Bob explained that he worried about his son picking up some of the "city stuff or "macho stuff" from attending West City. As he put it, this comes from the "project kids" who, he sympathetically guesses, "have to be tough to survive." While Alex's family lives in the middle of the Latino neighborhood where most of West City's Latino students come from, Alex does not have any friends from the neighborhood. In many ways the family is "in" rather than "of" the neighborhood. When I asked Bob why Alex did not have friends from nearby (I'd seen a bunch of kids playing outside when I'd arrived for the interview), Bob hesitated, stating haltingly: "Um, I think there's, I guess I should be honest, whatever, I think there's just the difference, you know, um the kids are different here, you know, its um, and a lot of his friends are from go to his old school (a white private school they'd stopped going to when they could no longer afford the tuition) and um people that we can *more relate to* and stuff."

In many different ways Alex receives messages that he is different from those around whom he lives and with whom he spends many hours at school. In school, Alex demonstrated a sense of sympathy for his school peers, but one that was imbued with a sense of separation and distance. This was something Alex's father indirectly explained as one of the things he hoped his son was learning in school. For example, Bob explained that he was initially quite upset about some of the (rather minor) diversity and "get-along" programs the school was doing. However, he'd come to see that it is important for "inner-city" kids:

> I came out of this meeting and they were changing the name and they
> said its gonna be this, this school for diversity and I said, "oh god I
> thought I came here to learn about how they were going to educate the
> kids and this was, you know, this is the day club." . . . But that was my
> first impression of this whole [diversity] thing, is that I was kind of upset
> about it, that they would spend the time trying to get into this whole
> thing about that. And then I heard about this little thing, "get-along
> sessions" or whatever they do on Friday, and I thought "oh God, what
> is this?" But then I think that maybe for a lot of kids it really is an issue
> and that its a good thing to do with a lot of the kids. I thought the most
> important thing was to *educate* them, which I still do, but maybe for
> inner-city school kids that you've gotta do that. Whereas for Alex you
> gotta teach him that there is, that they need help, they need to know how
> to do conflict management, and they need to know how to, how to work
> something out without their fists or whatever. At first I thought "I don't
> want him educated in that, its just ridiculous," but now I'm starting to
> see the sense in it.

Implicit in all of Bob's comments is a clear sense that the black and Latino
students at West City are different from him and his son. He cannot relate to
them, though he does sympathize.

Ascriptions of characteristics to other racial groups did not flow in only one
direction. Students and staff of color had their own notions of what whiteness
meant. One day, while driving three African-American boys (Darnell, Malik,
and Thompson) to watch a basketball game, I explained to them that I had never
been to the school but my understanding was that it was at a pretty "fancy" place.
Malik assured me that it wouldn't be a problem, "Don't worry Ms. Lewis, Darnell
knows how to talk white." Darnell proceeded through a series of impersonations
that the other boys practiced imitating in-between their fits of giggles. Darnell's
impersonations included among others, a haughty, refined accent ("Get me my
slippers, Geoffrey"), a hillbilly voice ("Whaddya say, Billy?"), a sort of military
toned ("alright son") and a repressed sounding teacher ("Okay class").

This particular incident was a window into two clear understandings about
whiteness. Not only did my signal about class status ("fancy") immediately get
read as a racial signifier ("don't worry, Darnell knows how to talk 'white' "), but
the boy's impersonations were almost all voices of authority giving instructions
to subordinates. In interviews, these and other boys talked about whites as people who were sometimes racist, often mysterious, and definitely powerful. The
conflation of race and class or whiteness with access to resources proliferated.
This did not by any means mean that these students of color had any desire to
be white. In several incidents black and Latino light-skinned students got angry

when either mistakenly or in jest called white. Malik wrote a story for Martin Luther King Day saying that he was grateful for King because his efforts allowed him to have white friends like Julio. Upon hearing the story read out loud, Julio exploded out of his seat and yelled "I know you ain't talkin about me. I ain't white." In his case specifically, Julio viewed whites as those who had treated his family poorly when they first immigrated to the Northwest three years earlier. This hostility towards whites was sometimes directed towards the few whites in the school, where the label of "white boy" was used disparagingly in the yard.

In adult discourse, whiteness remained more obtuse as an unspoken referent to the "cultural" behavior of their minority students. As Pamela Perry (2001) discusses, whiteness is often understood as a "postcultural" position within current discourse, wherein "multicultural" is deployed as a code word for racial minorities and thus tacitly labels only people of color as "cultural." To many, then, whiteness involved those to whom Alex's father Bob could easily relate, those whose families spoke in more normal tones, and those who helped their children with homework and sent them to school clean and well fed. Conversely, to many folks of color, "white" referred to those whose behavior the African-American school secretary had to watch carefully and to whom the African-American first-grade teacher had trouble talking. Staff of color were never unaware of the whiteness of the space in which they worked. On more than one occasion one of them referred to West City as a "white" school. Again, West City is demographically a very nonwhite place, but in relation to issues of culture and power it was not whole inaccurate to describe it as "white."

METRO 2

Metro 2 is a quite different community. It is an alternative-school setting in which many progressive teachers work and to which many liberal/progressive families send their children. The school curriculum includes long units on stereotypes, immigration, and the Civil Rights movement. Unlike in other settings, Metro 2 students, including white students, articulated a well-developed sense of history and had a coherent critique of the racial structure. For example, when I interviewed children and asked them to explain why some people are rich and others poor, Metro 2 students talked about how some people inherit money, how some do not have the same job opportunities because of discrimination, how some children get better education and thus have more opportunities to go to college.

There were, however very few—if any—explicit positive notions of whiteness available for kids to draw on (Giroux 1998). The response by many of these white students was to want to be "less white" "a different white" or "not white." For example one fifth-grade boy claimed that his friend's Salvadoran grandmother said that he was practically Latino because he liked her food. He claimed and embraced his "honorary Latinoness."

On the other hand, even though it was not represented as a good thing in relation to history, within the everyday life of the school, white was both in practice and in the social imaginary still a signifier for enfranchised, middle-class, influential families and children. For example, in recent schoolwide battles over school uniforms and school disciplinary policies, positions taken largely by the Latino community in the school for uniforms and stricter discipline lost out to the white middle-class preference for leniency. This is partly about social class, but race is used as a signifier to represent more than just class—it is used to represent the relatively empowered, the category of parents who control much of what goes on in the school, the category of children who have cultural capital and relatively higher skills. In Metro 2, "white" was not used to describe all that was good and virtuous nor all that was oppressive; it was a description of social status, marking who had power and resources. Thus some teachers spoke in very ambivalent ways about how their school also continued to be a "white" space despite many efforts to the contrary.

In all these settings whiteness was many different things—invisible, explicit, normative, conflictual, racist, powerful. Despite this variation/multiplicity, however, it was still a major player in shaping the culture of each space as well as the material circumstances of the lives of all those within. Whiteness was not always the same but it was always present with real implications for those operating in each community.

STUDYING WHITENESS

My overall argument and these examples raise interesting issues about studying race and whiteness in particular. In each case, studying race and white people is not necessarily always going to be about asking them directly, because they will sometimes deny that it has made any difference at all. This kind of work necessitates multiple kinds of data and analytic work and raises some interesting questions. Essentially a central aspect of this work will sometimes involve declaring that race matters for people who claim it does not or inferring racialized practices from differential outcomes. This flies in the face of recent judicial decisions that declared the necessity of showing intention to demonstrate discrimination—racially unequal outcomes were not seen as *prima facie* evidence. This understanding, however, does not reflect how race works today but rather how race worked in the past. Rather than explicitly rejecting (or explicitly discriminating *against*) anyone, it is quite possible for long-term patterns of exclusion to be repeated through the embracing of a select few. In essence the outcomes are identical but the means might be somewhat different.

As Bonilla-Silva and Doane discuss in Chapters 18 and 1, color-blind ideology is a key player in current racial struggles. Not only does color-blind ideology facilitate the ignoring of numerous troubling racial patterns in interactions and outcomes, but it co-opts a racially progressive *aspiration*—color blindness—and asserts it as a *reality*. Racial ideology generally and color-blind ideology in particular, at least in part in the claim that whites are not a social collective, naturalize racialized interactions that privilege whites. These interactions often seem not to be about race at all or to be just the normal way of operating. The unequal power relations that are enacted in such interactions are concealed almost completely. The everyday performances and deployments of whiteness are as powerful and consequential as they are subtle and allusive—in fact, they are often powerful and even more consequential precisely because they are hard to see (Essed 1991; Holt 1995). In Bernard Lefkowitz's (1997) *Our Guys,* we can see one example of the often covert nature of whiteness in action. In discussing the trial of a group of white teenagers convicted of raping a mentally impaired girl from their town, Lefkowitz (1997:485–486) describes the judge's deliberations over the boys' sentencing:

> When he recalled how they had appeared in court and the distress on the faces of their families and friends [the judge] also thought about how he had acted when he was a teenager. He asked himself, How much sense and discretion did I have? He told himself that there was no excuse for what they did, but then, he thought, if it hadn't been for that one horrible day, they would have been someone's all-American boys.

A judge's identification with the defendants provides them with the benefit of the doubt; it facilitates and fuels sympathy for the accused, as they remind him of himself at that age. In fact the boys initially served no jail time for their crime (including using broomsticks and baseball bats to penetrate the young woman). It is this sort of implicit process, in which a key decision-maker looks across a desk and sees someone who looks "like me," that whiteness and racial privilege gets enacted as a system of inclusion. This judge was not acting on behalf of his white (or male or middle-class) brethren but was drawing his intuition from what he knew "to be true." Here he was not acting as a member of a self-conscious group but as a member of a series, a social collectivity of those similarly located in a particular racialized social system. Here, identifying with "same" (as opposed to distancing oneself from "other') lead to a more complex understanding of events, to seeing all sides of the story, to empathy and to the assumption of primary if not inherent innocence (Peshkin 1991).

This assumption of white innocence is perhaps as powerful and possible as corrosive as the parallel assumption of black criminality. There has been much attention recently to the outrageous and pervasive practices of racial profiling which have lead to the targeting of blacks on interstate highways, in neighborhoods, and in stores. As Katheryn Russell (1998) captured in her book, *The Color of Crime,* the image of the "criminalblackman" is powerful, pervasive and destructive. What we too often fail to see is that this image has a negative— the "innocentwhite"—that is the flip side of the racial profiling of blacks. The racial profiling of whites as innocent, even in the face of evidence to the contrary, is one example of racial moments in which congealed histories of generations of racism translate into racial advantage (or disadvantage) today. These kinds of moments are most often recorded as patterns of outcomes in which blacks face some discriminatory behavior. Yet they are also patterns of whites being the beneficiaries of discriminatory behavior on their behalf, affirmative actions of various sorts that regularly give them the benefit of the doubt, allow them to get away with questionable if not illegal behavior, and provide them with the ability to move through the world (and down highways, through stores, and into the executive suite) relatively unencumbered.

Elsewhere I have talked about this pattern of white affirmative action as white symbolic capital (Lewis 2003a). As defined by Bourdieu, symbolic capital relates to symbolic systems that, as the means for making sense of the world, perform the multiple functions of "cognition, communication and social differentiation" (Swartz 1997:83).[6] These symbolic systems function as "codes" that convey deep meanings to those within a particular culture or context and therefore function as instruments of communication and knowledge. They are part of our social language referring to a whole set of social relationships or narratives the significance of which would be unintelligible to an outsider. These symbolic systems also function as instruments of domination in that they provide ways of distinguishing between groups and ranking them. Race can be thought of as a symbolic or signifying system that serves as an instrument of communication and knowledge (tells us things about people before we even know them) and as an instrument of domination that sorts and ranks groups. As David Swartz (1997:84) states: "The fundamental logic of symbolic processes and systems . . . is one of establishing differences and distinctions in the form of binary oppositions . . . symbolic systems, from this perspective, are classifications systems built upon the fundamental logic of inclusion and exclusion."

Race and, specifically within our current context, whiteness can then be considered as a form of symbolic capital—a resource that may be accessed or deployed to provide access to additional resources. As Paul Connolly (1998:21) argues, this can function in a number of different spaces, including schools:

It is clearly the case that white skin, for instance, can represent symbolic capital in certain contexts. Some teachers may be influenced (whether directly or indirectly) by a set of racist beliefs which encourages them to think of White children as being more intelligent and well behaved than Black children. In this sense, having White skin represents a form of symbolic capital which brings with it better treatment and more educational opportunities.

The value of this kind of symbolic capital is demonstrated whenever whiteness provides access to better treatment in a restaurant, better mortgage rates from brokers, a wider range of housing options from a realtor (Ayers and Siegelman 1995; Oliver and Shapiro 1995; Schuman, Singer, Donovan, and Sellitz 1983;

Yinger 1995), or alternatively when it provides shelter from suspicion, freedom of movement, or protection from encumbrance.

The challenge in studying whiteness is to find ways to study contemporary white experience in ways that situate and contextualize that experience—that pay attention to how race functions as symbolic capital, that uncover how racism is deployed in systems of inclusion, that highlight the seriality of race for whites— and that recognize that peoples' material realities are always at stake in racial struggles and negotiations. Race is never merely about signifying difference but about "meaning in the service of power" (Bonilla-Silva 2001:55). Racialization is not a phenomenon only for racial minorities; though the nature of whiteness may enable many whites to go through life without thinking about the racialized nature of their own experiences, it does not mean they are somehow outside of the system they have created for and projected onto others. It is especially important then, constantly to reinsert them into history and into our under- standings of the still appallingly unequal current racial realities, but to do so in ways that are true to the complexity of those realities.

12

Good Neighborhoods, Good Schools:
Race and the "Good Choices"
of White Families*

HEATHER BETH JOHNSON
THOMAS M. SHAPIRO

The community and school decisions that parents make are some of the most monumental decisions in the lives of their families. These decisions, made at critical points along the life course, not only affect the everyday lives of parents and their children but contribute significantly to a family's life chances, their future prospects, and their identities. In a system of persistently segregated neighborhoods and vastly unequal and increasingly resegregated schooling, the stakes are high: accessing "good" schools and "good" neighborhoods is not always easy to do, and ultimately not everyone gets the chance. While these are indeed individual choices, the community and school decisions made by parents are highly structured in a context of systematic socioeconomic and educational inequality.

In this chapter we discuss what white parents say about why they live in the neighborhoods that they do and send their children to the schools that they do, focusing on the role that race plays in their decision-making about two of the most important decisions they will ever make. Here we are interested in understanding what seems to be "going on" in the minds of whites in contemporary U.S. society when it comes to race, schools, and neighborhood choice, and how this mind-set informs behavior and action. This topic is important for understanding the processes through which race and class inequality are reproduced and how structures of segregation and inequality are recreated in everyday life.

Our research findings suggest that the process of school and community choice can be seen as a key mechanism that reproduces race and class stratification. Our data show that white parents' decisions are often based on

*An earlier version of this chapter was presented at a Special Session on "Interviewing Whites about Race" at the Annual Meeting of the American Sociological Association, Washington, D.C., August 12, 2000. Special thanks to the panelists and participants of that session and to Woody Doane and Eduardo Bonilla-Silva for helpful comments and suggestions that contributed to this chapter.

race and made possible by their own race and class privilege. These choices are made within an arena that is rigidly stratified and socially structured to reward those in advantageous positions for making decisions that will further their advantage and similarly situate their children. In this context of inequality, individual family's "choices" serve to perpetuate existing inequalities by passing along advantage (or disadvantage, as the case may be), to the next generation and thus contribute to the reproduction of social stratification.

The interview data presented here reveal depths of racialized actions previously hidden by survey research and public opinion polls. Our data show that in-depth interviewing can encourage candid discussions about race to occur, especially around concrete events in people's lives. We conclude with a brief discussion of the interview techniques and methodological strategies that we believe allowed the white families interviewed for our study to unburden themselves of their genuine and candid thoughts about race.

INTERVIEWING WHITE FAMILIES ABOUT RACE: RESEARCH APPROACH

The data for this paper come out of a larger project on race and wealth in America for which we interviewed approximately two hundred families in Boston, St. Louis, and Los Angeles. We completed interviews between January 1998 and June 1999, identifying participants through a structured snowball sampling method. We conducted interviews with black and white families representing a broad socioeconomic spectrum ranging from poor to working class to middle and upper middle class. Each participating family had at least one school-aged (or pre-school-aged) child living in the home, and we conducted interviews with parents—both couples and single heads of households. Interviews took place in participating families' homes or another place of their choosing and were semistructured, in-depth conversations that lasted between one and three hours each. We asked parents in depth about assets, income, family background, how they came to live where they do and send their children to the schools that they do, and the roles that wealth and race played in their decision-making. The interview sessions were recorded, were transcribed to over seven thousand pages of text, and were coded using NUD*IST qualitative data analysis software. The resulting qualitative data set is extensive, covering a broad range of topics related to the project's focus, and is the first of its kind.

This paper is based on interviews with the seventy-five white families who participated in the study. This particular set of data is uniquely well suited to provide insight into the role of race in the ways that white Americans make decisions about the communities and schools they choose and raise their children in. Our interviews provide clear evidence that race is paramount in the minds of white parents when they make school and community choice decisions for their families. We argue that the role their "choices" play in the social reproduction of racial stratification looms large in contemporary U.S. society.

SCHOOLS, NEIGHBORHOODS, AND RACE: RESEARCH FINDINGS

Laurie: Now it's not necessarily fair and it's not necessarily right, but I think certain neighborhoods are better, certain schools are better, and your children will have a better childhood and better educational background because of where they go. But it's not right. I don't think it's necessarily right, but I think everyone should have the same opportunities my children do, but they don't. . . . O.k., I'll rephrase that. I don't think it's right that my children get to go to a private school and get to wear Adidas and, and, there are other children living in the city who aren't even fed breakfast, who wear raggy, holey clothes, who have teachers who don't want to be there, and they get no educational benefits whatsoever.

Q: Do you feel like race has played a role in any of the decisions that you all have made?

Laurie: I have to be honest and . . . I'm probably wrong for even saying it, but truthfully, it's in the back of my mind, yes. . . . But I do want to clarify one thing. If there was a nice black family who my husband worked with at General Electric and they bought the house next door to us and had the same values and the same desires and goals that we had, I would have nothing, and I wouldn't be afraid to have my children carpool or sit by them. I guess I am racist deep down inside, and I feel guilty for admitting that, but those poor inner-city kids whose parents are on crack and who don't care about them and don't feed them and have drugs and guns lying around for them to bring to school, I'm afraid of them. I am afraid of them. And maybe I want to shelter my kids until they're older and they can handle it better. When they're young, I don't want them to be exposed to that type of situation. . . . Well, I shouldn't say that they have to work at General Electric, they don't have to work at General Electric, but they have to work and have to save and have to strive and try to better themselves. But if they're out selling drugs on the corner, I don't want my kids to be around that. And I don't want my kids being shipped into a school like that. . . . I feel guilty because I'm not doing anything to make their life better or try to help them. I'm hiding out here in my little nice neighborhood and my little private school and I'm like sticking my head in the sand and pretending like these problems don't exist. So I do have a sense of guilt over it.

Laurie, a parent interviewed for our study, lives in a white suburb of St. Louis with her husband and three children. Her explanation of her family's decision to live where they do and send their children to the schools that they do is strikingly candid and reveals a depth of racialized beliefs and action that was not uncommon in our interviews with white parents. For these parents, schools, neighborhoods, and race are intricately tied in complex ways that ubiquitously surround and concretely impact their decisions about community and education.

When asked how they chose their neighborhood, most white parents explained right away that it was for the school district. This is the case even for parents who send their children to private schools and do not use the public school system. For the vast majority of families, looking for a "good" neighborhood means looking for one that is in a "good" school district. And because property taxes fund school districts, residential location and school quality tend to go hand in hand. "Good" schools are in "good" neighborhoods, and "good" neighborhoods have "good" schools.

Barbara, one of the parents interviewed, says that the main reason that she and her husband chose the community they did was "schools for the kids." Paul says: "We looked at the city, and the bottom line was we weren't happy with the schools. We wanted to be in a public school in the county." Another parent explained: "we specifically did not look in certain areas because the school districts weren't that good."

Q: So, did you ask your broker to only look in certain areas?
Steve: Yes.
Q: And the area was south county?
Steve: Yes. Uh, well, specifically, uh, the Lindbergh school district.

These families are trying to make "good choices" for their families, but what do these phrases—"good neighborhoods" and "good schools"—mean to them? Inevitably, in explaining their thinking and decision-making, race became an integral part of parents' explanations. Interviews reveal that almost always, in the case of neighborhoods and schools, "good" is woven with ideas about race, and race is clearly a primary dimension of whites' choices. The specific kind of environment white parents want for their children (or do not want) and attempting to control that environment were integral dimensions of their school and community choices.

Q: How are you going to decide where to live?
Jean: I guess race would affect it a little bit. I don't know. . . . There's some parts of the city and just from the location that they are, and the incomes there, I really wouldn't want her to go to those types of schools. I don't know what kinds of education they have in those schools. I know most of them are probably public, and that would be something I would have to check out. I guess it's kind of sad to say that I would want her in an area maybe, I wouldn't want to say more *white*, but I guess it would really depend on the area, because I mean, it's like I said, there's some places . . . that I would be scared for her to go to school. I'm scared walking down by the school and things, and so I guess it would play a part, just in the fact . . . of where we buy our home.

Our interviews suggest that in contemporary American society, the school and community choices of white families are thoroughly permeated by race.

"WE TRY TO STAY WITH OUR OWN TYPE"

Many of our interview participants displayed open and overt racism in discussing their decisions about where to live and send their children to school. Our data reveal deep levels of explicit racism by whites against blacks in particular. This racism is often translated directly into action: often, in our interviews with whites, race alone was a major explanation for school and community choice, and overt racism itself propelled much of their decision-making.

Such is the case with Merilyn and Duane Fisher. The Fishers have a Nineteen-month-old daughter; Merilyn does clerical/secretarial work, and Duane is a butcher. They spoke openly of having considered moving into only a community that was predominantly or exclusively white.

Duane: My first impression of somebody is probably going to be the color of the skin. . . . Then I go on how they act, what kind of character they have . . . like I said, I wouldn't live in East St. Louis. The crime rate's too high there. There's also the race, you know the one, one race. I hate to say it, but that's, that's the issue. . . . I mean, I don't believe I am a bigot but I mean, in a lot of ways I gotta be because the first thing I think of is, you know, um, type.

Q: What do you mean?

Duane: Type cast, I guess. . . . It's hard not to look at someplace like East St. Louis and say, "well, you know, it's a black community" and people know what you mean when you say that. . . . It means that, um, maybe it's a little run down and the crime rate's a little higher and it's not a very desirable place to even drive through and you know?

Q: So as far as choosing a community, was that a factor for you? Were you looking for more of a white community?

Duane: Yeah.

In terms of school choice, the Fishers say that they *might* consider putting their daughter Sarah into a public school that had *some* black students. They say that as long as the black students "came from a neighborhood that has nice neat lawns and stuff, then it's OK."

Marilyn Masterson is a divorced mother of two children ages twelve and seven who works as a child care center administrator. The fact that the area Marilyn has recently moved her family into is much less racially diverse than where they lived previously is no coincidence:

Marilyn: I've known blacks, I've dated blacks. . . . But, but there is a category, you don't want to call them niggers anymore, but I, it's, it's lower than blue collar, it's a certain mental attitude toward, toward everybody, toward the world. . . . And I see it more in black people than in white. . . . The families aren't together, extended or otherwise, or, or the extended women half of the family are together, raising

> the kids, you know, the unmarried daughter with her baby and the
> mom and the grandmom kind of thing. But there's just not a lot of
> real sticking together protecting their own in, in this particular black
> community . . . the ones I don't want to call niggers.
>
> **Q:**   Is that part of the reason why you wanted to move?
>
> **Marilyn:** Because it is a part of the black population in "U City" [a section of
> the St. Louis metropolitan area] Yes.

Marilyn's openly racist rhetoric may seem shocking, but in fact was not uncommon in our interviews. She, like many of the whites we interviewed, expresses her overt racism with some apologies but at the same time seems to think that her views are completely justified. In explaining their move to a white suburb from a city neighborhood one father said: "We just thought, the *mix* of the group and then all of these people going to the same school, it didn't fit with what we wanted for our family." To avoid exposing their children to people that they find "undesirable" (as one participant explained it), many white parents simply moved. Many others decide to send their children to predominantly or exclusively white private schools.

Other white families find themselves living in what used to be exclusively white neighborhoods but which are now diversifying as more blacks and other minorities move in. In these cases the neighborhood and school discussions were steeped with worry and concern about what this meant for the future of the neighborhood and schools. In such cases the whites we interviewed expressed serious fear and often anger about what they perceive happening before their very eyes: as they see black families moving in, they see their white neighbors moving out. And often even more upsetting to these families is the neighborhood "deterioration" they believe to go hand in hand with the color change of their neighborhoods.

Patricia and James Keady have two children, ages six and three. Patricia is a homemaker and James is a union construction worker. They live in a predominantly white neighborhood but they are worried about "too many black families" moving in. They have decided to leave if this happens, and their incentive is to "get out" before their home's property value goes down. They figure that if they move out "before it's too late" they won't have to take a loss on their house investment. We can see that James and Patricia undoubtedly have overtly racist attitudes, but we can also see that their thinking about community choice takes place in a structural context that will ultimately reward them for acting on those attitudes. They will literally make more money on their house if they participate in white flight.

> **Q:**   Anything that you're unhappy with, or concerns you have about living
> here?
>
> **James:** Just there are a lot of homes going for sale, a lot of homes.

Q: And what's your concern about that?

James: Who might move in.

Q: Who are you concerned might move in?

James: Well, the blacks in the city are slowly moving to south St. Louis. The whites move out, the blacks move in, it turns into a pretty rough neighborhood. Deteriorates and so on. You know the old story. It seems to be moving in this direction. We're concerned how fast it's going to get here. Nothing against blacks, I work with them.

Q: What is it about that makes the neighborhood go down?

James: Don't ask me!—I'm getting out before it gets bad! . . . I think people need to kind of stay where they're in place. I'm telling you, if there's too many black families on the street, when you go to sell this house, you're not going to get what you think, you know? I mean, they don't do anything for property values—

Patricia: You know, we wouldn't move into an area that was predominantly black, or even probably—

James: Puerto Ricans. We're not prejudiced against blacks. I mean—you know, we try to stay with our own type of people.

These are not isolated comments. Similar statements were made again and again in interviews with white parents.

For some, a "good" community and school truly means, at least in part, having a certain amount of distance from people who are nonwhite. Others have shown that perceived risk of crime is directly related to perceived racial and ethnic composition of neighborhoods, and that for whites criminal threat is associated with perceived proximity of racial others (Chiricos, McEntire, and Gertz 2001). Our interviews support this "social threat" perspective by providing insight that moves beyond survey research about attitudes to the real-life mind-sets of a sample of white families. Charlene Quinlin and her husband Angelo are a poor couple with one teenage child. They live in a section of Boston that has for the most part been white working class. They are concerned about the recent influx of blacks into their community. This, in their minds, is not only a problem unto itself, but is also a problem because it seems to be motivating a lot of whites to move out. If they could afford it, they would like to move out too—to a suburb with a "higher class" of people. Here we see the "social threat" perspective in action:

Charlene: I mean, there's a lot of blacks that moved in. That I was starting to worry about, because I was afraid it was going to go down. I'm not prejudiced, but it's just that, I'm sorry, once certain type comes in, that's it! Well, my concern when a lot of blacks started moving in was with the drugs, okay? The pushing of the drugs on your kids. Maybe getting stabbed or something. Or shot. That's where my big

> concern is . . . they do try to make you afraid and threatened. A lot
> of people did move out because of that. . . . I'm just worried about
> it going down more. . . . I know a lot of whites moved out because
> of that problem—"I'm moving out, the blacks are moving in"—you
> know? All of them I met, they started selling their house. This one
> started selling their house. And you know what pissed me off? That
> they're selling to blacks!

This explicit racism is not necessarily class-based. We found such sentiments
to be present in many white interviews representing all points on the socioeconomic spectrum. Mary and Tony Kruger, a well-educated, middle-class couple
from St. Louis, also have concerns about the "type" of people moving in to their
neighborhood. They say that they feel like their neighborhood is "on the edge"
and it may "slip" at any moment because people of "different values" are moving
in. They say that their neighborhood is starting to have a reputation for being
"scuzzy" and Mary wishes that more "regular" people would move in.

Mary: We wouldn't mind people that move in that have education or a little
bit of money, or some sort of value system. . . . I'll tell you quite frankly
what I would look for is more people who look—regular. Because I go to
the shopping centers and there's just a lot of people there that I probably
wouldn't end up relating to. I feel a little bit sometimes like a fish out of
water, like when I'm in the shopping center, I feel like I'm more in an
inner-city slum.

These white families and many others we interviewed spoke of their concerns
about their neighborhoods deteriorating due to blacks moving in and told stories
of their successful "escapes" from such situations. When financially possible,
these families tended to flee to white suburbs or to other predominantly white
neighborhoods with what they consider "decent," middle-class values to raise
their children in. Here, they often find the "safe" schools they were looking for,
away from the "bad elements" and "negative influences," which in their minds
tend to be representative of more racially diverse—but particularly black—
communities. Their choices for neighborhoods and schools—whether acted
upon or simply dreamt about—were often motivated by a clear and explicit
racist belief system. Within a structure of unequal schools and greatly varying
neighborhoods, acting on this belief system is generally rewarded with often
genuinely superior school systems and more ample community resources.

"I Wouldn't Care, but . . . It Just Happens to Work out That Way"

Alice and Philip Hutcheson live in St. Louis with their two children, ages three
years and eight months. Alice describes herself as a stay-at-home mom, and

Philip is a medical resident. Alice and Philip moved to St. Louis from Utah to complete Philip's residency. They chose their neighborhood because they had friends from medical school who lived there, their real estate agent recommended the neighborhood, and it was close to a church they planned to join. In all of these ways, because their social network is white and middle-class, the decision to choose a white, middle-class neighborhood was structurally *encouraged* before the Hutchesons's decision-making (racially motivated or not) ever even entered the arena. But they were also looking for a certain type of neighborhood and were purposely avoiding others; Alice explains her desire to not be in a black neighborhood as rooted in the fact that "the nicer schools are in the white neighborhoods." She describes how their real-estate agent spoke to them of "black neighborhoods" and "white neighborhoods" and how they were told by her: "don't live in this neighborhood, don't live in that neighborhood." Still, when Alice is asked about the racial makeup of her neighborhood, she says she is disappointed by the fact that her neighborhood is all-white:

Alice: It's racially segregated. But I was surprised, because when we moved into this neighborhood, you know, people had said this is a nice neighborhood and stuff . . . and the realtor said that. And I just thought we would have some black neighbors, 'cause I think St. Louis is predominantly black. I thought, "Oh, you know, my kids will, you know, they'll be some black neighbors." And there's no black neighbors. . . . I thought, "Oh!" You know, I didn't want to live in an all-black neighborhood, necessarily . . . but I thought we'd have some black neighbors. And I could tell my family in Utah—"Yeah, we're branching out here." . . . But it's just too bad that it's like that—so segregated. . . . I wouldn't care a bit about having all black neighbors, but I want them to go to a nice school, and since probably the nicer schools are in the white neighborhoods—I mean, they are—so, yeah, I thought that was a factor . . . 'cause I think, "Well, a white neighborhood would have a better school." You know? It's very segregated.

Alice further explained that she "wouldn't care a bit having some black neighbors" but she would never put her children in "inner-city" schools because she has seen reports in the media about school violence and would not expose her children to that. She acts surprised by the degree of racial segregation: on one hand she says that she would not mind having black neighbors and would be proud to "branch out," but on the other hand she believes that the nicer schools are in white neighborhoods so she chooses white neighborhoods only. Alice is telling us that she chose her neighborhood for the "nicer" school and the fact that it is all-white is by default. But the fact that it is all-white is Alice's way of knowing that it is "nicer," and that the schools are "good" ones. Thus race, fundamentally, is a primary dimension of how she and her husband are making community and school choices. The structure of the unequal and racially segregated school system is such that indeed, Alice will be rewarded for choosing the white neighborhood: she will be able to access higher-quality education for her children.

Within this highly structured context, this kind of sense-making and logic in terms of racially defining "good" neighborhoods and schools dominated many of our interviews. In such cases, white families we interviewed stood in contrast to the examples of overt racism above because they were more conflicted in their racialized explanations for school and community choice. While their choices were still race-based, in these cases our white participants explain that it is not racial minorities *per se* that they are concerned about, it is simply the fact that the white neighborhoods and schools are the "good" ones. Eduardo Bonilla-Silva (2001) refers to this type of discourse as "rhetorical incoherence" and finds it prevalent when whites are discussing racially sensitive subjects. Nonetheless, it is no coincidence that "good" equals "white" and "bad" equals "black" in the minds of whites. While this is partially attitudinal, it is also the consequence of a racially stratified and segregated structure within which individual families make decisions. Ultimately, no matter how conflicted they are, the end result is the same as in the cases above: the white families choose to live in, and are rewarded for living in, white neighborhoods.

Jan and Steve Hadley have been married for twelve years and have three children. Jan is the supervisor of a research lab in a hospital. Steve works at a university as a research technician in an anatomy lab. After their third child was born they decided they wanted to move in order to live in one specific school district. Interestingly, even though Steve and Jan say they chose their community based on this school district, they have their children enrolled in private school. They say it was important to them that their children attend private schools so that they would be around "like-minded people."

Q: Can you tell me a few things you find particularly good about the school they're attending now?
Steve: It's a small school. Everybody, um, knows everyone pretty well. Um.
Jan: Fairly similar backgrounds. Um.
Steve: Yeah.
Q: In what ways?
Jan: White, middle class. So.
Q: OK.
Steve: That is a point. There is not one black in that school, is there? Is there?
Jan: No, but there are some, like girls, like Lee's friend Kayla, I mean she's Oriental and they, there are a couple, but as far as, um, African-American, no, there aren't any. So.
Q: Is that something that was intentional?

Steve: No, I mean, it, it just happened. So, um.

Jan: No, it's just, it's based on the churches, you know, the four churches that own the school and—

Steve: Yeah, and, they, they're from the south county area also so, and there just are, there aren't many blacks.

Jan: Unless they are part of the bussing program, and you will find that in the public school system, but not in the private sector. So. And that's, I mean, that's not a problem as far as I'm—see, we have black friends, but it just happens to work out that way.

According to Steve and Jan's logic, "it just happens to work out" that although they supposedly "have black friends," their children have none.

Color is a defining factor in determining a "good" neighborhood and a "good" school. In the minds of most of the whites we interviewed, the whiter, the better. But even more particularly, the fewer blacks, the better. A little diversity doesn't hurt (in fact, it might be nice), but in general our white participants saw the "nicer" neighborhoods and schools as being the least black. They claim that they would not care if racial minorities lived in their neighborhoods or schools but that in the best interest of their children's education it just happens to work out that the best schools and communities are the white ones. This is not necessarily overt racism, rather it is more of a perception-based logic. Others have shown similar findings on whites' claims of the "naturalization of racial matters" (Bonilla-Silva 2001:149) and whites' claims that "segregation just happened" or is viewed as "natural" and therefore somehow "acceptable" (Doane 1996:44). But again, regardless of their explanations, this logic is encouraged by a social structure that rewards white families for perpetuating segregation through their racialized decisions. As one interview participant said when asked about the diversity of the schools with the better reputations, test scores, and facilities: it just so happens that they are "A lot whiter!"

"I'm Not Going to Put My Family at Risk to Be Part of the Solution"

Freda and Flint Frey have three children and live in St. Louis in "the city." When asked where her children go to school, Freda says: "They go to city public school; it's a magnet school, however, which is nice." When asked why her children go to the magnet school, Freda says, "Because I did not want them to attend a regular St. Louis city public school, I think they're horrible, horrible, horrible. But the magnet schools are really great." Freda explains that she likes the magnet schools because they do not "have the magnitude of the, um, behavioral problems that regular city schools have." The magnet schools have a disproportionate number of white students enrolled compared to the regular city schools. Freda says she "feels bad" about this; she thinks it is wrong that the system is so unequal; and she recognizes that there is a "problem of racism."

Freda: The thing is that I really, I really think that racism is horrible, and I would like to be part of the solution. I know that sounds very cliché. But I'm not going to put my family at risk to be part of the solution.

Freda says that she would like to be "part of the solution" by putting her white children into the city schools rather than escaping them like all of the other white people she sees, but she feels that she just can't "risk" it.

Freda: I don't know anybody who's white that sends their kids to a regular St. Louis city school.
Q: Really?
Freda: Yeah, I mean I know there are obviously some but I don't personally know them. Because everyone that I know, if their kids don't get into a magnet, they don't buy [homes] here. 'Cause I know there really are race issues if you're not in a magnet school. It's like, it's just horror stories. . . . The black kids, you know, it's just a real thing, you know? So. Of course, I have to say too, that they are also violent against each other, the black people in these schools.

The Freys have recently decided that they want to move out of the city. They explain that despite their good intentions of staying in the city and "being part of the solution" they just aren't willing to make what they see as "sacrifices" in their potential quality of life and their children's schooling. Even the magnet school "solution" is not powerful enough to curtail the enticing incentives of moving to the suburbs.

But Freda, unlike some other white interview participants, argues that she intends well. Along with a handful of other white families in our sample, the Freys openly acknowledge the racial inequalities they see in the system and talk about wishing they could be part of the "solution." Yet most whites do not challenge a system of school districting and funding that maintains these inequalities. Other researchers have shown through survey research and census data that neighborhood racial composition is indeed directly related to "white flight" and that there is "a gap between attitude and behavior" (Farley and Frey 1994:40). Thus, while the majority of whites currently do support the idea of equal opportunity in the housing market for black families, they will not move into neighborhoods where they will have many black neighbors (Farley and Frey 1994:40). Our work provides the context of those mind-sets. Like many of the other white families interviewed, the Freys are making the same kinds of choices; the "quiet neighborhood" they move to will undoubtedly be predominantly white with white schools. And most likely, despite their desire to be "part of the solution," they will become part of what they themselves identify as "the problem" of racism and residential and educational segregation—and for it they will reap the benefits of superior community resources for their families and superior schools for their children.

WHITE FAMILIES, "GOOD CHOICES," AND RACE: RESEARCH CONCLUSIONS

Our interviews with white families tell us that race is a major factor, if not *the* major factor, in determining community and school choice. This concept is not new, but the data presented here move beyond survey research to give insight into white racialized belief systems, white racism, and ongoing systems of neighborhood and school segregation. Race is a key dimension of how whites define "good" neighborhoods and "good" schools, and the two are so intricately intertwined that they cannot be seen as separate choices. Interview participants were clear about their views, and it is obvious that race looms large in their minds when they make school and community choice decisions.

Some have argued that white racism is on the decline and that race relations have been improving in the United States in recent years (Thernstrom and Thernstrom 1997). But most of the recent literature on racial attitudes and beliefs has disagreed, arguing that while *explicit* racism is on the decline, we have moved into a new era of white racism and racialized belief systems defined as "symbolic racism" or "color-blind racism" (for example Bonilla-Silva 2001; Schuman et al. 1997; Sears, Sidanius, and Bobo 2000; Sleeper 1997). Based on this solid body of quantitative and qualitative research, one may be surprised by the depth and centrality of race to whites' thinking about community and schools revealed in these candid discussions. Perhaps more than anything, this points to how in-depth interviewing does indeed make an important contribution to our understanding.

The interviews documented here were not given time constraints and in most cases were quite long (up to three hours). In most interviews with white participants, they did not begin overtly and explicitly discussing their views on race until far into the interview, with many not including explicit discussions about race until an hour or more into the interview. In some cases, the most explicit racist dialogue occurred in the last few minutes.

Another important methodological point is that in this study participants were asked explicitly about race, questions were probed, and answers followed up on. It seems this is partly why participants' responses were often more explicit than previous research has shown. Prior studies have explored phrases such as "good neighborhoods" and "good schools" as "code words" that enable respondents to maintain "sincere fictions" (Feagin and Vera 1995) of nonracism, but such work has rarely presented data that reveal whites "decoding" those terms themselves. Unless people are pushed to define these terms concretely, it may be possible for them to create a nonracist presentation that rationalizes beliefs and behaviors (for example, on the use of "neighborhood schools" in a school desegregation controversy, see Doane 1996). However, in the case of the research presented here, participants' answers were probed and they were asked to define specifically what they understand "good" neighborhoods and "good" schools to mean. It is therein that we often hear more race-conscious

statements and uncover layers of more explicit racist beliefs and racially motivated actions.

Furthermore, conducting most of the interviews in the participants' homes
seemingly helped to make those interviewed feel more comfortable and at ease
in expressing their views. The participants felt, quite literally, "at home," and
this seems to have contributed to their sense of candidness.

Lastly, it is also important to note that the interviews that solicited the most
racialized discussions were always the ones conducted by white interviewers.
While nonwhite interviewers did conduct some of the interviews with whites
in which racist mind-sets were revealed, by far the most overt and explicit
racist statements were made by whites in interviews conducted by a white
interviewer.

An important dimension of our findings is the fact that *because* the interviews
highlighted here are with white families, for the most part they *do* have relatively
much more opportunity to act on their perceptions. Due to the structurally
advantaged/privileged position of whites as a social group, and in particular
because of the financial capabilities that many of them have in terms of assets,
they are able to make choices and act on their choices in very real ways (H. B.
Johnson 2001; Shapiro 2003; Shapiro and Johnson 2003). Assets enable more
options. This stands in contrast to other social groups, such as black Americans,
who due to structural disadvantages, in particular lack of assets, are not able to
make or act on their "choices" in the same ways. Although everyone, to some
degree, has constrained choices, whites have relatively more choices and are
relatively more able to act on them for themselves and their children. Within
these structural circumstances, "choice-making" by whites can have very real
consequences for the society as a whole.

Neighborhoods and schools are not equal: they are segregated and stratified. Property values differ dramatically, community services and quality of life
differ drastically, and everyone knows that schools are segregated and vastly unequal. When white parents choose the "good" neighborhoods and the "good"
schools, they choose to separate themselves from their black peers. While they
may be colleagues at work, they are not neighbors, and their children are not
classmates. Sometimes this might be unintended: some white Americans would
like to participate in diversity but simply are not willing to sacrifice (as they
see it) the best chances possible for themselves and their children. But sometimes this re-creation of segregation is not a coincidence. As we have seen, white
Americans often conscientiously decide to isolate themselves in white environments precisely to avoid diversity.

Race is on the minds of white Americans, and they are thinking about it in
when it comes to neighborhood and school choice. By making the choices they
do, white Americans reproduce segregation in neighborhoods and re-create segregated, unequal schooling for their children. The opportunities for white families to choose and their individual decisions to choose the "good" neighborhoods

and the "good" schools can hence be seen as a mechanism through which contemporary racial stratification is perpetuated in the United States. The structural context rewards whites for acting in a racist manner and a manner that perpetuates race and class inequality. Most whites do not challenge structural inequality or aspects of it such as systematic school districting and funding that maintains inequalities. Rather they participate, and are rewarded for doing so—often through the unearned benefits of simply being white. Ultimately, if the cycle continues, it is the children of those we interviewed who will go on to perpetuate further the systems of advantage and disadvantage that they are currently reaping the benefits of. One day they too will face the same decisions that their parents explain here.

13

White Views of Civil Rights: Color Blindness and Equal Opportunity

NANCY DITOMASO
ROCHELLE PARKS-YANCY
CORINNE POST

There are few subjects that generate as much conflict in U.S. history as race relations (Kinder and Sanders 1996), and yet few white Americans think race relations is a topic about them. Gunnar Myrdal made the same point in his famous book, *An American Dilemma* (Myrdal 1996 [1944]:37): "One can go around for weeks talking to white people in all walks of life and constantly hear about [the racism of other people], yet seldom meeting a person who actually identifies himself with it." Myrdal's point is underlined by Mary Jackman (1994:137), who argues that racial inequality is reproduced "without active participation by individual whites, and hidden from their view." Thus, when it comes to issues of race, as Jennifer Hochschild notes (1995:55–71), most white Americans cannot understand "what the fuss is about."

The seeming inconsistency between the pervasive concern about racial conflict and inequality in the country but lack of salience for many white Americans is captured in the controversial statement by Stephen and Abigail Thernstrom (1997:13), who claim: "There is no racism; there is nothing but racism." This seeming inconsistency is also empirically evident in one of the most researched puzzles in the study of race relations, namely, that traditional measures of prejudice suggest a growing liberalization of white racial attitudes, while whites continue to oppose public policies that are intended to bring about greater racial equality (See Bobo 1998; Kinder and Sanders 1996; Kluegel and Smith 1986; Sears 1998; Sniderman and Carmines 1997; Schuman et al. 1997). As a result of these unresolved issues, some scholars argue that there is genuine racial progress (Patterson 1997; Thernstrom and Thernstrom 1997), while others— often with the same evidence—argue that racism has just taken on a new or more subtle form (Bobo et al. 1997; Bonilla-Silva 2001; McConahay 1983; Sears 1988; Sears et al. 2000).

This chapter seeks to shed light on the seeming inconsistency by describing the responses of white interviewees regarding their views on racial inequality. Like Jackman (1994), we argue that one of the reasons that white racial attitudes have puzzled researchers is because they have misunderstood the implications of the commitment whites espouse toward color blindness, equal opportunity, and individual achievement. In this paper we argue that the ways whites frame racial issues take attention away from issues of power in the reproduction of inequality, and we also argue that they are mischaracterizations of what actually happens in the lives of people who are privileged by race and social position. Our failure to understand these issues reflects insufficient attention to the need for legitimacy in the reproduction of racial inequality (Jost and Major 2001).

First, as Jackman notes (1994:33–43), the study of race relations still gives primary emphasis to prejudice and/or to racism as the source of conflict among racial groups in the United States. Others have expressed similar views (Blauner 1972; Bonilla-Silva 2001; Wellman 1993), but despite their calling attention to the institutional or structural processes that reproduce racial inequality, they still insist on labeling these processes as "racism" of one sort or another. In addition to institutional racism (Blauner 1972; Wellman 1993), other new forms of "racism" include: laissez-faire, color-blind, everyday, aversive, modern, and symbolic (Bobo et al. 1997; Bonilla-Silva 2001; Essed 1991; Gaertner and Dovidio 1986; McConahay 1983; Sears 1988). In contrast to these efforts to reinterpret the meaning of racism and to preserve the label of racism toward white attitudes, we argue that one of the characteristics of white privilege (McIntosh 1988; Rothenberg 2002) is that whites do not have to be racists in order for racial inequality to be reproduced. Not only do whites not think of themselves as racists, but they also believe themselves to be part of the solution rather than part of the problem of racial inequality.

Second, we argue that there has been too much emphasis on "equal opportunity" (and by extrapolation on discrimination) in policy discussions about race relations, but there has been insufficient attention given to processes of favoritism or inclusion that help whites (instead of harming blacks and other nonwhites). While some may argue that discrimination and favoritism are different sides of the same coin, discrimination is illegal, whereas favoritism is not (McGinley 1997). In other words, we argue that the advantages that whites enjoy because of their access to social and cultural capital and to economic resources protect whites from having to face "equal opportunity"—that is, the market forces—that they so readily see as the solution to the disadvantage of blacks and other nonwhites.

White advantage, however, is hidden from view, because whites are subject to attribution error (Pettigrew 1979) which leads them to believe that they got ahead because of their own personal characteristics (hard work, effort, and persistence) while they cognitively minimize the situational or contextual factors that may have contributed to their life outcomes. Because of this, many whites can believe themselves to be innocent bystanders vis-à-vis black disadvantage.

Third, the focus on individual achievement rather than group relations has taken attention away from the power relations that exist between groups, a point that has been made by others (Bonilla-Silva 2001: Jackman 1994; Tilly

1998; and Wilson 1998). By thinking of their life outcomes as the result of individual choices and values, whites fail to see the relationship in their own lives to the lives of blacks and other nonwhites (Kluegel and Smith 1986; Spears, Jetten, and Doosje 2001). Jackman and Michael Muha (1984) argue that white emphasis on individualism is part of the strategy for deflecting attention from power issues, while Donald Kinder and Tali Mendelberg (2000:44–74) argue that individualism is an inherent part at this point in history of "racial resentment." We find that individualism is deeply embedded in the thinking of most Americans, including whites. Whites can easily point to the things they had to do to get to their current places in life, but they do not at the same time as easily recall the group basis of their life outcomes.

In this chapter, we examine how whites talk about civil rights and equal opportunity to explain why whites cannot understand "what the fuss is about" (Hochschild 1995). We argue that the focus whites give to color blindness and to equal opportunity and their belief that individuals are responsible for themselves have allowed whites to accept the premises of the Civil Rights movement and yet to maintain white privilege, in many cases, "without active participation" and "hidden from their view" (Jackman 1994:137).

RESEARCH METHODOLOGY

Data for this study come from semistructured interviews with 246 randomly selected whites from three areas of the country: New Jersey, Ohio, and Tennessee. Using the methodology outlined by Michele Lamont (1992, 2000), four zip codes were identified in each region, from which addresses were randomly selected. About a third of the participants in each region who were reached by phone agreed to participate in the study. The target areas were identified based on census data pertaining to their relative regional median income, the area's proportion of non-Hispanic whites, the percentage of the area's population holding managerial jobs, and the percentage of the area's population holding a bachelor's degree.

Participants were restricted to U.S.-born whites between the ages of twenty-five and fifty-five. The sample included approximately equal numbers of men and women and working-class and middle-class respondents in each area, although, reflecting the composition of the areas, there are more middle-class interviewees in New Jersey and more working-class interviewees in Ohio than in the other areas. Class was defined by education, with those having a college education or more being defined as middle class or above, and those with less education being defined as working class (McCall 2001).

Most of the interviews (all done by the first author in the last three years) were conducted in the participant's home and occasionally at a public place or nearby university. The interview included a detailed life history of the respondent, starting with high school, to the present regarding education and jobs, plus questions about self-identity, family, intergroup relations, and views of public policy. The interviews averaged about two hours each, and each interview was transcribed verbatim and then coded for analysis.

This study is qualitative and interpretive. It is both grounded in the qualitative data collected for the study and developed through interaction with the research literature. The purpose of reporting on what the interviewees said is to look for themes or meaning content more than to count how many people said what. For the purposes of this paper, we report on the interviewee responses to questions about "changes that have occurred in access to education and jobs in the last several decades" for African-Americans (separate questions were asked as well about such changes for women and for immigrants). This question was purposely worded so as to avoid the use of the words "equal opportunity" and "affirmative action." The question was asked after the interviewee had described his or her own education and job history. Although there was no explicit question about "color blindness" (i.e., color should not matter), it was a pervasive theme in the interviews. The interviewees were also asked toward the end of the interview what they thought "equal opportunity" should mean and then how they would ensure it, if it were up to them. While there are some differences in the interviews with regard to region, gender, and class, on these particular issues the responses are generally consistent.

Cᴏʟᴏʀ Bʟɪɴᴅɴᴇꜱꜱ

When asked about the "changes that have occurred for blacks over the last several decades," the interviewees generally expressed positive views about the Civil Rights movement and disavowed prejudice, racism, or discrimination on the basis of color, although this was less evident in the Tennessee interviews than in the New Jersey or Ohio interviews. Recurring comments in response to the question about changes for African-Americans in the last several decades were "good," "great," "wonderful," and even "not enough." For example, a middle-class male in Ohio said:

> I guess it's about the same, you know. I mean, if people have ability, it doesn't matter what their skin color is or what their gender is. I think they should have the opportunities for education and jobs. I don't think I have any discrimination against groups like that and have no notions that they shouldn't be at school or at certain jobs.

As this interviewee did, most of the interviewees portrayed their own views as supportive of the Civil Right movement and as opposed to "prejudiced people" or to "racists."

When talking about the Civil Rights movement, though, most of the interviewees espoused a general principle of "color blindness." Reflecting these views are claims such as "color shouldn't matter," "skin color is not the way to go," or "a person shouldn't be looked at by the outside, the color of their skin." The interviewees argued that people should be able to do whatever they are capable of and should be chosen on the basis of merit or qualifications rather than for who they are. The notion that outcomes depend on effort and that opportunities should be available based on qualifications or merit largely defines the view of egalitarianism held by these interviewees. For example, a working-class female from Ohio said: "the person qualified, I don't care what color they are, should get the job." A middle-class male from New Jersey provides another expression of color blindness in a very typical statement: "if someone is qualified, I don't care if they are purple, black, green, or white."

These views appear to serve several functions for the interviewees. It makes the interviewees "good guys." Racism and prejudice are attributed to other abstract people, but the interviewees themselves disavow such views. The standards that the white interviewees express are presumed on their part to be universal and impersonal: those who are qualified deserve to get rewarded, and in their view, people generally get what they deserve. The normative language of color blindness, as others have noted (see chapters in this volume, for example, by Doane and by Andersen), allows them to direct attention away from the larger patterns of racial inequality in society and places the responsibility for life outcomes on blacks themselves. For example, when the white interviewees commented on the changes that have occurred for blacks with regard to education and jobs, they prefaced the generally supportive comments with statements such as, "if they can do the job," "if they are willing to work hard," "if they have the qualifications." Some interviewees complained that blacks have not taken advantage of the opportunities they have been offered because of the Civil Rights movement.

The language of color blindness also makes civil rights personal (Emerson and Smith 2000). In this sense, the argument that "everyone deserves a chance" removes the white interviewee from having to think of him or herself as unfair (Bonilla-Silva 2001:137). It conjures up for the interviewee the assurance that he or she has never made a decision about someone based solely on the irrelevant characteristic of race. The emphasis on color blindness allows whites to believe that they are contributing to the elimination of racial problems, that is, by not acknowledging or giving attention to race. Instead, as Myrdal suggested, whites believe race to be an issue only for other people—the "racists"—but they do not include themselves in that category.

EQUAL OPPORTUNITY

The white interviewees in this study frequently argued that everyone deserves an equal opportunity and that no one should be denied opportunity because of "race, creed, or color." For example, a middle-class male from Ohio said: "I think equal opportunity would be to fill jobs and education opportunities without regard to race, gender, age, or anything else." A working-class woman from Ohio said something very similar: "I think everybody should have a chance to try for any job they think they're qualified for." A working-class woman from New Jersey was more explicit. She said: "Equal opportunity is suppose you were black and went for a job. If you are better qualified, you get the job. That's equal opportunity. Too bad on my part."

When it came to their own life experiences, however, many of the interviewees did not themselves rely on equal opportunity. Instead, they sought and accepted special favors, even unsolicited help, and it often made the difference in terms of what they were able to do in their lives. People in their social networks told them about jobs, helped them get jobs, or actually provided jobs. They also provided financial resources and cultural knowledge. In some cases, such help was made available even when the interviewee was clearly not "the best person for the job."

For example, a middle-class male from Ohio said that people should get what they deserve. He also argued that it is not fair if the person with the highest test score is not the one who gets the job. The details of his own life, however, do not conform to these principles. He had flunked out of college, had been fired from jobs, and had failed at several businesses. He even decried the fact that he had never tested his chances in the job market but had instead always relied on the help from family and friends to get jobs. He further reported that his daughter had gotten into law school despite having scores "at the low end of the scale." And regarding himself, he said: "I'm not the greatest student in the world, but I happen to think I'm a pretty good person. If you just looked at my grades, no, I'm not equal to a lot of people. . . . It's more than just my grades, my scores."

Another example can be seen in a working-class man from New Jersey. He was one of the more explicit regarding his negative view of blacks and his opposition to affirmative action. When asked about how he got his own job in the building trades, though, he explained:

> My cousin let my mother know when they were giving out the test, the application for the jobs. So I went down there. And I went to my cousin's job, and I had some of his men on the job put references down for me, because when I went back to the hall, they said how do you know these guys. So I says, well [this fellow], he's my cousin. And he says, all right.

When asked whether knowing when to take the test and having a cousin who could vouch for him helped, he replied, "Yeah, that helps. That helps. But you see, if you don't pass the test, it's not going to help one damn bit."

That is, the interviewees argued that equal opportunity should apply to people in general, but they did not apply it in their own lives. When asked in some interviews about the seeming discrepancy, most of the interviewees minimized or discounted the help that they had received by comments such as: "But that just got me in the door, then I had to prove myself." These attitudes were obviously self-serving, but they are more than that. As Jackman (1994) argues, they also hide or render invisible the privileges that the interviewees have available in their lives. The interviewees in our study, in other words, were subject to attribution errors (Pettigrew 1979), in that they emphasized dispositional or personal characteristics as the basis of their life outcomes while they minimized or forgot to mention the situational or contextual—the structural—advantages of which they were able to avail themselves.

In part because the interviewees were not especially conscious of the help that they had received and in part because they cognitively discounted or minimized it, they primarily constructed an understanding of their life experiences as being the result of their own effort, hard work, and talent. In contrast, many thought of those who had less than they did, and specifically blacks, as being undeserving because, in their view, they had not tried hard enough, gave up too soon, or were not flexible enough. They did not consider that perhaps the absence or lack of the same kind of social resources as they themselves had drawn upon contributed to life outcomes for blacks.

Hence while generally supportive of equal opportunity, many of the interviewees expressed strong opposition to affirmative action. Interestingly, most could not specifically name affirmative action as a policy, but instead, reduced it in their comments to "quotas." The interviewees opposed affirmative action because, they said, the use of policies like affirmative action violated the principle of people being chosen on qualifications or merits without regard to "race, creed, or color." In this regard, a number of the interviewees expressed concern that the government had "gone overboard" and had given extra advantages to blacks in a way that, in their view, harmed whites. Those who raised such issues said that it was not fair because "two wrongs don't make a right."

For example, a middle-class woman from Tennessee said: "I think we find it sometimes going the other direction. We bend over backwards for the minorities and the person that suffers is the white person." Such comments were more frequently heard in the Tennessee interviews, but they occurred in all three regions. The interviewees argued that the policies had done more harm than good and that blacks were getting jobs for which they were not qualified. The white interviewees also expressed concern about lowering standards and about poor attitudes or work habits among blacks hired through affirmative action. Thus despite the generally positive views expressed about the Civil Rights movement and antidiscrimination policies in general, the specific implementation of policies such as affirmative action engendered more negative reactions and even claims about reverse discrimination.

There is another important point, however. The interviewees were also asked later in the interview what they thought equal opportunity should mean if it were up to them. Most said things like: "Best man for the job." For example, a working-class male from Ohio said equal opportunity should mean: "throw color, gender, and everything out. If you're qualified to do the job, then you're qualified." A middle-class male in Tennessee said it should mean: "that the most skilled person gets the job without any other consideration." A middle-class female in New Jersey said: "Equal opportunity means no discrimination against race and creed or your color or whatever."

Despite the claim that equal opportunity should be available to all, when the interviewees were asked as a follow-up how they would ensure that the "best person" got the job, most of the interviewees said that it was not possible. In fact, many did not give a definition of equal opportunity at this point of the interview because they said that it would never be possible to evaluate qualifications without regard to personal ties and employer preferences for whomever they want to hire. In other words, the constant focus on equal opportunity hid the fundamental belief, applied in their own lives, that one cannot eliminate subjective judgment or personal bias in employment decisions.

Individual versus Relational Inequality

In many cases, the interviewees were explicit about their assumptions that no one helped them, even though their life stories suggested otherwise. For example, a working-class male from New Jersey who had been helped into a construction union by his father and then into a more stable job through help from his friends, said when asked whether he earned his place in life: "Did I earn it? Yeah, I worked for what I've got. Definitely. Nobody gave me nothing. Nothing."

Another working-class male, also from New Jersey, received help with every job he had obtained throughout his life. Given his relatively low skills, many of the jobs he got ended with plant closings or layoffs, but he was usually able to find a friend or family member to help him find another one. In one case, a friend also helped him by giving him a copy of the test and answer sheet that he would need to get the job, because he knew that he could not pass the test on his own. Yet, when asked about the reasons for the problems of the inner city, he said: "Bunch of fucking lazy people . . . they think the government owes them something. If you want something . . . you've got to go out and get it. It's not handed to me. . . . They just . . . to me, they're lazy. I mean, point blank. They're looking for the easy way out."

Most of the interviewees assumed that their achievements were due to their own efforts, and they frequently said that people can do whatever they want in life. Others have found that these views are very pervasive in American culture. For example, James Kluegel and Eliot Smith (1986:23) found that the majority of Americans believe in what they call "the dominant ideology," namely, that "opportunity for economic advancement is widespread," "that individuals are personally responsible for their positions," and that the "system of inequality is . . . equitable and fair" (see also Hochschild 1981).

One of the most important implications of these views for our purposes is that the interviewees (and apparently the population as a whole) do not see any relationship between their own life outcomes and those of others. Even more specifically, they do not see the group basis of their advantages and the relationship between their advantages and others' disadvantages. Charles Tilly makes this point as well. He argues that inequality in any society has to be seen with reference to the "cumulative, relational, often unnoticed organizational processes" (Tilly 1998:35). Tilly further argues that processes such as the opportunity-hoarding evident in these interviews reinforce boundaries between "categorical pairs," maintain inequality, and reproduce it. When jobs are passed among circles of friends, acquaintances, neighbors, and family, then those jobs are effectively taken "out of competition" (or hoarded). The result is to leave many fewer job opportunities that can be competed for among those who are not part of the same networks, friendship circles, or social categories. When the interviewees in my study repeatedly argued that blacks should try harder, prepare themselves more, or believe in themselves, they had in mind the image of themselves as having done it on their own. They did not have in mind their own advantaged lives.

CONCLUSION

In this chapter, we argue that white racial attitudes must be seen in the context of how whites live their lives. An affirmation of color blindness allows whites to ignore, deny, or disregard any notion that race matters in people's lives. Because the white interviewees in this study constructed an image of themselves as supportive of civil rights in the form of color blindness, they did not need to face the possible conflict that the acknowledgment of the existence of racial inequality might engender.

Intertwined with white views of color blindness is their frequently expressed belief that equal opportunity is the solution to racial (or gender) inequality. To the interviewees, equal opportunity means that the "best person" should get any given job and that jobs should not be set aside for some types of people over others. Yet the majority of the interviewees in this study had gotten their own jobs primarily through the help of family, friends, and acquaintances, and in many examples, the interviewee was presumably not the "best person for the job." When asked about these issues, the interviewees discounted such help with statements such as: "I could do the job; that just got me in the door." In other words, the interviewees themselves did not rely on equal opportunity. Instead, they sought and used advantage.

The whites in our study also espoused beliefs that opportunities are available for blacks and that they just need to take advantage of the opportunities that are already available to them. When they argued that blacks "should do it the way I did," they thought they were holding up as an example their special effort, hard work, and talent rather than the use of the social, economic, and cultural resources that most had in fact used in their own lives. By forgetting or minimizing their own advantages, the white interviewees failed to see any culpability on their part for the outcomes in the lives of blacks. They thought of themselves more as innocent bystanders than as active participants in the creation, maintenance, or reproduction of racial inequality. In this regard, they espoused what Joe Feagin and Hernán Vera (1995:xi) call "sincere fictions."

The white interviewees in this study argued that people get ahead as a result of their own efforts, hard work, and talent, and they generally believe their own life outcomes to be the result of their own efforts as well. The interviewees, however, are subject to attribution errors in giving more emphasis to their individual effort and forgetting or minimizing the structural advantages and economic resources that they had available. We found that the strong individualism expressed by the interviewees enabled them to miss the interconnection between their own lives and the lives of blacks and other nonwhites. By thinking of themselves only as individuals rather than as part of groups whose lives unfold in relationship to other groups in the society, the interviewees were able to hold themselves blameless and to believe that the reasons racial inequality exists—to the extent that they acknowledged that it did—was because of others, especially because of the actions of blacks themselves or because of the unnamed "racists" to which they occasionally referred.

Because their own advantages were not salient or visible to them, the white interviewees espoused a commitment to color blindness and equal opportunity that they did not adhere to in their own lives. The interviewees did not think of themselves as racists and most of them specifically condemned those who held racist views. Instead, because the white interviewees enjoyed the benefits of structural positioning that gave them access to social and cultural capital and economic resources, they could in a sense have the luxury not to be racists. Their belief that prejudice and racism by impersonal but unnamed others are the source of any continued disadvantage for blacks allowed the whites in our study to believe themselves to be blameless regarding racial inequality and not to notice the structural relationships from which they benefited.

As Jackman (1994:137) argued, by constructing an understanding of life outcomes as the result of impersonal principles like color blindness and of competition and equal opportunity, whites can be "blissfully unaware" of the institutional arrangements that reproduce inequality in their favor "without active participation" and "hidden from view." They can also, as she also argues, "feel quite blameless in the whole affair." This is a good description of what we found in the interviews with whites in this study. The white interviewees were concerned about issues of racial inequality and conflict but they did not think of themselves as participants in bringing these situations about. Further, they thought of themselves as supportive of the solutions, namely, the advocacy of equal opportunity and people getting ahead on their merits, but they were seemingly unaware of the extent to which they gave themselves permission to use advantage from their networks of social resources and of the extent to which they were able to benefit from opportunity-hoarding and other processes by which they obtained structural advantage. With this view of the world and their place in it, whites can continue to be puzzled by the "fuss" that blacks (and other nonwhites) apparently make about the issues of racial inequality.

14

"Racing for Innocence": Whiteness, Corporate Culture, and the Backlash against Affirmative Action

JENNIFER L. PIERCE*

> **Kingsley:** It's like they were just racing for innocence. . . .
> **Q:**   That's a great phrase! Tell me what you mean. . . .
> **Kingsley:** Racing for innocence? Racists for innocence. [He laughs.] It's like they are just working like crazy to convince me that they aren't racist when they know they have done something wrong. But they won't admit they've done anything wrong. You know, "Who me? I'm not a racist." So, they're racing to be the most liberal, most hip, non-racist white guy.
> —Interview with Randall Kingsley (a pseudonym),
> African-American lawyer

Many white, middle-class Americans consider affirmative action as a policy to be unfair because it is alleged to rely on racially based preferences (Dovidio et al. 1989; Drake and Holsworth 1996; Schuman, Steeh, Bobo, and Krysan 1997). Yet studies demonstrate that this same group of Americans choose to live in predominantly white neighborhoods, work in racially segregated occupations, and, if given the opportunity, hire white employees rather than African-Americans (Massey and Denton 1993; Tomaskovic-Devey 1993; Wilson 1997). The gap between their ideals and their day-to-day practices uncovers a fault line in American culture when it comes to matters of race. Middle-class Americans proclaim the virtues of a color-blind society at the same time as they do everything possible to be self-conscious about race and racial matters. What is it that

---

*This is a revised version of my article published in *Qualitative Sociology* 26, 1 (Spring 2003). I would like to thank Robert Zussman, Dan Clawson, and the anonymous reviewers for *Qualitative Sociology* for their critical comments on earlier drafts. I am also grateful to Maggie Andersen, Rod Ferguson, Doug Hartmann, Elizabeth Higginbotham, and Dave Roediger for encouragement and feedback on an early draft. And finally, many thanks to members of the SABLE seminar, especially Jean Allman, Lisa Disch and Jeani O'Brien.

enables the recipients of white privilege to deny the role they play in reproducing racial inequality? In other words, how is whiteness as a structural feature of inequality constituted and reconstituted in daily life?

As George Lipsitz so eloquently reminds us in answering such questions: "The problem with white people is not our whiteness, but our possessive investment in it. Created by politics, culture, and consciousness, our possessiveness in whiteness can be altered by those same processes, but only if we face the hard fact open and honestly and admit that whiteness is a matter of interests as well as attitudes, that it has more to do with property than with pigment" (1998:233). This article contributes to an understanding of our "possessive investment in whiteness" by looking at everyday practices through which it is created, maintained, and reproduced. Borrowing from Randall Kingsley, whom I quote in the epigraph above, I term such practices "racing for innocence."

The race for innocence is a historically specific discursive practice that draws from a broader American discourse, that of liberal individualism. In the United States, the language of liberal individualism enshrines the rights and efforts of individuals and defines social life as the sum total of conscious and deliberate individual activities. This language serves to recast long-standing, systematic racist practices such as discrimination against African-Americans and other people of color in employment and housing into seemingly individual, isolated incidents of personal prejudice. "Collective exercise of power that relentlessly channels rewards, resources, and opportunities from one group to another will not appear 'racist' from this perspective because they rarely announce their intention to discriminate against others" (Lipsitz 1998:20–21).

The race for innocence and the larger American discourse from which it draws informs many aspects of American life. In this chapter, I consider its pernicious consequences among professionals in a workplace, the legal department of a large northern California corporation. As I demonstrate, in this particular social and historical context, the race for innocence is part of the backlash against affirmative action. In popular culture and in the scholarship on racist attitudes and beliefs, white working-class men are often depicted as more rigid in their thinking and hence more likely to display racist attitudes and beliefs (Adorno 1950; Selznick and Steinberg 1969; Fine et al. 1997). Presumably, those with more education are less likely to rely upon stereotypical beliefs. By contrast, my research focuses on highly educated, middle-class professionals—lawyers—who, as I find, are no less likely than white working-class men to display such behavior and attitudes.

In what follows, I begin by reviewing the literature on whiteness studies and affirmative action and elaborate my theoretical point of departure. The next section details the methods used and the historical context for this study. In the third section, I draw from in-depth interviews with white lawyers as well as Randall Kingsley, an African-American lawyer who used to work for the in-house legal department in this corporation, to explore the meaning and consequences of "racing for innocence." His story of leave-taking is told along with the stories constructed by the white men who still work there about his departure from the company. I do so to make an argument about why these white men, by virtue of their social location, cannot see how they contributed to the hostile climate that forced Kingsley out of the department. Further, I contend that it is through such everyday practices that whiteness is reproduced as a structural relationship of inequality in workplaces.

WHITENESS STUDIES AND AFFIRMATIVE ACTION

Whiteness studies has emerged in recent years as a powerful means of critiquing the maintenance and reproduction of systems of racial inequality. As many of these scholars have noted, what is particularly insidious about whiteness is its seeming invisibility (Frankenberg 1993; Lipsitz 1998). Because it is an "unmarked category," George Lipsitz writes, "against which difference is constructed, whiteness never has to speak its name, never has to acknowledge its role as an organizing principle in social and cultural relations" (1998:1). The main thrust of this scholarship is to render this unmarked category visible as a central aspect of racial inequality.

In David Roediger's (1991) influential work, whiteness is theorized as a "public and psychological wage" invoked by mid-nineteenth-century, white, working-class men to garner "public deference" and preferential "personal treatment" vis-à-vis black Americans. In another important piece, legal scholar Cheryl Harris (1993) conceptualizes whiteness as assumptions about who has rights to own property (whites), who does not (American Indians), and those who are objects of property (blacks). And in another historical account, Mathew Frye Jacobson (1998), who provides a history of the political vicissitudes of whiteness, mapping its changing boundaries over three time periods from 1790 to 1965, argues that whiteness often devolves around changing notions of political "fitness for self-government." In all this literature, whether whiteness is defined as a structural position conferring power and privilege (Frankenberg 1993) or as an organizing principle in cultural and social relations (Lipsitz 1998), the central theoretical thrust emphasizes that whiteness is a social and historical construction and is tied to relations of domination and subordination.

Although there have been excellent historical studies on whiteness (Brodkin 1999; Jacobson 1998; Roediger 1991) as well as ethnographic studies that focus on the development of white-supremacist discourses and white racial identities (Crapanzano 1985; Ferber 1998b; Fine et al. 1997; Frankenberg 1993; Gallagher 1995), attention has yet to focus on how whiteness operates within contemporary American workplaces and organizations. Given the contemporary backlash against affirmative action in our post–civil rights era, the consequences it poses for people of color in the United States, and the small numbers of people of color in the professions, the need for such a study is particularly crucial.

In the literature on affirmative action, there has been little discussion of whiteness. But even more significantly, there are few actual empirical studies of the implementation of affirmative action policies or their effectiveness. Much of what has been written about affirmative action until quite recently has either been philosophical debates about "fairness," legal histories, or polemical tracks (Cahn 1997; Jones 1991; Martinelli 1989; Skrentny 1996). Although scholars on both the left and the right have written personal narratives about how affirmative action has helped or hurt them (Carter 1991; Rodriguez 1982; Steele 1990; P. Williams 1990), with the exception of William Bowen's and Derek Bok's (1998) influential book, *The Shape of the River: Long Term Consequences of Considering Race in College and University Admissions,* there have been very few systematic empirical studies that consider its implementation, its effectiveness, or the experiences of its beneficiaries.

My intent is to bring these two literatures together to examine how whiteness operates in a workplace with a federally mandated affirmative action program. My focus is on the effectiveness of this particular program and how it is experienced by those who benefited from it and those who did not. Analytically, whiteness is theorized as a set of unequal social relations and practices. Randall's metaphor, "racing for innocence," nicely captures my conceptualization of whiteness as reiterated through practice, a doing that is often unwitting in its reiteration of power and privilege.

METHODS

Data were collected over a two-year period in 1988 and 1989 and again over a one-year period in 1999 in a large in-house legal department with more than 150 lawyers within a large company in the San Francisco Bay area that I call Bonhomie Corporation (BC). Over the past thirty years, this company has been one of the largest and most successful businesses in the Bay area. Positions within its corporate hierarchy range from entry-level factory, sales, and clerical work to jobs at higher levels requiring college and professional degrees such as an MBA or a law degree. Compared to other large companies with an in-house counsel, what makes this one unique is its federally mandated affirmative action program, which was created in the early 1970s when a federal court ordered the corporation to implement an affirmative action program in response to a lawsuit filed against it for race and sex discrimination.[1]

The first phase of my study was an ethnographic investigation focusing on the gendering of occupations and legal workers. Data were collected through three means: nine months of fieldwork as a participant observer in the legal department; informal interviews and formal in-depth interviews with lawyers; and an analysis of company documents, such as records about the affirmative action program, and lawyers' résumés.[2] My field notes record page after page of negative comments about the alleged effects of the program. In the legal department, some of the white lawyers complained about "those unqualified clerks in the file room" who, as they observed, "just happened to be black or Latino [and female]." In fact, the adjective "unqualified" popped up time and time again in public conversations as a code word for racial or ethnic minority employees. Job candidates with unremarkable job histories were "unqualified" when they were African-American but "could use a boost up" when they were white men. Bad jokes about affirmative action abounded: "It's our quota system for lazy people." For the most part, white employees told jokes like these to other white coworkers in less public settings such as someone's office.

Historically, it is important to note that in 1989, when I began my fieldwork, a backlash against affirmative was already well under way across the United States. At this time, the media focused its attention on the culture wars on college campuses, the attack on multicultural education, and so-called "reverse discrimination and the "plight of the white male victim" (Feagin and Vera 1995). At the same time, there was a resurgence of a conservative agenda with Reagan and Bush in the 1980s, which led the assault against the welfare state, welfare recipients, immigrants, and affirmative action. (Chavez 1998; Hondagneu-Sotelo 1994). In addition, the small gains African-Americans had made in the corporate world through the affirmative action of the 1960s and 1970s were being eroded by the decisions of a more conservative Supreme Court during the Reagan and Bush years (S. Collins 1997; Higginbotham 2001). In the 1980s and 1990s, the numbers of African-Americans in corporate managerial positions in the United States declined sharply. Then, in the fall of 1995, the majority of California voters endorsed the so-called California Civil Rights Initiative (or Proposition 209) which was designed to end racial and gender-based preferences in employment and education in the state. California was followed by other states, such as Texas, that began to consider initiatives to repeal affirmative action programs and considerations. In this light, a California corporation provides an intriguing and timely window into raced workplace dynamics in our post–civil rights era.

By 1989, BC had improved the representation of racial and ethnic minorities as well as white women in the lower echelons of the corporate hierarchy in sales and in factory work. However, the corporation had been less successful in meeting goals and timetables for managerial positions at higher levels. In the litigation department where I conducted my fieldwork, three attorneys were African-American and forty were of white or European-American ancestry. Nine attorneys were women: eight white and one African-American.[3]

In 1999, the second phase of the study involved contacting the forty three lawyers who had worked at BC in 1989 when I first met them, and reinterviewing them. The turnover rates over the ten year survey period for both African-Americans and white women were higher compared to those of white men: 100 percent, 75 percent, and 60 percent respectively. Of the three African-American lawyers who had worked there in 1989, all three had left the firm. I eventually located these three individuals and interviewed them (see Table 4). Of the eight white women who had been there, six had left. I interviewed the two who remained at BC as well as five of the six who had resigned. Of the thirty two white men, thirteen were still employed at BC. Nine of the thirteen agreed to be interviewed, and I located fourteen of the nineteen who had departed for

Table 4 Interviews with Lawyers Who Stayed or Left (N = 43).

	WHITE WOMEN	WHITE MEN	BLACK WOMEN	BLACK MEN
Original	8	32	1	2
Number Stayed	2	13	0	0
Number Left	6	19	1	2
Interviewed	7	23	1	2
Unable to Interview	1	9	0	0

other positions. Overall, thirty three of the original forty three individuals who had been in the litigation department in 1989 were interviewed.[4]

Interviews began as job histories and often lasted from one to two hours. They were taped, and tapes were subsequently transcribed. The interviews drew from a general guideline and followed the same format but were open-ended enough to allow flexibility.[5]

My analysis compares the narratives of African-American men who left the litigation department with those of the white men who remained. In the following section, I begin with the interviews with white male litigators and their views on affirmative action. Next, I provide a lengthy interview excerpt from Randall Kingsley (a pseudonym), one of the African-American lawyers, because it best represents the stories told by the African-Americans who chose to leave and it also sets the stage for role Kingsley came to play in subsequent interviews. I use the term narrative purposefully to emphasize the socially constructed nature of the material from my interviews.[6] As I will demonstrate, Kingsley and the white litigators tell very different narratives about his departure from the firm, stories that not only reflect their different standpoints and personal biographies but also draw from larger cultural narratives about professional success and, implicitly, about race.

As in most professional legal settings, the numbers of African-American men are quite small in this occupational context. My intent, however, is not to generalize about the experiences of black men as litigators but rather to thematize critically and problematize the data relative to my theoretical questions about how race shapes and gives meaning to professional lives and to extend and reconstruct existing theory about how whiteness operates in this particular organizational context (cf. Burawoy 1991).

RACING FOR INNOCENCE

The majority of white male lawyers who worked in the litigation department from the late 1980s to 1999 described their work environment and their work in quite positive terms. Most expressed loyalty to the company and emphasized the role it played in building their careers. They described their success in terms of the legal cases they had defended and won, the increasing respect they had garnered over the years, their pride in their homes and families, and their sense of satisfaction in having worked hard and done well. This is not an especially surprising finding: people who leave jobs are more likely to have done so because they are unhappy or recognized better opportunities elsewhere, while those who stay are more likely to enjoy their work. These interviews took a surprising turn, however, when I asked them to talk about the firm's policy for affirmative action. Here, their upbeat, often self-congratulatory narratives of determination, hard work, and the rewards of success stopped short with long, uncomfortable silences.

The most common response to follow these lengthy silences was to complain in hushed tones about "having to be careful" about what was said at work. In probing for details, I often came up against either their reluctance or embarrassment to be to give a specific example. Here is a typical exchange from an interview with Jonathan Galaskiewitz (a pseudonym), a fifty-two-year-old white lawyer:

Q:	Be careful about saying what?
Galaskiewitz:	Oh, you know, certain things, you just don't say certain things.
Q:	But like what?
Galaskiewitz:	Just certain kinds of things, you just don't say them.
Q:	But what? I really don't know what you mean. Can you be specific?
Galaskiewitz:	Certain things, you know, you just don't say certain things, you can't make, um, [pauses] make certain comments or jokes, things that used to be, you know, okay. It makes me feel [pauses], it makes me feel like I am walking around on eggshells all the time, like I might say the wrong thing.
Q:	But what would be the wrong thing? You mean a joke that might be racist or sexist?
Galaskiewitz:	Well, no, I mean, I don't tell those kind of jokes. [Pauses,] But you know how it is, some people take every little thing personally— they're offended by the most innocent remark. I don't know, it's hard to say exactly, but I feel like I have to watch everything I say.

What is striking in this interview is how an otherwise articulate and highly educated middle-class man whose work requires him to make forceful arguments suddenly becomes stumbling and inarticulate. In fact, I often had the sense in interviews like this one that lawyers wanted to say much more but were afraid, as Jonathan said, of saying the "wrong thing," of saying something that might be construed as racist. For many white Americans, "color blindness," continues to be the " 'polite' language of race," and Jonathan's oblique references to "certain comments" is constructed in such a way that can hardly offend anyone.[7] However, there is more than simple politeness to his response. His stumbling language, "certain things, you know, you just can't say certain things," poses a contrast to his first person descriptions self-assertions of earlier in the interview—for example, "I worked very hard to make senior counsel," or "I won the case hands down." This shift to third person subtly operates to remove him from these seemingly presumably delicate conversations as if to imply "it's about what you all say, not me." And when I ask directly whether he's referring to racist or sexist jokes, his immediate response is: "I don't tell jokes like that," suggesting that he is not responsible for such behavior. He further deflects responsibility from himself in the next sentence by pointing the finger of blame at others: "some people take every little thing personally." Implicit throughout are not only the difficulty and discomfort he has in talking about race and racism directly (he actually never even mentions either word) but the sense that he, as an individual, is not responsible for such problems.

A few others who initially appeared uncomfortable with my questions explained the legal history of the company's policy to me in lawyerly terms and added that such a program was either unfair or no longer necessary because "things were better." But even in these legalistic discussions, their reluctance to say what they really thought and their defensiveness about the company's reputation for diversity came through. Here is one exchange I had with Randall's former supervisor, Sam Nelson (a pseudonym), a fifty-four-year-old lawyer, an exchange that became more and more heated as I probed for specifics to his evasive answers:

Q: Can you tell me what about this policy is unfair?

Nelson: Well, sometimes positions go to people who are unqualified. So it takes jobs away from people who are.

Q: Not qualified in what way?

Nelson: That they're not qualified. That they don't have the expertise.

Q: Do you have someone in mind?

Nelson: [Long pause.] Well, no, not really.

Q: So, none of the lawyers hired here lack expertise?

Nelson: [Quietly answers] Well, no.

Q: So, you're talking about affirmative action in general as opposed to what's happened here?

Nelson: Uh, huh. Uh, huh.

Q: Well, let me ask again, um, in a different way. How do you feel about the program here?

Nelson: I guess I would have to say it's outlived its usefulness.

Q: Because?

Nelson: Because things are better. Things are so much better. Look, we hire minorities. That's more than you can say for a lot of firms in the city.

Q: And you don't have any problems with their qualifications?

Nelson: I never said that I did! I never said that. [His tone becomes increasingly angry.] Look, the problem is with all these government regulations about who we're supposed to hire. I resent like hell all these regulations. [He repeats his criticism of regulations several times.] . . . Things are better here.

Q: So, about how many of the lawyers in this department are white women or people of color?

Nelson: I don't know. [Pauses, then says definitively] A lot. I don't have the exact numbers at my fingertips. You'll have to check with personnel.

Q: Well, what about retention issues? Do you know how many people have stayed and how many people have left?

Nelson: Look, you'll have to check with personnel. I don't keep track of these things. But I have to say, it's really not unusual for anyone to leave. It's a long haul to make senior counsel [the equivalent of partnership] and lots of young attorneys drop out along the way. They decide that corporate law is not for them, they want to move on, get different experience, better jobs, other opportunities or they just don't have what it takes.

Q: Yeah, I know that's true. I mean, I know it's difficult to make partner. But I was wondering, you know the ABA [American Bar Association] has published statistics about women and minorities in law, and the percentages who make partner are still very small nationwide. And, I was wondering, what your sense of that [the percentage of women and minorities who make partner] was here? I mean maybe not the actual numbers, but your sense of. . . .

Nelson: [He interrupts me,] Look, I already told you, I don't know the exact numbers.

Q: I know, but I was wondering. . . .

Nelson: [He interrupts me again,] But I will say this, if these people don't want to stay here, it's not my fault. If they want to move on, there's nothing that I can do about that.

Q: So some minorities have left?

Nelson: [With exasperation,] I don't know the numbers.

Q: But you do know someone who left?

Nelson: [Sighs loudly and pauses] Yes, I do remember someone who left. A young attorney named Randall. African-American. And yes, he left for a better job. And I've heard that he's done very well for himself. Now, I am sure you can appreciate that I am a very busy man and I don't have time for any more questions.

As in the other interviews I had conducted with these white men, once I raised questions about affirmative action and the retention of people of color, the upbeat progression of the narrative altered, the rapport I had worked hard to maintain broke down, and, in this case, I was summarily dismissed.[8] What's interesting about this interview is Sam's insistence that "things are better," despite the fact that he does not have the "exact numbers" to support his claim. The more I probe about numbers and retention of people of color, the more defensive he becomes, until he finally says: "if these people don't want to stay here, it's not my fault." As I mentioned earlier, the turnover rate for the 1989 cohort of African-Americans was 100 percent—a retention rate of zero. Furthermore, when I checked with personnel, I discovered that the percentage of litigators of color in the department in 1999 was 3 percent—one African-American and one Latino. So, despite Sam's claim, in numerical terms at least, things were actually not better but slightly worse.

Of additional interest in Sam's narrative are not only its factual inaccuracies but also its emotional tone and construction. The defensiveness and anger, and finally, his abrupt ending of the interview, all suggest that my questions about race provoked discomfort. Furthermore, like Jonathan, Sam moves to absolve himself of responsibility—it's not his fault if lawyers leave the department. This is an interesting sleight of hand. If Sam is not the perpetrator of racism, then the blame lies elsewhere. He is innocent. This theme of their innocence and blame of others resurfaced in almost all the interviews with white lawyers when I brought up questions about affirmative action and race.

In contrast to Sam's indirect references to race, the African-American litigators I interviewed talked frankly about race and racism at work. Moreover, unlike the narratives of hard work and professional success, the African-American lawyers who left the litigation department told stories of marginalization, alienation, and then exit from the company. In what follows I draw at length from Randall Kingsley's narrative not only because it best represents their narratives but also because his name came up in so many of the interviews.

In Kingsley's interview in 1998, he describes himself as "a sort of jack of all trades." Most of his cases are employment disputes, but he also does the occasional personal injury case or a simple will for a friend, or provides advice about getting a divorce. Though he enjoys his independence as a solo practitioner and finds his work interesting, he complains: "It's often difficult to make ends meet." His annual salary in 1998 was $47,000. In 1989, when I first interviewed Kingsley in the litigation department at Bonhomie Corporation, he was making $45,000. Although it would be inaccurate to describe him as downwardly mobile, he still practices law and considers himself to be "solidly middle-class"—within the stratification of the legal profession, he has moved from the top tier of highly paid corporate law to the lower strata of the lower-paying practice of the solo professional. Ten years have passed and he is making only $2,000 more a year than when he first left law school.

Kingsley's work history, like those of many other black professionals, began with the opportunities opened up by affirmative action programs and policies in the late 1960s and early 1970s (S. Collins 1997; Higginbotham 2001). In 1985, after he finished law school, he applied for jobs in several big firms in employment law, and he was eventually offered one position in the district attorney's office in Oakland and another in the litigation division within the legal department at BC. Both were known for hiring blacks and for their affirmative action recruitment policies. He decided to take the position at BC because "the salary was better and the opportunities seemed greater." Four years later, when he left BC, his initial move was not up but rather a lateral one to a legal department in another large corporation in the South Bay. His salary was commensurate to what he was making. "It had a good reputation as a kind of progressive place, but it turned out to be very conservative." In 1993, he decided that he had "had it" with the corporate environment and opened his own practice with an old friend who is also African-American from law school. Kingsley's reasons for leaving BC are, in his words, "a long story:"

Kingsley: Part of it has to do with how they hype their affirmative action program there. [He adopts a booming announcer voice:] We have the best affirmative action program and we are all one happy family. Diversity is excellence. Rah, rah, rah.... [He returns to regular voice] But they don't really believe that. It's just assumed that if you are black then you can't possibly be qualified for the job.

Q: So, did you feel like affirmative action was a kind of stigma there?

Kingsley: Yeah. In their heads, it went something like: "minority" equals "affirmative action hire" equals "unqualified." I don't mean everyone thought this way, but enough people did to make it matter.... So, yeah, it was disappointing. I mean part of the reason I went there was because they have a reputation for having a good [affirmative action] program. You know, it's like they made mistakes in the past, but they did something about it.... And, uh, to be completely fair, they did improve a lot some areas like clerical, sales, and craft [factory]. But there still aren't a lot of women and minorities in management level positions. In litigation, I was one of three African-Americans in the entire department....

Q: So why did you leave?

Kingsley: It started with a lot of small stuff, and the small stuff just added up....

The small stuff began when Sam Nelson, the head of the litigation section, whom Kingsley described sardonically as "pretty liberal for a white guy," gave him his first assignment, legal research in an area that lay outside Kingsley's area of expertise. Kingsley expressed some concern, but Sam told him not to worry about his inexperience in this area. "There's a whole department here of folks to help you out." "So I decided against my better judgment to take it on and get some help from some of the other litigators in the department." When Kingsley first approached one of the white lawyers, Bill Fischer, he was cool and brusque, and told Kingsley that he was "too busy." In the meantime, Kingsley, who felt he was "being brushed off," decided to approach other senior litigators in the department for advice.

Kingsley felt that these men reacted indifferently or even negatively to him and heard from some of the secretaries and paralegals that they joked among themselves about his style and manner. He experienced this undercurrent of resistance in different ways. One attorney lost a key memo Kingsley had spent days researching, another made jokes whenever Kingsley came into his office, still another ignored his remarks in meetings, and another "forgot" a lunch date he made with him. He began to see these multiple interactions as many small acts of discrimination and harassment. Moreover, it was clear to him that the new junior associate, who was European-American, was not treated in the same way. He began to feel alienated from his colleagues, isolated, and angry. His story of leave-taking continues:

Kingsley: So, I finally decided to call them on it. First, I went back to Sam and asked him why he had given me this assignment at the beginning. I wanted to know why my first project was outside my area. I mean I had been hired to do labor law and they had me working on a patent case? He got really defensive and he had all these excuses. Then I said that I felt like no one was really mentoring me, you know that they weren't helping me. And, I knew that Todd [a young, white, male attorney] was getting all kinds of help. He made more excuses. I said that I wanted to know what was going on. You know, because this was an incident of differential treatment. I used those words, "differential treatment," very carefully. Oh, he got so mad. He started yelling, "Are you calling me a racist?" And then [later] he tells everyone else in litigation that I said he was a racist and they all start acting weird— really nice, but really defensive.... Suddenly, Bill, who is like, you know, a cold fish, is like, saying hello all the time and telling me how he was really busy when I stopped by asking for advice. And how he was really sorry if there was any misunderstanding. And by the way, did I know that he belongs to the ACLU? ... And Ralph kept saying over and over that he really forgot that lunch date with me, "it doesn't have anything to do with [pause], you know...."

Q: It doesn't have to do with the fact that you are African-American?

Kingsley: Yeah, that's what he meant, but he wouldn't say it. So after that they all started doing it. It's like they were racing for innocence.... And things just got weird. It seemed like either I did the wrong thing or people just reacted weirdly to me.... And so I decided to move on.

The stories these European-American attorneys tell about Kingsley's career trajectory since he left the company are quite different from his own. Recall that Sam Nelson, his former supervisor, says that he is doing very well for himself. Bill Fisher described Kingsley in less flattering terms, saying that he had "cashed in on all the opportunities available for minorities" and had landed a much higher-paying job at another firm. He also confided that he found

Kingsley "demanding" and "abrasive" and doubted his "qualifications from the beginning," but hastened to add: "This assessment has nothing to do with the fact that Randall is African-American." Other lawyers told me that Kingsley had taken a much better job somewhere else, though they could not tell me the name of the firm. One remarked that he knew Kingsley must be doing well because "he's driving one of those BMW convertibles now." (He actually owned a Japanese economy car.) Although they all agreed that Kingsley was a "go-getter," they made disparaging comments about the way he dressed—"he's too flashy"—and complained about his requests for help—"he's too demanding." For these white men, each of whom has had two, maybe three, interactions with Kingsley, the issue was reduced to one of style and personality, and Kingsley just didn't "fit in." (Given the racially skewed proportion of lawyers in this workplace, white lawyers were likely to have had only a very small number of daily interactions with Kingsley.) He wore the wrong clothes, he said the wrong things, and he was much too obvious as a "go-getter." For them, each individual meeting with Kingsley was an isolated incident.

Looking at his leave-taking from the standpoint of the two groups—the perspective of the white male attorneys and Kingsley's perspective as one of three African-Americans—demonstrates that what looks "individual" to members of a dominant group is often "experienced as systematic bias by non-dominant group members" (Calvert and Ramsey 1996:470). This helps in part, to explain, why many of the white men I interviewed claimed to be innocent of racism. They are "innocent" in the sense that they are oblivious to the consequences of their actions. They simply do not experience the sum total of their actions toward Kingsley or their statements about him. Because they can treat each meeting as an isolated incident, it is difficult for them to see how making jokes or comments about his style of dress can be construed as racist. They simply act out of a sense of their right to act. As a consequence, they fail to see how they participate collectively in constructing what Kingsley experiences as an unfriendly work environment.

Their narrative of Kingsley's experiences fits neatly within the framework of individualist thinking.[9] They look at everything Kingsley does as an individual action, a product of "free" choices, individual will, and hard work. Kingsley left because he either chose not to "fit in," as one lawyer contends, or lacked the qualifications to begin with, as another suggests. On the other hand, Kingsley, for whom the majority of interactions have been with these white men, sees a pattern in their behavior, a practice and disavowal of everyday racism. What he experiences as systematic and unrelenting forms of indifference, derision, and exclusion, the white lawyers insist are isolated or individual events. Analytically, his story is a sociological one about the reiteration of whiteness through practice, a doing that is often unwitting in its reproduction of power and privilege, while theirs is a liberal individualist one, invoking Kingsley's failure to live up to liberal individualism's ideals.

In explaining the divergence in perspective between these two groups, my analysis in the last two paragraphs treats these narratives as equivalent accounts. However, there is additional evidence to suggest that Kingsley's story of departure from BC is in some sense a "truer" one. Much of his story is supported by observations and comments I recorded in my field notes ten years ago, such as the unfriendly joking by white attorneys about the affirmative action program and its "unqualified minorities," discussed in the methods section of this paper. In addition, I have detailed notes about lawyers making fun of his style of dress, about the day the memo he wrote was lost by another attorney, and counts of the number of times his comments were ignored in meetings. I was also able to verify his employment record and salary after he left BC.

By contrast, there are many inconsistencies in the white lawyers' narratives about Kingsley. They misrepresented (to me or perhaps to themselves) the kind of position and salary that Kingsley had after he left the company. And most, like Sam, were unwilling to discuss the specifics of Kingsley's departure from the company. Their inconsistent accounts, the reluctance to discuss why he left, and the defensive tone running through their interviews all suggest more complicated circumstances surrounding Kingsley's departure from the firm than the content of their narratives reveal.

CONCLUSION

> The American dream is innocence and clean slates and the future.
> —Toni Morrison, "A Conversation with Miriam Horn"
> (1987).

This chapter has argued that racing for innocence is a discursive practice that functions simultaneously to deny accountability for racist practices at the same time that everyday racism is practiced. This "race" surfaced in the defensive narratives white men constructed in their interviews, such as Sam Nelson's insistence that "things are better" when in fact the numbers of lawyers of color in his department continued to be quite small, or in white lawyers' collective insistence that Randall Kingsley left for a better job opportunity when, in his own account, he left because he faced an unfriendly working environment. From all indicators, his new job was a lateral move, not an advance. This "race" also appeared in African-American lawyers' descriptions of white lawyers' behavior toward them. They all provided accounts of being "brushed off" by white lawyers who were too busy to advise them but not too busy to assist other white junior colleagues and who became defensive when asked to explain their lack of interest. They also shared stories about forgotten professional or social engagements with white colleagues who, when asked about these missed appointments, recited their credentials as "good" white people who belong to the ACLU and have a black friend or even a distant relative "who is married to one." Because these collective and systematic practices of exclusion and denial typically remain unchallenged, whiteness continues to be maintained and reproduced as a structural relationship of inequality in this particular workplace.

Interestingly, the narratives white lawyers told about affirmative action are in many ways similar to those of white working-class men in other studies who viewed affirmative action as a threat because they saw their jobs being "taken away by people of color" (Fine et al. 1997). While these white men were not quite this explicit—they were more likely to launch a general critique about the alleged unfairness of the program, to invoke the problems of bureaucratic inefficiency, or to point to a seemingly ambiguous shift in the etiquette of workplace interactions—they arrived at a similar conclusion. For them, affirmative action was not necessary because people who work hard will reap the benefits of their initiative and efforts.

In this way, we can see how racing for innocence also draws from the larger cultural discourse of liberal individualism. By defining social life as the sum total of conscious and deliberate individual activities, these white lawyers are able to ignore the very systematic practices they themselves deploy, practices that exclude and marginalize African-American lawyers. Despite their insistent denial of responsibility for the small numbers of people of color in the litigation field, a hostile work environment, or Kingsley's departure from the firm, these narratives are not entirely seamless. The emotional tone of embarrassment and defensiveness running through them suggests that something is unsettling their stories, "a seething presence, acting on, and often meddling with taken-for-granted realities" (Gordon 1997:8). What is it that, in Avery Gordon's sense of the term, "haunts" and upsets their accounts?

In her influential study, *White Women, Race Matters,* Ruth Frankenberg (1993) found that, when confronted with race and racial issues, many of the white women she interviewed retreated into what she terms a "polite language of race," a color-evasive response which refuses to invoke racial terminology and yet insists that race does not matter, a practice Eduardo Bonilla-Silva (2001) has recently termed "color-blind racism." What appears to haunt these color-evasive accounts, then, is the understanding that recognizing race might be construed as racist. But why is it that recognizing one's culpability in racist practices, however small or subtle, is so difficult for them to acknowledge?

In her provocative article, "The Trickster's Play: Whiteness in the Subordination and Liberation Process," Aida Hurtado (1999:226) suggests that we: "lack an elaborate language to speak about those who oppress—how they feel about, think about it. . . . Missing in the puzzle of domination is a reflexive mechanism for understanding how we are all involved in the dirty process of racializing and gendering others, limiting who they are and who they can become." Given this nation's ideological emphasis on democracy and equality, it is not surprising that white Americans have a difficult time talking about power. Americans often assume that we live in a "classless" society; we presume we are all equal under the law. In this respect, white Americans are "innocent" of power.

Stories of innocence have long been part of the mythology about America's history and heritage. In American studies, the theme of "innocence" is central in the early historiography on America as an exceptional nation, a nation uncorrupted by the forces of feudalism and aristocratic excess, as "innocent" and unmarked by history, and as "innocent" of imperialism and fascism (Marx 1964; Miller 1953; Smith 1950). And stories about racism and genocide are profoundly shocking, as Coco Fusco (1995) reminds us, because they deeply upset white Americans' notion of self as good and tolerant people. Calling attention to the race for innocence draws attention to the profound denials white Americans must construct to ignore the experiences of racial and ethnic minorities. It is an embarrassing reminder of the part we play, unwittingly or not, in the collective construction of white privilege and power. By naming and acknowledging whiteness' haunting presence, we can begin to develop a reflexive mechanism for understanding "how we are all involved in the dirty process of racializing others (Hurtado 1999)."

15

Blinded by Whiteness: The Development of White College Students' Racial Awareness

MARK A. CHESLER
MELISSA PEET
TODD SEVIG

In this chapter we examine the precollege and in-college experiences of white students as they express their understanding of their own racial group membership and their views of other racial/ethnic groups. Whiteness develops and is affected by changing social conditions and discourses about racial issues. The current series of debates and litigation around race relations on campus is a particularly powerful part of the societal and university context in which racial identity is played out.

This inquiry into whites' racial consciousness brings together literatures on white racial attitudes and white racial identity and links them to changing cultural patterns. Racial identity is the meaning attached to self as a member of a group or collectivity in racial situations, and individuals may express this identity differently in different circumstances (Cornell and Hartman 1998). Since identity is formed by class and gender as well as race, there are many ways of being white or any other race/ethnicity. Racial attitudes and changing attitudes are the statements of a person's preferred views or positions about others and about contemporary (or historic) policies and events. Attitudes are also shaped by one's social location and are expressed differently in different circumstances. Social and institutional structures and cultures provide the limits and opportunities for both the creation of racial identities and the formation and expression of racial attitudes.

Throughout, we present the voices of white students attending the University of Michigan, a university with a tradition of student, faculty, and administrative engagement with issues of racism and affirmative action. Recently, Michigan has become one of the nation's battlegrounds for competing narratives and institutional policies around racial matters. The data reported here were gathered from white students of varied backgrounds in individual and small-group interviews conducted between 1996 and 2000. Although they are not geographically, temporally, or in terms of cohort representative of other white students' racial consciousness, they are useful windows into the ways in which racial processes become visible and are expressed.

Background

The social and cultural context of the modern university is one of racial plurality but also of racial separatism and tension. Students come to these settings from racially separated and often segregated neighborhoods and communities (Bonilla-Silva and Forman 2000; Massey and Denton 1993). For many, the university is the first place in which they have sustained contact with a substantial number of students of another race. Although there are more numerous formal and informal opportunities for racial interaction and growth in the university than in most secondary educational environs, white students' lives in these environs are often not very different from their separated lives in previous home and school communities (Hurtado et al. 1994).

In these collegiate circumstances, white students are often confronted for the first time with the need to think about their own racial location. Having been socialized and educated at home, in their neighborhoods, through the media, and in previous schooling to expect people of color to be different, less competent, and potentially threatening, most young white people are ignorant, curious, and awkward in the presence of "others." Some may be aware of their racial group membership and identity, but others may be relatively unaware. Furthermore, during this developmental stage of late adolescence and early adulthood, students' identities as racial beings, as well as their racial attitudes, are subject to challenge and change. Hence it is important to understand the potential developmental trajectory of students' views as they move from their communities of origin to and through diverse collegiate experiences.

Recent explorations of whiteness suggest that changes in the economic, political, and cultural landscape have promoted greater self-consciousness about race. As a result, for many students the invisibility of whiteness, the notion that white is normal and natural, has become harder to sustain. Challenges to white ignorance and/or privilege have also increased some whites' sense of threat to their place in the social order and to their assumptions about their lives and society (Feagin and Vera 1995; Pincus 2000; Winant 1997). Discussions of historic privilege, structural inequality, and racial oppression have caused some white students (and college administrators and faculties as well) to question their enmeshment in pervasive (if unintended) patterns of institutional discrimination. In addition, institutions that now see the education of a diverse citizenry as integral to their missions of education and public service are struggling to make changes in the demographics of their faculty and student bodies, curricular designs, pedagogical tactics, student financial aid programs, and support services.

CONTEMPORARY THEORIES OF WHITE RACIAL
ATTITUDES AND IDENTITIES

In the context of these shifts and struggles, scholars have described and explained the genesis and nature of whiteness and white racial attitudes and experiences as well as the developmental aspects of white racial identity and consciousness. When understood in the context of larger patterns of institutional racism and changing cultural narratives about race, these identity and attitude frames are useful guides—heuristic devices—to understanding white racial consciousness and conceptions of whiteness itself. However, almost all interpretations and typologies of white attitudes and identities focus on their views of "the other" rather than on views of oneself or one's own racial group. That is, surveys of racial attitudes generally ask white people about their views of or prospective behavior toward people of color or race-related policies, seldom inquiring into whites' views of their own racial selves or of their earned/unearned status (i.e., privileges).

Similarly, most white identity development models focus on how whites view people of color rather than themselves; thus their racial identity is conceived as a reflection of their views of "the other." The stance that overlooks one's own race and focuses on others' can itself be seen as a manifestation of the "naturalness" and dominance of whiteness. Certainly one's views of the other and of the self are interactive, and people learn about their racial identity and attitudes in an interactive context, but one's views of others (or of the meaning of others' race) and one's views of themselves (or of the meaning of their own race) are not the same thing.

Originating from models of black racial identity development and using similar terms, white identity models fail to attend seriously to the quite different ways in which whites of different social classes and genders experience and incorporate race into their personal identities, especially how they do or do not account for their power and privilege. The lack of attention to multiple identities and to the reality of intersectionality is a serious limitation (Myers et al. 1991; Sevig et al. 1993). Most people carry multiple identities (a race and a gender and a class, etc.), and often both an agent (privileged) and a target (oppressed) status. These multiple and intersecting statuses are, after all, the social contexts within which individual identity and interpretive schemes about race are grounded and negotiated.

Despite these shortcomings, theories of white racial identity occupy significant space in the literature of psychology, youth studies, and college development. They add an important developmental perspective to the generally cross-sectional nature of attitude studies. Although the work on both white identities and white attitudes needs further refinement and test, both help us understand how racial ideology, discourse, and the positionality of dominance are expressed in white students' construction of racial experiences on college

Table 5 Comparison of Theoretical Categories of Racial Attitudes with Theoretical Stages of White Identity Development.

ATTITUDE THEORY		IDENTITY DEVELOPMENT STAGE
Old fashioned racism	$\longleftrightarrow$	Unawareness/acceptance of stereotypes
Modern/symbolic racism	$\longleftrightarrow$	Questioning/confusion/dissonance
Aversive/self-interested racism	$\longleftrightarrow$	Reintegrative/dominative
Color-blind racism	$\longleftrightarrow$	Liberal/pseudo-acceptance
Liberationist/anti-racism	$\longleftrightarrow$	Integrative/internalized/anti-racist

campuses. Identities and attitudes are the microsites where macrolevel phenomena take root and lead to interracial behavior.

Indeed, we suggest that the categorizations of white racial attitudes toward "others" and of white racial identity development often parallel one another (See Table 5).

The notion of white racial "identity stages" suggests a developmental process that generally proceeds as follows (Helms 1990; Rowe et al. 1994; Tatum 1992): 1) from racial unawareness or conformity to traditional racial stereotypes, sometimes called an "unachieved" racial identity; 2) through questioning of these prior familial and societal messages, with attendant confusion, dissonance, and perhaps even "overidentification" with the other and attendant rebellion; 3) to retrogressive reintegration, where white culture is idealized, others are rejected, and a racially "dominative" ideology holds forth; 4) into a generally liberal (sometimes called pseudo-) acceptance or tolerance of people of color, often accompanied by adherence to notions of "color blindness" or denial and conflict around remaining prejudices; and 5) it is hoped to an antiracist stance, wherein understanding of others' oppression and one's own privilege is (more or less) fully integrated into a personal worldview called an "autonomous" or "integrative" white racial identity (at this stage the literature's focus begins to be more on whiteness than on the other).

However, as Thompson (1994) points out, it is often empirically unclear just what is meant by "development": does it imply temporality (change), cumulativity (one stage building on another), directionality (without reversal), or all three? And does one's location in a given stage vary by the social situation in which action occurs (home versus school, a monoracial setting versus a multiracial setting)? Despite these questions, it is obvious that identity change can occur, and this is one of the advantages of a developmental approach.

In contrast, research on whites' racial attitudes and behaviors has often gone beyond monolithic notions of whiteness and has explored the ways in which whites' views differ as a function of gender, age, and socioeconomic class background. Moreover, studies of attitude change often compare responses over different time periods, showing general shifts in public opinion. More focused studies of change have examined the effects of particular organizational, curricular, or student life interventions. However, very few longitudinal studies exist that clearly identify changes in individuals' racial attitudes over time or historical circumstance.

One historically prominent descriptor of white racial attitudes is "old-fashioned racism," involving the expression of traditional negative prejudice, bigotry, and stereotypic beliefs about the inferiority or even dangerousness of people of color (Dovidio and Gaertner 1986; McConahay 1986). Many surveys of white attitudes indicate that this explicit form of white racial belief has largely disappeared from the American scene or has gone underground and is no longer acceptable as public speech (Schuman et al. 1985). When encountered in the form of heated conversations, graffiti, slanderous writings, and verbal or physical attacks, these orientations are defined as aberrant and are shunned and sanctioned. White racial identity theorists have labeled these examples of "old-fashioned racism" as a form of naïve, unaware, or "unachieved" racial consciousness, steeped in notions of superiority and conformity, and contiguous with a notable lack of contact with or exposure to people who are different.

More common contemporary expressions of white racial beliefs have been labeled by scholars as "aversive racism," demonstrating an internal conflict between beliefs in fair play and egalitarian values and remnants of prejudicial beliefs about (or aversions to) people of color (Dovidio and Gaertner 1986). Closely related to aversive racism is "symbolic racism," wherein negative feelings about people of color are expressed primarily at the policy level (Kinder and Sanders 1996; Kinder and Sears 1981; McConahay 1986). Here ideological commitments to American traditions of meritocracy and individual achievement are expressed in opposition to what is seen as preferential treatment or "special rights and privileges" provided to people of color. Both the aversive and symbolic forms of "modern" racial ideology contain substantial ambivalence about the fairness of policies targeted to assist historically disadvantaged classes. To the extent that such ambivalence or conflict produces discomfort with racialized situations, a lack of awareness or even denial of prejudice and discrimination is often evident. Hence much of the content of these "modern racist" views is tied to what identity theorists have called disintegration or dissonance, marked by uncertainty and questioning of traditional stereotypes (Rowe et al. 1994). It is usually a product of some direct exposure to diverse people and debates about race and racism.

Implicit in several of these theories is the notion that many if not all attitudes, including racial attitudes, are based upon some degree of individual or group self-interest and position (Bobo 1999; Bobo et al. 1997). The self-interest or "laissez-faire" theory argues that white people gain from their overtly or covertly racialized attitudes and behaviors. These gains may be material (greater access to good jobs, educational opportunities, or public facilities) and/or symbolic (an increased sense of personal or group esteem by disparaging others). This attitudinal approach emphasizes whites' role as sustaining agents and beneficiaries of discrimination and oppression, even if they are unaware of its impact on themselves or on people of color. This sense of personal or group self-interest has surfaced recently in whites' expressions of a sense of "victimhood" or reverse discrimination in response to alleged losses due to the unearned advances of people of color (Pincus 2000). In the racial identity literature this category of white racial belief is labeled as reintegrative or dominative; however, it is seldom tied to the notion of self-interest or group position, perhaps because that framework is much more rooted in sociological than psychological traditions of inquiry.

Another common form of racial attitudes is captured in the notion of "color blindness," a rhetoric that professes not to see or be aware of differences between people of different racial groups or to minimize differences that do exist. Typically, whites link this view to a particular interpretation of the writings of Dr. Martin Luther King, Jr., proclaiming their desire to adopt here and now his vision of a society that judges people on the basis of the "content of their character, not the color of their skin." Since it is impossible for people truly not to "see" skin color (unless that color is indistinguishable from "white" or pinky-yellow) and therefore apparent racial difference, this unawareness is hard to sustain rationally. In racial identity development terms the color-blind view is seen as a more sophisticated form of unawareness or as liberal pseudoacceptance of the racial other. Recent governmental and federal Supreme Court policies promoting a Constitutional basis for color blindness help establish this as a permissible and legitimate stance on race, thus providing a historic context and structural support for such individual responses.

Given increased collegiate attention to racial injustice and the desire of some people and advocacy groups to challenge institutional racism, it is not surprising that some young white collegians are becoming more conscious of their racial membership and its privileges. Such consciousness is likely to be painful, as it requires acknowledging both systemic advantage and personal privilege and enmeshment (historically and contemporarily) in structural or institutional discrimination and oppression. A few scholars have pointed to the emergence of a "liberationist" or "antiracist" form of white racial attitudes, wherein white people acknowledge and grapple with their accumulated racial privileges and their role (intentional or not) in sustaining white advantage and the domination over people of color. The racial identity literature refers to this belief/action system as an integrated, autonomous, introspective, or antiracist racial consciousness.

Despite the limitations of these two literatures, they do help describe and illuminate white racial consciousness. The stages represent categories or types of white racial belief, in much the same way as do theories of white racial attitudes. The utility of these two frameworks is increased when we apply them to particular historic circumstances and situations; racial identities, attitudes, and (inter-) actions occur within specific organizational, cultural, and historic contexts. In particular, the milieu of the contemporary university serves as a context for both buffering and reinforcing societal messages and norms in the lifespaces and mindspaces of white students and their peers of color. It also can serve as an arena for challenging prior messages and experimenting with new racial identities, learning new meanings of whiteness, and expressing new forms of racial attitudes and behaviors.

In the following section, we examine the development and expression of these racial identity stages and these sets of racial attitude theories in the words of white students who are reflecting on their precollege and in-college racial encounters.

WHAT DO WHITE STUDENTS BRING WITH THEM TO THE UNIVERSITY?

In interviews, white students discussed the neighborhoods and schools in which they grew up and the effect these largely segregated experiences had on their conceptions of themselves, race, and racism. The major themes that characterize their precollege experience are lack of exposure, subtle and overt racism, racial tokenism, and lack of successful role models of people of color:

> I never really think about the fact that I am white. I just think that it is fortunate that we don't have to think about it, you know what I mean? It is one of the perks of being white.

> I consider myself white, but I don't think about it. The only time I think about it is when we have to do these dumb forms and think about what race we are.

According to Janet Helms (1990:3), racial identity is "a sense of group or collective identity based on one's perception that he or she shares a common racial heritage with a particular group." If the students above never thought about being white and didn't feel a sense of shared racial heritage, they could not possibly develop a self-conscious racial identity; they were at the unaware stage.

White students consistently indicated that their lack of prior contact with people of color, even in the midst of liberal rhetoric, failed to prepare them to engage meaningfully about race:

> I grew up in a very white community, and the church was really white. We talked about other cultures, but it was all about boys and girls are equal and worthy and so are people of different colors. It was all about "everything's OK."

> Where I grew up, everybody was white, and even though I knew (on some level) that not everyone was white, we never really had to deal with it, and so we didn't.

A few students reported coming from more diverse neighborhoods and schools, but they too indicated a relatively low level of sustained interaction or conscious educational attention to issues of diversity and intergroup relations.

In these "more diverse" settings, racial segregation was still the normative experience for white students (as well as for students of color):

> [The city] is very segregated in terms of housing, and there's all different kinds of people who live here. But there isn't a tremendous amount of communication and social interaction between the groups . . . unless you played sports or you were involved in something else, because it was tracked. Almost all of the kids on the college track were white and almost all of the kids on the other tracks were black . . . and then there were also Asian kids and they were generally in the white track.

This lack of meaningful contact with people from other races was often coupled with various forms of both subtle and overt racism. In fact, many students' comments indicate that intergroup separation supported the home and media-based racism they were exposed to, creating and sustaining conditions wherein remnants of "old-fashioned racism" and an identity stage of unawareness and acceptance of stereotypes could be maintained:

> So I grew up with my dad particularly being really racist, he didn't really say much about any other group except Black people. "Nigger" was a common word in my family. I knew that that was not a good thing in terms of race. I knew that there was the black side of town, there was the black neighborhood, and then the rest of it was white, and that's what I grew up in. . . . But we never had any personal interactions with anybody [from the black neighborhood].

> My whole town was white except for a few families who migrated from Mexico to work. I had the clear sense that they weren't supposed to be there. They were like some unspoken exception that was supposed to be invisible.

In addition to the lack of contact in school and neighborhood and the various forms of racism that students were exposed to, several students indicated that when they did learn about people from other races, they were usually token efforts of inclusion:

> The only thing I learned in school was that Washington Carver was a black man and he discovered peanuts or something like that. I think we might have peripherally dealt with Martin Luther King. But four years, two years of history, two years of government, we really didn't touch on African-American or any other issues at all . . . that just didn't even exist as far as anybody was concerned. In elementary school we dealt with the Indians. You know, you put your hand on a piece of paper and you draw around it and you cut it out and you make a turkey, or you make little Indian hats and things like that with feathers.

Finally, even students who experienced token efforts of inclusion as unsatisfactory found little opportunity to formulate openly meaningful questions about race. Several students commented that when they did have racial questions and concerns during their high school years, they were simply told that there was "nothing to talk about":

> The message that I got from the white teachers at the school and other people was that the way not to be racist was to just pretend that you don't see any differences between people. And so everybody had feelings about race, but nobody talked, there was no place to talk about those things. And you only have to just treat everybody as an individual and everything will be fine.

> In my high school government class I asked a question about the Civil Rights movement and racism. The answer I got was basically that it was bad back then, but now everything was fine.

Growing up with everyday processes of segregation, lacking contact with racially (or socioeconomically) different peers, being exposed to various forms of racism and racial tokenism, and not being educated meaningfully about race and racism deeply affect white students' social identity—their sense of themselves as well as their relations with others. In their homes, schools, and communities these students acquired habitual attitudes, expectations, and ways of making meaning about their world. White students were socialized to not see themselves as having a race and did not understand their own (and their communities') exclusionary attitudes and behaviors. This message was reinforced unconsciously and uncritically within dominant cultural narratives about people of color that were primarily negative:

> Where I grew up, it was all white and there was a clear sense that we were not like "others." Yes, we had it better, but that was because we worked harder—and they (people of color) simply did not. That was a given.

> We had one African-American student in my class, and he was really smart and on the college track with the rest of us. I remember that I kept expecting him to fall behind when we went on to Advanced Placement math, but he never did. I was surprised that he was still with us at the end.

The previous student's "surprise" with regard to the African-American student's success demonstrates white students' limited sense of the racial "other"; it also reflects an assumption of superiority—"I kept expecting him to fall behind."

WHITE STUDENTS' EXPERIENCES ON CAMPUS:
NEW CHALLENGES TO WHITENESS

Students' precollege socialization forms a grid of attitudes and expectations about race and whiteness that is often reenacted and reified through their collegiate experience. As several white students reported, once in college they still did not think about themselves as being white—even in the presence of diversity; no one and no program invited or required them to. Hence, as the racial majority on campus and the dominant group within the larger society, the experience of knowing themselves as white was primarily reactive. That is, white students' numerical and cultural dominance protected them from having to know or understand others' experiences. Consequently, in order to "see" their race, they had to have a critical encounter or be consciously challenged to think and reflect about the particular experiences (perhaps privileges) that they had as a result of their racial position. Unless this challenge occurs at a conscious level, their own racial identity remains unknown and invisible during their college years.

Even when white students do have a critical encounter that raises their awareness of their race, they may not have the skills and consciousness (or instructional and experiential assistance) to deal with or act on it productively. Compare, for instance, the level of insight conveyed in these two excerpts:

> I don't understand why all the black students sit together in the dining hall. They complain about people being racist, but isn't that racist?

> Something I see is that the different races tend to stick with people like themselves. Once, in a class, I asked why all the black students sit together in the dormitory cafeteria. A black student then asked: "Well, why do you think all the white kids sit together?" I was speechless. I thought that was a dumb question until I realized that I see white people sitting together as normal and black people sitting together as a problem.

The first student wonders, or perhaps is troubled, about a common white perception of a cultural phenomenon (very similar to material reported in depth in Tatum 1997). For the second student, however, the challenge a student of color posed to her/his own racial outlook opens up a new set of perceptions, questions, and potential learning. Such challenges and other experiences may serve to contrast public and politically correct discourses of equality and togetherness with private stances of separation, silence, innocence, and white superiority. The result of such (unguided and unprocessed) new encounters or challenges is often a confused or fragmented racial consciousness indicative of the confused or dissonance stage of white racial identity and contradictory expressions of racial attitudes categorized as "modern" or "symbolic."

These comments reflect larger social assumptions about race relations on campus, wherein the prevailing myth has been that minority students are "self-segregating" and the exclusionary behaviors of the majority white group remain unseen (Elfin and Burke 1993; Tatum 1997). However, longitudinal research with over 200,000 students from 172 institutions found that it was white students who displayed the most exclusionary behaviors—particularly when it came to dating (Hurtado et al. 1994). Thus the view that minority students are self-segregating is clearly a skewed perspective that does not take into consideration the separatist and/or exclusionary behaviors of white students. It also fails to account for the ways in which institutional norms and cultures help students misinterpret patterns of interracial interaction.

Other white behaviors took the form of promoting or reacting to patterns of racial marginalization and separation in daily interactions in classrooms, social events, or casual encounters. The result, of course, continues to be minimal opportunity for sustained interaction:

> My black friend invited me to a party with her. And the first thing I could think of was how many white people are usually there. I remembered thinking, this is probably going to be uncomfortable, and I would rather just go out with my white friends. I'm feeling apprehensive about meeting their friends and therefore spending time with them.

> I used to feel very guilty thinking I don't have many diverse friends. I thought: "I have to go out and get a black friend."

Some white students reported finding these and other situations so discomforting that they began to express resentment against students of color. This type of resentment is supported by the discourse of whites as victims:

> I think white males have a hard time because we are constantly blamed for being power-holding oppressors, yet we are not given many concrete ways to change. Then we just feel guilty or rebel.

> I think that black people use their race to get jobs. I've seen it happen. My friend should have had this job as a resident advisor, but a black guy got it instead. There's no way the black guy was qualified.

The particular reference to "my friend" in the excerpt above is referred to by Eduardo Bonilla-Silva as one of the main "story lines of color blindness (2001:159)." Views such as these, expressing the emergence of a self-interested form of racial awareness, are consistent with Lawrence Bobo's (1999) discussion of the group-position frame of racial attitudes.

Hence we encounter the view of the white person as the "new victim" of racism or as the target of "reverse discrimination" (Gallagher 1995; Pincus 2000). Victimhood, like all racial identities and views, is historically situated, and current public discourse about affirmative action and other race-based remedies stimulates and supports its development and expression. A lack of understanding of one's own prejudices, the realities of racial discrimination, and the advantages whites have leads to the view that minority advance is unmerited and a reflection of special privilege. The result often is aversive or self-interested racism that facilitates the interpretation of interracial encounters or circumstances as overprivileging minorities and victimizing whites. This also is referred to as the reintegrative or dominative stage of white racial identity.

The inability to understand racial membership is compounded by denial of any racial prejudice or racism. As a result of professed innocence about the meaning and implications of their own racial status and privileges, white students are often "blind" to the reality and status of students of color and regard themselves as "color-blind." If white students do not understand the personal or structural implications of being white and are unable to see how their racial behaviors affect others, they blindly negotiate racial encounters with the sense that all that matters is their good intentions. Their structural position of racial dominance, together with precollege socialization and color-blind ideology, makes it very difficult to distinguish between good intentions (or innocence) and a reflective consciousness that can enact just racial encounters:

> I am a pretty open person and someone who wouldn't even think about race, who would try to be color-blind.

> When I was asked in a class to describe my beliefs about race it was easy. I said that I think that the whole idea of race has gone too far, that we need to stop thinking about race and start remembering that everyone is an individual.

Robert Terry (1981) identifies this pervasive color-blind ideology as an attempt to ignore or deny the relevance of race by emphasizing everyone's "humanness." Others have pointed out that the changing discourse of affirmative action—from a need to remediate past injustice to a concern about reverse discrimination—has affected how white people construct racial meaning (Gamson and Modigliani 1987). The new discourse of white victimhood not only acts to obscure the experiences of students of color but also further reinforces barriers to white students' ability to acknowledge their own racial identity as members of the dominant or privileged group.

Despite these reports of unawareness, negativity, blindness, and victimhood, there are also signs that some white students develop more sophisticated and progressive views of race. As they encounter themselves and others, some white students report moving out of the stage of "conformity" or "dissonance," going beyond "color blindness," and acknowledging their racism, prejudices, and stereotyped assumptions or expectations. This occurs partly as a function of structured educational experiences and informal contacts:

> It took me a long time to be able to get to a point where I can say that I have prejudices.

> Something I learned is that people have stereotypes. I learned that having stereotypes about other groups is part of the environment that we grow up in.

For a number of white students, these realizations led to a sense of shame or guilt: several scholars have also referred to these responses as the symbolic or emotional "costs" of white racism (Feagin and Vera 1995; Rose 1991):

> But I was so guilt-ridden, just horribly liberal guilt-ridden, paralyzed and unable to act. I was totally blowing every little minor interaction that I had with people of color way out of proportion and thinking that this determines whether or not I'm a good white person or a bad white person, and whether I'm racist or not. I saw how hard it was for me to stop doing that and start being more productive. And how hard it was for me to not be scared.

Such strong feelings, when combined in sensitive ways (as contrasted with self-pitying or defensive ways) with new educational input, helped some white students understand some of the privileges that were normally accorded them as a function of their white skin color (and associated socioeconomic and educational status):

> I learned that being white, they're so many privileges that I didn't even know of . . . like loans from the bank, not being stopped by the police, and other things me and white kids can get away with.

> I had not noticed the extent to which white privilege has affected and continues to affect many aspects of my everyday life. I thought "I" had accomplished so much, but how much of where I am is due to my accumulated privilege—my family, economic status, school advantages?

Although these last expressions may represent an evolving racial consciousness, they still exhibit an underlying sense of confusion and hesitant grappling with racial contradictions. It is difficult, as Bonilla-Silva and Forman point out (2000), to tell whether some whites' generally progressive responses to attitude surveys accurately represent the complexity of their behaviors in a racialized situation. The test, after all, is in behavior, in action, in attempts to "walk the talk," not only during college but afterwards. But for some white students, these new understandings were clearly reported as stepping stones to the "fuller integration," "integrative awareness," and "autonomy" referred to by Hardiman (2001), Helms (1990), and others. Terry (1981) has referred to this form of racial consciousness as the "new whiteness," and Bennett and colleagues (1993) discuss it as "active achieved white racial consciousness." It involves a desire to take action to reduce racism as it is experienced and confronted in oneself or in other whites. Indeed, a progressive or antiracist white racial identity suggests the beginning of a new narrative made possible by learning, reflecting, testing, and engaging in action for justice:

> Now that I've made the decision to try to deal with that oppression, it is something I feel I have to be constantly working at it. Whereas if I were

just ignorant about racism and didn't really think about it, it would be less of a responsibility.

By now my friends know not to make stupid racial comments around me ... they know I will call them out on it.

White students' integrative awareness involves recognition that racism and oppression exist in everyday thoughts and activities and that vigilance and counteraction are constantly required.

White Attitudes, Whiteness, and Views of Affirmative Action on Campus

These expressions and recent studies of racial attitudes suggest the contradictions present in many white students' views of racial relations. They are often tolerant and even progressive in rhetoric but more often contradictory and hesitant in practice or behavior. For instance, when it comes to issues of affirmative action, a "hot" issue on predominantly white campuses, a diversity of white students' views is evident. A large national cross section of first-year public university students shows that 52.4 percent feel that: "Affirmative action in college admissions should be abolished" and 21.8 percent feel that: "Racial discrimination is no longer a problem in America" (CIRP 2000). These represent major shifts in students' attitudes, with "should be abolished" up from 15.8 percent six years ago and "no longer a problem" up from 12 percent twelve years ago (Hurtado 1992). The changing social and political context of race in America has obviously affected the racial views of college students.

The national discourse surrounding affirmative action not only reflects whites' racial attitudes and ideologies, it also reproduces different understandings of whiteness and white identities. Several major themes or perspectives seem to characterize student outlooks on this issue (Chesler and Peet 2002): 1) while racial inequality and discrimination existed in the past, there is now equal (educational) opportunity hence affirmative action is unnecessary; 2) although some degree of past racial inequality and discrimination may still exist, affirmative action is an unfair and inappropriate remedial measure. This stance leads some to an emerging and increasingly vocal sense of white victimhood; 3) affirmative action is ineffective in promoting advance for people of color, both currently and in their future careers; and 4) some students argue that racial inequality and discrimination, and reciprocal white privilege and oppression, must be challenged by affirmative action as a strategy to create a more equitable and just society.

The view that racial discrimination no longer exists or is minimal reflects a shift in focus: "from who is excluded to the unfair advantage of those who benefit from affirmative action. Affirmative action gives minorities something they have not earned and do not deserve. Whatever happened in the past is over; this is now" (Gamson and Modigliani, 1987:146–147). Minimizing racial discrimination facilitates the argument that supporting equal opportunity requires opposition to affirmative action.

The moral claim that affirmative action is unfair rests on the principle that all people should be judged (or admitted to college) based on their individual academic merits. In this view college board tests and high school grade point averages are seen as bias-free measures of merit (of talent and hard work), and inequalities rooted in history, economic disadvantage, and poor schooling are not problematic for a meritocracy. Both the "unfair" and "ineffective" views reflect a relatively naïve sense of white consciousness and a lack of awareness by many white students of their own privileged status.

In addition, some white students feel their personal or group self-interest challenged and themselves systematically placed at a disadvantage because of the presence of students of color. Predicated on stereotypic beliefs about the inferiority of people of color, this view reflects the attitudinal system that supports "old-fashioned racism" (Dovido and Gaertner 1986). It also articulates the emerging white "victim" identity that is supported and reified through the discourse of "reverse discrimination" in the affirmative action debate (Pincus 2000) and provides further evidence of the group-position perspective on racism. This is similar to the reintegrative or dominant stage of white racial identity development. To be sure, the sense of white victimhood is supported by the reality that some whites may fail to gain admission to certain colleges or positions due to advances by people of color. But such "reverse discrimination" is rare and is experienced at an individual level, if at all. It is hardly institutional and pervasive, while continued discrimination against people of color (and white working-class and poor people) clearly still is.

Some students argue that when unqualified or underqualified students are admitted to the university, they cannot "make it." Poor prior educational experience, lack of talent, or unwillingness to work hard are suggested as reasons affirmative action will not really help and may even harm students of color. However, the view that affirmative action does not work is countered by recent studies that show that students of color, despite the pain and discomfort they often experience at the hands of white peers and faculty, generally do well in college and afterwards (Bowen and Bok 1998; Lempert et al. 2000). It also overlooks white students' reports of the educational benefits of racial (and other forms of) diversity (Gurin 2001).

Finally, some white students appear to have developed a more complex and racially progressive understanding of the issues and are prepared to advocate for affirmative action efforts. Their view suggests a deeper understanding of the nature of racial discrimination and paves the way for the development of a liberationist set of attitudes with a more integrative and antiracist racial identity. Indeed, some white students have gone beyond the prodiversity and antidiscrimination models of affirmative action and see it as part of a necessary challenge to entrenched white privilege. These students appear to recognize the role that their own racial positionality—white privilege—plays in their perceptions of racial issues in general and affirmative action in particular. They see affirmative action as part of a broader program of social change and are prepared (at least rhetorically) to play an active role in that effort.

CONCLUSION

We have suggested that white students typically arrive at college from prior lives of race and class separation and privilege and that many of these patterns of separation continue through college. Racial identities and attitudes formulated in these environs often include ignorance, a sense of superiority, the mystification of racial relationships, and an inability to see or understand themselves as "white" or as enacting racist views and behaviors. These students also generally carry a set of ahistoric and astructural views of race relations that stem from and lead to ignorance and innocence. As they encounter diverse groups of students, whites often act on the basis of their stereotypes, are fearful or awkward in intergroup interactions, and may seek the safety of in-group exclusivity. When challenged, they often experience resentment, conscious or unconscious feelings of threat fueled by expectations of danger to themselves and their accumulated interests and privileges. This resentment currently takes shape as resistance to affirmative action programs, to their perception that such efforts permit people with inferior talent to succeed via special treatment, and to the view that whites are the current or future victims of "reverse racism." Hence reactions to affirmative action permit us to see some of the impacts of social and historical forces on the psychological development of white college students.

Innovative educational programs must be designed and implemented to address these issues in students' racial identities and attitudes. However, even such innovations will not be effective or sustained without parallel changes in the operations of departments and the larger collegiate or university environment. Without changes in this broader organizational landscape, it is unlikely that individual white students' attitudes will change or that their racial identities will continue to "progress"—or that such change programs, if initiated, can be maintained. Moreover, students' consciousness and the academy itself are enmeshed in our society's continuing struggle with racial discrimination and racial privilege. There are real limits for any change toward more liberationist or antiracist white identities or racial attitudes within a highly racialized and racist society and higher educational system.

PART IV

Whiteness and Antiracism

16

Diverse Perspectives on Doing Antiracism: The Younger Generation

KARYN D. MCKINNEY

JOE R. FEAGIN

In what was perhaps the first extended analysis of whiteness, in a chapter in his autobiography "Darkwater," W. E. B. Du Bois (1920:497–498) noted that: "the discovery of personal whiteness among the world's people is a very modern thing.... The ancient world would have laughed at such a distinction...we have changed all that, and the world in a sudden, emotional conversion has discovered that it is white and by that token, wonderful!"

In this chapter, we use new qualitative data from extended autobiographies to explore some dimensions of this "wonderful whiteness." Here we construct whiteness as a racialized category related to a larger-scale system of racism, one developed primarily by elite whites and sustained by whites at all class levels over nearly four centuries. In other work, we have demonstrated that the racism central to U.S. society is *systemic,* for it has long been a central foundation of this country (Feagin 2000). This systemic racism has five major components, consisting of racist 1) attitudes, 2) emotions, 3) ideology, 4) practices, and 5) institutions. Only the first of these categories has been thoroughly examined by social scientists—and mostly by means of multiple-choice surveys of white attitudes toward Americans of color. These surveys have not examined how white Americans think or feel about antiracist actions nor are they capable of probing deeply into such matters. In addition, very little research has ever been done on the racist ideology that provides the overarching framework for the various prejudices and stereotypes that are held by white Americans.

In this chapter we use data that are much deeper and more nuanced than that provided in survey studies and we also provide conceptual linkages to this larger framework of theory about systemic racism. Much has been made of how white Americans view Americans of color, yet no in-depth research had been done on how white men and women saw themselves until the mid-1990s work of Feagin and Vera (see rev. ed., Feagin, Vera, and Batur 2001). In that pioneering work on institutionalized racism and white identities, Feagin and Vera examined in detail the "sincere fictions" that white men and women hold not only about others but also, for the first time, about themselves (on views of white women, see also Frankenberg 1993). These sincere fictions involve collective misrecognitions of both the white self and of other racial selves (Bourdieu 1980; Feagin, Vera, and Batur 2001). Sincere fictions rationalize white privilege as a taken-for-granted foundation of the society. Whites as a group not only come to see outgroups such as African-Americans in negative and stereotypical terms but they also come to see themselves in very positive terms—often in sugarcoated images and stereotypical descriptions of being "good people" and of "not being racist." In the data on younger whites below, we see many of the commonplace sincere fictions of the white self, how whites use these images in constructing individual and group identities, and how these in turn shape the perceptions they have of their responsibilities to help end racism.

In asking them to construct a "racial/ethnic autobiography," one question we asked of these mostly young whites was how they view their role in antidiscrimination efforts both now and in the future. They gave a range of responses depending on how committed they were to white privileges and the existing system and how much understanding they had of institutionalized racism. Since most whites, including these respondents, have little knowledge of the country's racist history—and because they have not reflected much on their position as whites in society—they usually construct their white identities as normal and routine, yet often also as being empty, passive, and even socially disadvantaged. Their unreflectiveness means that their whiteness is viewed as unconnected to their social, psychological, and material privileges.

Indeed, many view white Americans as now under siege from outside by Americans of color and by programs favoring these groups, such as affirmative action. White privileges are usually omitted from their images of themselves and of whiteness generally—and thus the white-dominated racial system of inequality is seen as just and fair (see McKinney 2003 for a complete discussion of all these elements of whiteness found in the data). We should underscore the point that the complex set of sincere fictions expressed by these and other white Americans are *not* isolated attitudes, but they fit together to help sustain an old and overarching racist ideology. This racism in turn generates and buttresses a great range of discriminatory actions. Hence we agree strongly with Andersen (Chapter 2 in this volume) that, if they are to dig deeply into this society, whiteness studies must deal centrally with the material and other privileges garnered by white Americans and, we would add, how these privileges are rationalized or ignored in the overarching racist ideology.

In this article we analyze racial/ethnic autobiographies written by sixty-one mostly young (eighteen to twenty-one) white students at three Southeastern universities. All students (twenty-four males and forty-two females) now live in the Southeast, although many have lived in other regions of the United States. These students were asked to write a racial/ethnic autobiography as part of course requirements for some and extra credit for others. After many of the white students (though interestingly, *none* of the students of color in the classes) expressed concerns that they had "nothing to write about," they were given an "autobiography guide" which suggested certain questions that they should try to address in the body of their papers. Among other questions, these young white students were asked what role they see themselves taking in current issues and debates regarding racism, both now and in the future.

White students constitute an important population for those concerned with racism and whiteness, for several reasons. First, in their often more subtle and covert racism, they exhibit a different style of racism from their parents' or grandparents' generations, who engaged in more overt and blatant hostility and discrimination. Second, with acts of young, white, male violence being commonplace and often racialized, more research is needed to address the racial components of their hostility and alienation. Third, because of the nation's changing racial demography, most young whites will have more contact with people of color than their parents and grandparents did. Finally, it is likely that younger whites will have a greater impact on whether racism will be eradicated than older generations will.

PASSIVE OBSERVERS OF WHITENESS

Previous research indicates that many whites have given little thought to what it means to be "white." Indeed, when asked about this issue, many whites will say they have not thought about it, or they will pause for a moment before groping for an answer. In a previous study, one college student gave a typical reply when asked what it is like being white:

> You really don't think about that much, at least I don't. It has its advantages; and then again it has its disadvantages. There is always a feeling of comfort, usually, but sometimes disadvantages because you feel you may miss out because they are looking for a minority or something like that, so it has its good points and bad points. But . . . I don't think about it much. (Feagin, Vera, and Batur 2001:191)

For many white Americans, being white means rarely or never having to think about it. Indeed, Beth,[1] who was often one of the more reflective respondents in this study, wrote in her autobiography "Whiteness, to me, is not having to think about being white. . . . I can make myself invisible in a majority of situations . . . I could definitely tell my life story without mentioning race." Most whites, unlike Beth, live their entire lives without realizing that this perspective contrasts with the experiences of many people of color, whose racial identities are forced into their consciousness by recurring contacts with white Americans (see Feagin and Sikes 1994).

Moreover, when whites are prompted to discuss the matter, as in this research, they often view whiteness as obscure, empty, or boring. Many use racialized "others," particularly African-Americans, to construct a white identity—in other words, they write of who they are by referring to who they are not. As we will see, some view whiteness as a victimized identity. Even those who recognize personal white privilege and individual prejudice often lack an understanding of the systemic racism that has long been central to the United States (Feagin 2000:105–136).

The young whites in our research for the most part view themselves as passive in regard to the many racialized aspects of their lives. They often describe themselves as recipients of racial messages and claim that certain attitudes are the result of what was put into their minds about "race" by others. Thus, writing about his middle school years, Stephen describes white, black, and Latino gangs, and then adds: "I was an observer, and what I was observing was very discouraging, not only as a white person, but also as a human being. It started to make me question my own heritage and upbringing." As young adults, these respondents tend to view themselves not as actors but as *reactors* in interracial interactions and as empty vessels to be filled with data gathered in personal experiences with people of color, rare as these experiences might be.

With these general characteristics in mind of whiteness seen in the autobiographies, we can turn to the various perspectives that were expressed by these white students regarding how they see their role in antiracist efforts now and in the future. We observed an interesting range of answers to this important question, from relatively negative and reluctant responses to much deeper and more activist responses. We theorize that it is the level of understanding that whites have of systemic or institutionalized racism that makes the difference in how they see antiracist action, both for themselves and for other whites.

In this article we roughly group the responses into the following categories: fearful, dismissive/resentful, directionless, antiprejudiced, and antiracist. We analyze each perspective and see how they are linked to the students' understandings of racism. We also comment in each section and in the conclusion on how critical conceptions of whiteness can and do further the cause of antiracist action, including antiracist teaching and instruction.

Ours is not an attempt to categorize each individual student into a specific category on a continuum of antiracism. Instead, it is important to note that our interest is in *collective* whiteness, and hence the unit of analysis is not the individual white person but the individual story or unit of text. For many reasons, including current demographic changes, whiteness is in a state of flux, and the corresponding complexity of white identity is exemplified in these data. In the same autobiography, a respondent often writes from one perspective, only to take another perspective later. All of these perspectives or positions on race are part of whiteness for young people in the new millennium.

Fearful Responses

Numerous respondents stated or implied that they have postponed their involvement in antiracism because of fears regarding social tensions or awkwardness. Like other whites (see Feagin, Vera and Batur 2001), some students perceived that while *they* have been trying to act in opposition to racism, people of color are *the real problem,* in that they are less open than whites or resistant to whites' efforts. These students view actions opposing racism as fraught with the danger of their own victimization or rejection. Discussing her workplace, Brittany illustrates this perspective:

> [My] company is very, very racially diverse. As far as I know, everyone gets along professionally and personally. This serves as a perfect example that different cultures can coexist in harmony. In my department there are two black women.... Over time I have grown extremely close to them and I credit this to our ability to have an open relationship. We talk freely about everything from our love lives to our shoe sizes. Naturally, racial issues arise in these conversations and we are all able to ask each other questions without fear of offending or being offended.... At one point in my cultural diversity class, I experienced some discomfort about this issue, however. A particular article ... explained that at times non-minorities ask questions or do things that are offensive without knowing it. A black student in class reflected on this and said that when whites ask them questions it is sometimes derogative. As I explained earlier, I feel that we should be understanding of each other's ignorance and interpret these inquiries as an attempt to understand and I felt a bit frustrated at the young man's opinion on the matter.

Brittany has developed a relationship with black women at work such that they are able to discuss various subjects without, at least according to Brittany, offending one another. When a black student in her class expresses the opinion that sometimes the questions that white people ask are offensive, she is frustrated. Brittany constructs his opinion as being in opposition to *her* experience and hence incorrect. In fact, both experiences could be equally valid—perhaps Brittany is able to discuss racial issues with her friends that would be offensive if a white stranger inquired about them.

Similarly, Felicia comments:

> My awareness finally started to broaden when I came to college.... This process made me realize what my first thoughts about people were, and I was disappointed in myself. For instance, I would clutch my purse when an African American would pass me at night.... One experience that broadened my thoughts on race and ethnicity was the process of getting to know my Jewish roommate. While I had always thought my prejudices were strictly addressed at race, I was proven wrong when I could express no knowledge of the Jewish culture.... My next big step towards unlearning my racism was when I registered for [the race and ethnicity] class. I was tentative about the class, probably because I already knew the dreary truth that I was going to have to face about racism.... After the first couple of classes I felt hopeful that I was making a change within

myself and becoming more aware, but then I experienced a set back. One night, walking out of class, I saw a group of my African American classmates walking ahead of me, one of which I knew from a previous class. I debated whether or not to say hello because of the ratio of them to me, but convinced myself through my newfound hope to end my racist thoughts. As I said hello everyone was friendly, but looked somewhat suspicious of me. My friend and I began to talk about the class we had together previously, which was about the psychology of women. I joked with him that at least he was no longer the minority in this class like he was in the other and he replied, "yeah, now you are." The words were harsh and rebuilt my wall of defense.

Felicia, who in an earlier passage discussed overcoming her defensive reaction to African-American students' comments about racism, begins this college course believing racial tensions will not be a problem. She is surprised when in response to an intended joke to a black classmate, he points out that she is a minority in the class, instead of him. It may be that what Felicia perceives as a relationship that can accommodate this type of joking is not experienced as such by the black student. It is also possible that he realized she was joking, but still believed it reasonable to point out what he did. Many respondents, believing themselves to have made progress in becoming more racially "aware," expect their efforts to be taken at face value by people of color and feel victimized or fearful of further interaction if they believe they have been misunderstood.

DISMISSIVE AND RESENTFUL ACCOUNTS

Some respondents, believing that they are personally blamed for racial problems, become dismissive, resentful, and unreceptive in response to further discussions of racism as well as to antiracist action. Some view college lessons about the racist realities of the United States as indicting them individually. When ordinary whites understand racism this way, they often become defensive and unwilling to assist in the work against discrimination (Blauner 1995; Bonilla-Silva 2001). This also may lead to a feeling of social or cultural victimization (see Feagin and Vera 1995, Chapter 7).

Jerry, the grandson of a former leader of the Ku Klux Klan, first asserts in his autobiographical statement that this had no direct impact on his upbringing, but later admits that it may have had *some* influence, since his father was raised by this Klan activist. Throughout his autobiography, Jerry describes each negative encounter he has had with African-Americans, inserting an occasional comment that, although coded in different terms, seems to ask the reader "Given all these things, how could I *help* but think negatively about them?" Again, one can see the passivity implied as part of whiteness—white people are given certain messages, data, and experiences about people of color and in effect cannot help the attitudes they develop as a result. These attitudes are naturalized as beyond their control. In other data collected as part of this ongoing study (McKinney 2003), a young woman raised in a small rural town in the Northeast stated, after telling how she had offended a black roommate: "I told her that I came from a small, all white town and I could not help what I say sometimes." In this case, the cultural climate of a "small town" is invoked as the cause of passive whites' racial attitudes.

Asked about his role in the future of U.S. racial relations, Jerry writes about his experiences in his race and ethnicity course:

> I am realizing that my feelings are not shared by many and that everyone grew up quite differently than me. We have had several discussions about affirmative action and the only problem with the class is that they want you to go along with whatever they say. If you do, you are encouraged and told [that] you are making good points. If you decide to go against what they are saying or even worse make a comment against the book that was written by our professor, you are ridiculed and called a racist. I enjoy the class just because it is a lesson in adversity.

Jerry first positions himself as an outsider in the class by asserting that his upbringing was different from everyone else's. He constructs his experience as "a lesson in adversity" characterized by accusations of racism. It is important to consider *how* Jerry has constructed himself as the victim in his class and how instructors might work against constructions of victimization, which only further ensconce certain students in their positions. Seeing himself as a victim, this young man has no motivation to oppose racism. Interestingly, elsewhere in his autobiography Jerry says that he wishes that he were African-American, because the latter are today more privileged than whites. This view is not unique with Jerry, for many other white men also believe it to be the case. Indeed, the leading New York real-estate entrepreneur, Donald Trump, once commented to an interviewer "I've said on one occasion, even about myself, if I were starting off today, I would love to be a well-educated black, because I believe they have an actual advantage" (quoted in Porter 1989:G1).

Another student, Joseph, expresses resentment toward people of color based on his understandings of course materials:

> All of my close friends throughout life have been white and I believe this to be a result of the commonalities that exist between us. I have never been subject to discrimination based on my color or ethnicity. I feel that this may be a result of my actions toward those of other races. I never feel that I have the right to treat anyone different. I only realize that they are in fact different. I did not come to this conclusion about race relations till I finished a semester of [race and ethnicity]. The material and class lectures showed me a side of other races that I did not see before. Before I took this class I genuinely had no problems with people of color, now

> I see that they are bitter and unforgiving about the past. This is a very
> ignorant standpoint for them to take and causes their equality to be
> prolonged even further. I believe that it is my responsibility as a white
> citizen not to repay these people for things that should be long forgotten
> but to show them equal respect.

Before taking a race and ethnicity course, Joseph was unaware of the perspectives
of people of color. He now generalizes from his own experience of matters of
racism: Because *he* has never believed in treating people differently, he assumes
others have acted the same, and so reasonable requests for equity from people
of color are seen as demands representing an "ignorant standpoint." Elsewhere,
Joseph discusses his beliefs about his whiteness:

> It is my view that every factor of our genetic make up can affect our per-
> sonality and development. . . . I would be classified as a white American.
> I find joy and happiness in my whiteness. I am considered by many to
> be at the top of the social structure of our system. There is nothing that I
> would trade for the color of my skin. When I think of being white I think
> of my superiority in society. There is a lack of worry in being white.

Joseph's statement is perhaps the strongest one of this type in the sample, as
he recognizes white privilege, yet celebrates it without mentioning changing it.
Further, Joseph is the only student who gives explicit, and insightful, attention
to how white people feel a sense of group interest based on race.

Classroom experiences can be a source of defensiveness for whites. For example, in their courses many respondents saw a film called *The Color of Fear*, in
which a small group of men of various racial backgrounds go on a weekend retreat to discuss racial issues (Wah 1994). There are two white men in the group,
one who is more or less antiracist and the other, David, who denies that racism
even exists. The group spends much time trying to get David to see the reality of
racism in the lives of people of color. However, many white students believe the
group is "blaming" David for racism. For example, Briana writes this comment
in her autobiographical account:

> We watched . . . "The Color of Fear" in class and I was very discouraged.
> I felt that the anger that these men of color had towards every white
> man was being vented on this individual white man. I felt it was not
> this particular individual's fault, it was the fault of the whole race. This
> anger should not have been targeted specifically at him. I felt I could
> sympathize with this white man because he was at a loss as to what to
> [do] about racism as a whole.

Briana empathizes with what she believes is David's uncertainty about how to
oppose racism personally as well as with his position of having anger "towards
every white man" directed at him. She may have perceived herself being in this
position at some time or may fear someday being in that position. Whichever

is true, Briana constructs a bond of whiteness with the man in the movie based on a shared sense of victimization.

A Directionless Perspective

Some respondents have relatively nonracist attitudes but lack direction in regard to putting those attitudes into action. In these autobiographies they write about what they learned in courses but complain that these courses did not offer actions that a person can take to help dismantle racism. Put simply, the courses elucidated the "disease" in depth without offering any "cures."

These students' words can serve instructors as a call to action. In our view, instructors should offer students ways that they may act to help end racism (for a similar point about sociology in general, see Feagin and Vera 2001). In their lack of direction, one can read in these respondents' words a sense of frustration about engaging in further discussions of racism. For example, Trent is unsure of his place in opposing racism. He comments that:

> So the question is whether being white gives any privileges or benefits, a question which is almost laughable. Of course it does. There are still a lot of people around who are ... racist, and not being black or some other ethnicity can be a great benefit. So, if there are benefits, and if *respon-sibilities* always come with benefits, then what are my *responsibilities?* I haven't figured that out yet. I know I have a responsibility to try to end racism, within myself at the very least. Do I also have a responsibility to go on protests against racism? Do I have a *responsibility* to give away belongings that I obtained because of the privileges associated with my race? I haven't yet figured out just how far my responsibility goes, and whether I should be morally obligated to go even farther than just what I am responsible for.... As you can see, this hasn't been an important part of my life until recently.

Trent has a unique view among the respondents. He questions what "responsibility" means in terms of his future behavior. Trent is unsure of how to decide what action to take and perhaps has not gleaned from any other sources how to be "responsibly white." In our view it is the responsibility of white antiracist scholars not only to expose white racism but also of suggest how whites might be accountable allies of people of color. As more of our data will show and we will conclude, these ideas must be taken beyond intellectual musings and made practically applicable in the lives of well-meaning whites.

One female student, Abigail, considers carefully both white privilege and several options that she as a white person has for responding to it:

> The Race/Ethnic Minorities class ... is opening my eyes to the inequal-ities the different races possess. These inequalities affect me in all that I do, and I am only beginning to recognize them for what they entail. These inequalities are unspoken privileges that I have been given due to

my race. From the moment I wake up in the morning and listen to a white newscaster report the white man's successes of the day, until the time I go to bed listening to a white radio broadcaster playing predominantly white music; I am unconsciously reminded of the status I own. Being born a white person in a country where white is considered normative has put me in a position where I can reliably expect to encounter people of my race wherever I choose to go. I will generally be welcome and feel comfortable in most situations when I leave my home, and if I don't, it probably won't have anything to do with my race. Realizations such as these weren't always in my conscious thought; it wasn't until recently that I came to recognize these privileges.

After discussing other specific privileges, such as in hiring and treatment in the criminal justice system, she goes on to discuss her options for handling these privileges:

First, I can continue to naively accept these privileges as the way the United States works and continue to go through life without acknowledging the inequalities that exist in our society. Second, I can make an effort to be more appreciative of these privileges. In doing so, I would still be accepting, but I would consciously make an effort to recognize these things as they happen. This option, I believe is almost as bad as the first one, because it may lead a white person to feel superior or even grandiose. A third option would be to disregard these options and try to live in a way that promotes equality. I feel that this is the only acceptable option for me, but how to go about actively doing this isn't as clear. I do feel that it is my responsibility to point out racial discrimination when I see it. I feel I should inform people of their biased views, even if it offends them. I feel that I need to continue educating myself on the inequalities that exist in American society, because knowledge is truly the key to social change.

Understanding that to be just "more appreciative" of white privilege is not an effective strategy, Abigail wants to instead "promote equality." However, she is unsure of how to take action to do this. She has completed a course in race and ethnicity, has learned about white privilege, and has realized that she is responsible for trying to end it, but Abigail did not glean from the course concrete ways actively to oppose racism.

THE ANTIPREJUDICED VIEW

Many theorists have discussed the current trend toward "color-blind" racism (see, e.g., Bonilla-Silva 2001; Carr 1997; Frankenberg 1993). Instead of openly noting differences between whites and people of color and then asserting white superiority, many whites today state that they "don't notice color," and yet go on actively or passively to support institutionalized racism. The claim that one can be "color-blind" about race and that this stance is even *desirable* is one of the sincere fictions of whiteness.

Although certainly color blindness was a discernable element in many of the autobiographies, a distinct perspective expressed at least as often, and perhaps a relatively new sincere fiction of whiteness observed in the autobiographies, we call the "antiprejudiced" view. Antiracist action involves an active resistance to discriminatory behavior, whether individual or institutionalized. The antiprejudiced perspective involves only stated resistance to negative *attitudes* about people of color, those held by the respondent or by other whites.

This perspective is not the same as color blindness, in that these antiprejudiced whites usually do not claim to overlook the meaningful, although socially constructed, "racial" differences that elicit prejudices. However, theirs is not a strong antiracist response either, but is at best only a tentative move in an activist direction. While ending prejudice can be a useful step in ending racism, it is not the only step. For most of those who are targets of racism, an end to *discrimination* is likely the primary concern, separate from how or when whites' attitudes become friendlier toward them. The antiprejudiced approach can waste precious energy fighting the battle of ending all prejudiced attitudes while the larger war of dismantling racist practices is unfought.

When asked what they believe their future role will be in combating racism, numerous respondents write in their autobiographical statements about being sure that they themselves do not harbor negative attitudes about people of color and about raising their children this way, and some mention helping other whites become less prejudiced or more "aware." Few speak of ending prejudice as *only a first step* toward ending racism. Briana puts it this way:

> I acknowledge that white people have the power and the privilege and I understand that discrimination does take place. It is the moral responsibility of whites to admit that racism and discrimination exist and to work toward combating them. I have taken several college courses that were geared toward cultural awareness and diversity. I have shared some of the knowledge I have gained with some of my family members. In the future, I plan to instill the same values in my children that my parents instilled in me.

Briana clearly states that it is *white people's* responsibility to combat racism. However, the only ways that she suggests they do so is through acknowledging and admitting there is a problem, becoming more aware of diversity individually, and helping to educate other whites, primarily in their own families.

Similarly, Lisa writes of working only on a "small scale," in part to keep from disrupting her life:

> I see myself trying to help race relations on a small scale. I try to correct people when they make ethnic jokes or slurs. I am not going to try and change the world because I want a quiet life. I feel that I can do good

everyday just by treating people as equals. If I can get even one person to think before they say something racist, I believe I have done well. I also believe I will raise my children to look beyond race. I don't have kids yet but I have already decided to expose them to different lifestyles whenever I have the chance. I won't teach them they are good because they're white.

Like many respondents, Lisa combines various perspectives on racial matters. After asserting a color-blind position, she then switches to more diversity-conscious language. One reads here the complexity of whiteness and the impossibility of categorizing ordinary whites easily in terms of their perspectives on racial matters. These perspectives are discursive tools, used in telling stories of whiteness and constructing collective white identity, rather than static positions of individual identity.

An older student, Ted, has a teenage son whom he believes he is raising to be unprejudiced:

I have taken it upon myself to raise an unbiased, objective thinking child on the subject of race and ethnicity . . . hopefully what I have been teaching him in the form of non-prejudicial thinking will have an influence. . . . My role in the future of racial/ethnic relations is to take an individual stand against this social parasite in my home, school, workplace and community by not partaking in slur type language and jokes and by treating my fellow humans as I wish to be treated in all interactions. . . . I feel that a national solidarity must take place here in our nation if we are to overcome this destructive social disease that racial/ethnic discrimination brings to the table. When our founding fathers wrote the preface to the constitution they stated that all men were created equal—it is high time we as a nation practiced that belief. . . . I hold a race conscious view that is void of any overt discriminatory bias towards any other race or ethnic group. I am not perfect, I did not choose to be born white anymore than African or Native Americans chose to be born into oppression or poverty, but I am aware! . . . Perhaps, someday if we all do our share, America really can become the "land of the free!"

Again, Ted emphasizes overcoming prejudice, teaching one's children to do so, and, as do other antiprejudiced respondents, "being aware" as individuals in order to dismantle racism. Unlike other respondents, Ted does mention the contradiction between the ideals of the United States and racial oppression. Yet in his account he does not suggest specific ways that "we as a nation" might begin to practice the stated belief in equality.

Taking an Actively Antiracist Perspective

Though much less often expressed than other positions, elements of a stronger antiracist position are conveyed in the autobiographical accounts of some students. These tell stories of having taken action against racism or speak of doing so in the future. The antiracist perspective suggests that the respondent opposes not just prejudiced attitudes but *racist behavior* or *institutionalized racism.*

Some student accounts reveal awareness of structural racism and how traditional views are inadequate to address that reality. Chris writes in his reply to the key question about antiracist action in the future:

> There is no quick fix cure for racism. I now know that people can't just take the position "why can't we all just get along," it goes much deeper than that. The video that we watched in class opened up my eyes a great deal. I realize that people need to learn about themselves before they can start to learn about people they know nothing about.

Chris has learned that racism is too embedded in society to be dismantled by pleas that we all "get along," in other words that friendly attitudes and relationships between whites and people of color alone will not end racism. His statement suggests that whites must turn the gaze on whiteness to gain the consciousness necessary to have real understanding of institutional racism.

Similarly, Rianne asserts that a color-blind position towards antiracism can often do more harm than good:

> I think there are a lot of Davids [the white man in *The Color of Fear*] out there who really have no idea that their color-blind attitudes are just as racist as discrimination and prejudice are. I do not feel that racism is for only whites to resolve. However, I do think that as the dominant power in our society today, whites will have to put forth more effort than other races will in order to make a significant impact.

Rianne is unwilling to assign *all* the responsibility for ending racism to whites. Yet she does acknowledge that because whiteness is dominant, white people presently have more responsibility than do people of color.

Characteristic of the stronger statements of active antiracism in the autobiographies is the recognition of structural racism. Stephanie explains the problem in her account:

> Despite efforts on the part of racial and ethnic groups to make society change, there has not been much progress in the big picture. People individually are more open and accepting now days than in the past and a greater effort towards equality is being made on a personal level than ever before. But, still there is not equality on a corporate and economic level.

Stephanie realizes that individuals being more "open and accepting" will not, alone, end racism—progress must also be made on an institutional level.

Several respondents mention the demographic changes that the United States is undergoing and how these will affect race relations. They argue that because of the increasing population of people of color in the United States, whites, by being more often in the "minority" position, will be forced to learn to get along better with people of color. Rhonda discusses first how she is preparing her children to interact with people of color and then these changing demographics:

> Race continues to be a significant factor in my life. I have two children, and I want to make sure that I teach them correctly from the start.... My children have had a lot of exposure to people who are different races and ethnicities than them. They have a multiracial collection of dolls and Barbies. They are currently taking Spanish classes, and enjoy it very much. In this class they not only learn the language, but they also learn about customs, food, and history.... When my daughters come home talking about Christopher Columbus I tell them the real story. I ask them—did they teach you that he took the Native people from America and made them slaves? Or did they tell you that there were 20 million Native Americans living here when Columbus came? Their answers to these questions is always "no." I try to be careful to give them information that they are ready for. I don't want to continuously tell them that white people were bad because this could affect the way they see themselves. Raising children can be very tricky....
>
> The demographic changes that are underway will be positive for our society. Power will shift and begin to be more evenly distributed. There are always problems when one particular ideological group has dominant power. This can be seen over and over again in history. The demographic shifts in the United States will be ground breaking in so far as so many diverse groups living under the same government. I would hope that institutional racism and all the other kinds of racism lessen rather than gain momentum with the anticipated demographic shifts in the future.

Rhonda does not try to raise her children to be color-blind. Instead, she is focusing on correcting much of the misinformation that they are taught in mainstream schools. She does this with a sensitivity to the need for a positive identity, however, and struggles with how to make whiteness part of that identity. She discusses the impact of current demographic changes and, most importantly, acknowledges that whites do sometimes act as part of "one particular ideological group." Often white people believe that only people of color have group interests and culture.

Few respondents write stories of having actually taken antiracist action. Those who do, interestingly, are mostly male. Jordan tells of an incident that occurred in his early teens:

> We were hungry one morning so we walked over to a [doughnut shop].
> While in the restaurant, a couple of black kids a little younger than
> ourselves walked in and ordered breakfast themselves. At the time [the
> doughnut chain] was running a promotion for free doughnuts and cof-
> fee. This contest consisted of scratch-off tickets that were given to you for
> each item that you bought. While eating I noticed that one of the black
> kids had apparently won a free doughnut. However, the Asian woman
> refused to give this boy his prize because she claimed that he scratched
> off a part that he was not supposed to. I went over to him and asked what
> was going on. After he explained what happened, he asked if I would
> try to redeem the ticket. I agreed but did not think she would accept it
> [from] me. To my dismay, they did not even question the ticket. I was
> totally shocked and outraged that this happened. After we confronted
> these women and I gave my new buddy his prize, I apologized on the
> employee's behalf. He told me it was not a big deal and that this kind of
> stuff happens to him and his friends all the time.

In his autobiography to this point, Jordan has not portrayed himself as a particularly antiracist person. However, in this instance we see that, taking the situation
at face value, he believes he has witnessed a clear act of racism. The portion of
this passage that makes Jordan's action antiracist is when he got involved by
asking the young man what was going on. Most white people would not cross
racial boundaries in order to involve themselves in a dispute involving a black
stranger.

Larry has challenged racism actively on both a structural and a personal
level. Some might construct his behavior and that of other antiracist respondents as "white messiah" stories (Vera and Gordon 2003), in which whites are
intentionally made the saviors of African-Americans. However, because these
accounts do not rhetorically reassert white privilege and because the accounts
were prompted by the questions asked in the autobiography guide and not
produced for a mass audience, it seems these particular respondents were not
seeking personal recognition by engaging in dramatic rescuing behavior but
instead simply responded to situations of racial discrimination with which they
were confronted.

Larry describes the segregated neighborhoods he has lived in, the racist attitudes his parents expressed, the more positive attitudes of his grandparents,
and then tells of his reaction to an incident in which two of his friends refused
to eat dinner with an interracial couple:

> When I experience racism, prejudice, and sheer stupidity first hand like
> I did that night it made me very angry and made me realize, that people

who you thought were your friends can be racist and judge a person, not by getting to know them, but simply by the color of their skin.

Because of this incident, Larry ends his friendship with these two young men. He also describes an instance of institutional racism:

> Last summer when I was applying for a job at a sporting goods store . . . as I was going into the manager's office to be interviewed, an African American man about my age was just leaving his interview with the same man who was about to interview me. After the very brief interview, he told me I had the job and that he trusts me more and told me I would be a better worker than the man he just interviewed. I was very stunned that he could and would hire me and make that statement even though he knew nothing about that other man and myself. And he made this decision based on the fact that the other man was African American and I was white. That was a summer job I wanted very much to work at but I definitely did not want to work for a person who was a bold face racist.

This is the only clear rejection of privilege in the student autobiographies. Most respondents, even those who recognize that they receive privileges, do not suggest dismantling the racist system by rejecting those privileges.

Finally, Larry ponders the future role of whites in challenging racism:

> The role I see my racial/ethnic group playing in current racial/ethnic relations . . . is trying to get rid of racial stereotypes whether it's regarding Latinos, Asian Americans, African Americans, or Native Americans. Also, trying to get rid of racism in the workplace and in the schools.

Larry later suggests that getting rid of workplace racism entails getting the white decision-makers to give up enough power to allow more people of color to be hired, and that this is a formidable challenge.

CONCLUSION: TOWARD AN ANTIRACIST PEDAGOGY

These commentaries from younger white Americans demonstrate that white racist attitudes, emotions, and ideology remain central and *systemic* in this society. The views expressed here are of great consequence to those whites who express them, regardless of the fact that they may not have given conscious thought to whiteness before, and they are very consequential for the racial present and future of the United States. It is the views of "everyday" whites that motivate racist practices that in turn sustain institutionalized racism.

As can be seen in the data, in constructing their racial identities, our respondents use a range of fictions. Their white identities have three commonplace elements: they are constructed as empty, passive, and disadvantaged—socially, politically, or economically. Mirrored against the cultures of people of color, whiteness often seems to lack content. Whiteness is explicitly perceived as being overwhelmed by other cultural intrusions. Without the historical context with which to understand current racism, whites often construct themselves as passive recipients of racial knowledge and observers of racist actions. Also in part because of ignorance of history, socioeconomic privileges are usually omitted from white identity, leaving whites fictionalized as victims of racial disadvantages. Indeed, white identity is frequently seen as a liability. Further, because the white-dominated system is believed to be just and equal, whites are being victimized by government policies such as affirmative action.

Given this set of beliefs, it is not surprising that whites often translate their views into action—or harmful inaction (Feagin and Vera 1995:9–10). Whites vary not only in the degree of their racist attitudes but also in the level of their racist actions. White officiants are usually the most active in perpetrating antiblack discrimination, as they make the key decisions and articulate the important racist attitudes. Other white actors act the part of acolytes, for they discriminate against African-Americans or other people of color partly or mainly because they are told to do so by their employers. Yet other whites stand by and observe while the officiants and/or acolytes carry out overt discrimination against people of color. Passivity is a very important buttress of contemporary racism.

Yet the exciting aspect of these findings is that many students have been moved toward questioning at least some of the sincere fictions they have been taught. Even one racial and ethnic relations course has moved many of them to reflect on the views, attitudes, and images they hold about African-Americans and people of color. These courses have helped many of them begin to see structural racism, which this study suggests is a crucial element in motivating antiracism. They are at least questioning, and some have gone to the point of taking antiracist action. Many, indeed, seem to be more concerned than previously at least with being antiprejudiced, if not being antiracist in terms of action. This is a hopeful finding.

Our research has important implications for antiracist theory and practice. Because this generation's view of everyday whiteness is different from that of previous generations, new antiracist strategies must be employed to confront everyday racism. If we continue to use models for combating racism devised for the parents and grandparents of young whites, we will not address the specific issues that lead the latter to endorse actively or to support passively societal racism. Young white students will one day be the influential adults who may perpetrate everyday racism against African-Americans and people of color. Hence, particularly when speaking with students, for whom in-class discussions of racism are often the first they have away from home, instructors should carefully define their terms, making clear the distinctions between the key types of racism, such as covert, subtle, overt, and unintentional racism, or individual and institutional racism. Broader and narrower definitions of "racism" can be acknowledged in antiracist education (Blauner 1994).

In antiracist education we must counter the commonplace discourses of white privilege. Our youthful autobiographies suggest that many whites most often understand themselves to be privileged only in minor ways. For example, many students have read an article that includes a list of white privileges at all levels, both "microlevel" and structural (McIntosh 1998). Many refer to the article in their autobiographies. The privilege they mention most often is that white people can buy flesh-colored bandages while people of color must announce every wound with an unmatched strip across their bodies. Although a recognition of all levels of privilege is important, young whites should be reminded that white privileges not only make their everyday lives easier but give them major economic resources and stability, and enable them to live, on the average, six to seven years longer than African-Americans (for an in-depth discussion of the health costs of racism, see Feagin and McKinney 2002).

This study shows that one good venue for white reeducation is the college classroom. The Latin American educator Paulo Freire once explained that the *true vocation* of human beings is not the dehumanization of others that they too often engage in but rather the humanization of the world. Teaching antiracism involves creating greatly expanded awareness not only among the oppressed but also among the oppressors (Freire 1995:17; see also Feagin and Vera 2001:21–22). Sadly, we currently have few college courses that begin to deal candidly with systemic racism in the United States, past or present. Many more are needed, with instructors who are as diverse as the society itself. Instructors teaching about the nation's racist history and current reality are in a position to disrupt or refute the many fictions of whiteness. A first major step in dealing with white racism is to confront firmly its many myths and misconceptions. However, progressive educators must be certain not only to point out the seriousness of the problem of institutionalized racism but also to suggest how whites may become antiracist activists in the field and allies to people of color. Instructors should suggest various antiracist activist groups, publications, and Web sites for their students to visit and should be available for further conversations about racism when the course is over.

In addition, instructors can provide important information on how to counter racism in everyday practice and on how students can play a role in reducing prejudice and discrimination in their own spheres of interaction, such as family and friendship networks. Instructors can also bring in members of local organizations of color that are working against racial discrimination, in order to provide students with practical information on actions that are being taken against discrimination. By bringing in adults of color who have long suffered from racial discrimination and who are now taking action against it, instructors not only can better inform their students about racism in the "outside world," but also can help students to build linkages with people of color outside the classroom. For many white students, particularly those who have grown up in rural settings, these may be some of the first relationships with people of color that they will have had. The learning experiences with the greatest potential for disrupting sincerely held fictions of the white self are likely those that involve crossing racial boundaries and learning new racial attitudes while unlearning racist behaviors. Yet such interracial experiences must not be accepted as proof of the end of racism or conceived of as the final goal of antiracism.

Instructors who teach about racism must recognize one of the primary obstacles students cite to becoming active in antiracism: fears of social awkwardness or interpersonal discomfort and tension. Although some use this as an excuse, we as teachers of antiracism have a responsibility to try not to alienate white students who are part of our classrooms. Yet we have an often conflicting responsibility to combat the denial of white privilege that is so evident in the words of young white people (see Kincheloe et al. 1998). Instructors should not try to remove all tension from discussions, because expression of these tensions can be enlightening for young people. Indeed, while being sympathetic to white students is very important, it is equally important to encourage them to take action in their own lives.

Giving up racism means not only abandoning racist attitudes but also relinquishing power and privilege. This study demonstrates that antiracist instructors have a unique opportunity to show young people not only how racism has developed and been maintained in the United States, but how they can actively resist it and renounce white power and privilege. As Feagin, Vera, and Batur have recently stated: "those committed to antiracist thought and action, whatever their background or group, need to interfere regularly in the transmission and redefinition of this commonplace racist imagery and iconography—if it is to be started on the road to eradication. . . . Whether blatant or subtle, the racist understandings that are imbedded in daily life can be actively challenged every day" (2001:17).

17

The Political Is Personal: The Influence of White Supremacy on White Antiracists' Personal Relationships

EILEEN O'BRIEN

Whites and people of color in the United States are separated by a vast "perception gap"—whites feel that racism ended in the 1960s and see people of color as complaining or overreacting, while people of color see continued racial discrimination (Steinhorn and Diggs-Brown 2000). This perception gap means that substantial white support for antiracist policies is lacking. Because whites are a majority in numbers and power in this nation, the "conversion" of whites to antiracism is a crucial part of the larger political struggle for human rights. Yet we seldom hear about whites who have taken the step to antiracism. This step is a substantial one, far from simply being nonracist. Joe Barndt writes: "Nonracists try to deny that the prison exists. Antiracists work for the prison's eventual destruction" (1991:65). Whereas nonracists merely profess tolerant attitudes and think everyone should be treated equally, antiracists not only acknowledge that not everyone is treated equally but work "daily [and] vigilantly" (hooks 1995:158) to combat this inequality.

Recently writers have been engaged in the process of describing what this antiracist path might look like. Paul Kivel (1996) advises whites to become "allies" of people of color, while Noel Ignatiev and John Garvey (1994) suggest a "race traitor" stance, where one refuses to partake in the "white club" of privileges accorded to those who appear "white" in our society. Anthologies such as *Off White* (Fine et. al. 1997) and *Critical White Studies* (Delgado and Stefancic 1997) offer perspectives on how whites can challenge the centrality of whiteness, thereby upsetting the very foundation of racism in North American culture. However, there has been little empirical analysis of white antiracists themselves, and nothing to my knowledge has been written on how taking such a political stance affects the *interpersonal relationships* of these whites. In this analysis, I will demonstrate how whites' relationships with people of color and their relationships with other whites are impacted by their commitments to being antiracist. In particular, I will argue that just because whites have dedicated their lives to antiracism does not mean that they exhibit *empathy* in their relationships with people of color, nor does it mean that they have developed the *autonomy* of a secure white identity that enables them to interact with other whites. Indeed, empathy and autonomy are so difficult to achieve for white antiracists because of the pervasiveness of white supremacy and racism.

Joe Feagin and Hernán Vera (1995) found that what set white antiracists apart from the general white population was their ability to empathize with people of color. For whites, developing empathy means having to step across that perception gap, grasping the extent to which racism still exists, and validating the experiences of people of color. Because white denial about modern racism is so pervasive, we might expect that people of color would instantly bond to those few whites who are actually antiracist. However, this is seldom the case. During my first presentation of some of my research on white antiracists, one African-American woman responded: "those are the people I don't trust." My first instinct was to clarify who my sample was—perhaps she had not understood that I was studying white *anti*racists, not white racists. Yet she assured me she had not misspoken. Indeed, this woman echoes the sentiments of many African-Americans, including 1960s activists such as Dick Gregory and Malcolm X, who said they preferred a white bigot to a white liberal because at least the former was under no false pretenses of being well-intentioned. Three decades later, Richard Delgado developed the concept of *false empathy* to explain how well-intentioned whites can actually do more harm than good without realizing it:

> False empathy is worse than none at all, worse than indifference. It makes you overconfident, so that you can easily harm the intended beneficiary. You are apt to be paternalistic, thinking you know what the other really wants or needs. You can easily substitute your own goal for his. You visualize what you would want if you were he, when your experiences and needs are radically different. (Delgado 1996:31)

Because white antiracists can easily fall into the behavior that Delgado describes above, people of color often choose to keep their distance until a white antiracist has earned their trust. Hence white antiracists face the challenge of establishing *empathy*, rather than false empathy, when creating relationships with people of color.

Empathy is often more easily achieved by those who have a secure racial identity. Janet Helms (1990) has developed a stage theory of racial identity development, noting that both whites and people of color go through parallel but not identical six-stage processes. For whites, the first three stages (contact, disintengration, reintegration) represent those who are ignorant about racism, due to either lack of exposure or limited exposure without fully understanding. The second three (pseudo-independence, immersion-emersion, autonomy) represent a journey "toward a nonracist white identity" (Jones and Carter 1996:7). Beverly Tatum (1992, 1994) has observed that for whites, pseudo-independence is often characterized by avoidance of other whites. That is, once they become aware of racism and accept that it exists, it may seem like their only option is associating with predominantly people of color since most whites do not share their newfound perspective. Viewing whites as the primary perpetrators of racism, they may feel that in order to be good antiracists they must stay away from other whites. It also may be uncomfortable for them to connect with whites who are not antiracist, because they would face the daunting task of educating them. Pseudo-independents believe themselves to be confident as white antiracists, yet they are confident in this identity only around those who already agree with them—usually people of color. Whites typically emerge out of this stage when they are able to discover white antiracist role models. This search for others like them is part of the immersion-emersion stage, and once they have successfully incorporated this acceptance of a white antiracist identity as part of their self-concept, they reach autonomy (Helms's final stage.)

Helms's racial identity theory has direct implications for white antiracists' personal relationships with other whites. If whites are in the pseudo-independence stage, their political stance of antiracism may be intact, but their personal relationships with other whites could be either suffering or nonexistent. They may sever ties with white people who have previously meant a lot to them or miss out on opportunities to connect with whites who are not necessarily antiracist but still could be receptive to their point of view. On the other hand, if they have reached autonomy, they should be more likely to extend empathy to other whites whether or not they are antiracist. They may even use those relationships with whites as opportunities to share an antiracist perspective. Hence, in moving towards empathy and autonomy, white antiracists create the greatest possibilities for successful *inter*racial and *intra*racial relationships.

This movement, however, is not easy in today's white-supremacist/racist society. In contrast with older traditional definitions of racism which focus on attitudes and behaviors, modern racism is often less overt and barely detectable to most whites. It is reproduced in the everyday normal functioning of society, resulting in countless material advantages or "privileges" for whites (Bonilla-Silva 2001; Feagin 2000). This system does not change simply because individual whites become antiracist. Even white antiracists carry white-supremacist expectations about the everyday dynamics of their lives. For one thing, it is less imperative for whites to have to consider alternative perspectives when embarking upon a course of action, whereas for people of color such considerations are much more common for reasons of survival. It is under this context that white false empathy occurs—even though they may mean well by suggesting solutions for racism, they may not stop to consider alternatives because it has not been in their everyday experience to have to do so.

Another everyday privilege of whiteness is that whites assume or expect that they will be trusted and taken seriously. However, all of these privileges flow much more smoothly to whites who support the dominant color-blind ideology. Once they challenge this ideology, their fellow whites are not automatically receptive to them. Another privilege is for them to withdraw into supportive communities and not face that challenge with other non-antiracist whites (the choice against autonomy).

In these ways, then, their movement towards empathy with people of color and autonomy with other whites is a direct struggle against white supremacy. It is a struggle to translate a political commitment (to antiracism) into one's personal relationships—that everyday realm where white supremacy is reproduced.

Methods

The data analyzed in this chapter are part of a larger research project on white antiracist activists which utilized a multiple method strategy of interviews, participant observation, and archival analysis of organizational literature of two major antiracist groups: Anti-Racist Action (ARA) and the People's Institute for Survival and Beyond (PISB). Here I draw primarily from thirty in-depth interviews collected between 1996 and 1999 using a purposive snowball sampling technique. The sample is split evenly with respect to gender (fifteen women and fifteen men), and a variety of ages are represented (ten are age thirty or under, seventeen are between the ages of thirty-one and sixty, and three are over age sixty.) The interviewees also represent different regions of North America. Two interviewees reside in Toronto, two reside west of the Mississippi River (in North Dakota and Arizona), and the rest are from east of the Mississippi River in the United States—nine from the Midwest (Ohio, Illinois, and Michigan), five from the Northeast (Massachusetts, New York, and Washington DC), five from the Southeast (Florida and North Carolina) and seven from Louisiana.

About half of the sample consists of members of ARA or PISB, and the other half represent other organizations or were not part of any organization. Elsewhere (O'Brien 2001), I have focused more specifically on the differences between these two organizations, since each group has distinct foci and methods of action, but here I focus on the influence of organizational ideology only as it is relevant to personal relationship development. I also quote some activists of color who have been interviewed about their perceptions of white antiracists.

Relationships with People of Color
Journeys to Empathy

Delgado (1996) and Feagin and Vera (1995) emphasize the importance of moving from false empathy to empathy for whites. Yet false empathy can be common for those in these early stages of antiracism. Jason, a young white antiracist, displayed an example of false empathy as he described an incident at the Lollapalooza tour (a concert event) where he was "tabling" for his antiracist organization (distributing newsletters and brochures and signing people up for the mailing list).

> There was a table almost beside us . . . who were in MTV's Choose or Lose thing, the voter registration drive. There was probably about fifteen

to twenty people staffing it, and they were all black people. And when they were setting up, [we asked them] "Oh who are you guys with?" [they said] "MTV's Choose or Lose," and I was like, "Oh that's pretty cool." And one of the people there asked us who we were with, and we said "Anti Racist Action" and I heard a snicker. [laughs] Like that. And my guard just went up, and I was like, "what was that for?" I almost wanted to say to him, "You should be working with us, rather than working for MTV!"

Here Jason faced a common situation for white antiracists, where credibility as whites doing antiracist work needs to be established in order to foster trusting relationships with people of color. When Jason sensed his credibility was being challenged, rather than reaching out to establish that credibility, he became defensive and assumed a paternalistic attitude toward this black young man, implying he himself knew better than this person of color how his activist energies should be spent. This type of false empathy prevented a potential relationship between the two young men from developing. Had the two of them talked openly, a white person might have learned how important lack of voter registration has been to black freedom struggles both historically and currently, and a black person might have learned about a white young man who put his life on the line to challenge police brutality. Yet this did not occur.

It might be useful to contrast this account with a viewpoint from Lorenzo, an activist of color, who faced a similar situation in organizing a campuswide coalition against racism:

I saw a lot of whites that talked the talk, but never really sort of gave up their white supremacy beliefs, whether conscious or unconscious. And for example when we were pushing a particular agenda, these folks came behind and tried to tell us how to basically organize and how to proceed in the movement.... These are the folks, in terms of practical matters were middle class, settled, nothing would happen to them and still they sort of chastised us because in their estimation we were not radical enough and they wanted us to be more radical. I was like, "look, this is not a revolution, this is a very restricted struggle here and the conditions are not such to be aspiring for a revolution."... I'm talking about socialist folks who claim to be on our side, but in truth were more interested in telling us how to run the movement.

Here we can begin to understand what it might feel like for a person of color to try and interact with white antiracists who perceive him as "not radical enough." Being told what to do by white people, whether they claimed to be antiracist or not, for him felt like just another manifestation of white supremacy.

Rosalind, another white antiracist, a bit older than Jason, who struggled with her tendency to adopt a paternalistic attitude towards people of color, described a maturation process. She was beginning to try to understand why people of color might opt for different methods of antiracism and community organizing from those she would have them select:

> I still sort of feel like I'm beating my head against the wall when I try to work with [African-American community]. I don't know how much you know about them, but they are unusual about being pretty far along in self-determination and community empowerment in terms of [a] really oppressed community. But I've been very frustrated in the partnership areas. They'll demand that we meet and work together, and then they won't [pause] they won't do it! And I understand the[ir] resistance to doing it. So I'm not as impatient with that as I used to be, but it's still real frustrating.

Like Jason, Rosalind revealed her frustration that people of color do not necessarily choose to do their community organizing with *her* (predominantly white) antiracist group. Yet unlike Jason, she expressed some willingness to understand the reasoning behind these African-Americans' decisions. Both Jason and Rosalind demonstrated that false empathy is an easy pattern to fall into and that it takes a conscious effort to resist it.

Part of the journey to empathy for whites is facing the historical atrocities committed by whites against people of color and realizing that the distrust of whites that people of color may have is grounded in a long history. White antiracists who grasp this reality may be more likely to wait out the initial distrust and work towards forming relationships with people of color. Pam explained:

> A white antiracist is looked at very skeptically from the community of color, and *rightfully so*. . . . Until that person, that group, whatever gets to know an individual and understand why [they are antiracist], I think, their skepticism—I can't condemn them for that. If a white person comes around, there's gotta be a reason why they're doing something that they're doing. Why did the army men give all those warm blankets to the Indians that were infected with smallpox? They gave those blankets to those people for a reason, they wanted to get rid of them! So why am I doing something then? Do I wanna get inside so I can find out the inner workings of the community so I can destroy it, or am I a curiosity-seeker, or do I really want to help? So I think people of color should look at white antiracists a little questionably at first and until they realize that this person's OK. They have *every reason* for being skeptical.

While earlier Rosalind stated that she "understand[s] the resistance" of people of color to working with antiracist whites, here Pam elaborated on the source of that resistance, described it, and seemed truly empathic. Rather than exhibiting false empathy, Pam spoke from a place of wanting to understand where people of color were coming from, even though in condoning those actions she condoned some treatment of her as a white person that could be uncomfortable for her.

One of the many unfortunate consequences of racism is that truly intimate interracial relationships are difficult to form. White antiracists are not exempt from this consequence. Those who approach their relationships with people of color with false empathy probably will not be successful in building lasting interracial relationships. Those who strive for empathy have no less of a thorny road to travel. They must persevere in the face of rejection. But their openness to facing constructive criticism without becoming defensive is exactly what their allies of color may desire. Lorenzo, the activist of color quoted earlier in this section, explained this perspective:

> Whites obviously feel afraid of many of us minorities thinking that we're not going to trust them, that we're not really going to be on their side, and this and that. That fear . . . has a limited basis in reality because my impression of the situation is that, if you walk the walk, after the first encounter or two when I see or we see that you are on our side you become a brother, OK? But anyway, because many people are not willing to expose themselves and be vulnerable to misunderstandings, which is part of the game, then they develop a shield and never really go beyond sort of appearances and always remain sort of aloof. That sense of aloofness has always been an issue in developing true interracial organizations and struggles. So you need to break those barriers and the only way is by making mistakes, by saying silly things occasionally, and then getting mad and then learning and then sort of getting smart and then moving on.

This vulnerability to face one's own mistakes and willingness to learn and grow from them is the first step to building authentic relationships with people of color.

AUTHENTIC RELATIONSHIPS AND ACCOUNTABILITY

As whites learn how to develop empathy, rather than false empathy, with people of color, they begin to develop meaningful relationships with them. While most whites may go through their entire lives thinking they have a token "black friend," in actuality this person may be nothing more than an acquaintance who does not feel comfortable sharing his or her thoughts about racial matters with this white "friend." Whites have a history of *rereading* or *looping* (Rosenblum and Travis 1996) upon being told about instances of discrimination—that is, they will tend to suggest that the tellers were either overreacting or perhaps provoked the incident themselves. Such behavior obviously thwarts the establishment of empathy. When these interracial relationships can survive discussions that confront racism head-on, "authentic relationships" are established, according to PISB. In a similar vein of Delgado's (1996) discussion of false empathy, PISB asserts that well-intentioned white antiracists may be doing more harm than good if they do not have "accountability" to people of color through these authentic relationships. Hence, interracial relationships are not just sites of personal connection but also are crucial to ensuring effective activism. David, an organizer and trainer with PISB, addressed why the concept of accountability is important for whites:

> There's got to be *accountability* to oppressed peoples . . . otherwise, even though we [whites] would claim to be antiracist, we'd change the subject. We would, by the very nature of what it means to be white, if all of us get into a room talking, and meeting, and doing whatever, if we're not held *accountable*, the forces will take us off course. And we will either start fighting with each other on the things that white folks fall out with each other on, or we would begin to take over the study of what it means to be white in a way that doesn't mesh with peoples of color's reality.

For white antiracist activists, the method for keeping oneself in check is not adherence to some abstract code of ethics or to a board of directors; rather it is in interpersonal relationships that accountability is sustained. The personal is indeed political, as one's political action is inspired and adjusted by the personal connection of authentic relationships.

These dynamics come into play more specifically in white antiracists' lives. PISB member Kendra described the tenacity and commitment that goes into sustaining authentic relationships, even when being held accountable causes humiliation and pain:

> The first year that I was working in relation to the community I worked in [an African-American community] . . . I was very excited about their model of organizing and I wrote two articles about it, and had them published. And I had passed them around the community beforehand, and stuff, but when it came out, [pause] it was a shock to people . . . this was not what they expected. And they felt used, and they felt abused, and they felt that their lives had been taken from them and put in a book and by someone they trusted—it really breached the trust that we had very, very deeply. . . . So I had to sit down with the community, and talk about it. And the people were *really* angry at me, and I made a commitment that I was going to accept responsibility. . . . What I've learned [from this] is an understanding that, to really make the change happen that needs to happen in this world, it's gonna take commitment and staying in there and hanging in there when things get difficult.

Although the concepts of authentic relationships and accountability are unique to PISB, other white antiracists who are not members of that organization also rely on their personal relationships with people of color to keep them vigilant on their antiracist journeys. Angela, for example, found herself challenged about her white privilege during a heated argument with her African-American partner about how they celebrated Christmas:

> [My partner] said, "Look, we cannot resolve this until we start talking about the class part of this." And that of course intrigued me enough to sort of keep me in there. . . . She began to explain to me, "we do Christmas the way you did it . . . you take weeks and weeks to do it. . . . And I grew up in a situation where I was working and my mother was working and my father was working up until the afternoon of Christmas Eve. And our tradition was always running up to Woolworth's and getting gifts for each other." . . . I devote three to four weeks leading up to it . . . but some of the way that I can do that is really about my privilege, and I had a mom at home and aunts living right next door to me, I had the advantage and the privilege I guess of some sorts of making that happen and making it possible.

White supremacy encroached upon the most intimate relationship in Angela's life. The way she approached the holiday season was embedded in her privilege in a way she had not recognized until her African-American partner pointed it out to her. A common denominator in these situations of accountability is that the white antiracists resisted acting out of defensiveness or false empathy. They remained open to a person of color's interpretation of racism and their own role in it, and strove to use that information to inspire their own further growth as an antiracist. In these cases, empathy is achieved, and interpersonal relationships become potential sites of social change.

Another activist of color, Vanessa, explained what she is looking for in those white antiracists whom she can truly trust, and it resembles what Kendra and Angela described above:

> I look for that self-analysis. . . . I look for a willingness to take whatever criticisms I may have without being defensive. Sort of accepting that and [being] willing to have the conversation that that might be true. Not to be caught up in yes I do or no I don't or this person does it more. A willingness to work on solutions from both parties about whatever the behavior is.

Vanessa does not only look at how whites respond to her, she also looks at how they respond to their white "peers," the issue to which I now turn.

RELATIONSHIPS WITH OTHER WHITES

BEING "DISGUSTED" WITH WHITES

The literature on white racial identity development acknowledges that whites may go through a period of abhorrence of whiteness when first committing to antiracism (Tatum 1992, 1994). Although not using the language of these stages, the white antiracist respondents in this study agree that it was a "progression" on their journey to move out of a pseudo-independence, or white-avoiding, stage. Mike, for example, stated:

> I've seen a lot of white people go through this. They get real disgusted with white culture, because when you become aware of the reality of what has been done by the white collective, it's kind of disgusting. I personally went through a process where there was very few [white] people that I wanted to be around . . . I just wasn't wanting to be around most of the people that had been my support system. And that was real disappointing for a long time, it put me in a real difficult place. And that's progressed to the point where I understand that . . . there's work for me to do within the white community.

As Mike pointed out, one moves beyond this avoidance of whites by coming to understand the importance of bringing other whites to awareness. But this progression is sometimes not an easy one. Nancy's progression was at least thirty years in the making, dating back to the 1960s and extending into the 1990s. She recalled:

> I think from the earliest times I thought it was unjust and I wanted to be part of the solution. I didn't understand how to be a part of that solution within the white community—at all! I mean, even when Malcolm started saying go back to your own community, I was like, you don't know where I come from! [laughs] . . . because we knew we couldn't go home, I mean our parents would never speak to us again. . . . But then on the other hand, I'm showing absolute respect for what he meant by that, so I'm not trying to make light of that. . . . I've learned over the years how much I have to do to be willing to come back and work in the white community and work on antiracism with white people. . . . And that was the hardest trip I've ever had to make . . . was from living very, very comfortably in African-American neighborhoods, and living with my friends, and surrounded by predominantly African-American culture and stuff, to saying it is my responsibility, if I mean that sincerely, to make this move and work with white people.

Nancy spent most of her adult life avoiding whites. She lived comfortably in black neighborhoods, worshipping in black churches, and being an activist in predominantly black political organizations. Indeed "the hardest trip [she] ever had to make" was reestablishing significant personal attachments to other whites and accepting that as part of her antiracist work.

This "pseudo-independent" behavior is not perceived favorably by people of color, and hence it alienates whites not only from other whites but from people of color as well. Interestingly, both activists of color quoted in the previous section mentioned their perceptions of white antiracists who separate themselves as the "good whites" from other white peers. Both Lorenzo and Vanessa perceived this behavior as arrogant and judgmental:

> Humility is something that white people need big time, because even in this antiracist organization I have found that many of them develop this notion that I am better than anybody. Some of them develop the belief that they are better than the average white because they're "beyond" and then some of them believe they're better than us because they "understand."

> Often times I find white antiracist workers a bit judging. I think that they set themselves above their white peers. I think that often this marker of antiracism gets worn as a banner that yeah, I'm down with the black people, the colored people, the "whatever" people.

While the more obvious consequence of pseudo-independent behavior is the lack of relationships with other whites, a latent consequence is that the alliances whites forge with people of color based upon that premise will not be solid either.

David, quoted previously, drew upon the PISB philosophy as he explained the difficulty of but necessity for antiracist whites to maintain relationships with other whites:

> The [People's] Institute would later talk to me about how important it would be for me to maintain my relationship with my family and thus model, [or] attempt to model, how other whites must always keep the connection, must not write each other off, must try to keep from being split all the time in the many ways that white folks split themselves and divide themselves from each other. . . . Who had resisted this construct of race who were white? Who had stood against it? What were their names? What did they look like? They're invisible in history. We would hear about other peoples being invisible-ized, but those whites who stood against it, with one or two exceptions, were not there either. . . . None of us got here on our own, we all stand on the shoulders of others.

A major source of the difficulty in moving out of the "pseudo-independent" stage is the lack of white antiracist role models (Tatum 1992, 1994). It is not that they never existed; rather, there is a historical silence about them. Malcolm X pointed out there was a reason behind the silencing and/or discrediting of white antiracists. If we were told that white people like John Brown (who was executed for inciting a slave rebellion) were lunatics instead of heroes, then whites would be less likely to break the status quo and join in the struggle.

The effects of this silence are political and personal. Whites not only lose out on opportunities to advance antiracism but also decrease their capability for intimate connections with other whites. Nowhere was this more evident than in the story of Nancy's relationship with her white son:

> My biggest disappointment is that I didn't understand well enough about dealing with whiteness to make the life of my white son [long pause]— I wasn't able to give him the tools that he needed to understand the complicated world that he was living in racially. . . . He always knew that I valued black culture, and blackness, and that I valued societal change. He grew up a kid who always chose black friends. . . . I don't think I was ever the kind of person who bashed people. But I didn't know how to make him feel really good about being a white person and an antiracist and a resistor. I didn't help him to have a positive [pause] white identity or male identity. I sort of thought if you're white and male in this culture, everything's positive. . . . But . . . he didn't want to be like those white men. It took me years before I realized that I had ill-equipped him. . . . We're just learning how to deal with ourselves as white people and be proud of ourselves by choosing role models who are white that we can be like.

White antiracists face unique challenges in developing and maintaining interpersonal relationships with other whites. The political divide-and-conquer strategies which define racism as a "black issue" about which whites should have no concern keep us from seeing the long history of whites who *have* been concerned and lived lives dedicated to that concern. Yet these politics trickle down and have a very personal impact on people's lives. Although white antiracists may find it easier to connect with people of color, the "hardest trip" but most necessary trip may be the one towards autonomy, in which they maintain their connections with other whites.

STAYING CONNECTED TO OTHER WHITES

As with their journeys to true empathy with people of color, these white antiracists also described journeys to greater openness to other whites as they continued their work. Paul, a teacher, described his movement from separating himself from other whites to a more nonjudgmental attitude that allowed him to connect more with others:

> I can tend to get excited about things and tend to become evangelistic. And so I was the person at the school, once I began to see it, I was talking about it, and I knew that I was quickly getting marginalized. And so a lot of the work for me has been, how do I do this work holding people with love that I'm working with and not be judgmental?

At some point Paul began to realize that becoming "marginalized" would not ultimately help him do his antiracist work effectively. Mac discussed a similar evolution in his own work, and explained in more detail the practical implications of staying connected for further antiracism:

> I'm a real practical person and I don't try to convince anyone beyond the amount I think I can. . . . I am more skilled as a revolutionary now than I was when I believed that every time somebody said "nigger" I had to throw a fit. I don't have to do anything, except whatever is the most effective right then to get them closer to fixing it. So, if shutting your mouth and walking out is the smartest thing—well, actually, if any other choice will create more harm than good—then your responsibility as a revolutionary is to shut your mouth, smile, act like you didn't hear it, and move on, because we have to win. We can't be just making stands in the abstract and being unpopular. We have to get people's ideas to change, and ranting sometimes pushes them the other way.

Both Mac and Paul realized that behaving in an aggressively self-righteous way with other whites was not the best way to "get people's ideas to change."

Maintaining relationships with other whites means that white antiracists are not just "preaching to the choir," or spending time only with whites who agree with them, as pseudo-independents would. They are increasing the span of the lives that they touch by maintaining those connections. They are continually challenging other whites to question the ways in which they unknowingly contribute to racism. In this way, they further their goal of fighting racism through their interpersonal relationships. However, as the above quotes point out, this goal cannot be met by becoming angry and indignant at every turn. This presents a special challenge when dealing with family members, since people often are more likely to be candid and emotional in familial settings. Kendra recounted one such challenge in the following anecdote:

> One night I was sitting at the dinner table with my [black] husband, and my [white] stepmother, and my little daughter, and we needed some napkins. And my little brother was in the other room and I said, "[Name], will you grab me a napkin?" Then [he] came into the room with a roll of paper towels. And my mother says, "[Name], there's napkins in there, come on, let's eat like the white folks." [pause] And [laughs] [my husband] and I are looking at her, you know? And she's like, "Oh, I'm so sorry, I'm so sorry," and she said, " Oh, I spent too many years hanging around your father." So she was blaming it on him and [laughs] I said, "Well, that wasn't him, that was *you, you* said that!" [laughs] . . . If [my husband] had wanted to get up and walk out, we would've. But . . . I don't think it would have changed her. I think that having her realize that she had just hurt someone who's a member of our family, who she says she loves and respects, made more of a difference. And if I had, on my own, gotten up and stormed out of the house, I don't think I would

have helped, it would have hurt more. And I think it would have been arrogant of me. If [my husband] had just said, "I cannot sit at the table with this woman," I would have left. . . . But it was like he took it with a certain grace and sense of humor, and I think I had an obligation to do the same thing. And I don't think she says stuff like that anymore.

Rather than making a scene, Kendra spoke of her concern for effectiveness and success when she said, "I don't think it would have changed her," and "I don't think it would have helped, it would have hurt more." Additionally, like Paul and Mac, she referred to minimizing the self-righteous attitude when she remarked that it would have been "arrogant" for her to storm out of the house in retaliation. Kendra selected a course of action that still called a racist comment into question without disrupting the family dinner, and without severing her relationship with her stepmother.

In using her husband's reaction as a guide, Kendra was practicing accountability to people of color as discussed previously. Often, a person of color will not want to "make a scene" when racism occurs because it happens so often that they would not have the energy to endure every such "scene." In becoming indignant in such situations, as if speaking for the person of color, whites can lapse into the false empathy that Delgado (1996) describes. In actuality, people of color may view nonresponse to a racist situation as most appropriate, especially when action could detain them or put them in danger. Having not lived their lives with such regular possibilities of danger looming, whites may be unaware of these kinds of considerations. This is when accountability to people of color can be especially useful, even lifesaving. The practices of accountability to people of color and of maintaining connection to other whites came together effectively in Kendra's example. Indeed, one activist of color quoted previously, Vanessa, asserted that how white antiracists respond to their white peers is *the* most important criterion for her in determining whether she can truly have an authentic relationship with that person:

> Call your peers to the table! My main quest would be that this is all good and great, but we would get along even better if I saw you sticking your neck out there, calling your own folks to the table. Not in a condescending way, not in a way that says you're better than they are, but really call them to the table to have the discussion.

CONCLUSION

"Condescending," "arrogant," and "judgmental" are just some of the adjectives used to describe white antiracists throughout these interviews. Yet it is crucial that these barriers to empathy and autonomy are understood not as personality shortcomings but as collective inheritances that whites as a group receive under white supremacy. Hence, increasing the number of whites who are politically committed to antiracism will not alone eradicate racism. As Eduardo

Bonilla-Silva aptly points out, the focus on a struggle between the "good whites" and "bad whites" misses the point, since white supremacy is continually reproduced in the "everyday rituals" of society (2001:196). White antiracists must not only cease being prejudiced and discriminatory and fight racist institutional practices, but they must also tend to their everyday interactions with others, where white supremacy also resides.

False empathy as a barrier to white antiracists' relationships with people of color is not a problem of these whites' personal prejudices. Rather, under white supremacy, whites have been trained to not have to take into consideration "other" worldviews, so any strategy they propose for ending racism may unintentionally come across as arrogant to people of color who have had to adopt a "double consciousness" to survive. Further, whites have had the privilege of being judged solely as individuals and hence expect that. Those white antiracists who struggle for empathic relationships with people of color not only strive to reduce personal prejudice and discrimination but humble themselves to alternative interpretations of their actions, understanding that they occupy a privileged position in white supremacy that has little to do with their individual convictions.

Beyond their relationships with people of color, it may seem surprising that white antiracists' relationships with other whites are also constrained by white supremacy. Yet indeed, we see here how the choice either to separate from other whites or to relate to them only with arrogant admonitions (in the "good white/bad white" model) further perpetuates racism, even though no overt act of antiblack discrimination is taking place. The individualistic orientation to life that is a white privilege gives whites the idea that they can be one-man or one-woman islands of political antiracism and still be effective in their work. Ironically, Helms has named her most developed stage of white identity "autonomy," which refers to someone who maintains a subversive antiracist ideology despite the pressures to conform to the dominant ideology. One cannot maintain this orientation if constantly cut off from those who hold the dominant ideology, whether through avoidance or arrogance. If being antiracist means challenging the modern existence of racism, then white antiracists must continue to be present in those "everyday rituals" of white supremacy if they expect to interrupt it effectively. This means that remaining connected to other whites is a decisively antiracist act both personal and political.

In describing true white antiracism as "daily [and] vigilant," bell hooks (1995:158) understood the pervasiveness of white supremacy. Only antiracism which struggles against these everyday manifestations of white supremacy in the most personal and intimate of relationships can be effective in today's "new racist" society.

PART V

Conclusion

18

"New Racism," Color-Blind Racism, and the Future of Whiteness in America

EDUARDO BONILLA-SILVA

In most postmodern writing, whiteness is regarded as an identity, a performance, a mere cultural construct or, is framed as a moral problem. In sharp contrast, we anchored this volume on the idea that whiteness is the foundational category of "white supremacy" (Mills 1997). *Whiteness, then, in all of its manifestations, is embodied racial power.* Whether expressed in militant (e.g., the Klan) or tranquil fashion (e.g., most members of the white middle class) and whether actors deemed "white" are cognizant of it, *whiteness is the visible uniform of the dominant racial group.* Therefore all actors socially regarded as "white"—and, as I shall argue later, as "near white"—receive systemic privileges by virtue of wearing the white—or virtuallly white—outfit, whereas those regarded as nonwhite are denied those privileges.[1] This explains, for instance, why "not-yet-white" ethnic immigrants (Roediger 2002) historically strove to become white as well as why immigrants of color always attempt to distance themselves from dark identities (blackness) when they enter the United States' racial polity (Bonilla-Silva 1997, Bonilla-Silva and Lewis 1999).

The authors in this volume have addressed various aspects of whiteness as embodied racial power (e.g., whiteness in neighborhoods, whiteness by class, whiteness among biracials, whiteness in certain professions, whiteness among Latinos, etc.). In this chapter I attempt to explain how whiteness survives in a country that proclaims to be "beyond race" and to forecast how whiteness will play out in the twenty-first century. First, I discuss the nature of the "new racism"—the racial structure (specific set of social arrangements and practices that produce and reproduce a racial order) that replaced Jim Crow in the 1960s and 1970s. I follow this with a description of the basic contours of "color-blind racism," or the racial ideology that bonds the "new racism." After explaining the structural and ideological context for whiteness in post–civil rights America, I suggest in the next section that whiteness will undergo a major transformation in the twenty-first century and become Latin America–like. I conclude this chapter with an analysis of the political implications of the "new racism," color-blind racism, and the Latin-Americanization of whiteness and offer various strategies to challenge them.

NOW YOU SEE IT, NOW YOU DON'T: POST–CIVIL RIGHTS WHITE SUPREMACY

Although whites' common sense on racial matters ("We used to have a lot of racism, but things are so much better today!") is not totally without foundation (e.g., traditional forms of racial discrimination and exclusion as well as Jim Crow—based racist beliefs have decreased in significance), it is ultimately false. A number of researchers have documented the manifold subtle yet systematic ways in which racial privilege is reproduced in the United States (Feagin 2000; R. C. Smith 1995). I have labeled this new, kinder and gentler, white supremacy as the "new racism" and have argued that it is the main force behind contemporary racial inequality (Bonilla-Silva 2001; Bonilla-Silva and Lewis 1999).

Although the "new racism" seems to be racism lite, it is as effective as slavery and Jim Crow in maintaining the racial status quo. The central elements of this new structure are: 1) the increasingly *covert* nature of racial discourse and practices; 2) the avoidance of racial terminology and the ever-growing claim by whites that they experience "reverse racism"; 3) the invisibility of most mechanisms to reproduce racial inequality; 4) the incorporation of "safe minorities" (e.g., Clarence Thomas, Condeleeza Rice, or Colin Powell) to signify the nonracialism of the polity; and 5) the rearticulation of some racial practices characteristic of the Jim Crow period of race relations. In what follows, I explain why this "new racism" emerged and succinctly, because of space constraints, discuss how it operates in the area of social interaction (for a full discussion on how it works in other areas, see Bonilla-Silva 2001).

WHY A "NEW RACISM"?

Systems of racial domination, which I have labeled elsewhere as "racialized social systems" (Bonilla-Silva 1997, 2001; Bonilla-Silva and Lewis, 1999) are not static. Much like capitalism and patriarchy, they change due to external and internal pressures. The racial apartheid that blacks and other people of color experienced in the United States from the 1860s until the 1960s was predicated on 1) keeping them in rural areas, mostly in the South; 2) maintaining them as agricultural workers; and 3) excluding them from the political process. However, as people of color successfully challenged their socioeconomic position by migrating initially from rural areas to urban areas in the South and later to the North and West, by pushing themselves by whatever means necessary into nonagricultural occupations (Tuttle 1970), and by developing political organizations and movements such Garveyism, the NAACP, CORE, La Raza Unida Party, Brown Berets, and SNCC (Payne 1995; Montejano 1987), the infrastructure of apartheid began to crumble.

Among the external factors leading to the abolition of the Jim Crow racial order, the most significant were the participation of people of color in World Wars I and II, which patently underscored the contradiction between fighting for freedom abroad and lacking it at home; the Cold War, which made it a necessity to eliminate overt discrimination at home in order to sell the United States as the champion of democracy; and a number of judicial decisions, legislative acts, and presidential decrees that have transpired since the forties.

These demographic, social, political, and economic factors and the actions of various racial minority groups made change almost inevitable. But ripe conditions are not enough to change any structural order. Hence the racial order had to be directly challenged if it was going to be effectively transformed. That was the role fulfilled by the Civil Rights movement and the other forms of mass protest by blacks that took place in the sixties and seventies (Payne 1995). Organized and spontaneous challenges (e.g., the over three-hundred racial riots in the 1960s) were the catalysts that brought down Jim Crow white supremacy.

"NEW RACISM" IN SOCIAL INTERACTION

Despite the real progress that the abolition of most of the formal, overt, and humiliating practices associated with Jim Crow represented, this did not mean the end of practices to reproduce racial hierarchy. Instead, new racism practices have replaced Jim Crow ones in all areas of life. In terms of social interaction among the races in neighborhoods, schools, stores, and other areas, whites and minorities (but blacks in particular) have very limited and regimented interactions.

Yet the way in which racial inequality is reproduced in this area is vastly different from how it was reproduced in the past. For instance, residential segregation today, which is almost as high as it was forty years ago (Lewis Mumford Center 2001; Yinger 1995), is no longer accomplished through clearly discriminatory practices, such as real-estate agents employing outright refusal or subterfuge to avoid renting or selling to minority customers, federal government redlining policies, antiminority insurance and lending practices, and racially restrictive covenants on housing deeds (Massey and Denton 1993). In contrast, in the face of equal housing laws and other civil rights legislation, covert behaviors and strategies have largely replaced Jim Crow practices and have maintained the same outcome—separate communities. For example, housing audits indicate that blacks are denied available housing from 35 percent to 75 percent of the time, depending on the city in question (Smith 1995; Yinger 1995). These housing studies have shown that, when paired with similar white counterparts, minorities are likely to be shown fewer apartments, be quoted higher rents, or offered worse conditions, and be steered to specific neighborhoods (Galster 1990a, 1990b; Turner, Struyk, and Yinger 1991).

In the realm of everyday life, several recent works have attempted to examine the experiences blacks have with discrimination (S. Collins 1997; Feagin and Sikes 1994). In his interviews of middle-class blacks who have supposedly "made it," Ellis Cose (1995 [1993]) repeatedly discovered a sense among these "successful blacks" that they were being continually blocked and constrained (see also Hochschild 1995). Cose cites the cases of a trade association vice president who is kept is charge of "minority affairs," a law partner always viewed as a "*black litigator*," a prominent journalist who is demoted for pointing out how race affects news reporting, and a law professor at Georgetown who is embarrassed by Harvard in a recruitment effort (Chapter 1, Cose 1995 [1993]. The same pattern was evident in Sharon Collins's work in the Chicago area).

In 1981 Howard Schuman and his colleagues replicated a 1950 study of restaurants in New York's Upper East Side and found a substantial amount of discrimination remained (Schuman et al. 1983). Similar to the housing audits, the discrimination was of a subtle nature. Lawrence Otis-Graham reports in his book *Member of the Club* (1995) that in ten of New York's best restaurants he and his friends visited, they were stared at, mistaken for restaurant workers, seated in terrible spots, and buffered so as to avoid proximity to whites in most of them. He reports that they were treated reasonably well in only two of the ten restaurants. The suits recently filed against Denny's, Shoney's, and the International House of Pancakes suggest that discrimination in restaurants is experienced by blacks of *all* class backgrounds (Feagin and Sikes 1994).

The existence of everyday discrimination is also confirmed by existing survey data. For instance, one study found that 38 percent of blacks report discrimination as a result of being unfairly fired or denied a promotion, 37 percent report harassment by the police, and 32 percent report not being hired for a job (Forman, Williams, and Jackson 1997). Similar to other studies, the rates of discrimination reported by blacks on any single item were quite modest (see also Bobo and Suh 2000; Sigelman and Welch 1991). However, a shift to the question of how many blacks have experienced at least one form of discrimination in their lifetime provides some intriguing results (they were asked about six different types): 70 percent of blacks report experiencing at least one form of major discrimination in their lifetime (Forman, Williams, and Jackson 1997). Students of color on predominantly white college campuses have also reported extensive patterns of daily discrimination (Feagin, Vera and Imani 1996).

Joe Feagin and Melvin Sikes (1994) also document the dense network of discriminatory practices confronted by middle-class blacks in everyday life. Although they correctly point out that blacks face discriminatory practices that range from overt and violent to covert and gentle, the latter seem to be prevalent. In public spaces the discriminatory behavior described by black interviewees included poor service, special requirements applied only to them, surveillance in stores, being ignored at retail stores selling expensive commodities, receiving the worst accommodations in restaurants or hotels, being constantly confused with menial workers, along with the usual but seemingly less frequent epithets and overtly racist behavior (see Chapter 2 in Feagin and Sikes 1994).

Moreover, many of these patterns experienced by middle-income blacks are more apparent only because they have at least secured access to previously inaccessible social space. For low-income racial minorities, these kinds of experiences with daily discrimination are perhaps less rampant because they are, for the most part, physically excluded from white environs (neighborhoods, board meetings, classrooms, etc.; however, see my arguments about light-skinned Latinos and many Asians below). For example, in a study of families in several different school communities, low-income Latino families reported very little racial discrimination because they had contact primarily with other low-income Latinos in their neighborhoods and in the workplace. Discrimination was most apparent in those moments when these parents had to interact with large public institutions, where they reported rampant disrespect and disregard if not explicit racism (Fine and Weis 1998). Tyrone Forman and colleagues also found a similar pattern in their study of African-Americans in the Detroit metropolitan area. That is, blacks who have attended college or received a college degree report experiencing more discrimination than those who have not (Forman, Williams, and Jackson 1997).

This almost invisible racial structure maintains the "wages of whiteness" (Du Bois 1969) at the social, economic, political, and even psychological levels. By hiding their racial motif, new racism practices have become the present-day Trojan horse of white power.

COLOR-BLIND RACISM: HOW WHITES JUSTIFY CONTEMPORARY RACIAL INEQUALITY

If Jim Crow's racial structure has been replaced by a "new racism," what happened to Jim Crow racial ideology? What happened to beliefs about minorities' mental, moral, and intellectual inferiority?—to the idea that "it is the [blacks'] own fault that he is a lower-caste...a lower-class man" or the assertion that blacks' lack initiative, are shiftless, and have no sense of time; in short, what happened to the basic claim that minorities (but again, blacks in particular) are subhuman? (Dollard 1949:372). Social analysts of all stripes agree that most whites no longer subscribe to these tenets in a traditional, straightforward fashion. However, this does not mean the "end of racism," as a few conservative commentators have suggested (D'Souza 1995; Thernstrom and Thernstrom 1997). Instead, a new powerful racial ideology[2] has emerged that combines elements of liberalism with culturally based antiminority views to justify the contemporary racial order: color-blind racism. Yet this new ideology is a curious one. Although it engages, as all such ideologies do, in "blaming the victim," it does so in a very indirect "now you see it, now you don't" style that matches perfectly the character of the "new racism." In this section, I discuss briefly its central frames with examples drawn from in-depth interviews conducted as part of the 1997 Survey of College Students' Social Attitudes and the 1998 Detroit Area Study (DAS henceforth)[3] and from the material presented by some of the authors in this volume (for a full discussion of all the features of this ideology, see Bonilla-Silva 2003).

THE FRAMES OF COLOR-BLIND RACISM

Color-blind racism has four central frames, namely, *abstract liberalism, naturalization, cultural racism,* and *minimization of racism.* I illustrate here the first two frames and explain how whites use them to defend and, ultimately, justify contemporary racial inequality.

Abstract Liberalism: Unmasking Reasonable Racism   When minorities were slaves, contract laborers, or *"braceros,"* the principles of liberalism and humanism were not extended to them. Today whites believe minorities are part of the body-politic but extend the ideas associated with liberalism in an *abstract* and *decontextualized* manner ("I am all for equal opportunity, that's why I oppose affirmative action") that ends up rationalizing racially unfair situations. An archetypal example of how whites use this frame to oppose racial fairness is Sue, a college student in a Southern university. When asked if minority students should be provided unique opportunities to be admitted into universities, Sue stated:

> I don't think that they should be provided with unique opportunities. I think that they should have the same opportunities as everyone else. You know, it's up to them to meet the standards and whatever that's required for entrance into universities or whatever. I don't think that just because they're a minority that they should, you know, not meet the requirements, you know.

Sue, like most whites in contemporary America, ignores the effects of past and contemporary discrimination on the social, economic, and educational status of minorities. Therefore, by supporting equal opportunity for everyone without a concern for the savage racial inequalities between whites and minorities, her stance safeguards white privilege.

Naturalization: Decoding the Meaning of "That's the Way It Is"   A frame that has not yet been brought to the fore by social scientists is whites' naturalization of race-related matters. Whites invoke this frame mostly when discussing school or neighborhood matters to explain the limited contact between whites and minorities and to justify whites' preference for whites as significant others. The word "natural" or the phrase "that's the way it is" is often interjected to normalize events or actions that could otherwise be interpreted as racially motivated (residential segregation) or racist (preference for whites as friends and partners). For instance, Bill, a manager in a manufacturing firm, explained the limited level of school integration as follows:

Bill: I don't think it's anybody's fault. Because people tend to group with their own people. Whether it's white or black or upper-middle-class or lower-class or, you now, upper-class, you know, Asians. People tend to group with their own. Doesn't mean if a black person moves into your neighborhood, they shouldn't go to your school. They should and you should mix and welcome them and everything else, but you can't force people together. If people want to be together, they should intermix more.

Interviewer: OK. So the lack of mixing is really just kind of an individual lack of desire?

Bill: Well, individuals, it's just the way it is. You know, people group together for lots of different reasons: social, religious. Just as animals in the wild, you know. Elephants group together, cheetahs group together. You bus a cheetah into an elephant herd because they should mix? You can't force that [laughs].

Bill's crude, unflattering, and unfitting metaphor comparing racial segregation to the separation of species, however, is not the only way of using the naturalization frame. Many whites naturalize in a gentler fashion. For instance, Steve and Jan Hadley, two of the respondents cited by Johnson and Shapiro, Chapter 12 in this volume, explain their lack of racial mix in their neighborhood and in the schools their children attended as follows:

Steve: No, I mean, it, it just happened. So, um.

Jan: No, it's just, it's based on the churches, you know, the four churches that own the school and—

Steve: Yeah, and, they, they're from the south county are also so, and there just are, there aren't many blacks.

Jan: Unless they are part of the bussing program, and you will find that in the public school system, but not in the private sector. So. And that's, I mean, that's not a problem as far as I'm—see, we have black friends, but it just happens to work out that way.

Despite whites' belief that residential and school segregation, friendship, and attraction are natural, raceless occurrences, social scientists have documented how racial considerations affect all these issues. For example, residential segregation is created by white buyers searching for white neighborhoods and aided by realtors, bankers, and sellers. As white neighborhoods develop, white schools follow—an outcome that further contributes to the process of racial isolation. Socialized in a "white habitus" (Bonilla-Silva 2003) and influenced by our Eurocentric culture, it is no wonder whites' interpret their racialized choices for white significant others as "natural." All these "choices" are the "natural" consequences of a white socialization process.

Although this frame seems to contradict the color-blind script, it is in fact used to deflate charges of racism. If someone argues that whites go to school, live with, befriend, and date other whites, whites can say "It's a natural thing" and that all groups do it. Hence something that presumably everybody does "naturally" is something that is "beyond race."

The Latin-Americanization of Whiteness in the United States

What will be the cartography of whiteness in twenty-first-century America? Who will be "white" and who will be "nonwhite"? Will the traditional (albeit always somewhat porous) lines of whiteness and nonwhiteness remain or will

"Whites"
Whites
New Whites (Russians, Albanians, etc.)
Assimilated light-skinned Latinos
Some multiracials
Assimilated (urban) Native Americans
A few Asian-origin people

"Honorary Whites"
Light-skinned Latinos
Japanese-Americans
Korean-Americans
Asian Indians
Chinese-Americans
Middle Eastern Americans
Most multiracials

"Collective Black"
Filipinos
Vietnamese
Hmong
Laotians
Dark-skinned Latinos
Blacks
New West Indian and African immigrants
Reservation-bound Native Americans

Figure 4   Preliminary map of triracial system in the United States[1].

they be reconfigured? In what follows I suggest that whiteness will shed its traditional garb and slip into Latin American–like clothes. Specifically, I argue that the United States will develop a triracial system with "whites" at the top, an intermediary group of "honorary whites"—similar to the coloreds in South Africa—and a nonwhite group or the "collective black" at the bottom (see Figure 4). In addition, as is the case in Latin America and the Caribbean, I expect the color logic of white supremacy to become more salient. "Shade discrimination" (Kinsbrunner 1996), or preference for people who are light-skinned, will become a more important factor in all kinds of social transactions.

There are multiple reasons why I posit that whiteness will become Latin-Americanized. The most basic one is demographic-political in nature. The white population, which has always been a numerical majority in the country—with

---

[1]This is a heuristic rather than an analytical device. Hence not all groups are included, and the position of a few groups may change.

Table 6 Projected Population of the United States by Race and Ethnicity (%) in 2020, 2045, 2070, and 2100.

	2220	2045	2070	2100
Whites	63.8	54.5	46.8	40.3
Latinos	17.0	23.1	28.6	33.3
Blacks	12.0	13.2	13.2	13.0
Asians	5.7	8.4	10.6	12.6
Native Americans	0.8	0.8	0.8	0.7

Source: U.S. Census Bureau, Population Projections Branch. Maintained by: Laura K. Yax (Population Division). Last revised: August 02, 2002 at 01:55:31 PM. Available from http://eire.census.gov/popest/estimates.php

a few notable exceptions during some historical junctures in some regions—is decreasing in size and by the middle of this century may have become a numerical minority (see Table 6). This rapid darkening of America is creating a situation similar to that of many Latin American and Caribbean countries in the sixteenth and seventeenth centuries (e.g., Puerto Rico, Cuba, and Venezuela), or of South American countries such as Argentina, Chile, and Uruguay in the late eighteenth and early nineteenth centuries. In both historical periods, white elites realized their countries were becoming majority nonwhite and devised a number of strategies (unsuccessful in the former and successful in the latter) to whiten their population and preserve racial power (Helg 1990). Although whitening the population through immigration or by classifying many newcomers as white (Gans 1999b; Warren and Twine 1997) is a possible solution to the new American dilemma, a more plausible one is to create an intermediate racial group to buffer racial conflict, allow some newcomers into the white racial strata, and incorporate most immigrants of color into a new bottom strata.

Even though Latin-Americanization will not fully materialize for several more decades, many social trends that correspond to the emerging stratification order are already evident. For example, the standing of the groups in Figure 4 in terms of income, education, wealth, occupations, and even social prestige largely follows the expected patterns. Hence in general terms, whites have higher income, education, and better occupations than "honorary whites," who in turn have a higher standing than members of the collective black in all those areas.

If these groups develop significant status differences, those differences should be reflected in their consciousness. Specifically, if my Latin-Americanization thesis is accurate, whites should be making distinctions among "honorary whites" and the "collective black" (exhibiting a more positive outlook toward "honorary whites" than toward members of the "collective black"). Similarly, "honorary whites" should exhibit attitudes toward the "collective black" similar to those of whites (see them as "inferior," etc.). Finally, members of the "collective black" should exhibit a less coherent and more disarticulated racial consciousness than in the past,[4] as is the case of the subordinated caste in Latin America and the Caribbean (Hanchard 1994; Twine 1998).

Although assessing some of these matters is very problematic as few data sets include information on skin tone, the available data are very suggestive as they mostly fit my Latin-Americanization thesis. For example, various surveys on Latinos confirm that they tend to self-identify as "white." However, the proportion varies tremendously by groups in a manner that is congruent with my expectations. Whereas over 75 percent of Cubans, Argentines, Chileans, and Venezuelans identify as white, fewer than 45 percent of dark-skinned or Indian-looking Latinos such as Puerto Ricans, Salvadorans, and Dominicans do so (Rodriguez 2000). In line with this finding, data from the Latino National Political Survey reveal that Mexicans and Puerto Ricans—two groups primarily composed of people who will belong to the "collective black"—are more likely than Cubans—a group that will mostly be comprised of "honorary whites"—to be sympathetic toward blacks. More significantly, the degree of closeness toward blacks *was greater* among those Latinos who self-identify as black while those who self-identify as white who were more sympathetic toward whites and Asians (Forman, Martinez, and Bonilla-Silva unpublished).

Various studies have documented that Asians tend to hold antiblack and anti-Latino attitudes. For instance, Lawrence Bobo and associates (1995) found that Chinese residents of Los Angeles expressed negative racial attitudes toward blacks. One Chinese resident stated: "Blacks in general seem to be overly lazy" and another asserted: "Blacks have a definite attitude problem" (Bobo et al. 1995:78; see also Bobo and Johnson 2000). Studies of Korean shopkeepers in various locales have found that over 70 percent of them hold antiblack attitudes (Weitzer 1997; Yoon 1997; Min 1996). In a more recent study of Asians (Chinese, Koreans, and Japanese) in Los Angeles (Bobo and Johnson 2000), Asians were more likely than even whites to hold antiblack and anti-Latino views. In line with this finding and with my thesis, they held more positive views about whites than about Latinos and blacks. Not surprisingly, as the racial attitudes of whites and Asians are converging, their views on racial policies are too. For example, in a recent poll in California, 78 percent of blacks and 66 percent of Latinos supported maintaining affirmative action, but only 27 percent of whites and 49 percent of Asians did so (Hajnal and Baldassare 2001). Similarly, as the views of Asians and whites converge, their political allegiances may too. The same recent study in California found that Latinos and blacks register mostly as Democrats, whiles Asians lean slightly toward the Democratic Party and whites split their party allegiances.

If groups develop status differences and translate them to their consciousness, they should also show signs of behavioral and associational patterns consistent with their new position. Whites should exhibit a clear preference for associating with "honorary whites" and vice versa. "Honorary whites" should not favor mingling with members of the "collective black" but members of the "collective black" should favor associating with members who are higher in the racial order. The rates of interracial marriage (the bulk of it is with whites) tend to fit the Latin-Americanization expectations. Whereas 93 percent of whites and blacks marry within-group, 70 percent of Latinos and Asians do so and only 33 percent of Native Americans marry Native Americans (Moran 2001:103). More significantly, when one disentangles the generic terms "Asians" and "Latinos," the data fit the Latin-Americanization thesis even more closely. For example, among Latinos, the groups that potentially include more members of the "honorary white" category, such as Cubans, Mexicans, Central Americans, and South Americans, have higher rates of intermarriage than the groups that have more individuals belonging to the "collective black" category, such as Puerto Ricans and Dominicans (Gilbertson et al. 1996). Although interpreting the Asian-American outmarriage patterns is very complex (groups such as Filipinos and Vietnamese have higher-than-expected rates in part due to the Vietnam War and the military bases in the Philippines), it is worth pointing out that the highest outmarriage rate belongs to Japanese-Americans and Chinese (the Asian overclass) (Kitano and Daniels 1995) and the lowest to Southeast Asians.

Data on racial assimilation through marriage ("whitening") show that the children of Asian-white and Latino-white unions are more likely to be classified as white than the children of black-white unions. Hence whereas only 22 percent of the children of black fathers and white mothers are classified as white, the children of similar unions between whites and Asians are twice as likely to be classified as white (Waters 1997). For Latinos, the data fit my thesis even closer, as Latinos of Cuban, Mexican, and South American origin have high rates of exogamy compared to Puerto Ricans and Dominicans (Gilbertson et al. 1996). This may reflect the fact that these latter groups have far more dark-skinned members, which would limit their chances for outmarriage in a highly racialized marriage market.

REPERCUSSIONS OF LATIN AMERICANIZATION FOR THE FUTURE OF WHITENESS IN AMERICA

With some trepidation, given the data limitations I have pointed out, I suggest that the Latin Americanization of race relations in the United States is already under way. If this is the case, what will be the repercussions for whiteness? First, the category white, which has always been fluid, as evidenoed by the fact that over the last two hundred years it has incorporated "ethnic" groups such as Irish, Jews, Italians, Polish, Greeks, and so on, will undergo a major transformation. The white category will *darken* and include unexpected company as a segment of the "multiracial" community joins its ranks (Rockquemore 2002, 2003). "Whites" will also include assimilated light-skinned Latinos (Barry Alvarez, the football coach at the University of Wisconsin, Lauro Cavazos, former secretary of education under Reagan, etc.), some well-to-do assimilated Asians, and maybe even a few "blacks" who "marry up" (Ward Connelly, Tiger Woods, etc.).

Second, Latin-Americanization will force a reshuffling of *all* ethnic identities. Certain "ethnic" claims may dissipate (or, in some cases, decline in significance) as mobility will increasingly be seen as based on 1) whiteness or near-whiteness; and 2) intermarriage with whites (this seems to be the case among many Japanese-Americans, particularly those who have intermarried). This dissipation of ethnicity will not be limited to "honorary whites," as members of the "collective black" strata strive to position themselves higher on the new racial totem pole based on degrees of proximity or closeness to whiteness. Will Vietnamese, Filipinos, and other members of the Asian underclass coalesce with blacks and dark-skinned Latinos or will they try to distance themselves from them and struggle to emphasize their "Americanness"?

Third, whiteness will have a new ally in near-whiteness. "Honorary whites" will do the bulk of the dirty work to preserve white supremacy as they will think their fate is tied to whites. Two incidents reported by Norman Matloff in an op-ed piece in the *San Francisco Chronicle* (1997) are examples of things to come:

> In the newsletter of the Oakland chapter of the Organization of Chinese Americans, editor Peter Eng opined: "Chinese-Americans will need to separate and distance ourselves from other ethnic immigrant groups" and suggested that Latino immigration was a burden to society.

> Elaine Kim, a Korean-American UC Berkeley professor, has written that a major Latino organization suggested to her [actually to Korean community activist Bong-Huan Kim—added by Matloff] that Asians and Latinos work together against blacks in an Oakland redistricting proposal. And an Asian/Latino coalition is suing Oakland, claiming it awards too many city contracts to black-owned firms.

Lastly, the space for contesting whiteness and white supremacy will be drastically reduced, as is the case all over Latin America. As the mantra of "We are all Americans" becomes part of the fabric of the United States, traditional racial politics will become harder to maintain. Activists trying to organize in the future around the "we" versus "them" dynamic will be declared "racist" and accused of trying to divide the "long and hard-fought national unity."

HOW TO FIGHT WHITENESS AND WHITE SUPREMACY IN THE TWENTY-FIRST CENTURY

How can we organize to fight a racial structure that is almost invisible, an ideology that denies being racial, and a whiteness that will be stretched out and be seemingly "inclusive." In what follows, I outline a political strategy to fight the three heads of postmodern white supremacy in the United States.

The first head of contemporary white supremacy is the "new racism." I argued that because post-1960s racial practices tend to be covert, subtle, institutional, and apparently nonracial, white privilege is maintained in a "now you see it, now you don't fashion." Furthermore, because systemic advantage is less dependent on virulent actions by individual actors,[5] the average white person does not see "racism" or is less likely than ever to understand minorities' complaints. Instead, whites believe the passage of civil rights legislation leveled the playing field and thus regard any talk about racism as an "excuse" used by minorities to avoid dealing with the real problems in their communities. The filler for whites' racial narratives comes from the second head of postmodern white supremacy, color-blind racism or the dominant post–civil rights racial ideology.

I have suggested elsewhere that the task for progressive social scientists and activists fighting contemporary white supremacy and color-blind racism is to unmask the racial character of many of these practices and accompanying beliefs; to make visible what remains invisible (Bonilla-Silva 2001). To this effect, we can follow the lead of the department of Housing and Urban Development, which has developed the audit strategy of sending out testers evenly matched on all characteristics except race to investigate claims of housing discrimination. This strategy can be used by researchers and activists alike in a variety of venues: banks, retail stores, jobs, and so on.

Another strategy that may prove useful is to do undercover work on racial affairs. Investigative news shows such as *Prime Time, 20/20,* and others have used this technique quite successfully to document discrimination. Lawrence Otis-Graham used this strategy for gathering data for his book *Member of the Club* (1995). Otis-Graham, who is a black lawyer, worked at a private golf club as a waiter and showed that elite whites talk about race in an old-fashioned manner when they are in the comfort of their (almost) all-white environments. We can use this technique in an even more effective manner if white progressives do the undercover work.

Yet uncovering these new racism practices and documenting the whiteness of color blindness, as important as this is, will not lead to a major change unless we can organize a new Civil Rights movement. The task at hand is to demand what whites do not want to give us: *equality of results.* Equal opportunity is not equal if the groups in competition do not have similar foundations (e.g., levels of income, education, etc.) and if some groups still suffer from discrimination. This new movement should demand proportional representation in everything. If blacks and Latinos represent 25 percent of the nation, that should be their proportion among lawyers, doctors, and engineers as well as among people in the nations' prisons. How to achieve this (reparations, affirmative action, a Marshall-like program?) is a matter to be fought and discussed by this new Civil Rights movement (for details, see Bonilla-Silva 2001).

I have left the last head for the end—the Latin-Americanization of whiteness—because I believe this will be the hardest one to slay. Why?

Because if whiteness becomes Latin American–like, then race will disappear from the social radar, and contesting racial issues will be an extremely difficult thing to do (How can we fight something that is not *socially* accepted as real?). That said, my point is that race relations will become Latin American–*like*, not *exactly like* in Latin America. Hence, for example, the black-white fracture will remain in place, albeit in a changed format. Similarly, the deep racism experienced by dark-skinned Latinos will also form part of the future. Lastly, the discrimination that Asian-Americans have experienced will not dissipate totally in years to come.

Therein lies the weakness of the emerging triracial order and the possibilities for challenging Latin American–like whiteness. Members of the "collective black" must be the backbone of the new Civil Rights movement as they are the ones who will remain literally "at the bottom of the well." However, if they want to be successful, they must wage, in coalition with progressive Asian and Latino organizations, a concerted effort to politicize the segments I label "honorary whites" and make them aware of the *honorary* character of their status. As Dr. Moses Seenarine (1999), professor and a South-Asian-Indian organizer, recently put it:

> as long as a particular minority community continue to exclude others, they themselves will be excluded. As long as one group discriminates and are prejudiced to those who are poorer or "blacker" than themselves and their communities, they continue to reinforce and maintain the system of white racism. It is of no use of Indo-Caribbeans trying to distance themselves from Africans, or for South Asians distancing themselves from Indo-Caribbeans and Africans, because ultimately, these groups are all considered "black" by the dominant whites. Instead of excluding others, all "Indian-looking" peoples should build alliances with each other, and with African, Latino and other minority groups, to prevent racism in all of our communities.

This is the way out of the new quandary. We need to short-circuit the belief in near-whiteness as the solution to status differences and create a coalition of all "people of color" and their white allies. If the Latin-American model of race prevails and "pigmentocracy" crystallizes, we will all scramble for the meager wages that near-whiteness will provide to all who are willing to play the "we are all American" game.

Notes

Notes to Chapter 1

1. A representative list of works includes Roediger 1991; Frankenberg 1993; C. Harris 1993; W. Allen 1994, 1997; Gallagher 1995; Ignatiev 1995; Gibson, 1996; Haney López 1996; Lucal 1996; Doane 1997a; Delgado and Stefancic 1997; Fine et al. 1997; Hill 1997; Winant 1997; Wray and Newitz 1997; Gabriel 1998; Kincheloe et al. 1998; Lipsitz 1998; Hartigan 1999.
2. On critiques of the neglect of the sociology of majorities, see Bierstedt 1948; Hughes and Hughes 1952; Doane 1997b.
3. For discussions of the academic impact of whiteness studies, see McMillen 1995; Stowe 1996; R. Rodriguez 1999; Bennefield 1999; Nguyen 2000.

Notes to Chapter 6

1. When "Black" is capitalized in this chapter, it denotes a national group and is synonymous with African-Americans. When in lower case, it denotes a racial group.
2. Because I discuss only people of mixed Black/white parentage, "biracial" is used instead of "multiracial," unless in a direct quote.
3. Terry is a pseudonym, per his/her request.
4. This does not include multiple-race responses that included "Some other race."
5. The Add Health data set provided only 108 respondents Harris determined to identify as biracial.

Notes to Chapter 9

1. This is similar to research on other deviant activities (see Bulmer 1982; Ronai and Ellis 1989). When the population is hard to reach and/or when the subject matter is highly sensitive—as is racetalk—then covert methods are a viable method for obtaining data (Miller and Tewksbury 2001).
2. This project was an Undergraduate Research Apprenticeship Program (URAP) project within the College of Liberal Arts and Sciences at our home university. In a URAP, a faculty contracts to do original research with an undergraduate as a form of professional mentoring. The undergraduate receives a stipend for one semester's work. The original data were, therefore, collected within one semester.
3. Because this project emerged in reaction to Bonilla-Silva and Forman (2000), I chose to study college students as they did.
4. Most incidents were clearly one type and not others. However, others overlapped. For instance, an incident of surveillance may contain racial epithets. In such a case, I counted both the interracial surveillance and the epithets separately.
5. This etiquette was far-reaching, delineating how "Negroes" should share sidewalks and highways, how to speak to whites, when to remove your hat, and how to act around white women (see C. Johnson 1943). The punishments for violating the etiquette were, of course, severe.

Notes to Chapter 10

1. The sample included eight focus groups of white students from a large urban university and a small elite liberal arts college. Through personal contacts and snowball sampling

we located thirty-two adults for individual in-depth interviews. Respondents were raised in urban, suburban, and rural environments.

Notes to Chapter 11

1. For more on this kind of phenomenon, see Bonilla-Silva and Forman 2000.
2. All names of locations, schools, and people have been changed to protect the confidentiality of those involved. Hence all names included herein are pseudonyms created by the author.
3. I am using the term "typical" here to mean several things. First, a school that is generally similar to the kind most either white or nonwhite students attend and thus one that offers a fairly typical experience. In this case, most students of color in the United States, particularly Latino and African-American students, attend urban public schools that are primarily demographically nonwhite in their student population and have predominantly white staff. Most white students, on the other hand, attend schools that are all or almost all white. However, in selecting schools I was careful to pick those that, if anything, would yield an underestimate of effects. Hence I limited my selection of urban schools to those that were not in the lowest tier for performance, disciplinary problems, or socioeconomic status. In selecting a suburban school I looked for districts that were neither particularly wealthy nor particularly working-class and whose student populations were between 80 and 90 percent white. I also looked for districts that were part of the Hillside metropolitan area rather than more closely associated with other urban areas near by.
4. This is a normative aspect of dominant identities: e.g., we see St. Patrick's Day as an "Irish Holiday" but we don't see Thanksgiving as a "WASP Holiday." Thanks to Woody Doane for pointing this out.
5. This is similar to what Salvatore Saporito and Annette Lareau (1999) found in their studies of parents' school choice processes. Race is factored in initially to eliminate certain schools and then other criteria are used to make a final decision among the remaining schools.
6. For more on this see Bourdieu and Passeron 1990.

Notes to Chapter 14

1. The existence of such a program in a private corporation makes this case unique. For a discussion of different types of affirmative action programs, see Baebaea Reskin (1998).
2. For a full discussion of the sites and methods used in my earlier study of contemporary law firms, see Pierce (1995).
3. None of the attorneys in the Legal Department was Latino, Asian-American, or American Indian.
4. Among the ten people I was unable to interview, one had retired and moved away from the Bay area, several others claimed to be too busy, another canceled interview after interview, and finally, there were six individuals who had moved on to other jobs and whom I was unable to locate.
5. Some of the questions included: What has your professional trajectory been since I last interviewed you in 1989? How would you characterize your current practice? Why did you stay in (or leave) BC's legal department? How would you characterize BC's policies for women and minorities? Names of individuals and organizations were changed at their request to protect confidentiality.
6. I borrow the usage of narrative from Susan Chase (1995) who argues that " narrative[s] share a fundamental interest in making sense of experience, in constructing and communicating meaning" (p. 8). Further, narratives are always constructed in particular contexts, most immediately within the interview situation itself, but more broadly within particular social and historical times and places. In this sense, "[n]arration is a cultural practice, in making sense of experience, any narrative draws on and is constrained by the culture in which it is embedded" (1995:8). This is not to say that narratives do not contain individual biographical or idiosyncratic elements, but rather to underscore the point that they always draw from larger cultural discourse.

7. See Ruth Frankenberg (1993) for a discussion of the "polite" language of race. Also, see Bonilla-Silva (2001) for a discussion of color blindness as a form of racism in our post–civil rights era.
8. In this interview, I used a more confrontational style to push the lawyer to answer my questions. Other ethnographers have used argumentation as a method for getting answers in difficult interviews. See for example, Robert Zussman (1995).
9. David Wellman (1993) also finds that individualism is used to mask white racism in his oral histories with white Americans. Also, see Joe Feagin's and Hernán Vera's (1995) discussion of what they call "sincere fictions" used by white people to deny racism.

Notes to Chapter 16

1. All of the respondents' names have been changed to pseudonyms to protect their privacy. Names of places, universities, and courses have also been changed or removed when their inclusion might rish the privacy of respondents.

Notes to Chapter 18

1. Although the profitability of whiteness varies by class and gender (e.g., elite white men earn more than poor white women), *all* actors socially designated as "white" receive a better deal—more social, economic, political, and psychological benefits—than their nonwhite equivalents. Hence, poor white men do better than poor black men, poor white women than poor black women, and so on.
2. By racial ideology I mean the racially based frameworks used by actors to explain and justify (dominant race) or challenge (subordinate races) the racial status quo. I have suggested that it can be operationalized as comprised of frames, style, and racial stories (see Bonilla-Silva 2001, 2003). In this chapter I discuss only its frames.
3. I was the principal investigator in these two projects. For details on these projects, see Bonilla-Silva and Forman (2000) and Bonilla-Silva (2001).
4. This new disarticulated consciousness will reflect 1) the effects of a triracial order, which blunts the "us" versus "them" racial dynamic; and 2) the fact that members of the "collective black" can expect some real degree of racial (and class) mobility through association and marriage with lighter-skinned people.
5. Most whites, unlike during slavery and Jim Crow, need not take direct action for "keeping minorities in their place." By just following the post-1960s white script (i.e., living in white neighborhoods, sending their children to white schools, and associating primarily with whites) they help produce the geopolitical and cultural conditions needed for white supremacy.

References

Aanerud, Rebecca. 1997. "Fictions of Whiteness: Speaking the Names of Whiteness in U.S. Literature." Pp. 35–59 in *Displacing Whiteness: Essays in Social and Cultural Criticism,* ed. Ruth Frankenburg. Durham, NC: Duke University Press.

Abbott, Edith. 1936. *The Tenements of Chicago, 1908–1935.* Chicago, IL: University of Chicago Press.

Adorno, Theodor. 1950. *The Authoritarian Personality.* New York: Harper.

Alba, Richard. 1990. *Ethnic Identity: The Transformation of White America.* New Haven, CT: Yale University Press.

Alcoff, Linda Martín. 1999. "Towards a Phenomenology of Racial Embodiment." *Radical Philosophy* 95.

Aldrich, Nelson W., Jr. 1989. *Old Money.* New York: Knopf.

Allen, Theodore W. 1994. *The Invention of the White Race:* Racial Oppression and Social Control. New York: Verso.

———. 1997. *The Invention of the White Race: The Origin of Racial Oppression in Anglo-America.* New York: Verso.

Allen, Walter, Edward Telles, and Margaret Hunter. 2000. "Skin Color, Income, and Education: A Comparison of African Americans and Mexican Americans." *National Journal of Sociology* 12: 129–180.

Allport, Gordon. 1954. *The Nature of Prejudice.* New York: Addison-Wesley.

Almaguer, Tomas. 1994. *Racial Fault Lines: The Historical Origins of White Supremacy in California.* Berkeley, CA: University of California Press.

Amin, Samir. 1988. *Eurocentrism,* trans. Russell Moore. New York: Monthly Review.

Amory, Cleveland. 1947. *The Proper Bostonians.* New York: Dutton.

Andersen, Margaret. 1984. "Race and the Social Sciences: A Teaching and Learning Discussion." *Radical Teacher* (November): 17–20.

———. 1987. "Denying Difference: The Continuing Basis for Exclusion in the Curriculum." Working Papers, Memphis State University Center for Research on Women.

———. 1999. "The Fiction of Diversity without Oppression: Race, Ethnicity, Identity, and Power." In *Critical Ethnicity: Countering the Waves of Identity Politics,* ed. Robert Tai and Mary Kenyatta. Boulder, CO: Rowman and Littlefield.

Anderson, Elijah. 1999. *Code of the Street.* New York: Norton.

Ansley, Frances Lee. 1989. "Stirring the Ashes: Race, Class and the Future of Civil Rights Scholarship." *Cornell Law Review* 74.

Appel, R. W. 2000. "Polishing Nashville's Twang." *New York Times* (July 28): 1.

Apple, Michael. 1998. "Foreword." Pp. ix–xii in *White Reign: Deploying Whiteness in America,* ed. Joe L. Kincheloe, Shirley R. Steinberg, Nelson M. Rodriguez, and Ronald E. Chennault. New York: St. Martin's.

Arce, Carlos A., Edward Murguia, and W. Parker Frisbie. 1987. "Phenotype and Life Chances among Chicanos." *Hispanic Journal of Behavioral Sciences* 9: 19–32.

Association of MultiEthnic Americans. n.d. "About AMEA: Mission Statement." Available from http://www.ameasite.org/about.asp.

———. 2001. Press Release, "AMEA Responds to Multiracial Census Data." March 12. Available from http://www.multiracial.com/news/pr20010312amea.html.

Ayres, Ian, and Peter Siegelman. 1995. "Race and Gender Discrimination in Bargaining for a New Car." *American Economic Review.* 85(3): 304–321.

Baker, Lee D. 2001. "Profit, Power, and Privilege: The Racial Politics of Ancestry." *Souls* 3: 66–72.

Baldwin, James. 1984. "On Being 'White' . . . And Other Lies." *Essence* (April): 90–92.

Banton, Michael. 1983. *Racial and Ethnic Competition.* Cambridge, UK: Cambridge University Press.

Barndt, Joseph. 1991. *Dismantling Racism: The Continuing Challenge to White America.* Minneapolis, MN: Augsberg Fortress.

Barnes, Charles B. 1915. *The Longshoremen.* New York: Survey Associates.

Baron, Harold. 1985. "Racism Transformed: The Implication of the 1960s." *Review of Radical Political Economics* 17: 10–33.

Barrera, Mario. 1979. *Race and Class in the Southwest: A Theory of Racial Inequality.* South Bend, IN: University of Notre Dame Press.

Barrett, James, and David Roediger. 1997. "In between Peoples: Race, Nationality and the 'New Immigrant' Working Class." *Journal of American Ethnic History* 16: 3–44.

Bederman, Gail. 1995. *Manliness and Civilization: A Cultural History of Gender and Race in the United States, 1880–1917.* Chicago: University of Chicago Press.

Bennefield, Robin M. 1999. "Whiteness Studies: Deceptive or Welcome Discourse? An Interview with Maulana Karenga." *Black Issues in Higher Education* (May 13): 26–27.

Bennett, L., D. Atkinson, and W. Rowe. 1993. "White Racial Identity: An Alternative Perspective." Paper presented at the meetings of the American Psychological Association, Toronto, Canada. August, 1993.

Bernal, Martin. 1987. *Black Athena: The Afroasiatic Roots of Classical Civilization,* vol. I. New Brunswick, NJ: Rutgers University Press.

Berry, Mary Frances. 1971; repr. 1994. *Black Resistance, White Law: A History of Constitutional Racism in America.* New York: Allen Lane.

Bierstedt, Robert. 1948. "The Sociology of Majorities." *American Sociological Review* 13: 700–710.

Blauner, Robert. 1972. *Racial Oppression in America.* New York: Harper & Row.

———. 1992. "Talking Past Each Other: Black and White Languages of Race." *The American Prospect* 10: 55–64.

———. 1994. "Talking Past Each Other: Black and White Languages of Race." Pp. 27–34 in *Race and Ethnic Conflict,* ed. H. J. Ehrlich and F. L. Pincus. Boulder, CO: Westview.

———. 1995. "White Radicals, White Liberals and White People: Rebuilding the Anti-Racist Coalition." In *Racism and Anti-Racism in World Perspective,* ed. B. Bowser. Thousand Oaks, CA: Sage.

Blaut, J. M. 1993. *The Colonizer's Model of the World: Geographical Diffusionism and Eurocentric History.* New York: Guilford.

Blumer, Herbert. 1958. "Race as a Sense of Group Position." *Pacific Sociological Review* 1: 3–7.

———. 1965. "Industrialisation and Race Relations." Pp. 220–253 in *Industrialisation and Race Relations,* ed. Guy Hunter. London: Oxford University Press.

Bobo, Lawrence. 1988. "Group Conflict, Prejudice, and the Paradox of Contemporary Racial Attitudes." Pp. 85–114 in *Eliminating Racism: Profiles in Controversy,* ed. Phylis A. Katz and Dalmas A. Taylor. New York: Plenum.

———. 1998. "Race, Interests, and Beliefs about Affirmative Action: Unanswered Questions and New Directions." *American Behavioral Scientist* 41: 985–1003.

———. 1999. "Prejudice as Group Position: Microfoundations of a Sociological Approach to Racism and Race Relations." *Journal of Social Issues* 55: 445–472.

———. 2000. "Race and Beliefs about Affirmative Action." Pp. 137–164 in *Racialized Politics: The Debate about Racism in America,* ed. David O. Sears, Jim Sidanius, and Lawrence Bobo. Chicago and London: University of Chicago Press.

Bobo, Lawrence, and Devon Johnson. 2000. "Racial Attitudes in a Prismatic Metropolis: Mapping Identity, Stereotypes, Competition, and Views on Affirmative Action." Pp. 81–166 in *Prismatic Metropolis,* ed. Lawrence Bobo, Melvin Oliver, and James Johnson, and Abel Valenzuela. New York: Russell Sage Foundation.

Bobo, Lawrence, and James Kluegel. 1997. "Status, Ideology and Dimensions of Whites' Racial Beliefs and Attitudes: Progress and Stagnation." In *Racial Attitudes in the 1990s: Continuity and Change,* ed. Steven A. Tuch and Jack K. Martin, Westport, CT: Praeger.

Bobo, Lawrence, James Kluegel, and Ryan Smith. 1997. "Laissez-Faire Racism: The Crystallization of a Kinder, Gentler, Antiblack Ideology." Pp. 15–44 in *Racial Attitudes in the 1990s: Continuity and Change,* ed. Stephen Tuch and Jack Martin. Westport, CT: Praeger.

Bobo, Lawrence, and Susan Suh. 2000. "Surveying Racial Discrimination: Analyses from a Multiethnic Labor Market." Pp. 523–560 in *Prismatic Metropolis: Inequality in Los*

Angeles, ed. Lawrence Bobo, Melvin Oliver, James Johnson Jr., and Abel Valuenzuela Jr. New York: Russell Sage.

Bobo, Lawrence, Camille Zubrinksy, James Johnson Jr., and Melvin Oliver. 1995. "Work Orientation, Job Discrimination, and Ethnicity." *Research in the Sociology of Work* 5: 45–85.

Bonacich, Edna. 1972. "A Theory of Ethnic Antagonism: The Split Labor Market." *American Sociological Review* 37: 547–559.

———. 1980. "Class Approaches to Ethnicity and Race." *The Insurgent Sociologist* 10(2): 9–24.

Bonilla-Silva, Eduardo. 1997. "Rethinking Racism: Toward a Structural Interpretation." *American Sociological Review* 62: 465–480.

———. 2000. "'This Is a White Country': The Racial Ideology of the Western Nations of the World-System." *Sociological Inquiry* 70: 188–214.

———. 2001. *White Supremacy and Racism in the Post-Civil Rights Era*. Boulder, CO: Lynne Rienner.

———. 2003. *Racism without Racists: Color Blind Racism and the Persistence of Racial Inequality in the United States*. Boulder, CO: Rowman and Littlefield.

Bonilla-Silva, Eduardo, and Tyrone A. Forman, 2000. "'I Am Not a Racist But...': Mapping White College Students' Racial Ideology in the USA." *Discourse & Society* 11: 50–85.

Bonilla-Silva, Eduardo, Tyrone Forman, Amanda Lewis, and David Embrick. 2003. "It Wasn't Me: How Will Race and Racism Work in 21st Century America." *Research in Political Sociology* 12: 111–135.

Bonilla-Silva, Eduardo, and Karen Glover. Forthcoming. "'We Are All Americans': The Latin Americanization of Race Relations in the USA." In *The Changing Terrain of Race and Ethnicity*, ed. Maria Krysan and Amanda Lewis. New York: Russell Sage.

Bonilla-Silva, Eduardo, and Amanda Lewis. 1999. "The New Racism: Toward an Analysis of the U.S. Racial Structure, 1960s–1990." In *Race, Ethnicity and Nationality in the United States: Toward the Twenty-First Century*, ed. Paul Wong. Boulder, CO: Westview.

Bonnett, Alastair. 1996a. "Anti-racism and the Critique of 'White' Identities." *New Community* 22: 97–110.

———. 1996b. "'White Studies': The Problems and Projects of a New Research Agenda." *Theory, Culture & Society* 13: 145–155.

———. 1997. "Constructions of Whiteness in European and American Anti-Racism." In *Debating Cultural Hybridity: Multi-cultural Identities and the Politics of Anti-Racism*, ed. P. W. and T. Modood. London: Zed.

———. 1998. "Who Was White? The Disappearance of Non-European White Identities and the Formation of European Racial Whiteness." *Ethnic and Racial Studies* 21: 1029–1055.

———. 2000. "Whiteness in Crisis." *History Today* 50 (December): 38–40.

Bourdieu, Pierre. [1973] 1977a. "Cultural Reproduction and Social Reproduction." Pp. 487–511 in *Power and Ideology in Education*, ed. Jerome Karabel and A. H. Halsey. New York: Oxford University Press.

———. 1977b. *Outline of a Theory of Practice*. New York: Cambridge University Press.

———. 1980. *The Logic of Practice*. Stanford, CA: Stanford University Press.

———. 1986. "The Forms of Capital." Pp. 241–258 in *Handbook of Theory and Research for the Sociology of Education*, ed. J. G. Richardson. New York: Greenwood.

Bourdieu, Pierre, and Passeron, Jean-Claude. 1990. *Reproduction in Education, Society and Culture*. London: Sage.

Bowen, W. and D. Bok. 1998. *The Shape of the River: The Long-Term Consequences of Considering Race in College and University Admissions*. Princeton, NJ: Princeton University Press.

Brimelow, Peter. 1995. *Alien Nation: Common Sense about America's Immigration Disaster*. New York: Random House.

Brodkin, Karen. 1999. *How Jews Became White Folks and What That Says about Race in America*. New Brunswick, NJ: Rutgers University Press.

Brown, Michael K. 1999. *Race, Money, and the American Welfare State*. Ithaca, NY: Cornell University Press.

Brown, M. Neil, and Stuart M. Keeley. 1998. *Asking the Right Questions: A Guide to Critical Thinking*. Upper Saddle River, NJ: Prentice Hall.

Brundage, W. Fitzhugh, ed. 1997. *Under Sentence of Death: Lynching in the South*. Chapel Hill, NC: University of North Carolina Press.

Buchanan, Patrick. 2001. *The Death of the West: How Dying Populations and Immigrant Invasions Imperil Our Country and Civilization.* New York: Dunne.

Bulmer, M. 1982. "When Is Disguise Justified?" *Qualitative Sociology* 5: 251–264.

Bultman, Bethany. 1996. *Redneck Heaven: Portrait of a Vanishing Culture.* New York: Bantam, Doubleday, Dell.

Burawoy, Michael, ed. 1991. *Ethnography Unbound.* Berkeley, CA: University of California Press.

Byrd, Charles Michael. 1998. "Census 2000 Protest: Check American Indian!" on *Interracial Voice.* Available from http://www.webcom.com/~intvoice/protest.html.

Cahn, Steven. 1997. "Two Concepts of Affirmative Action." *Academe* (January-February): 14–19.

Calvert, Linda McGee and V. Jean Ramsey. 1996. "Speaking as Female and White: A Non-Dominant/Dominant Group Standpoint." *Organization* 3(4): 468–485.

Campisi, Paul. 1942. "The Adjustment of the Italian Americans to the War Crisis." M.A. thesis, Department of Sociology, University of Chicago, Chicago, IL.

Carmichael, Stokely and Charles V. Hamilton. 1967. *Black Power: The Politics of Liberation in America.* New York: Vintage.

Carr, Howie. 2001. "Clinton Departure Removes Trash from the White House." *Boston Herald,* January 21: 14A.

Carr, Leslie G. 1997. *Color-Blind Racism.* Thousand Oaks, CA: Sage.

Carter, Stephen. 1991. *Reflections of an Affirmative Action Baby.* New York: Basic.

Cell, John W. 1982. *The Highest Stage of White Supremacy: The Origins of Segregation in South Africa and the American South.* Cambridge, UK: Cambridge University Press.

Chabram-Dernersesian, Angie. 1997. "On the Social Construction of Whiteness within Selected Chicana/o Discourses." Pp. 107–164 in *Displacing Whiteness: Essays in Social and Cultural Criticism,* ed. Ruth Frankenberg. Durham, NC: Duke University Press.

Cha-Jua, Sundiata Keita. 2001. "Racial Formation and Transformation: Toward a Theory of Black Racial Oppression." *Souls* 3: 25–60.

Cha-Jua, Sundiata Keita, and Clarence Lang. 1999. "Strategies for Black Liberation in the Era of Globalism: Retronouveau Civil Rights, Militant Black Conservatism, and Radicalism." *The Black Scholar* 29: 25–40.

Chan, Sucheng. 1991. *Asian Americans: An Interpretive History.* London: Twayne.

Chase, Susan. 1995. *Ambiguous Empowerment: Work Narratives of School Superintendents.* Amherst, MA: University of Massachusetts Press.

Chavez, Lydia. 1998. *The Color Bind: California's Battle to End Affirmative Action.* Berkeley, CA: University of California Press.

Cheng, Lucie, and Yen Le Espiritu. 1989. "Korean Businesses in Black and Hispanic Neighborhoods: A Study of Intergroup Relations." *Sociological Perspectives* 32: 521–534.

Chennault, Ronald E. 1998. "Giving Whiteness a Black Eye: An Interview with Michael Eric Dyson." Pp. 299–328 in *White Reign: Deploying Whiteness in America,* ed. Joe L. Kincheloe, Shirley R. Steinberg, Nelson M. Rodriguez, and Ronald E. Chennault. New York: St. Martin's.

Chesler, Mark, and Melissa Peet. 2002. "White Students' Views of Affirmative Action on Campus." *The Diversity Factor.* 10(2): 21–27.

Chicago Commission on Race Relations. 1922. *The Negro in Chicago: A Study of Race Relations and a Riot.* Chicago: University of Chicago Press.

Chicago Defender. 1928. July 7.

Chicago Herald Examiner. 1927. April 2.

Chicago Tribune. 1910a. June 7.

———. 1910b. August 19.

———. 1915a. June 11.

———. 1915b. June 13.

———. 1919. July 30.

———. 1926a. February 13.

———. 1926b. February 16.

———. 1926c. February 22.

———. 1926d. March 7.

———. 1926e. March 8.

———. 1927. March 26.

Chiricos, Ted, Ranee McEntire, and Marc Gertz. 2001. "Perceived Racial and Ethnic Composition of Neighborhood and Perceived Risk of Crime." *Social Problems* 48: 322–340.

Churchill, Ward. 1992. *Fantasies of the Master Race: Literature, Cinema and the Colonization of American Indians.* Monroe, ME: Common Courage.

CIRP: Cooperative Institutional Research Program. 2000. "Entering Student Survey." Los Angeles, CA: Higher Education Research Institute, University of California at Los Angeles.

City of Joy. 1992. Director: Roland Joffe. Story: Dominique LaPierre. Screenplay: Mark Medoff. Starring: Patrick Swayze, Pauline Collins, Om Puri, Art Malik.

Clark, Christine. 1999. "The Secret: White Lies Are Never Little." Pp. 92–110 in *Becoming and Unbecoming White: Owning and Disowning a Racial Identity,* ed. Christine Clark and James O'Donnell. Westport, CT: Bergin and Garvey.

Clark, Christine, and James O'Donnell. 1999. *Becoming and Unbecoming White: Owning and Disowning a Racial Identity.* Westport, CT: Bergin and Garvey.

Clark, Lorenne M. G., and Lynda Lange, eds. 1979. *The Sexism of Social and Political Theory: Women and Reproduction from Plato to Nietzsche.* Toronto: University of Toronto Press.

Cocker, Mark. 1998. *Rivers of Blood, Rivers of Gold: Europe's Conflict with Tribal Peoples.* London: Jonathan Cape.

Collins, Patricia Hill. 1998. *Fighting Words: Black Women and the Search for Justice.* Minneapolis, MN: University of Minnesota Press.

Collins, Sharon. 1997. *Black Corporate Executives: The Making and Breaking of the Black Middle Class.* Philadelphia, PA: Temple University Press.

Connolly, Paul. 1998. *Racism, Gender Identities and Young Children: Social Relations in a Multi-Ethnic, Inner-City Primary School.* New York: Routledge.

Cornell, Stephen. 1988. *The Return of the Native: American Indian Political Resurgence.* New York: Oxford University Press.

Cornell, Stephen and D. Hartman. 1998. *Ethnicity and Race: Making Identities in a Changing World.* Thousand Oaks, CA: Pine Forge.

Cose, Ellis. 1995[1993]. *The Rage of a Privileged Class.* New York: Harper Collins.

Coser, Lewis A. 1978. "American Trends." Pp. 287–320 in *A History of Sociological Analysis,* ed. Tom Bottomore and Robert Nisbet. New York: Basic.

Covello, Leonard. 1967. *The Social Background of the Italo-American School Child.* Leiden: Brill.

Cox, Oliver. 1948. *Caste, Class, and Race: A Study in Social Dynamics.* New York: Modern Reader.

Crapanzano, Vincent. 1985. *Waiting: The Whites of South Africa.* New York: Random House.

Crenshaw, Kimberle Williams. 1988. "Race, Reform, and Retrenchment: Transformation and Legitimation in Antidiscrimination Law." *Harvard Law Review* 101.

———. 1997. "Color-Blind Dreams and Racial Nightmares: Reconfiguring Racism in the Post–Civil Rights Era." Pp. 97–168 in *Birth of a Nation'hood,* ed. Toni Morrison and Claudia Lacour. New York: Pantheon.

Crenshaw, Kimberle, Neil Gotanda, Gary Peller, and Kendall Thomas, eds. 1995. *Critical Race Theory: The Key Writings That Formed the Movement.* New York: New Press.

Cressey, Paul F. 1930. "The Succession of Cultural Groups in the City of Chicago." Ph.D. dissertation, Department of Sociology, University of Chicago, Chicago, IL.

Cunningham, George E. 1965. "The Italian, A Hindrance to White Solidarity, 1890–1898." *The Journal of Negro History* 50: 22–36.

Cuomo, Chris J., and Kim Q. Hall, eds. 1999. *Whiteness: Feminist Philosophical Reflections.* Lanham, MD: Rowman and Littlefield Publishers.

Dallas Morning News. 1999. "Oklahoma Governor Criticized: Keating's Trash Talk Labeled as Offensive." *Dallas Morning News,* November 13: 32A.

Daniel, G. Reginald. 1992. "Beyond Black and White: The New Multiracial Consciousness." Pp. 333–341 in *Racially Mixed People in America,* ed. M. Root. Newbury Park, CA: Sage.

Daniels, Jessie. 1997. *White Lies: Race, Class, Gender, and Sexuality in White Supremacist Discourse.* New York, NY: Routledge.

Daniels, Roger. 1990. *Coming to America: A History of Immigration and Ethnicity in American Life.* New York: Harper.

de la Garza, Rodolfo, Angelo Falcon, F. Chris Garcia, and John A. Garcia. 1998. *Latino National Political Survey, 1989–1990* [Computer file]. 3rd ICPSR version. Philadelphia,

PA: Temple University, Institute for Social Research [producer], 1992. Ann Arbor, MI: Inter-University Consortium for Political and Social Research [distributor], 1998.

Delgado, Richard, ed. 1995. *Critical Race Theory: The Cutting Edge*. Philadelphia: Temple University Press.

———. 1996. *The Coming Race War?* New York: New York University Press.

Delgado, Richard, and Jean Stefancic, eds. 1997. *Critical White Studies: Looking behind the Mirror*. Philadelphia: Temple University Press.

Dempsey, William J. n.d. "Gangs in the Calumet Park District." Department of Sociology, University of Chicago, Chicago, IL. Unpublished manuscript. Ernest W. Burgess Papers, Box 148, Folder 5, University of Chicago Special Collections, Chicago, IL.

Dennis, Rutledge M. 1993. "Participant Observations." In *Race and Ethnicity in Research Methods*, ed. John H. Stanfield and Rutledge M. Dennis. Newbury Park, CA: Sage.

Denzin, Norman K. 1995. *The Cinematic Society: The Voyeur's Gaze*. Thousand Oaks, CA: Sage.

Dickie, John. 1997. "Stereotypes of the Italian South, 1860–1900." In *The New History of the Italian South: The Mezzogiorno Revisited*, ed. Robert Lumley and Jonathan Morris. Exeter, UK: University of Exeter Press.

Di Leonardo, Micaela. 1999. "Why Can't They Be Like Our Grandparents?" In *Without Justice for All: The New Liberalism and Our Retreat from Racial Equality*, ed. Adolph Reed Jr. Boulder, CO: Westview.

Dirlik, Arif. 2000. *Postmodernity's Histories: The Past as Legacy and Project*. Boulder, CO: Rowman and Littlefield.

Doane, Ashley W., Jr. 1996. "Contested Terrain: Negotiating Racial Understanding in Public Discourse." *Humanity and Society* 20(4): 32–51.

———. 1997a. "White Identity and Race Relations in the 1990s." Pp. 151–159 in *Perspectives on Current Social Problems*, ed. Gregg Lee Carter. Boston, MA: Allyn and Bacon.

———. 1997b. "Dominant Group Identity in the United States: The Role of 'Hidden' Ethnicity in Intergroup Relations" *Sociological Quarterly* 38: 375–397.

Dobratz, Betty A., and Stephanie L. Shanks-Meile. 1997. *White Power, White Pride: The White Separatist Movement in the United States*. New York: Twain.

Dollard, John. 1949. *Caste and Class in a Southern Town*. NY: Harper.

Doob, Christopher Bates. 1999. *Racism: An American Cauldron*. New York: Longman.

Dovidio, J., and S. Gaertner. 1986. "Prejudice, Discrimination and Racism: Historical Trends and Contemporary Approaches." Pp. 1–34 in *Prejudice, Discrimination and Racism*. eds. J. Dovidio and S. Gaertner. Orlando, FL., Academic.

Dovidio, J. F., Mann, J, and Gaertner, S.L. 1989. "Resistance to Affirmative Action: The Implications of Aversive Racism." Pp. 83–97 in *Affirmative Action in Perspective*, eds. F. A. Blanchard and F. J. Crosby. New York: Springer-Verlag.

Drake, St. Clair, and Horace R. Cayton. 1993. *Black Metropolis: A Study of Negro Life in a Northern City*, rev. ed. Chicago: University of Chicago Press.

Drake, W.A. and R. D. Hosworth. 1996. *Affirmative Action and the Stalled Quest for Black Progress*. Urbana, IL: University of Illinois Press.

Dray, Philip. 2002. *At the Hands of Persons Unknown: The Lynching of Black America*. New York: Random House.

D'Souza, Dinesh. 1995. *The End of Racism*. New York: Free Press.

Du Bois, W. E. B. 1969 [1920]. *Darkwater*. New York: Schocken.

———. 1996 [1920]. *Darkwater*. As reprinted, Pp. 481–623 in *The Oxford W. E. B. Du Bois Reader*, ed. E. J. Sundquist. New York: Oxford University Press.

———. 1956 [1935]. *Black Reconstruction in America*. New York: Russell.

Durkheim, Emile. 1964 [1895]. *The Rules of Sociological Method*. New York: Free Press.

Dyer, J. A. Vedlitz, and S. Worchel. 1989. "Social Distance among Racial and Ethnic Groups in Texas: Some Demographic Correlates." *Social Science Quarterly* 70: 607–616.

Dyer, Richard. 1997. *White*. New York: Routledge.

———. 1998. "White." *Screen* 29 (Fall): 44.

Eagle, Morris. 1984. *Recent Developments in Psychoanalysis: A Critical Evaluation*. Cambridge, MA: Harvard University Press.

Elfin, M., and S. Burke. 1993. "Race on Campus: Segregation is Growing." *U.S. News and World Report*. (April 19): 52–56.

Ellison, Ralph. 1952; repr. 1972. *Invisible Man.* New York: Vintage.

Emerson, Michael O., and Christian Smith. 2000. *Divided by Faith: Evangelical Religion and the Problem of Race in America.* NY: Oxford University Press.

Eminem. 1999. "If I Had." *The Real Slim Shady.* Interscope Records.

Essed, Philomena. 1991. *Understanding Everyday Racism: An Interdisciplinary Theory.* Beverly Hills, CA: Sage.

Fanon, Frantz. 1952; repr. 1967. *Black Skin, White Masks,* trans. Charles Lam Markmann. New York: Grove Weidenfeld.

Farley, Reynolds. 1996. *The New American Reality.* New York: Russell Sage.

Farley, Reynolds, and William H. Frey. 1994. "Changes in the Segregation of Whites from Blacks during the 1980s: Small Steps toward a More Integrated Society." *American Sociological Review* 59: 23–45.

Feagin, Joe R. 2000. *Racist America: Roots, Current Realities, and Future Reparations.* New York: Routledge.

Feagin, Joe R., and Clairece Booher Feagin. 1978. *Discrimination American Style: Institutional Racism and Sexism.* Englewood Cliffs, NJ: Prentice-Hall.

———. 1996. *Racial and Ethnic Relations,* 5th ed. Upper Saddle River, NJ: Prentice-Hall.

Feagin, Joe R., and Karyn D. McKinney 2002. *The Many Costs of Racism.* Lanham, MD: Rowman and Littlefield.

Feagin, Joe R., and Melvin P. Sikes. 1994. *Living with Racism: The Black Middle-Class Experience.* Boston, MA: Beacon.

Feagin, Joe R., and Hernán Vera. 1995. *White Racism: The Basics.* New York: Routledge.

———. 2001. *Liberation Sociology.* Boulder, CO: Westview.

Feagin, Joe R., Hernán Vera, and Pinar Batur. 2001. *White Racism: The Basics,* 2nd ed. New York: Routledge.

Feagin, Joe R., Hernán Vera, and Nikitah Imani. 1996. *The Agony of Education: Black Students at White Colleges and Universities.* New York, NY: Routledge.

Ferber, Abby L. 1998a. "Constructing Whiteness: The Intersections of Race and Gender in U.S. White Supremacist Discourse." *Ethnic and Racial Studies* 21: 48–63.

———. 1998b. *White Man Falling: Race, Gender, and White Supremacy.* Boulder, CO: Rowman and Littlefield.

Ferguson, Andrew. 1996. "Who is this Sex-Crazed Hillbilly?" *Wall Street Journal,* January 26: A9.

Fields, Barbara. 1990. "Slavery, Race and Ideology in the United States of America." *New Left Review* 181: 95–118.

Fine, Michelle, and Lois Weis. 1998. *The Unknown City.* Boston, MA: Beacon.

Fine, Michelle, Lois Weis, Linda C. Powell, and L. Mun Wong, eds. 1997. *Off White: Readings on Race, Power, and Society.* New York: Routledge.

Firebaugh, Glenn, and Kenneth E. Davis. 1988. "Trends in Antiblack Prejudice, 1972–1984: Region and Cohort Effects." *American Journal of Sociology* 94: 251–272.

Flagg, Barbara J. 1997. " 'Was Blind, but Now I See': White Race Consciousness and the Requirement of Discriminatory Intent." Pp. 629–631 in *Critical White Studies: Looking Behind the Mirror,* ed. Richard Delgado and Jean Stefancic. Philadelphia, PA: Temple University Press.

Flores-Gonzalez, Nilda. 1999. "The Racialization of Latinos: The Meaning of Latino Identity for the Second Generation." *Latino Studies Journal* 10(3): 3–31.

Foley, Neil. 1997. *White Scourge: Mexicans, Blacks, and Poor Whites in Texas Cotton Culture.* Berkeley, CA: University of California Press.

Forman, Tyrone, David Williams, and James Jackson. 1997. "Race, Place, and Discrimination." *Perspectives on Social Problems.* 9: 231–261.

Forman, Tyrone A., Gloria Martinez, and Eduardo Bonilla-Silva. unpublished. "Latinos' Perceptions of Blacks and Asians: Testing the Immigrant Hypothesis."

Frankenberg, Ruth. 1993. *White Women, Race Matters: The Social Construction of Whiteness.* Minneapolis, MN: University of Minnesota Press.

———, ed. 1997. *Displacing Whiteness: Essays in Social and Criticism.* Durham, NC: Duke University Press.

———. 2000. "Contexts and Attachments: Reflections of the Psyche of Whiteness." Paper presented at the Annual Meeting of the American Sociological Association, Washington, DC, August, 2000.

Franklin, John Hope and Alfred Moss, Jr. 1994. *From Slavery to Freedom: A History of African Americans,* 7th ed. New York: Knopf.

Fredrickson, George. 1971; repr. 1987. *The Black Image in the White Mind: The Debate on Afro-American Character and Destiny, 1817–1914.* Hanover, NH: Wesleyan University Press.

———. 1981. *White Supremacy: A Comparative Study in American and South African History.* New York: Oxford University Press.

Freeman, Alan David. 1996 [1990]. "Legitimizing Racial Discrimination through Antidiscrimination Law: A Critical Review of Supreme Court Doctrine." Abridged in *Critical Race Theory: The Key Writings that Formed the Movement,* ed. K. Crenshaw, N. Gotanda, G. Peller and K. Thomas. New York: New Press.

Freire, Paulo. 1995. *Pedagogy of the Oppressed.* New York: Continuum.

Fromm, Eric. 1955. *The Sane Society.* New York: Rinehart.

Füredi, Frank. 1998. *The Silent War: Imperialism and the Changing Perception of Race.* New Brunswick, NJ: Rutgers University Press.

Fusco, Coco. 1995. *English is Broken Here: Notes on Cultural Fusion in the Americas.* New York: New Press.

Gabriel, John. 1998. *Whitewash: Racialized Politics and the Media.* New York: Routledge.

Gaertner, Samuel L., and John F. Dovidio. 1986. "The Aversive Form of Racism." Pp. 61–89 in *Prejudice, Discrimination, and Racism,* ed. John F. Dovidio and Samuel L. Gaertner. Orlando, FL: Academic.

Gallagher, Charles A. 1995. "White Reconstruction in the University." *Socialist Review* 94(1–2): 165–187.

———. 1997. "White Racial Formation: Into the 21st Century." Pp. 6–11 in *Critical White Studies: Looking behind the Mirror,* ed. Richard Delgado and Jean Stefancic. Philadelphia, PA: Temple University Press.

———. 1999. "White Racial Formation: Into the Twenty-First Century." Pp. 24–29 in *Race and Ethnic Conflict: Contending Views on Prejudice, Discrimination, and Ethnoviolence,* 2nd ed., ed. Fred L. Pincus and Howard J. Ehrlich. Boulder, CO: Westview.

———. 2000. "White Like Me? Methods, Meaning and Manipulation in the Field of White Studies." Pp. 67–99 in *Racing Research, Researching Race,* ed. Frances Windance Twine and Jonathan Warren. New York: New York University Press.

Gallup Organization. 1997. "Black/White Relations in the U.S." June 10, 1997. Available from http://www.gallup.com/poll/specialReports/pollSummaries/SR010711.PDF.

Galster, George C. 1990a. "Racial Steering by Real Estate Agents: Mechanisms and Motives." *The Review of Black Political Economy* 18 (Spring): 39–61.

———. 1990b. "Racial Steering in Urban Housing Markets: A Review of the Audit Evidence." *Review of Black Political Economy* 48(3): 105–129.

Gamson, William and Andrew Modigliani. 1987. "The Changing Culture of Affirmative Action." *Research in Political Sociology.* 3: 137–177.

Gans, Herbert. 1979. "Symbolic Ethnicity: The Future of Ethnic Groups and Cultures in America." *Ethnic and Racial Studies* 2: 1–20.

———. 1999a [1979]. "Symbolic Ethnicity: The Future of Ethnic Groups and Cultures in America." Pp. 417–429 in *Majority and Minority: The Dynamics of Race and Ethnicity in American Life,* 6th ed., ed. Norman Yetman. Boston, MA: Allyn and Bacon.

———. 1999b. "The Possibility of a New Racial Hierarchy in the Twenty-First Century United States." Pp. 371–390 in *The Cultural Territories of Race,* ed. Michelle Lamont. Chicago, IL: University of Chicago Press

Garrow, David J. 1981. *The FBI and Martin Luther King, Jr.: From "Solo" to Memphis.* New York: Norton.

Gerstle, Gary. 1997. "Liberty, Coercion, and the Making of America." *Journal of American History* 84: 524–558.

Gibson, Jane W. 1996. "The Social Construction of Whiteness in Shellcracker Haven, Florida." *Human Organization* 55: 379–388.

Gibson, Timothy A. 1998. "I Don't Want Them Living around Here: Ideologies of Race and Neighborhood Decay." *Rethinking Marxism* 10: 141–154.

Gilanshah, Bijan. 1993. "Multiracial Minorities: Erasing the Color Line." *Law and Inequality: A Journal of Theory and Practice* 12: 183–204.

Gilbertson, Greta, Joseph P. Kitzpatrick, and Lijun Yang. 1996. "Hispanic Outmarriage in New York City: New Evidence from 1991." *International Migration Review* 30: 445–450.

Gilman, Sander L. 1998. *Creating Beauty to Cure the Soul: Race and Psychology in the Shaping of Aesthetic Surgery.* Durham, NC: Duke University Press.

Giroux, Henry A. 1997. "Racial Politics and the Pedagogy of Whiteness." Pp. 294–315 in *Whiteness: A Critical Reader,* ed. Mike Hill. New York: New York University Press.

———. 1998. "Youth, Memory Work, and the Racial Politics of Whiteness. Pp. 123–136 in *White Reign: Deploying Whiteness in America,* ed. J. L. Kincheloe, S. Steinberg, N. Rodriguez, and R. Chennault. New York: St. Martin's.

Glaser, Barney, and Anselm Strauss. 1967. *The Discovery of Grounded Theory.* Chicago IL: Aldine.

Goad, J. 1997. *The Redneck Manifesto: America's Scapegoats: How We Got That Way and Why We're Not Going to Take It Anymore.* New York: Simon & Schuster.

Goldberg, David Theo. 1993. *Racist Culture: Philosophy and the Politics of Meaning.* Cambridge, MA: Blackwell.

———. 2001. *The Racial State.* New York: Blackwell.

Gordon, Avery. 1989. *Ghostly Matters: Haunting and the Sociological Imagination.* Minneapolis, MN: University of Minnesota Press.

Gordon, Lewis R. 1994. *Bad Faith and Antiblack Racism.* Atlantic Highlands, NJ: Humanities Press.

———. 1995 "Critical 'Mixed Race'?" *Social Identities* 1: 381–395.

Gordon, Milton M. 1964. *Assimilation in American Life: The Role of Race, Religion, and National Origins.* New York: Oxford University Press.

Gossett, Thomas F. 1963; new ed. 1997. *Race: The History of an Idea in America.* New York: Oxford University Press.

Goster, G., and H. Richard. 1997. "Wham, Bam, Thank You, SAM: Critical Dimensions of the Persistence of Hillbilly Caricatures." *Sociological Spectrum* 17: 157–177.

Gould, Mark. 1999. "Race and Theory: Culture, Poverty, and Adaptation to Discrimination in Wilson and Ogbu." *Sociological Theory* 17: 171–200.

Gould, Stephen Jay. 1981. *The Mismeasure of Man.* New York: Norton.

Graham, Susan. 1997. "From the Executive Director." October 29, 1997. Available from http://www.projectrace.com/fromthedirector/archive/fromthedirector-102997.php.

———. 2000. "Project RACE Vows to Continue the Fight for the Multiracial Community!" April 14, 2000. Available from http://www.projectrace.com/fromthedirector/archive/fromthedirector-041400.php.

Gramsci, Antonio. 1971. *Selections from the Prison Notebooks.* London, Lawrence and Wishart.

Grant, Madison. 1916. *The Passing of the Great Race.* New York: Scribners.

Grebler, Leo, Joan Moore, and Ralph Guzman. 1970. *The Mexican American People: The Nation's Second Largest Minority.* New York, NY: Free Press.

Green Berets, The. 1968. Directors: John Wayne, Ray Kellogg, Mervyn LeRoy. Story: Robin Moore. Screenplay: James Lee Barrett, Col. Kenneth B. Facey. Starring: John Wayne, David Janssen, Raymond St. Jacques.

Gribaudi, Gabriella. 1997. "Images of the South: The Mezzogiorno as Seen by Insiders and Outsiders." In *The New History of the Italian South: The Mezzogiorno Revisited,* ed. Robert Lumley and Jonathan Morris. Exeter, UK: University of Exeter Press.

Grieco, Elizabeth, and Rachel Cassidy. 2001. *Overview of Race and Hispanic Origin 2000.* Washington, DC: U.S. Government Printing Office.

Griffin, John Howard. 1961; repr. 1996. *Black Like Me.* New York: Signet.

Grossman, James R. 1989. *Land of Hope: Chicago, Black Southerners, and the Great Migration.* Chicago: University of Chicago Press.

Guglielmo, Thomas A. 2003a. *White on Arrival: Italians, Race, Color, and Power in Chicago, 1890–1945.* New York: Oxford University Press.

———. 2003b. " 'No Color Barrier': Italians, Race, Color, and Power in the US, 1890s–1918." In *Are Italians White?* ed. Jennifer M. Guglielmo and Salvatore Salerno. New York: Routledge.

Gurin, Patricia. 2001. "Expert report of Patricia Gurin: The compelling Need for Diversity in Higher Education." In *Grutz et al. v. Bollinger et al.* No 97-75-321, E.D. Mich.

Hajnal, Zoltan, and Mark Baldassare. 2001. *Finding Common Ground: Racial and Ethnic Attitudes in California.* Sen Francisco, CA: Public Policy Institute of California.

Hale, Grace Elizabeth. 1998. *Making Whiteness: The Culture of Segregation in the South, 1890–1940.* New York: Pantheon.

Hall, Stuart. 1991. "Ethnicity, Identity and Difference" *Radical America* 12: 57.

Hammen, Scott. 1985. *John Huston.* Boston, MA: Twayne.

Hanchard, Michael G. 1994. *Orpheus and Power.* Princeton, NJ: Princeton University Press.

Haney López, Ian. 1995. "The Social Construction of Race." In *Critical Race Theory: The Cutting Edge,* ed. Richard Delgado. Philadelphia: Temple University Press.

———. 1996. *White by Law: The Legal Construction of Race.* New York: New York University Press.

Hannaford, Ivan. 1996. *Race: The History of an Idea in the West.* Baltimore, MD: Johns Hopkins University Press.

Hansen, Marcus L. 1952. "The Third Generation in America." *Commentary* 14: 492–500.

Hardiman, R. 2001. "Reflections on White Identity Development Theory." In *New Perspectives on Racial Identity Development,* ed. C. Wijeysinghe and B. Jackson. New York: New York University Press.

Harding, Sandra, ed. 1993. *The "Racial" Economy of Science: Toward a Democratic Future.* Bloomington, IN: Indiana University Press.

Harris, Cheryl I. 1993. "Whiteness as Property." *Harvard Law Review* 106: 1707–1791.

Harris, David. 2002. "Does It Matter How We Measure? Racial Classification and the Characteristics of Multiracial Youth." Pp. 62–101 in *The New Race Question: How the Census Counts Multiracial Individuals,* ed. Joel Perlmann and Mary Waters. New York: Russell Sage.

Hartigan, John J. 1992. "Reading Trash: Deliverance and the Poetics of White Trash." *Visual Anthropology Review* 8(2): 8–15.

———. 1996. "Name Calling and Objectifying 'Poor Whites' and 'White Trash.'" Pp. 41–56 in *White Trash: Class, Race and the Construction of American Identity,* ed. M. Wray and A. Newitz. New York: Routledge.

———. 1997a. "Unpopular Culture: The Case of 'White Trash.'" *Cultural Studies* 11: 316–343.

———. 1997b. "Establishing the Fact of Whiteness." *American Anthropologist* 99: 495–505.

———. 1999. *Racial Situations: Class Predicaments of Whiteness in Detroit.* Princeton, NJ: Princeton University Press.

Helg, Aline. 1990. "Race in Argentina and Cuba, 1880–1930: Theory, Policies, and Popular Reaction." Pp. 37–61 in *The Idea of Race in Latin America, 1870–1940,* ed. Richard Graham. Austin, TX: University of Texas Press.

Heller, Zoe 2001. "When All Else Fails, Tell Her She Has Got Lumpy Thighs." *Daily Telegraph* August 4, 2001: 23.

Helms, Janet E., ed. 1990. *Black and White Racial Identity: Theory, Research and Practice.* New York: Greenwood.

———. 1994. "Racial Identity and Career Assessment." *Journal of Career Assessment* 2: 199–209.

———. 1996. "Toward a Methodology for Measuring and Assessing Racial as Distinguished from Ethnic Identity." Pp. 143–192 in *Multicultural Assessment in Counseling and Clinical Psychology,* ed. Gargi R. Sadowsky and James C. Impara. Lincoln, NE: University of Nebraska Press.

Henry, Charles. 1980. "Black-Chicano Coalitions: Possibilities and Problems." *Western Journal of Black Studies* 4: 222–232.

Henry, Charles, and Carlos Munoz. 1991. "Ideological and Interest Linkages in California Rainbow Politics." In *Racial and Ethnic Politics in California,* ed. Byron O. Jackson and Michael B. Preston. Berkeley, CA: IGS Press.

Herrnstein, Richard J. and Charles Murray. 1994. *The Bell Curve: Intelligence and Class Structure in American Life.* New York: Free Press.

Hickman, Christine B. 1997. "The Devil and the One Drop Rule: Racial Categories, African Americans, and the U.S. Census." *Michigan Law Review* 95: 1163–1265.

Higginbotham, A. Leon, Jr. 1978. *In the Matter of Color: Race and the American Legal Process—The Colonial Period.* New York: Oxford University Press.

———. 1996. *Shades of Freedom: Racial Politics and Presumptions of the American Legal Process.* New York: Oxford University Press.

Higginbotham, Elizabeth. 2001. *Too Much to Ask: Black Women in an Era of Integration.* Chapel Hill, NC: University of North Carolina Press.

Higham, John. 1988. *Strangers in the Land: Patterns of American Nativism, 1860–1925,* 2nd ed. New Brunswick, NJ: Rutgers University Press.

Hill, Mike, ed. 1997. *Whiteness: A Critical Reader.* New York: New York University Press.

Hochschild, Jennifer. 1981. *What's Fair?* Cambridge: Harvard University Press.

———. 1995. *Facing Up to the American Dream: Race, Class and the Soul of the Nation.* Princeton, NJ: Princeton University Press.

Hoetink, Harmannus. 1962. *Caribbean Race Relations: A Study of Two Variants.* London: Oxford University Press.

Holt, Thomas. 1995. "Marking: Race, Race-Making, and the Writing of History." *The American Historical Review* 100: 1–20.

Hondagneu-Sotelo, Pierrette. 1994. *Gendered Transitions: Mexican Experiences of Immigration.* Berkeley, CA: University of California Press.

hooks, bell. 1995. *Killing Rage: Ending Racism.* New York: Henry Holt.

Horowitz, Donald L. 1973. "Color Differentiation in the American Systems of Slavery." *Journal of Interdisciplinary History* 3: 509–541.

Horsman, Reginald. 1981. *Race and Manifest Destiny: The Origins of American Racial Anglo-Saxonism.* Cambridge, MA: Harvard University Press.

Hoyt, Homer. 1933. *One Hundred Years of Land Values in Chicago.* Chicago: University of Chicago Press.

Hubbard, Lee. 2001. "Charles Byrd: Forging an Identity Between Black and White." Retrieved from http://www.africana.com/index_20010405_2.htm on May 24, 2000.

Hughes, Everett C., and Helen M. Hughes. 1952. *When Peoples Meet: Racial and Ethnic Frontiers.* Glencoe, IL: Free Press.

Hurtado, Aida. 1999. "The Trickster's Play: Whiteness in the Subordination and Liberation Process." In *Race, Identity, Citizenship,* ed. R. Torres, L. Miron, and J. Inda. Malden, MA: Blackwell.

Hurtado, S. 1992. "The Campus Racial Climate: Contexts of Conflict." *Journal of Higher Education.* 63 (5): 539–569.

Hurtado, S., Dey, E., & Trevino, L. 1994. "Exclusion or Self-Segregation: Interaction Across Racial/Ethnic Groups On Campus." Presented to meetings of the American Educational Research Association. New Orleans, LA.

Ignatiev, Noel. 1995. *How the Irish Became White.* New York: Routledge.

Ignatiev, Noel, and John Garvey, eds. 1993–1994. *Race Traitor.* Published at Box 603, Cambridge, MA 02140.

———. 1996. *Race Traitor.* New York: Routledge.

Il Progresso Italo-Americano. 1919. July 31.

Indiana Jones and the Temple of Doom. 1984. Director: Steven Spielberg. Producer: George Lucas. Screenplay: Willard Huyck and Gloria Katz. Starring: Harrison Ford, Kate Capshaw, Ke Huy Quan.

Interracial Voice a. n.d. "About *Interracial Voice.*" Available from http://www.webcom.com/~intvoice/about.html.

Interracial Voice b, Letters to the Editor. Available from http://www.webcom.com/~intvoice/letters.html. Byrd, Charles: Reply to Myneca Ojo, February 21, 1999; Reply to Felipe Simmons, March 24, 1999. Martin, Liam, February 3, 1999; September 8, 1999. Powell, A. D., March 25, 1999; May 12, 2001; June 2, 2001. Simmons, Felipe, March 24, 1999. Winkel, George, July 2, 1999; May 21, 2001.

Interracial Voice c, Point-Counterpoint. Available from http: //www.webcom.com/~intvoice/point20.html. Powell, A. D., December 7, 1999.

Interracial Voice d, Point-Counterpoint. Available from http://www.webcom.com/~intvoice/point54.html. Becky, October 2, 2000. September 27, 2000. Miller, Candi, September 28, 2000. Powell, A. D., September 27, 2000. Whittaker, Tiffani, September 26, 2000, September 29, 2000.

Interracial Voice e, Point-Counterpoint. Available from http: //www.webcom.com/~intvoice/point33.html. Miller, Richard, June 17, 2000. Byrd, Charles, Comments in Candi Miller November 30, 2000.

Interracial Voice f, Point Counterpoint. Available from http://www.webcom.com/~intvoice/point20b.html. Powell, A. D., August 6, 2000.

Jackman, Mary R. 1994. *The Velvet Glove: Paternalism and Conflict in Gender, Class, and Race Relations*. Berkeley, CA: University of California Press.

Jackman, Mary R., and Michael J. Muha. 1984. "Education and Intergroup Attitudes: Moral Enlightenment, Superficial Democratic Commitment, or Ideological Refinement." *American Sociological Review* 49: 751–769.

Jackson, Byran, Elisabeth Gerber, and Bruce Cain. 1994. "Coalitional Prospects in a Multi-Racial Society: African American Attitudes toward Other Minority Groups." *Political Research Quarterly* 47: 277–294.

Jackson, Kenneth T. 1985. *Crabgrass Frontier: The Suburbanization of America*. New York: Oxford University Press.

Jacoby, Russell, and Naomi Glauberman, eds. 1995. *The Bell Curve Debate: History, Documents, Opinions*. New York: Random House.

Jacobson, Matthew Frye. 1998. *Whiteness of a Different Color: European Immigrants and the Alchemy of Race*. Cambridge, MA: Harvard University Press.

Jaggar, Alison. 1983. *Feminist Politics and Human Nature*. Totowa, NJ: Rowman & Allanheld.

Janis, P. 2001. "Of Gratitude and Platitudes: In Search of Civility in an Age of Indifference" *Washington Post* (August 12): B5.

Jaret, Charles. 1995. *Contemporary Racial and Ethnic Relations*. New York: Harper Collins.

Jenkins, Richard. 1997. *Rethinking Ethnicity: Arguments and Explorations*. London: Sage.

Jennings, Francis. 1975; repr. 1976. *The Invasion of America: Indians, Colonialism, and the Cant of Conquest*. New York: Norton.

Jennings, James, and Clarence Lusane. 1994. "Racial Hierarchy and Ethnic Conflict in the United States." Pp. 144–157 in *Blacks, Latinos, and Asians in Urban America: Status and Prospects for Politics and Activism*, ed. James Jennings. Westport, CT: Praeger.

Jessen, W. 2000. "Country Corner." *Billboard* 112: 60.

Johnson, Charles S. 1943. *Patterns of Negro Segregation*. New York: Harper.

Johnson, Deborah J. 1992. "Developmental Pathways: Toward an Ecological Theoretical Formulation of Race Identity in Black-White Biracial Children." Pp. 37–49 in *Racially Mixed People in America*, ed. M. Root. Newbury Park, CA: Sage.

Johnson, Heather Beth. 2001. "The Ideology of Meritocracy and the Power of Wealth: School Selection and the Reproduction of Race and Class Inequality." Ph.D. dissertation, Department of Sociology, Northeastern University, Boston, MA.

Johnson, Parker C. 1999. "Reflections on Critical White(ness) Studies" Pp. 1–9 in *Whiteness: The Communication of Social Identity*, ed. Thomas K. Nakayama and Judith N. Martin. Thousand Oaks, CA: Sage.

Jones-Correa, Michael. 1998. *Between Two Nations: The Political Predicament of Latinos in New York City*. Ithaca, NY: Cornell University Press.

Jones, James. 1991. "The Rise and Fall of Affirmative Action." In *Race in America*, ed. Herbert Hill and James Jones. Madison, WI: University of Wisconsin Press.

Jones, James M., and Robert T. Carter. 1996. "Racism and White Racial Identity: Merging Realities." Pp. 1–23 in *Impacts of Racism on White Americans*, ed. Benjamin P. Bowser and Raymond G. Hunt. Thousand Oaks, CA: Sage.

Jones, Nicholas, and Amy Symens Smith. 2001. "The Two or More Races Population: 2000." Available from http//:www.census.gov/population/www/cen2000/briefs.html.

Jordan, Winthrop. 1968; repr. 1977. *White over Black: American Attitudes toward the Negro, 1550–1812*. New York: W. W. Norton.

Jost, John T., and Brenda Major 2001. *The Psychology of Legitimacy: Emerging Perspectives on Ideology, Justice, and Intergroup Relations*. Cambridge, UK: Cambridge University Press.

Kairys, David, ed. 1982; rev. ed. 1990. *The Politics of Law: A Progressive Critique*. New York: Pantheon Books.

Kaiser Family Foundation. 1997. "The Four Americas: Government and Social Policy through the Eyes of America's Multi-racial and Multi-ethnic Society." June 5, 1997. Available from http://www.kff.org/content/archive/1105/.

Kaminsky, Stuart. 1978. *John Huston: Maker of Magic*. Boston, MA: Houghton Mifflin.

Keith, Verna M., and Cedric Herring. 1991. "Skin Tone and Stratification in the Black Community." *American Journal of Sociology* 97: 760–778.

Kelley, Kitty. 1997. *The Royals*. New York: Warner.

Kelly, Michael. 2001. "Not Us? Tough Luck." *Washington Post*, July 25: A21.

Kiernan, V. G. 1969; repr. 1981. *The Lords of Human Kind: Black Man, Yellow Man, and White Man in an Age of Empire.* New York: Columbia University Press.

Kincheloe, Joe L., and Shirley R. Steinberg. 1998. Pp. 3–29 in *White Reign: Deploying Whiteness in America,* ed. Joe L. Kincheloe, Shirley R. Steinberg, Nelson M. Rodriguez, and Ronald E. Chennault. New York: St. Martin's.

Kincheloe, Joe L., Shirley R. Steinberg, Nelson M. Rodriguez and Ronald Chennault, eds. 1998. *White Reign: Deploying Whiteness in America.* New York: St. Martin's.

Kinder, Donald R., and Tali Mendelberg. 2000. "Individualism Reconsidered: Principles and Prejudice in Contemporary American Opinion." Pp. 44–74 in *Racialized Politics,* ed. Donald Sears, Jim Sidanius, and Larry Bobo. Chicago: University of Chicago Press.

Kinder, Donald R., and Lynn M. Sanders. 1996. *Divided by Color: Racial Politics and Democratic Ideals.* Chicago: University of Chicago Press.

Kinder, D., and J. Sears. 1981. "Prejudice and Politics: Symbolic Racism versus Racial Threats to the Good Life." *Journal of Personality and Social Psychology.* 40: 414–431.

King, Desmond. 1995. *Separate and Unequal: Black Americans and the U.S. Federal Government.* Oxford: Clarendon.

King, Rebecca Chiyoko. 2000. "Racialization, Recognition, and Rights: Lumping and Splitting Multiracial Asian Americans in the 2000 Census." *Journal of Asian American Studies* 3: 191–217.

Kinsbrunner, Jay. 1996. *Not of Pure Blood: The Free People of Color and Racial Prejudice in Nineteenth-Century Puerto Rico.* Durham, NC: Duke University Press.

Kirkendall, R. 1995. "Who's a Hillbilly?" *Newsweek* (November 27): 22.

Kitano, Harry H. L. and Roger Daniels. 1995. *Asian Americans: Emerging Minorities.* Upper Saddle River, NJ: Prentice Hall.

Kivel, Paul. 1996. *Uprooting Racism: How White People Can Work for Racial Justice.* Gabriola Island, BC: New Society.

Klor de Alva, Jorge, Earl Shorris, and Cornel West. 1997. "Our Next Race Question: The Uneasiness between Blacks and Latinos." Pp. 482–492 in *Critical White Studies: Looking behind the Mirror,* ed. Richard Delgado and Jean Stefancic. Philadelphia: Temple University Press.

Kluegel, James R. 1990. "Trends in Whites' Explanations of the Black-White Gap in Socioeconomic Status." *American Sociological Review* 55: 512–525.

Kluegel, James R., and Eliot R. Smith. 1982. "Whites' Beliefs about Blacks' Opportunity." *American Sociological Review* 47: 518–532.

———. 1986. *Beliefs about Inequality: Americans' Views of What Is and What Ought to Be.* Hawthorne, NY: Aldine de Gruyter.

Kohut, Heinz. 1971. *The Analysis of the Self.* New York: International Universities Press.

Kolker, C. 2000. "Scrutiny Yielding a Clouded Picture, Texans Say." *Los Angeles Times* (October 25).

Korgen, Kathleen Odell. 1998. *From Black to Biracial: Transforming Racial Identity among Americans.* Westport, CT: Praeger.

Kovel, Joel. 1970; repr. 1984. *White Racism: A Psychohistory.* New York: Columbia University Press.

Lambert, Wallace, and Donald Taylor. 1990. *Coping with Cultural and Racial Diversity in Urban America.* Westport, CT: Praeger.

Lamont, Michele. 1992. *Money, Morals, and Manners.* Chicago: University of Chicago Press.

———, ed. 1999. *The Cultural Territories of Race: Black and White Boundaries.* Chicago: University of Chicago Press.

———. 2000. *The Dignity of Working Men: Morality and the Boundaries of Race, Class, and Immigration.* Cambridge: Harvard University Press, and New York: Russell Sage Foundation.

Landrith, James, Jr. n.d. "Councils, Caucuses and Consequences." Available from http://www.multiracial.com/editors/ccc.html.

La Parola dei Socialisti. 1913. January 4.

Lawrence, Charles R. III. 1995. "The Id, the Ego, and Equal Protection: Reckoning with Unconscious Racism." Abridged in Crenshaw et al., 1995.

Lee, Sharon M. 1993. "Racial Classification in the US Census: 1890–1990." *Ethnic and Racial Studies* 16: 75–94.

Lefkowitz, Bernard. 1997. *Our Guys.* New York: Vintage.

Leiserson, William M. 1924. *Adjusting Immigrant and Industry*. New York: Harpers.

Lempert, R., D. Chambers and T. Adams. 2000. "Michigan's Minority Graduates in Practice: The River Runs through the Law School." *Law and Social Inquiry* 25: 395.

Lewis, Amanda. 2001. "There is No 'Race' in the Schoolyard: Colorblind Ideology in an (Almost) All White School." *American Educational Research Journal* 38(4): 781–812.

———. 2003a. *Race in the Schoolyard*. New Brunswick, NJ: Rutgers University Press.

———. 2003b. "What Group? Studying Whites and Whiteness in the Era of 'Colorblindness.'" *Sociological Theory*.

Lewis Mumford Center. 2001. "Ethnic Diversity Grows, Neighborhood Integration Lags Behind." Report by Lewis Mumford Center. Albany, NY: University at Albany. Available from http://mumford1.dyndns.org/cen2000/WholePop/WPreport/MumfordReport.pdf.

Lieberson, Stanley. 1991. "A New Ethnic Group in the United States." Pp. 444–457 in *Majority and Minority*, 5th ed., ed. Norman Yetman. Boston, MA: Allyn and Bacon.

Lipsitz, George. 1998. *The Possessive Investment in Whiteness*. Philadelphia, PA: Temple University Press.

L'Italia. 1904. October 15.

———. 1909. April 10.

———. 1910a. April 30.

———. 1910b. September 10.

———. 1912. September 22.

———. 1927. April 3.

Litwack, Leon F. 1998. *Trouble in Mind: Black Southerners in the Age of Jim Crow*. New York: Alfred A. Knopf.

Local Community Research Committee. n.d. "History of the Lower North Side Community," vol. 3, pt. 2, Document 27a, pp. 9–10, Chicago Historical Society, Chicago, IL.

Lofland, John, and Lyn H. Lofland. 1995. *Analyzing Social Settings: A Guide to Qualitative Observation and Analyses*. Belmont, CA: Wadsworth.

Lopez, S. 2000. "A Visit to Bush Country." *Time* 155 (February 28): 36–38.

Lott, Juanita Tomayo. 1994. "Blacks and Latinos in the Unites States: The Emergence of a Common Agenda." Pp. 47–56 in *Blacks, Latinos, and Asians in Urban America*, ed. James Jennings. Westport, CT: Praeger.

Lucal, Betsy. 1996. "Oppression and Privilege: Toward a Relational Conceptualization of Race." *Teaching Sociology* 24: 245–255.

Lumley, Robert, and Jonathan Morris, eds. 1997. *The New History of the Italian South: The Mezzogiorno Revisited*. Devon: University of Exeter Press.

Mahoney, Martha R. 1997. "The Social Construction of Whiteness." Pp. 330–333 in *Critical White Studies: Looking behind the Mirror*, ed. Richard Delgado and Jean Stefancic. Philadelphia: Temple University Press.

Makalani, Minkah. 2001. "A Biracial Identity or a New Race? The Historical Limitations and Political Implications of a Biracial Identity." *Souls* 3: 73–102.

Malik, Kenan. 1997. "The Mirror of Race: Postmodernism and the Celebration of Difference." Pp. 112–133 in *In Defense of History: Marxism and the Postmodern Agenda*, ed. E. Meiksins Wood and J. Bellamy. New York: Monthly Review.

Mannheim, Karl. 1936. *Ideology and Utopia*. New York: Harcourt.

Man Who Would Be King, The. 1975. Director: John Huston. Screenplay: John Huston and Gladys Hill. Starring: Sean Connery, Michael Caine, Christopher Plummer, Saeed Jaffrey.

Marchand, N. 1997. "American Redneck Society." *Outdoor Life* 199: 12.

Marcuse, Herbert. 1964. *One-Dimensional Man: Studies in the Ideology of Advanced Industrial Society*. London: Sphere.

Martin, Judith N., Robert L Krizek, Thomas K. Nakayama, and Lisa Bradford. 1996. "Exploring Whiteness: A Study of Self-Labels for White Americans." *Communication Quarterly* 44: 125–144.

Martinelli, Arthur. 1989. "Affirmative Action: A Divided Supreme Court." *John Marshall Law Review* 22: 99–109.

Marx, Anthony W. 1998. *Making Race and Nation: A Comparison of the United States, South Africa, and Brazil*. New York: Cambridge University Press.

Marx, Leo. 1964. *The Machine in the Garden: Technology and the Pastoral Ideal in America.* New York: Oxford University Press.

Massey, Douglas S., and Nancy A. Denton. 1993. *American Apartheid: Segregation and the Making of the Underclass.* Cambridge, MA: Harvard University Press.

Matloff, Norman. 1997. "Asians, Blacks, and Intolerance." *San Francisco Chronicle.* (May 20).

Mauss, Marcel. 1966. *The Gift.* London: Cohen and West.

McCall, Leslie. 2001. *Complex Inequality: Gender, Class, and Race in the New Economy.* New York: Routledge.

McConahay, John B. 1983. "Modern Racism and Modern Discrimination." *Personality and Social Psychology Bulletin* 9: 551–558.

———. 1986. "Modern Racism, Ambivalence, and the Modern Racism Scale." Pp. 91–126 in *Prejudice, Discrimination and Racism,* ed. J. Dovidio and S. Gaertner. New York, Academic Press.

McCumber, John. 2001. *Time in the Ditch: American Philosophy and the McCarthy Era.* Evanston, IL: Northwestern University Press.

McDaniel, Antonio. 1995. "The Dynamics of Racial Composition in the United States." *Daedalus* 124: 179–198.

McGinley, A. C. 1997. "The Emerging Cronyism Defense and Affirmative Action: A Critical Perspective on the Distinction between Colorblind and Race-Conscious Decision Making Under Title VII." *Arizona Law Review* 39: 1004–1059.

McIntosh, Peggy. 2001 [1988]. "White Privilege and Male Privilege: A Personal Account of Coming to See Correspondences through Work in Women's Studies." In *Race, Class, and Gender: An Anthology,* ed. Margaret L. Andersen and Patricia Hill Collins. 2001. Belmont, CA: Wadsworth.

———. 1989. "White Privilege: Unpacking the Invisible Knapsack." *Peace and Freedom* (July/August): 10–12.

McKee, James B. 1993. *Sociology and the Race Problem: The Failure of a Perspective.* Urbana, IL: University of Illinois Press.

McKinney, Karyn. 2003. *White Kids: Everyday Whiteness and the Meaning of Race and Racism.* New York: Routledge.

McLaren, Peter. 1997. *Revolutionary Multiculturalism: Pedagogies of Dissent for the New Millennium.* Boulder, CO: Westview.

———. 1999. "Unthinking Whiteness: Rethinking Democracy: Critical Citizenship in Gringolandia." Pp. 10–55 in *Becoming and Unbecoming White: Owning and Disowning a Racial Identity,* ed. Christine Clark and James O'Donnell. Westport, CT: Bergin and Garvey.

McMillen, Liz. 1995. "New Field of 'Whiteness Studies' Challenges a Racial 'Norm.'" *Chronicle of Higher Education* (September 8).

McNamara, Robert S., and Brian VanDeMark. 1995. *In Retrospect: The Tragedy and Lessons of Vietnam.* New York: Times Books.

McPherson, T. 2000. "I'll Take My Stand in Dixie-Net: White Guys, the South, and Cyberspace." In *Race in Cyberspace,* ed. L. N. Beth Kolko and Gilbert Rodman. London: Routledge.

McSweeney, Edward F., and J. S. Rogers, Richard Campbell, and Victor Safford. June 26, 1898. RG 85, Entry no. 9, Box 143, File 52,729–9, National Archives I, Washington, D.C. Report submitted to T. V. Powderly, Commissioner General of Immigration.

Mead, A. 1995. "An Invisible Minority: Appalachians Find Prejudice Awaiting in Urban Settings." *Dallas Morning News* (March 13).

Merriam, Charles. n.d. "The Campaign Opens." Charles E. Merriam Papers, Box 90, Folder 4, University of Chicago Special Collections, Chicago, IL.

Meyers, Julie. 2001. "Age: 2000." *Census Briefs* (September). Available from http://www.census.gov/population/www/cen2000/briefs.html.

Miller, J. Mitchell, and Richard Tewksbury. 2001. *Extreme Methods: Innovative Approaches to Social Science Research.* Boston: Allyn and Bacon.

Miller, Perry. 1953. *The New England Mind: From Colony to Province.* Cambridge, MA: Harvard University Press.

Miller, Richard. n.d. "From History to Destiny." Retrieved from http://internettrash.com/users/mulatto/histdest.htm on May 24, 2000.

Millman, Marcia, and Rosabeth Moss Kanter, eds. 1975. *Another Voice: Feminist Perspectives on Social Life and Social Science.* New York: Doubleday.

Mills, Charles. 1997. *The Racial Contract.* Ithaca, NY: Cornell University Press.

———. 1998. *Blackness Visible: Essays on Philosophy and Race.* Ithaca, NY: Cornell University Press.

Min, Pyong Gap. 1996. *Caught in the Middle: Korean Communities in New York and Los Angeles.* Berkeley, CA: University of California Press.

Mindiola, T., M. Rodriguez, and Yolanda Flores Niemann. 1996. *Intergroup Relations between Hispanics and Blacks in Harris County.* Houston, TX: University of Houston, Center for Mexican American Studies.

Minority Rights Group, ed. 1995. *No Longer Invisible: Afro-Latin Americans Today.* London: Minority Rights Publications.

Montagu, Ashley. 1974. *Man's Most Dangerous Myth: The Fallacy of Race.* 5th ed. New York: Oxford University Press.

Montejano, David. 1987. *Anglos and Mexicans in the Making of Texas, 1836–1986.* Austin, TX: University of Texas Press.

Morago, Greg. 2001. "Summer of Shame." *Hartford Courant* (August 2).

Moran, Rachel. 2001. *Interracial Intimacy.* Chicago, IL: University of Chicago Press.

Morning, Ann. 2000. "Who Is Multiracial? Definitions and Decisions." *Sociological Imagination* 37: 209–229.

Morrison, Toni. 1970; repr. 2000. *The Bluest Eye.* New York: Penguin.

———. 1987. " 'Five Years of Terror.' A Conversation with Miriam Horn. *US News and World Report,* (October 19): 75.

———. 1992. *Playing in the Dark: Whiteness and the Literary Imagination.* Cambridge, MA: Harvard University Press.

———. 1993. "On the Backs of Blacks." *Time* (Fall): 57.

Mosley, Albert. 1997. "Are Racial Categories Racist?" *Research in African Literatures* 28: 101–111.

Mudimbe, V. Y. 1988. *The Invention of Africa.* Bloomington, IN: Indiana University Press.

———. 1994. *The Idea of Africa.* Bloomington, IN: Indiana University Press.

Mulatto People a. n.d. "Myths of the Multi-racial Movement and/or the Establishment of the Mulatto Race and Culture." Retrieved from http://internettrash.com/users/mulatto/myths.html on May 24, 2000.

———b. n.d. "What We Are Against." Retrieved from http://internettrash.com/users/mulatto/against.html on May 24, 2000.

Multiracial Activists. n.d. "What the Multiracial Activist Opposes." Retrieved from http://www.multiracial.com/about.html.

Mumford, Kevin J. 1997. *Interzones: Black/White Sex Districts in Chicago and New York in the Early Twentieth Century.* New York: Columbia University Press.

Murguia, Edward. 1991. "On Latino/Hispanic Ethnic Identity." *Latino Studies Journal* 2: 8–18.

Murguia, Edward, and Edward E. Telles. 1996. "Phenotype and Schooling Among Mexican Americans." *Sociology of Education* 69: 276–289.

Murray, Albert. 1970. *The Omni-Americans: New Perspectives on Black Experience and American Culture.* New York: Outerbridge & Dienstfrey.

Murray, Charles. 1993. "The Coming White Underclass." *Wall Street Journal,* October 29: 14A.

Myers, Kristen A., and Passion Williamson. 2001. "Race Talk: The Perpetuation of Racism through Private Discourse." *Race & Society* 4(1): 3–26.

Myers, L., Speight, S., Highlen, P., Cox, C., Reynolds, A., Adams, E., and Hanley, T. 1991. "Identity Development and World View." *Journal of Counseling And Development.* 70: 54–63.

Myrdal, Gunnar. 1944. *An American Dilemma: The Negro Problem and Modern Democracy.* New York: Harper.

Nadeau, Richard, Richard G. Niemi, and Jeffrey Levine. 1993. "Innumeracy About Minority Populations." *Public Opinion Quarterly* 57: 332–347.

Nagel, Joane. 1996. *American Indian Ethnic Renewal: Red Power and the Resurgence of Identity and Culture.* New York: Oxford University Press.

Nakayama, Thomas, and Robert Krizek. 1999. "Whiteness as Strategic Rhetoric." Pp. 87–106 in *Whiteness: The Communication of Social Identity,* ed. Thomas K. Nakayama and Judith N. Martin. Thousand Oaks, CA: Sage.

Nakayama, Thomas K., and Judith N. Martin, eds. 1999. *Whiteness: The Communication of Social Identity.* Thousand Oaks, CA: Sage.

Nelson, Bruce. 2001. *Divided We Stand: American Workers and the Struggle for Black Equality.* Princeton, NJ: Princeton University Press.

Neville, Helen A., Roderick L. Lilly, Richard M. Lee, Georgia Duran, and Lavonne Browne. 2000. "Construction and Initial Validation of the Color-Blind Racial Attitudes Scale (Cobras)." *Journal of Counseling Psychology* 47: 59–70.

Newitz, Annalee, and Matthew Wray. 1997. "What is 'White Trash'? Stereotypes and Economic Conditions of Poor Whites in the United States." Pp. 168–184 in *Whiteness: A Critical Reader,* ed. Mike Hill. New York: New York University Press.

New York Times. 1991. "Whites Still Cling to Stereotypes." (January 10): B10: 6.

Nguyen, Alexander. 2000. "The Souls of White Folk." *American Prospect* 11 (July 31): 46–49.

Niemann, Yolanda, Leilani Jennings, Richard Rozelle, James Baxter, and E. Sullivan. 1994. Use of Free Response and Cluster Analysis to Determine Stereotypes of Eight Groups. *Personality and Social Psychology Bulletin.* 20(4): 379–390.

———. 1999. "Social Ecological Contexts of Prejudice between Hispanics and Blacks." Pp. 170–90 in *Race, Ethnicity, and Nationality in the United States: Toward the Twenty-First Century,* ed. Paul Wong. Boulder, CO: Westview.

Nobles, Melissa. 2000. *Shades of Citizenship: Race and the Census in Modern Politics.* Stanford, CA: Stanford University Press.

Novak, Michael. 1971. *The Rise of the Unmeltable Ethnics.* New York: Macmillan.

Obermiller, P., and W. Philiber. 1987. *Too Few Tomorrows: Urban Appalachians in the 1980s.* Boone, NC: Appalachian Consortium Press.

O'Brien, Eileen. 2001. *Whites Confront Racism: Antiracists and Their Paths to Action.* Boulder, CO: Rowman and Littlefield.

Okazawa-Rey, Margo and Marshall Wong. 1997. "Organizing in Communities of Color: Addressing Interethnic Conflicts." *Social Justice* 24(1): 24–39.

Okihiro, Gary Y. 1994. *Margins and Mainstreams: Asians in American History and Culture.* Seattle, WA: University of Washington Press.

Oliver, Melvin, and James Johnson Jr. 1984. "Inter-Ethnic Conflict in an Urban Ghetto." *Research in Social Movements, Conflicts, and Change* 6: 57–94.

Oliver, Melvin L., and Thomas M. Shapiro. 1995. *Black Wealth/White Wealth.* New York: Routledge.

Omi, Michael. 1999. "Racial Identity and the State: Contesting the Federal Standards of Classification." In *Race, Ethnicity and Nationality in the United States: Toward the Twenty-First Century,* ed. Paul Wong. Boulder, CO: Westview.

Omi, Michael, and Howard Winant. 1986. *Racial Formation in the United States: From the 1960s to the 1980s.* New York: Routledge & Kegan Paul.

———. 1994. *Racial Formation in the United States,* 2nd. ed. New York: Routledge.

O'Reilly, Kenneth. 1989; repr. 1991. *Racial Matters: The FBI's Secret File on Black America, 1960–1972.* New York: Free Press.

O'Rourke, P. J. 2001. "Who the Heck Are These People?" *Forbes* (March 5).

Otis-Graham, L. 1995. *Member of the Club: Reflections on Life in a Racially Polarized World.* New York: Harper Collins.

Ozarks, Just That Much Hillbilly in Me, The. 1999. Mark Biggs. Ozarks Studies Institute, Southwest Missouri State University. Video.

Pappas, B. 1999. "Transparent Eyeball." *Forbes* 164: 45.

Parker, David, and Miri Song. 2001. "Introduction: Rethinking 'Mixed Race.'" Pp. 1–22 in *Rethinking "Mixed Race,"* ed. D. Parker and M. Song. London: Pluto.

Pasternak, J. 1994. "Bias Blights Life Outside of Appalachia." *Los Angeles Times* (March 29).

Pateman, Carol, and Elizabeth Gross, eds. 1987. *Feminist Challenges: Social and Political Theory.* Boston: Northeastern University Press.

Patterson, Monica Beatriz Demello. 1998. "America's Racial Inconscious: The Invisibility of Whiteness." Pp. 103–122 in *White Reign: Deploying Whiteness in America,* ed. Joe L. Kincheloe, Shirley R. Steinberg, Nelson M. Rodriguez, and Ronald E. Chennault. New York: St. Martin's.

Patterson, Orlando. 1997. *The Ordeal of Integration: Progress and Resentment an America's "Racial" Crisis.* Washington, DC: Civitas.

Payne, Charles. 1995. *I've Got the Light of Freedom.* Berkeley, CA: University of California Press.

Pearlman, Jeff. 1999. "At Full Blast: Shooting Outrageously from the Lip, Braves Closer John Rocker Bangs Away at His Favorite Targets: The Mets, Their Fans, Their City, and Just about Everyone in It. *Sports Illustrated,* (December 27): 60.

Peck, Gunther. 2000. *Reinventing Free Labor: Padrone and Immigrant Workers in the North American West, 1880–1930.* Cambridge, UK: Cambridge University Press.

Pedraza, Silvia. 1996. "Origins and Destinies: Immigration, Race, and Ethnicity in American History," Pp. 1–20 in *Origins and Destinies: Immigration, Race, and Ethnicity in America,* ed. Silvia Pedraza and Rubén Rumbaut. Belmont, MA: Wadsworth.

Perry, Pamela. 2001. "White Means Never Having to Say You're Ethnic: White Youth and the Construction of 'Cultureless' Identities." *Journal of Contemporary Ethnography* 30: 56–91.

Peshkin, Alan. 1991. *The Color of Strangers, The Color of Friends.* Chicago: University of Chicago Press.

Pettigrew, Thomas F. 1979. "The Ultimate Attribution Error." *Personality and Social Psychology Bulletin* 5: 461–476.

Philpott, Thomas Lee. 1991. *The Slum and the Ghetto: Immigrants, Blacks, and Reformers in Chicago, 1880–1930,* rev. ed. Belmont, CA: Wadsworth.

Pierce, Jennifer L. 1995. *Gender Trials: Emotional Lives in Contemporary Law Firms.* Berkeley, CA: University of California Press.

Pieterse, Jan Nederveen. 1990; repr. 1992. *White on Black: Images of Africa and Blacks in Western Popular Culture.* New Haven, CT: Yale University Press.

Pincus, Fred. 2000. "Reverse Discrimination vs. White Privilege: An Empirical Study of Alleged Victims of Affirmative Action." *Race and Society* 3: 1–22.

Piven, Frances Fox, and Richard A. Cloward. 1971. *Regulating the Poor.* New York: Vintage, Random House.

Porter, David D. 1989. "What Must Blacks Go Through? An Experiment Will Let You See." *Orlando Sentinel* (September 13): G1.

Portes, Alejandro, and Rubén G. Rumbaut. 1996. *Immigrant America: A Portrait.* 2nd ed. Berkeley, CA: University of California Press.

Postone, Moishe, and Elizabeth Traube. 1985. "*Indiana Jones and the Temple of Doom:* The Return of the Repressed." *Jump Cut* 30: 12–14.

powell, john A. 1997. "The Colorblind Multiracial Dilemma: Racial Categories Reconsidered." *University of San Francisco Law Review* 31: 789–806.

Prashad, Vijay. 2000. *The Karma of Brown Folk.* Minneapolis, MN: University of Minnesota Press.

Project RACE. n.d. "Mission Statement." Available from http://www.projectrace.com/about.html.

Rawick, George. 1972. *From Sundown to Sunup.* Westport, CT: Greenwood.

Reskin, Barbara. 1998. *The Realities of Affirmative Action.* Washington, DC: American Sociological Association.

Rocker, John. 2000. ESPN interview, January 12.

Rockquemore, Kerry Ann. 1998. "Between Black and White: Exploring the 'Biracial' Experience." *Race and Society* 1: 197–212.

———. 2002a. "Negotiating the Color Line: The Gendered Process of Racial Identity Construction among Black/White Biracial Women." *Gender & Society* 16: 485–503.

———. 2002b. "The End of Innocence: Choice, Fluidity and Racial Construction in Post–Civil Rights America." Paper presented at the Annual Meeting of the Association of Black Sociologists, Chicago, IL, August, 2002.

———. 2003. "Socially Embedded Identities: Theories, Typologies, and Processes of Racial Identity among Biracials." *The Sociological Quarterly.*

Rockquemore, Kerry A., and David L. Brunsma. 2001. *Beyond Black: Biracial identity in America.* Thousand Oaks, CA: Sage.

Rodney, Walter. 1972; repr. 1974. *How Europe Underdeveloped Africa.* Washington, DC: Howard University Press.

Rodriguez, Clara. 2000. *Changing Race: Latinos, the Census, and the History of Ethnicity in the United States.* New York: New York University Press.

Rodriguez, Clara, Aida Castro, Oscar Garcia, and Analisa Torres. 1991. "Latino Racial Identity: In the Eye of the Beholder." *Latino Studies Journal* 2: 33–48.

Rodriguez, Nelson M. 1998. "Emptying the Content of Whiteness: Toward an Understanding of the Relation between Whiteness and Pedagogy." Pp. 31–62 in *White Reign: Deploying*

Whiteness in America, ed. Joe L. Kincheloe, Shirley R. Steinberg, Nelson M. Rodriguez, and Ronald E. Chennault. New York: St. Martin's.

Rodriguez, Richard. 1982. *Hunger of Memory.* Boston: D.R. Godine.

Rodriguez, Roberto. 1999. "The Study of Whiteness." *Black Issues in Higher Education* (May 13): 20–25.

Roediger, David R. 1991. *The Wages of Whiteness: Race and the Making of the American Working Class.* New York: Verso.

———. 1994. *Toward the Abolition of Whiteness: Essays on Race, Politics, and Working Class History.* New York: Verso.

———, ed. 1998. *Black on White: Black Writers on What It Means to Be White.* New York: Schocken.

———. 2002. *Colored White: Transcending the Racial Past.* Berkeley, CA: University of California Press.

Rogers, Prentis and Carroll Rogers. 2001. "Rocker Talkin' Trash About Ex-Teammates." *Atlanta Journal Constitution,* June 28: 1G.

Ronai, Carolyn Rambo, and Carolyn Ellis. 1989. "Turn-ons for Money." *Journal of Contemporary Ethnography* 18: 271–298.

Rose, L. 1991. "White Identity and Counseling White Allies about Racism." Pp. 24–47 in *Impacts of Racism on White Americans,* 2nd ed., ed. B. Bowser and R. Hunt. Thousand Oaks, CA: Sage.

Rosenblum, Karen E., and Toni-Michelle C. Travis. 1996. *The Meaning of Difference: American Constructions of Race, Sex and Gender, Social Class and Sexual Orientation.* New York: McGraw Hill.

Rothenberg, Paula S., ed. 2002. *White Privilege: Essential Readings on the Other Side of Racism.* New York: Worth.

Rowe, W., S. Bennet, and D. Atkinson. 1994. "White Racial Identity Models: A Critique and Alternative Proposal." *The Counseling Psychologist.* 22: 129–146.

Rumbaut, Rubén G. 1996. "Prologue." Pp. xvi–xix in *Origins and Destinies: Immigration, Race, and Ethnicity in America,* ed. Silvia Pedraza and Rubén G. Rumbaut. Belmont, CA: Wadsworth.

Russell, Katheryn. 1998. *The Color of Crime.* New York: New York University Press.

Russell, Kathy, Midge Wilson and Ronald Hall. 1992. *The Color Complex: The Politics of Skin Color among African Americans.* New York: Harcourt Brace Jovanovich.

Sager, Gertrude. 1914. "Immigration Based upon a Study of the Italian Women and Girls of Chicago." M.A. thesis, Department of Sociology, University of Chicago, Chicago, IL.

Said, Edward. 1993. *Culture and Imperialism.* New York: Knopf.

Saito, Leland T. 1995. "Reassserting Whiteness: Whites as a Minority in an Asian American and Latino Community in Los Angeles County." Paper presented at the annual meeting of the American Sociological Association, Washington, DC.

Santiago, Roberto. 2001. "Lizzie's Trash Talk Offends." *Daily News* (July 28): 17.

Saporito, Salvatore, and Annette Lareau. 1999. "School Selection as a Process: The Multiple Dimensions of Race in Framing Educational Choice." *Social Problems* 46: 418–439.

Saxton, Alexander. 1990. *The Rise and Fall of the White Republic: Class Politics and Mass Culture in Nineteenth-Century America.* New York: Verso.

Scherman, Tony. 1994. "Country." *American Heritage* 45: 38–52.

Schuman, Howard, and Maria Krysan. 1999. "A Historical Note on Whites' Beliefs about Racial Inequality." *American Sociological Review* 64: 847–855.

Schuman, H., E. Singer, R. Donovan, and C. Sellitz. 1983. "Discriminatory Behavior in New York Restaurants." *Social Indicators Research* 13: 69–83.

Schuman, H., C. Steeh, and L. Bobo. 1985. *Racial Attitudes in America: Trends and Interpretations.* Cambridge, MA: Harvard University Press.

Schuman, Howard, Charlotte Steeh, Lawrence Bobo, and Maria Krysan. 1997. *Racial Attitudes in America: Trends and Interpretations.* Cambridge, MA: Harvard University Press.

Sears, David O. 1988 "Symbolic Racism." Pp. 53–84 in *Eliminating Racism: Profiles in Controversy,* ed. Phyllis A. Katz and Dalmas A. Taylor. NY: Plenum.

———. 1998. "Racism and Politics in the United States." Pp. 76–100 in *Confronting Racism: The Problem and the Response,* ed. Jennifer Eberhardt and Susan T. Fiske. Thousand Oaks, CA: Sage.

Sears, David O., Jim Sidanius, and Lawrence Bobo, eds. 2000. *Racialized Politics: The Debate about Racism in America.* Chicago: University of Chicago Press.

Seenarine, Moses. 1999. "South Asians and Indo-Caribbeans Confronting Racism in the US." *Cricket Int'l.*

Seltzer, Richard, and Robert C. Smith. 1991. "Color Differences in the Afro-American Community and the Differences They Make." *Journal of Black Studies* 21: 279–286.

Selznick, Gertrude Jaeger and Stephen Steinberg. 1969. *The Tenacity of Prejudice.* New York: Harper and Row.

Sennett, Richard, and Jonathan Cobb. 1973. *The Hidden Injuries of Class.* New York: Vintage.

Sevig, T., P. Highlen and E. Adams. 2000. "Development and Validation of the Self-Identity Inventory (SII): A Multicultural Identity Development Instrument." *Cultural Diversity and Ethnic Minority Psychology* 6(2): 168–182.

Shapiro, Herbert. 1988. *White Violence and Black Response: From Reconstruction to Montgomery.* Amherst, MA: University of Massachusetts Press.

Shapiro, Thomas M. 2003. *Racial Legacies: The Reproduction of Inequality.* New York: Oxford University Press.

Shapiro, Thomas M., and Heather Beth Johnson. 2003. "Family Assets and School Access: Race and Class in the Structuring of Educational Opportunity." In *Inclusion in Asset Building: Research and Policy,* ed. Michael Sherraden. New York: Oxford University Press.

Sheets, Rosa Hernández. 2000. "Advancing the Field or Taking Center Stage: The White Movement in Multicultural Education." *Educational Researcher* 29: 15–23.

Shome, Raka. 1999. "Whiteness and the Politics of Location." Pp. 107–128 in *Whiteness: The Communication of Social Identity,* ed. Thomas K. Nakayama and Judith N. Martin. Thousand Oaks, CA: Sage.

Sigelman, Lee, and Susan Welch. 1991. *Black Americans' Views of Racial Inequality.* New York: Cambridge University Press.

Simon, S. 2001. "It May Be Hillbilly, But These Kids Love Their Mountain Music." *Los Angeles Times* (March 29).

Skandinaven. Chicago Foreign Language Press Survey. 1900. (May 8).

Skrentny, John. 1996. *The Ironies of Affirmative Action.* Cambridge, MA: Harvard University Press.

Sleeper, Jim. 1997. *Liberal Racism.* New York: Viking.

Smith, Henry Nash. 1950. *Virgin Land: The American West as Symbol and Myth.* Cambridge, MA: Harvard University Press.

Smith, Robert Charles. 1995. *Racism in the Post–Civil Rights Era.* Albany, NY: State University of New York Press.

Smith, Rogers. 1997. *Civic Ideals: Conflicting Visions of Citizenship in U.S. History.* New Haven, CT: Yale University Press.

Sniderman, Paul M., and Edward G. Carmines. 1997. *Reaching Beyond Race.* Cambridge, MA: Harvard University Press.

Spann, Girardeau. 1995. "Pure Politics." In *Critical Race Theory: The Cutting Edge,* ed. Richard Delgado. Philadelphia, PA: Temple University Press.

Spear, Allan. 1967. *Black Chicago: The Making of a Negro Ghetto, 1890–1920.* Chicago, IL: University of Chicago Press.

Spears, Russell, Jolanda Jetten, and Bertjan Doosje. 2001. "The (Il)legitimacy of Ingroup Bias." Pp. 332–362 in *The Psychology of Legitimacy: Emerging Perspectives on Ideology, Justice, and Intergroup Relations,* ed. John T. Jost and Brenda Major. Cambridge, UK: Cambridge University Press.

Spencer, Jon Michael. 1997. *The New Colored People: The Mixed-Race Movement in America.* New York: New York University Press.

Spencer, Rainier. 1999. *Spurious Issues: Race and Multiracial Identity Politics in the United States.* Boulder, CO: Westview.

Spickard, Paul R. 2001. "The Subject Is Mixed Race: The Boom in Biracial Biography." Pp. 76–98 in *Rethinking "Mixed Race,"* ed. D. Parker and M. Song. London: Pluto.

Stargate. 1994. Director: Roland Emmerich. Screenplay: Dean Devlin, Roland Emmerich. Stars: Kurt Russell, James Spader, Jaye Davidson.

Steeh, Charlotte, and Howard Schuman. 1992. "Young White Adults: Did Racial Attitudes Change in the 1980s?" *American Journal of Sociology* 98: 340–367.

Steele, Shelby. 1990. *The Content of Our Character.* New York: St. Martin's.

Steinberg, Stephen. 1989. *The Ethnic Myth: Race, Ethnicity and Class in America,* rev. ed. Boston, MA: Beacon.

————. 1995. *Turning Back: The Retreat from Racial Justice in American Thought and Policy.* Boston, MA: Beacon.

Steinhorn, Leonard, and Barbara Diggs-Brown. 2000. *By the Color of Our Skin: The Illusion of Integration and the Reality of Race.* New York: Plume Books.

Stoddard, Lothrop. 1920. *The Rising Tide of Color against White World Supremacy.* New York: Charles Scribner's Sons.

Stowe, David W. 1996. "Uncolored People: The Rise of Whiteness Studies." *Lingua Franca* (September-October): 69–77.

Sugrue, Thomas J. 1996. *The Origins of the Urban Crisis: Race and Inequality in Postwar Detroit.* Princeton, NJ: Princeton University Press.

Swartz, David. 1997. *Culture and Power: The Sociology of Pierre Bourdieu.* Chicago, IL: University of Chicago Press.

Takaki, Ronald. 1979; repr. 1990. *Iron Cages: Race and Culture in 19th-Century America.* New York: Oxford University Press.

————. 1989. *Strangers from a Different Shore: A History of Asian Americans.* New York, NY: Penguin.

————. 1993. *A Different Mirror: A History of Multicultural America.* Boston, MA: Little Brown.

Tamale, Sylvia R. 1996. "The Outsider Looks In: Constructing Knowledge about American Collegiate Racism." *Qualitative Sociology* 19: 471–495.

Tatum, Beverly Daniel. 1992. "Talking about Race, Learning about Racism: The Application of Racial Identity Development Theory in the Classroom." *Harvard Educational Review* 62: 1–24.

————. 1994. "Teaching White Students about Racism: The Search for White Allies and the Restoration of Hope." *Teachers College Record* 95: 462–476.

————. 1997. *"Why Are All the Black Kids Sitting Together in the Cafeteria? And Other Conversations about Race."* New York: Basic.

Taylor, Clyde. 1996. "The Rebirth of the Aesthetic in Cinema." Pp. 15–37 in *The Birth of Whiteness: Race and the Emergence of U.S. Cinema,* ed. Daniel Bernardi. New Brunswick, NJ: Rutgers University Press.

Telles, Edward E., and Edward Murguia. 1990. "Phenotypic Discrimination and Income Differences among Mexican Americans." *Social Science Quarterly* 71: 682–696.

"Terry," May 31, 2001. Electronic correspondence with author (Makalani).

Terry, Robert W. 1981. "The Negative Impact on White Values." Pp. 119–151 in *Impacts of Racism on White Americans,* ed. Benjamin P. Bowser and Raymond G. Hunt. Beverly Hills, CA: Sage.

Thernstrom, Stephen, and Abigail Thernstrom. 1997. *America in Black and White: One Nation, Indivisible.* New York: Simon and Schuster.

Thompson, Becky. 1996. "Time Traveling and Border Crossing." Pp. 93–109 in *Names We Call Home: Autobiography on Racial Identity,* ed. Becky Thompson and Sangeeta Tyagi. New York: Routledge.

————. 1999. "Subverting Racism from Within: Linking White Identity to Activism." Pp. 64–77 in *Becoming and Unbecoming White: Owning and Disowning a Racial Identity,* ed. Christine Clark and James O'Donnell. Westport, CT: Bergin and Garvey.

Thompson, C. 1994. "Helms' White Racial Identity Development (WRID) Theory: Another Look." *The Counseling Psychologist* 22: 645–649.

Thornton, Russell. 1987. *American Indian Holocaust and Survival: A Population History Since 1492.* Norman, OK: University of Oklahoma Press.

Three Kings. 1999. Director: David Russell. Story: John Ridley. Screenplay: David O. Russell. Starring: George Clooney, Mark Wahlberg, Spike Jonze, Ice Cube, Nora Dunn.

Tilly, Charles. 1998. *Durable Inequality.* Berkeley: University of California Press.

Tomaskovic-Devey, Donald. 1993. *Race and Gender at Work.* Ithaca, NY: Cornell University Press.

Trinh, T. M. 1991. *When the Moon Waxes Red: Representation, Gender, and Cultural Politics.* New York: Routledge.

Tuch, Stephen A., and Jack K. Martin, eds. 1997. *Racial Attitudes in the 1990s: Continuity and Change.* Westport, CT: Praeger.

Turner, Margery A., Raymond Struyk, and John Yinger. 1991. *The Housing Discrimination Study.* Washington DC: The Urban Institute.

Turner, Patricia A. 1994. *Ceramic Uncles and Celluloid Mammies: Black Images and Their Influence on Culture.* New York: Anchor Books.

Tuttle, William M., Jr. 1970. *Race Riot: Chicago in the Red Summer of 1919.* New York: Atheneum.

Twine, France Winddance. 1996. "Brown Skinned White Girls: Class, Culture and the Construction of White Identity in Suburban Communities." *Gender, Place and Culture* 3: 205–224.

————. 1998. *Racism in a Racial Democracy: The Maintenance of White Supremacy in Brazil.* New Brunswick, NJ: Rutgers University Press.

————. 1999. "Bearing Blackness in Britain: The Meaning of Racial Difference for White Birth Mothers of African-Descent Children." *Social Identities* 5: 185–210.

Uhlaner, Carole. 1991. "Perceived Discrimination and Prejudice and the Coalition Prospects of Blacks, Latinos, and Asian Americans." Pp. 339–371 in *Racial and Ethnic Politics in California,* ed. Byron O Jackson and Michael B. Preston. Berkeley, CA: IGS Press.

U.S. Census Bureau. 2000. Census 2000 Redistricting Data (public Law 94–171) Summary File; Table PL3.

U.S. Congress. 1912. House Committee on Immigration and Naturalization. *Hearings Relative to the Further Restriction of Immigration.* 62d Cong., 2d sess., Pp. 77–78.

————. 1919. *Congressional Record.* 66th Cong., 1st sess., Pp. 3392–3393.

————. 1924. *Congressional Record.* 69th Cong., 1st sess., 5456.

————. 1998. Federal Measures of Race and Ethnicity and the Implications for the 2000 Census: Hearings before the Subcommittee on Government Management, Information, and Technology of the Committee on Oversight: April 23; May 22; and July 25, 1997. Washington, DC: U.S. Government Printing Office.

U.S. Department of Health and Human Services. 1994. *Vital Statistics of the United States, 1990. Part I, Natality,* Washington, DC: U.S. Government Printing Office, Table 1-34.

————. 1995. *Vital Statistics of the United States, 1991. Part I, Natality,* Washington, DC: U.S. Government Printing Office, Table 1-34.

————. 1996. *Vital Statistics of the United States, 1992. Part I, Natality,* Washington, DC: U.S. Government Printing Office, Table 1-34.

————. 1999. *Vital Statistics of the United States, 1993. Part I, Natality,* Washington, DC: U.S. Government Printing Office, Table 1-34.

————. 2000. *Vital Statistics of the United States, 1997. Part I, Natality,* National Center for Health Statistics. Retrieved May 14, 2000, available from www.cdc.gov/nchs/datawh/statab/unpubd/natality/natab97.htm. Table 1-11.

U.S. Immigration Commission. 1911. *Dictionary of Races and Peoples.* Washington, DC: Government Printing Office.

van den Berghe, Pierre. 1978. *Race and Racism,* 2d ed. New York: Wiley.

van Dijk, Teun. 1993. "Analyzing Racism through Discourse Analysis: Some Methodological Reflections." In *Race and Ethnicity in Research Methods,* ed. John H. Stanfield and Rutledge M. Dennis. Newbury Park, CA: Sage.

Vecoli, Rudolph J. 1963. "Chicago's Italians prior to World War I: A Study of Their Social and Economic Adjustment." Ph.D. dissertation, Department of History, University of Wisconsin, Madison, WI.

Vera, Hernán, and Andrew Gordon. 2003. *Screen Saviors: Hollywood Fictions of Whiteness.* Lanham, MD: Rowman and Littlefield.

Wah, Lee Mun. (Producer and Director). 1994. *The Color of Fear.* (Film). Available from Stir Fry Seminars and Consulting, 154 Santa Clara Avenue, Oakland, CA 94610.

Walker, David. 1993 [1830]. *Appeal.* Baltimore, MD: Black Classic Press.

Wander, Philip C., Judith N. Martin, Thomas K. Nakayama. 1999. "Whiteness and Beyond: Sociohistorical Foundations of Whiteness and Contemporary Challenges." Pp. 13–26 in *Whiteness: The Communication of Social Identity,* ed. Thomas K. Nakayama and Judith N. Martin. Thousand Oaks, CA: Sage.

Warren, Jonathan, and France Winddance Twine. 1997. "White Americans, the New Minority? Non-Blacks and the Ever-Expanding Boundaries of Whiteness." *Journal of Black Studies.* 28: 200–218.

Wartofsky, A. 1999. "Eminem's Hard Shell." *Washington Post* (July 27).

Waters, Mary C. 1990. *Ethnic Options: Choosing Identities in America.* Berkeley, CA: University of California Press.

———. 1996. "Optional Ethnicities: For Whites Only?" Pp. 444–454 in *Origins and Destinies: Immigration, Race, and Ethnicity in America,* ed. Silvia Pedraza and Rubén G. Rumbaut. Belmont, CA: Wadsworth.

———. 1997. "Prepared Testimony of Professor Mary C. Waters, Department of Sociology, Harvard University." House Committee on Government Reform and Oversight, Subcommittee on Government Management, Information, and Technology. Washington, DC: Federal News Service.

———. 1999. *Black Identities: West Indian Immigrants' Dreams and American Realities.* Cambridge, MA: Harvard University Press.

Weber, Max. 1958 [1922]. *From Max Weber: Essays in Sociology.* H. H. Gerth and C. Wright Mills, ed., trans. New York: Oxford University Press.

———. 1978. *Economy and Society: An Outline of Interpretive Sociology,* ed. Guenther Roth and Claus Wittich. Berkeley, CA: University of California Press.

Weitzer, Ronald. 1997. "Racial Prejudice among Korean Merchants in African-American Neighborhoods." *The Sociological Quarterly* 38: 587–606.

Wellman, David. 1993. *Portraits of White Racism,* 2nd ed., Cambridge, UK: Cambridge University Press.

———. 1997. "Minstrel Shows, Affirmative Action Talk, and Angry White Men: Marking Racial Otherness in the 1990s." Pp. 311–331 in *Displacing Whiteness: Essays in Social and Cultural Criticism,* ed. Ruth Frankenberg. Durham, NC: Duke University Press.

Welton, Donn, ed. 1998. *Body and Flesh: A Philosophical Reader.* Malden, MA: Blackwell Publishers.

White, Armond. 1984. "Temple of Gremlins." *Films in Review* (August/September): 411–413.

White, Shane, and Graham White. 1998. *Stylin': African American Expressive Culture from its Beginnings to the Zoot Suit.* Ithaca, NY: Cornell University Press.

Wildman, Stephanie M. 1996. *Privilege Revealed: How Invisible Preference Undermines America.* New York, NY: New York University Press.

Williams, Eric. 1944; repr. 1966. *Capitalism and Slavery.* New York: Capricorn.

Williams, Patricia. 1990. *Alchemy of Race and Rights.* Cambridge, MA: Harvard University Press.

Williams, Robert A., Jr. 1990. *The American Indian in Western Legal Thought: The Discourses of Conquest.* New York: Oxford University Press.

Williams, Robin. 1964. *Strangers Next Door.* Englewood Cliffs, NJ: Prentice-Hall.

Wilson, William J. 1973. *Power, Racism, and Privilege: Race Relations in Theoretical and Sociohistorical Perspective.* New York: Macmillan.

———. 1978. *The Declining Significance of Race.* Chicago, IL: University of Chicago Press.

———. 1987. *The Truly Disadvantaged: The Inner City, the Underclass, and Public Policy.* Chicago: University of Chicago Press.

———. 1997. *When Work Disappears.* Chicago, IL: University of Chicago Press.

———. 1998. "The Role of the Environment in the Black-White Test Score Gap." Pp. 501–510 in *The Black-White Test Score Gap,* ed. Christopher Jencks and Meredith Phillips. Washington, DC: The Brookings Institute.

Winant, Howard. 1994. *Racial Conditions: Politics, Theory, Comparisons.* Minneapolis, MN: University of Minnesota Press.

———. 1997. "Behind Blue Eyes: Whiteness and Contemporary U.S. Racial Politics." Pp. 40–53 in *Off White: Readings on Race, Power, and Society,* ed. Michelle Fine, Lois Weis, Linda C. Powell, and L. Mun Wong. New York: Routledge.

———. 1999. "Racism Today: Continuity and Change in the Post–Civil Rights Era." In *Race, Ethnicity and Nationality in the United States: Toward the Twenty-First Century,* ed. Paul Wong. Boulder, CO: Westview.

Wray, Matt and Annalee Newitz, eds. 1997. *White Trash: Race and Class in America.* New York: Routledge.

X, Malcolm. 1971. *The End of White World Supremacy,* ed. Imam Benjamin Karim. New York: Arcade.

Yinger, J. Milton. 1995. *Closed Doors, Opportunities Lost: The Continuing Costs of Housing Discrimination.* New York, NY: Russell Sage.

Yoon, In-jin. 1997. *On My Own: Korean Businesses and Race Relations in America.* Chicago, IL: University of Chicago Press.

Young, Iris. 1994. "Gender as Seriality: Thinking about Women as a Social Collective." *Signs* 19(3): 713–738.

Zack, Naomi. 1993. *Race and Mixed Race.* Philadelphia: Temple University Press.

———. 1999. "White Ideas." Pp. 77–84 in *Whiteness: Feminist Philosophical Reflections,* ed. Chris J. Cuomo and Kim Q. Hall. Lanham, MD: Rowman and Littlefield.

———. 2001. "American Mixed Race: The U.S. 2000 Census and Related Issues." *Harvard BlackLetter Law Journal* 17: 33–46.

Zorbaugh, Harvey Warren. 1929. *The Gold Coast and the Slum: A Sociological Study of the Near North Side.* Chicago, IL: University of Chicago Press.

Zussman, Robert. 1995. *Intensive Care.* Berkeley, CA: University of California Press.

Contributors

Margaret L. Andersen (B.A., Georgia State University; M.A., Ph.D., University of Massachusetts, Amherst) is Professor of Sociology and Women's Studies at the University of Delaware. She is the author of *Thinking about Women: Sociological Perspectives on Sex and Gender,* 6th ed. (Allyn and Bacon, 2003); *Sociology: Understanding a Diverse Society,* 2nd ed. (Wadsworth, 2002; coauthored with Howard F. Taylor); *Sociology: The Essentials,* 2nd ed. (Wadsworth, 2003; also coauthored with Howard F. Taylor); *Understanding Society: An Introductory Reader* (Wadsworth, 2001; coedited with Kim Logio and Howard F. Taylor); *Race, Class, and Gender: An Anthology,* 4th ed. (Wadsworth, 2001; coedited with Patricia Hill Collins); and *Social Problems* (Addison Wesley Longman, 1997; coauthored with Frank R. Scarpitti and Laura L. O'Toole). She is a recipient of the University of Delaware's Excellence-in-Teaching Award, former President of the Eastern Sociological Society, and a member of the National Advisory Board for the Center for Comparative Studies in Race and Ethnicity at Stanford University, where she has been a Visiting Professor.

Eduardo Bonilla-Silva is an associate professor of Sociology at Texas A&M University. He is best known for his 1997 *American Sociological Review* article, "Rethinking Racism: Toward a Structural Interpretation," where he challenged sociology to abandon the sterile soil of the prejudice paradigm. His work has appeared in journals such as *Sociological Inquiry, Research in Politics and Society, Discourse and Society, Journal of Latin American Studies, Race and Society,* and the *Journal of Political Ideology,* among others. He has also published two books, *White Supremacy and Racism in the Post–Civil Rights Era* (Lynne Rienner Publishers 2001), cowinner of the 2002 Oliver Cromwell Cox Award given by the Section of Race and Ethnicity of the American Sociological Association, and *Racism without Racists: Color Blind Racism and the Persistence of Racial Inequality in the United States* (Rowman and Littlefield 2003). He is currently working on a book project (with Gianpaolo Baiocchi and Hayward Horton) titled *Anything but Racism: How Social Scientists Limit the Significance of Racism* (Routledge), an edited book with Tukufu Zuberi titled *White Logic, White Methods: Racism and Methodology,* and a project examining the transformations in the nature of racial stratification in contemporary America.

Mark A. Chesler (Ph.D.) is Professor of Sociology at the University of Michigan and Executive Director of Community Resources Ltd. He has written extensively about race and racism in higher education and is an active consultant on multicultural and socially just organizational processes and changes.

Nancy DiTomaso is Professor of Organization Management at Rutgers Business School–Newark and New Brunswick. Her research specialties include the management of diversity and change, the management of knowledge-based organizations, and the management of scientists and engineers. Her Ph.D. is from the University of Wisconsin–Madison. She has coauthored and coedited four books and many articles and has had articles published in such journals as *Academy of Management Journal, Sex Roles, Leadership Quarterly,* and *California Management Review.*

Ashley "Woody" Doane is Associate Dean for Academic Administration and Associate Professor of Sociology at the University of Hartford. His research interests include racial discourse, white racial identity, and the history and political economy of race and ethnic relations. Publications relevant to this work include "White Identity and Race Relations in the 1990s" (1997), "Dominant Group Ethnic Identity in the United States: The Role of "Hidden" Ethnicity in Intergroup Relations" (1999), and "Contested Terrain: Negotiating Racial Understandings in Public Discourse" (1996). He is a past President (1999) of the Association for Humanist Sociology.

Joe R. Feagin (Ph.D., Harvard University) is Professor of Sociology at the University of Florida. His primary research interests concern the development and structure of racial and gender oppression. His books include *Double Burden: Black Women and Everyday Racism,* coauthored with Yanick St. Jean (M. E. Sharpe, 1998); *Racial and Ethnic Relations,* 7th ed. coauthored with Clairece Feagin (Prentice-Hall, 2003); *Racist America* (Routledge, 2000); *White Racism,* coauthored with Hernán Vera and Pinar Batur (Routledge, 2001); and *The First R: How Children Learn Race and Racism,* coauthored with Debra Van Ausdale (Rowman & Littlefield, 2001). He was the 1999–2000 President of the American Sociological Association. Email: Feagin@ufl.edu

Tyrone A. Forman is an Assistant Professor of Sociology and African American Studies, Faculty Fellow at the Institute for Research on Race and Public Policy, and Faculty Affiliate at the Institute of Government and Public Affairs at the University of Illinois at Chicago. His primary research interests are intergroup prejudice and discrimination, American youth and public opinion, and survey research methods. He is currently conducting research in three areas: 1) studies of intergroup relations among people of color; 2) studies of the patterns, trends, and social determinants of young whites' racial attitudes; and 3) studies of the social psychological consequences of racial stratification for

African-American well-being. His work on these topics has appeared in *Social Problems, Discourse and Society, Perspectives on Social Problems, Youth and Society, Sociological Studies of Children and Youth, Research in Political Sociology, Health Education and Behavior,* and *Journal of Studies on Alcohol.*

Andrew Gordon is Associate Professor of English and Director of the Institute for the Psychological Study of the Arts (IPSA) at the University of Florida. He has also been a Fulbright Lecturer in American Literature in Spain, Portugal, and Serbia, and a Visiting Professor in Hungary and Russia. He teaches contemporary American fiction, Jewish-American fiction, and science-fiction literature and film.

His publications include *An American Dreamer: A Psychoanalytic Study of the Fiction of Norman Mailer; Psychoanalyses/Feminisms* (coedited with Peter L. Rudnytsky); and *Screen Saviors: Hollywood Fictions of Whiteness* (coauthored with Hernán Vera; Rowman and Littlefield, 2003). He has written many essays on Jewish-American fiction, especially on the works of Saul Bellow, and on science fiction and science-fiction film, especially on the films of Robert Zemeckis, George Lucas, and Steven Spielberg.

Charles A. Gallagher, Assistant Professor in the Department of Sociology at Georgia State University in Atlanta, received his Ph.D. from Temple University in 1997. He teaches classes on race and ethnic relations, urban sociology, and inequality. Based on interviews and focus groups with 150 whites from around the country, Professor Gallagher's work focuses on the political and cultural meaning whites attach to their race and the rhetorical strategies whites use to explain racial inequality. His book, *Beyond Invisibility: The Meaning of Whiteness in Multiracial America* is forthcoming from NYU Press. He is the editor of *Rethinking the Color Line: Readings in Race and Ethnicity,* 2nd ed. (McGraw-Hill, 2003).

Thomas A. Guglielmo received his Ph.D. in History from the University of Michigan in 2000. He is now an Assistant Professor in the Department of American Studies at the University of Notre Dame. His book *White on Arrival: Italians, Race, Color, and Power in Chicago, 1890–1945* was published by Oxford University Press in 2003. He is presently at work on a history of the U.S. racial order during World War II.

John Hartigan, Jr. teaches in the Americo Paredes Center for Cultural Studies and the Department of Anthropology at the University of Texas, Santa Cruz. He is the author of *Racial Situations: Class Predicaments of Whiteness in Detroit* (Princeton, 1999) and *Odd Tribes: White Trash, Whiteness and the Uses of Cultural Analysis* (Duke, 2004).

Heather Beth Johnson is Assistant Professor of Sociology at Lehigh University. Her research interests focus on race and class inequality in the contemporary United States, the sociology of wealth, the sociology of children and childhood, ideology, and qualitative methodology. Recent publications include: "From the Chicago School to the New Sociology of Children: The Sociology of Children and Childhood in the United States, 1920–1999," in *Children at the Millenium: Where Have We Come From, Where Are We Going?* and "Race, Assets, andk Choosing Schools: Current School Choices and the Future of Vouchers," with Thomas M. Shapiro, in the forthcoming *Bringing Equity Back: Research for a New Era in American Educational Policy.*

Amanda E. Lewis (Ph.D., University of Michigan, 2000) is an Assistant Professor in the Departments of Sociology and African-American Studies at the University of Illinois at Chicago. Her primary areas of research and teaching include race and ethnic relations, sociology of education (particularly urban schools), gender, and qualitative and ethnographic research methods. She has recently completed an in-depth ethnographic study of the reproduction of racial meaning and racial inequality in schools; the manuscript based on this work, *Race in the Schoolyard: Negotiating the Color-Line in Classrooms and Communities,* will be published in early 2003 by Rutgers University Press. Examples of other recent publications include "The Impact of Color-Blind Ideologies on Students of Color: Intergroup Relations at a Predominantly White University" (with Mark Chesler and Tyrone Forman), *Journal of Negro Education* (2000); "Contestation or Collaboration: A Comparative Study of Home-School Relations" (with T. Forman), *Anthropology and Education Quarterly* (2001), and "Whiteness Studies: Past Research and Future Directions," *African American Research Perspectives* (2001).

Minkah Makalani is a Ph.D. candidate in History at the University of Illinois at Urbana-Champaign and an Erskine A. Peters Fellow at the University of Notre Dame. His work on biracial identity has also appeared in *Souls.* His dissertation is a study of the African Blood Brotherhood and the rise of Black Radicalism during the New Negro Movement.

Karyn D. McKinney (Ph.D., University of Florida) is an Assistant Professor of Sociology at Penn State Altoona. Her areas of research interest are race, ethnicity, and gender. Currently, her research focuses on how racial and ethnic identity informs interaction between members of various ethnic groups. She is working on a book about young whites' understandings of race, racism, and identity (Routledge, 2003), and on a coauthored book on Middle-Eastern-Americans (Rowman and Littlefield, 2003). She recently published a chapter in an edited book, *Race in the College Classroom* (Rutgers University Press, 2002), which addresses the challenges of teaching race and ethnicity to college students.

Charles W. Mills is Professor of Philosophy at the University of Illinois at Chicago. He works in the area of oppositional political theory and has two books, both with Cornell University Press, *The Racial Contract* (1997) and *Blackness Visible: Essays on Philosophy and Race* (1998). He is currently working on a third book, tentatively titled *From Critical Class Theory to Critical Race Theory.*

Edward Murguia is Associate Professor in the Department of Sociology at Texas A&M University. His publications on the Mexican American experience include studies of colonialism, intermarriage, skin color and its effect on life chances, generational differences, community, drug use, and religion. He served as Director of the Minority Affairs Program at the Executive Office of the American Sociological Association from 1998 to 2000, and directed the ASA Minority Fellowship Program during those years.

Kristen Myers is an Associate Professor of Sociology at Northern Illinois University. She received her Ph.D. in Sociology with an emphasis on inequality from North Carolina State University in 1996. She has published articles and book chapters on teaching racism in diverse classrooms, private racist talk, children reared in feminist households, gay and lesbian police officers, standpoint epistemology, and antiracist work. She is the coeditor of a book entitled *Feminist Foundations: Toward Transforming Sociology* (1998), a book dedicated to creating a comprehensive body of feminist sociology as well as a community of feminist scholars. She is currently writing a book on private racetalk.

Eileen O'Brien is Assistant Professor of Sociology at SUNY–Brockport where she teaches courses in Sociology, Women's Studies, and African-American Studies. Among her publications are *Whites Confront Racism: Antiracists and Their Paths to Action* (Rowman and Littlefield, 2001) and a book with Joe R. Feagin entitled *White Men on Race* (Beacon Press, 2003) about elite white men's racial attitudes.

Rochelle Parks-Yancy is a Ph.D. candidate in Organization Management at Rutgers University. She has papers accepted for presentation at the annual meetings of the Academy of Management, the American Sociological Association, and the Society for the Advancement of Socio-Economics. One of her papers was published in the Best Paper Proceedings at the 2002 Academy of Management meetings and received a Best Paper Award from Prentice Hall Business Publishing and the Careers Division of the Academy of Management. Her research interests include social capital, cultural capital, careers, and social group inequalities.

Melissa Peet (MSW) is a doctoral student at the Center for the Study of Higher and Postsecondary Education at the University of Michigan. Her research and teaching interests focus on social justice scholarship and pedagogies, the creation of collaborative learning environments, the development of critical consciousness in students, and organizational change.

Jennifer L. Pierce is Associate Professor of Sociology in the Department of American Studies at the University of Minnesota. She is affiliated with the Center for Advanced Feminist Studies, the Law School, the Sociology Department, and Women's Studies. She has published a book, *Gender Trials: Emotional Lives in Contemporary Law Firms* (University of California Press, 1995), an anthology, *Is Academic Feminism Dead? Theory in Practice* (New York University Press, 2000), and a number of articles and review essays for journals such as *Signs: Journal of Women in Culture and Society, American Sociological Review, Gender & Society, Qualitative Sociology, Contemporary Sociology,* and *Women's Studies.* She is currently working on a book-length manuscript on the backlash against affirmative action in a California workplace.

Corinne Post is completing her doctorate in Organization Management at Rutgers Business School. Her doctoral thesis is entitled: "The Role of Race, Gender, Family Characteristics, and Organizational Setting in the Distribution of Favorable Work Experiences among Scientists and Engineers in Industrial R&D." She holds a Masters in International Management from the University of Lausanne, HEC, Switzerland, and a Bachelor's degree in Business Administration from the University of Geneva, HEC, Switzerland. In the fall of 2003, she will be joining the Lubin School of Business, Pace University as Assistant Professor of Management.

Todd Sevig (Ph.D.) is Director of Counseling and Psychological Services and Clinical Instructor in Psychology at the University of Michigan. His research interests center on spirituality and multicultural counseling, experiences of white people in multicultural endeavors, and issue facing counseling centers.

Thomas M. Shapiro is Professor of Sociology and Anthropology at Brandeis University in Waltham, Massachusetts. Professor Shapiro's primary interest is racial inequality and public policy. With Dr. Melvin Oliver, he wrote *Black Wealth/White Wealth,* which received the 1997 Distinguished Scholarly Publication Award from the American Sociological Association. This book also won the 1995 C. Wright Mills Award from the Society for the Study of Social Problems. Oxford University Press is publishing his next book, *Racial Legacies,* scheduled for fall, 2003. Recent publications include *Assets for the Poor: The Benefits of Spreading Asset Ownership,* edited with E. Wolff, *Great Divides: Readings in Inequality in the United States,* and "Wealth and Racial Stratification," in *America Becoming.*

Hernán Vera was born and grew up in Santiago, Chile, where he practiced law until, at the age of thirty one, he came to the United States to teach political institutions of Latin America at the University of Notre Dame. In 1974 he obtained a Ph.D. in Sociology from the University of Kansas and joined the faculty at the University of Florida, where he is now a Professor of Sociology. He has taught at the State University of Utrecht, in the Netherlands, and at the Universidad de Chile in Santiago, Chile. He is author of seven books, among which is *Screen Saviors: Hollywood Fictions of Whiteness* (with Andrew Gordon); *White Racism: The Basics,* and *Liberation Sociology* (both with Joe R. Feagin); and *The Agony of Education: Black Students at Predominantly White Universities* (with Joe Feagin and Nikitah Imani). Hernán Vera is married to María I. Vera, and they have three children and three grandchildren. He teaches Sociology of Knowledge, Sociological Theory, and courses in Race Relations. His current project is the creation of a Latin-American film collection at the University of Florida.

Index